This compelling and wide-ranging new study focuses upon the heated controversies that have surrounded the meaning and shifting significance of Social Darwinism.

Through a careful survey of the enormous secondary literature on the subject, Mike Hawkins clarifies the nature of Social Darwinism and its complex relationship to the theories of Darwin, Lamarck and Herbert Spencer. In the first comprehensive comparison of the myriad European and American developments of these theories, the author explores their use in a number of crucial ideological debates and social movements, including eugenics and Fascism. Dr Hawkins shows how so many political positions – from anarchism and cooperation to socialism, imperialism, liberalism, Fabianism, democracy and anti-democracy – could draw on the Darwinian tradition. The study finishes with a topical discussion of late twentieth-century sociobiology in order to assess the continuing vitality of Social Darwinism.

Historians and social scientists from across many disciplines will enjoy this cogent and subtle analysis of Social Darwinism and will find it an invaluable guide through an often complex subject.

Social Darwinism in European and American thought, 1860–1945

Social Darwinism in European and American thought, 1860–1945

Nature as model and nature as threat

Mike Hawkins

Kingston University

CAMBRIDGE
UNIVERSITY PRESS

PUBLISHED BY THE PRESS SYNDICATE OF THE UNIVERSITY OF CAMBRIDGE
The Pitt Building, Trumpington Street, Cambridge CB2 1RP, United Kingdom

CAMBRIDGE UNIVERSITY PRESS
The Edinburgh Building, Cambridge CB2 2RU, UK http://www.cup.cam.ac.uk
40 West 20th Street, New York, NY 10011–4211, USA http://www.cup.org
10 Stamford Road, Oakleigh, Melbourne 3166, Australia

First published 1997
Reprinted 1998

Printed in the United Kingdom at the University Press, Cambridge

A catalogue record for this book is available from the British Library

Library of Congress cataloguing in publication data

Hawkins, Mike, 1946–
Social Darwinism in European and American thought, 1860–1945: nature
as model and nature as threat / Mike Hawkins.
    p.   cm.
Includes bibliographical references.
ISBN 0 521 57400 5 (hardback). – ISBN 0 521 57434 X (pbk.)
1. Social Darwinism – History.   I. Title
HM106.H38   1997
304′.09–dc20   96–20946 CIP

ISBN 0 521 57400 5 hardback
ISBN 0 521 57434 X paperback

CE

To my parents, Alec and Joan Hawkins

Contents

Acknowledgements

This book has been a long time in the making, as a result of which I have incurred many debts from friends, colleagues and family. Since it is those closest to me who have borne the brunt of my absences and mood swings, I would like to record my gratitude to Jacquie, Sarah and Elizabeth for their support, encouragement and forbearance over many years, and additionally for Jacquie's editing and proofreading skills. As to friends and colleagues, special thanks are due to Steve Woodbridge for his help in tracing sources, discussing ideas and reading drafts; to Keith Reader, Steve Bastow and Andrea Hawkins for their assistance with translations; and to Mike Giddy for enabling me to approach matters from a different – if not always sober – angle. The following also contributed ideas, criticisms and documents: Chris Alderman, Paul Auerbach, Phylomena Badsey, Joe Bailey, Peter Beck (who suggested the project in the first place), Gail Cunningham, Chris French, the late Ivan Hannaford, John Ibbett, Simon Locke, Bill Pickering, Anne Poole, Christine Pullen, Phil Spencer, Terry Sullivan, Marie Turner and Keith Weightman. Thanks also to two anonymous readers for Cambridge University Press, and to Richard Fisher, the Social Science Publishing Director at Cambridge, for his encouragement and patience. The Faculty of Human Sciences at Kingston University provided me with two small research grants which enabled me to devote time to the book at crucial stages in its development. None of the above are, of course, responsible for the interpretations and any errors this book contains, but without them it would not have been written.

Part I

Defining Social Darwinism

Only that which has no history is definable.
Nietzsche, *On the Genealogy of Morals*, II, 13.

Introduction: the identity of Social Darwinism

What is Social Darwinism, and what role has it played in the history of social and political ideas? These questions, the point of departure for the present study, are simple to formulate but, as the historiography of Social Darwinism attests, difficult to answer. Anyone consulting the vast literature on Social Darwinism in the hope of resolving them is likely to experience confusion rather than enlightenment. What he or she will encounter are heated controversies over a number of issues. First, scholars dispute the definition of Social Darwinism and, as a consequence, who is to count as a 'genuine' Social Darwinist. Second, they disagree over the ideological functions of Social Darwinism with some insisting on its conservative bias whereas others emphasise its reformist – even radical – orientation. Third, there is controversy over the significance of Social Darwinism, with positions ranging from the claim that it was both widespread and influential, to the contrary view that its importance has been grossly exaggerated by hostile commentators. Finally, scholars contest the relationship between Social Darwinism and Darwin himself, broadly dividing between those who see a connection and those who insist on a radical difference between the work of the English naturalist and the ideological uses to which his ideas were put.

This dissension has helped to define the aims and the contents of this book. Indeed, it is my view that any attempt to understand the emergence and history of Social Darwinism must first come to grips with these disputes: appreciating the points at issue and the controversies they have aroused is a first step towards a different approach to the subject. For this reason, it is useful to review each of these areas of disagreement in turn.

The nature of Social Darwinism

There are several ways of categorising Social Darwinism. One widespread and seemingly straightforward tactic is to do so in terms of a series of catchphrases. This approach was implicit in Hofstadter's

influential study of Social Darwinism in American thought, in which he
referred to the 'struggle for existence' and 'survival of the fittest' as
popular catchphrases of Darwinism.[1] Subsequent historians have added
'natural selection', and sometimes 'adaptation' and 'variation', to this
list.[2]

Not all commentators agree, however, that these catchphrases
adequately convey the sense of Darwinian theory. The American
historian Bannister, though adopting this approach himself, maintains
that after the publication of *On the Origin of Species* in 1859 Darwin
assigned less importance to natural selection, the struggle for existence,
and survival of the fittest in evolution and attributed a greater role to
other mechanisms such as the inheritance of acquired characters. For
Bannister, this makes questionable the extent to which these catchphrases can be taken as encapsulating Darwin's theory.[3] Other scholars,
in an attempt to dissociate Darwin from Social Darwinism, have even
suggested that natural selection was not the most important idea in the
Origin.[4] Since the expression 'survival of the fittest' was coined by
Herbert Spencer rather than by Darwin, and only adopted by the latter
from the fifth edition (1869) of the *Origin*, such considerations cast
doubt on the legitimacy of singling out certain ideas as specifically
Darwinian, thereby undermining the utility of the catchphrase approach.

There are important issues here concerning the continuity of Darwin's
ideas over time and their relationship to Spencer's theories which will be
taken up in later chapters. For the moment I want to raise a different
objection to the catchphrase approach: any attempt to define Darwinism
by means of a list of concepts – even if there is complete agreement on
what is to be included in this list – encounters difficulties in classifying
theorists who only subscribe to some of its features. For example, it has
been claimed of English Social Darwinism that it persistently presented
'evolution as the growth of rationality'.[5] It is unquestionably the case
that many Social Darwinists did perceive the growth of rationality as an
important facet of evolution. But there were others, considered by

[1] R. Hofstadter, *Social Darwinism in American Thought, 1860–1915* (Boston: Beacon, 1955), 6.
[2] For example, K. E. Bock, 'Darwin and Social Theory', *Philosophy of Science*, 22(1955), 124; R. M. Young, 'Malthus and the Evolutionists', *Past and Present*, 43(1969), 112; R. Bannister, *Social Darwinism: Science and Myth in Anglo-American Thought* (Philadelphia: Temple University Press, 1979), 7, 20; J. W. Burrow, 'Social Darwinism', in *The Blackwell Encyclopaedia of Political Thought* (Oxford: Blackwell, 1987), 481.
[3] R. Bannister, 'The Survival of the Fittest is our Doctrine: History or Histrionics?', *Journal of the History of Ideas*, 31(1970), 377, 378.
[4] J. Bronowski, 'Introduction', in M. Banton, ed., *Darwinism and the Study of Society* (London: Tavistock, 1961), x.
[5] G. Jones, *Social Darwinism and English Thought* (Brighton: Harvester, 1980), 176.

themselves and their contemporaries to be Darwinists, who placed the emphasis elsewhere. Benjamin Kidd, for instance, asserted that: 'The evolution which is slowly proceeding in human society is not primarily intellectual but religious in character.'[6] Should, then, Kidd be excluded from the Social Darwinist camp? Such a decision would be perverse given that this statement occurs in his *Social Evolution*, which was an explicit attempt to apply Darwinism to human social and mental evolution.[7]

Similar considerations apply to the claim that a belief in historical progress is an essential attribute of Social Darwinism.[8] This belief certainly was upheld by a number of Social Darwinists (e.g. Kidd), but in Europe during the late nineteenth and early twentieth centuries there was, alongside the belief in progress, a widespread fear of moral and physical degeneration, and a sense of decadence and the imminent demise of Western civilisation.[9] This was sometimes fuelled by the spectre of the total destruction of humanity wrought by the cooling of the sun. The second law of thermodynamics was represented in some late nineteenth-century literature in the form of a dead earth, rendered lifeless by the cooling sun.[10] These preoccupations were sometimes wedded to evolutionary theory, giving rise to modes of Social Darwinism in which progress was either seen as a rare and contingent phenomenon or else denied outright. Thus, far from believing in the inevitability of progress, the French 'anthropo-sociologist' Vacher de Lapouge was convinced that the rigorous application of Darwinism to social and political change exposed the chimerical nature of progress.[11] As will be demonstrated in later chapters, Lapouge was by no means alone in this conviction.

The point of these examples is this: what is required for an understanding of Social Darwinism is not simply an enumeration of its various components but an indication of how these components relate to one another, and of the importance of each to the overall configuration.

---

[6] B. Kidd, *Social Evolution* (London: Macmillan, 1894), 245.
[7] This is acknowledged by Jones, *Social Darwinism*, 122.
[8] R. Williams, 'Social Darwinism', in J. Benthall, ed., *The Limits of Human Nature* (London: Allen Lane, 1973), 117.
[9] On the prevalence of notions of degeneration during this period, see J. Chamberlin and S. Gilman, eds., *Degeneration* (New York: Columbia University Press, 1985); D. Pick, *Faces of Degeneration* (Cambridge University Press, 1989).
[10] C. Watts, *A Preface to Conrad* (London: Longman, 1982), 182–3. Watts discusses the cultural impact of this nightmare, 86–8. See also G. Myers, 'Nineteenth Century Popularizations of Thermodynamics and the Rhetoric of Social Prophesy', *Victorian Studies*, 29(1985), 35–66.
[11] G. Vacher de Lapouge, *Les Sélections sociales* (Paris: Fontemoing, 1896), 446, 449; Lapouge, *L'Aryen* (Paris: Fontemoing, 1899), vii, 512.

Focusing on the interrelationships and relative weighting of the different ingredients of Social Darwinism produces a richer and more useful understanding of it. This is not to say that all problems pertaining to the classification of particular theorists are eliminated. Any definitional framework is bound to encounter 'hard cases' – instances where it is difficult to determine whether the relevant criteria have been satisfied. The framework proposed in the next chapter is no exception in this respect. But it has the advantage of discriminating between thinkers who embrace the configuration as a whole, including the 'rules' for inter-connecting its different components, and those who make use of some of these components within a different, perhaps even antithetical, dis-cursive framework. Social Darwinism must be seen as a *network* of inter-linked ideas, subject to change over time – particularly with regard to the relationships among these ideas – but retaining its overall identity notwithstanding these modifications.

Some commentators have defined Social Darwinism as the explicit endorsement of Darwin's theory of evolution, leaving open the issue of the actual content of this theory.[12] The problem with this approach is that it includes theorists who, while seeking to legitimate their ideas by claiming their provenance in Darwin, in fact propounded doctrines which were at variance with the fundamental premises of Darwinism. This is true of much of what has been labelled 'reform Darwinism'. On the other hand, this tactic would lead to the exclusion of Spencer who objected to being referred to as a Darwinist because he had arrived at this theory independently of Darwin's work.[13] Defining Social Darwin-ism in terms of an express commitment to Darwin's ideas in the context of social theory is, therefore, unsatisfactory.

In an effort to introduce more specificity into the notion of Social Darwinism, some historians have recommended equating it with eugenics, or at least including the latter as part of the definition.[14] The problem with conflating Social Darwinism with eugenics, however, is that it was possible to support one and not the other. Thus Benjamin Kidd, though a Social Darwinist, was a severe critic of eugenics, while

---

[12] J. R. Moore, 'Varieties of Social Darwinism', Open University Course A309, *Conflict and Stability in the Development of Modern Europe* (Milton Keynes: Open University Press, 1980), 37. See also A. Kelly, *The Descent of Darwin* (Chapel Hill: University of North Carolina Press, 1981), 103.

[13] See H. Spencer, 'Réponse à M. Emile de Laveleye', in E. Laveleye, *Le Socialisme contemporaine*, fourth edn (Paris: Alcan, 1888), 409.

[14] For the first tactic, see R. J. Halliday, 'Social Darwinism: A Definition', *Victorian Studies*, 14(1971), 401; for the second, see D. P. Crook, 'Darwinism: The Political Implications', *History of European Ideas*, 2(1981), 19. Not all historians, however, regard eugenicists as bona fide Social Darwinists. See Bannister, *Social Darwinism*, 166; C. Degler, *In Search of Human Nature* (Oxford University Press, 1991), 42.

George Bernard Shaw endorsed eugenics with enthusiasm but was dismissive of Darwinism.[15] Hence while there was often a very close association between eugenics and Social Darwinism, it provides insufficient warrant for conflating them.

If this last approach is overly restrictive, then equating Social Darwinism with a belief in the beneficial effects of warfare sins in the opposite direction. This connection was made at the start of the present century by the Russian-born businessman and sociologist, Jacques Novicow (1849–1912), who proclaimed Social Darwinism to be a doctrine which believed human progress had occurred through 'collective homicide'.[16] He then proceeded to label as Social Darwinist anybody who proffered a positive assessment of warfare irrespective of the basis upon which this assessment was made. As a result Novicow included many writers who were manifestly not Darwinists, in addition to misrepresenting the views of genuine Social Darwinists who were explicitly opposed to warfare between civilised nations – Spencer being a notable but by no means the only example.[17] The result of this type of procedure is to deprive the notion of Social Darwinism of any specific content and hence of any value in the analysis of ideas.

These disagreements over the intention of the term Social Darwinism are not trivial matters of academic hair-splitting, for, as we shall see, they have important ramifications for other areas of controversy.

The ideological functions of Social Darwinism

There tend to be two positions in the secondary literature on the discursive functions of Social Darwinism. One position links it to specific ideologies such as *laissez-faire* liberalism, racism or imperialism.[18] A variant of this view regards Social Darwinism as performing

[15] For Kidd's attitude to eugenics, see the study by D. P. Crook, *Benjamin Kidd: Portrait of a Social Darwinist* (Cambridge University Press, 1984), 78, 255. Shaw's ideas are discussed below, chap. 7.

[16] J. Novicow, *La Critique du darwinisme social* (Paris: Alcan, 1910). This connection had already been made by opponents of Social Darwinism, e.g. Laveleye in *Le Socialisme*, 397–400, 410. For a detailed assessment of the relationship between Darwinism and warfare, see P. Crook, *Darwinism, War and History* (Cambridge University Press, 1994).

[17] Spencer believed that struggle had evolved from warfare in primitive times to industrial competition in advanced societies. Novicow repudiated the identification of economic competition with struggle, although earlier in his career he had made precisely this identification himself and overtly endorsed Darwinism. See Novicow, *Les Luttes entre les sociétés humaines et leurs phases successives* (Paris: Alcan: 1893), 218.

[18] Ball and Dagger, in their textbook on political ideologies, define Social Darwinism as the adaptation of Darwinism to classical liberal theories of *laissez-faire* and limited government. T. Ball and R. Dagger, *Political Ideologies and the Democratic Ideal* (New

broader but still politically distinctive functions. Thus Kelly, in his analysis of German Social Darwinism, depicts it as legitimating 'the competitive, hierarchical, bourgeois society'.[19] Degler, in an account of Darwinism in American social theory, likewise maintains that 'the aim of Social Darwinism was frankly conservative ...'.[20] In contrast, a second position regards Social Darwinism as multivalent, capable of adaptation to a wide range of ideological stances.[21] In this perspective, Darwinism could be, and was, enlisted in the services of opposed political positions – militarism and pacifism, capitalism and socialism, patriarchy and feminism, totalitarianism and anarchism. So, to take the German case again, proponents of the multivalent perspective stress the variety of ideological contexts in which Social Darwinism was used rather than confining it to conservative apologetics.[22]

One aim of the present study is to explore the ideological roles played by Social Darwinism and its discursive boundaries. But this requires a satisfactory definition of Social Darwinism, one not inherently predisposed to a particular political perspective or ideological function. This involves a separation between the content and the function of Social Darwinism, a distinction which, I shall argue in the next section, is not always adhered to.

The significance of Social Darwinism

One of the most contested areas in the historiography of Social Darwinism pertains to its significance. Early critics like the Belgian, Emile Laveleye (1822–92), and Novicow portrayed it as a pervasive set of ideas in European culture, a viewpoint reinforced by Hofstadter's study of the USA. Many scholars have upheld these verdicts. Thus some have ascribed an influential role to Social Darwinism in the social sciences during the last half to a third of the nineteenth century.[23] Raymond Williams has extended this influence to the realm of popular culture, arguing that the struggle for existence and the survival of the fittest were daily realities for many ordinary people in the nineteenth

York: HarperCollins, 1991), 257. Yet the authors acknowledge that Social Darwinism was readily adapted in the service of non-liberal causes: *ibid.*, 193.

[19] Kelly, *The Descent of Darwin*, 100. Kelly is aware of more radical uses of Darwinism (101), but for some reason refuses to regard such usages as true Social Darwinism.

[20] Degler, *In Search of Human Nature*, 13. Cf. also 112.

[21] For example Jones, *Social Darwinism*, 77; Crook, *Darwinism, War and History*, 192.

[22] R. Weikart, 'The Origins of Social Darwinism in Germany, 1859–1895', *Journal of the History of Ideas*, 54(1993), 469–88.

[23] W. Stark, 'Natural and Social Selection', in Banton, *Darwinism and the Study of Society*, 49; C. Shaw, 'Eliminating the Yahoo: Eugenics, Social Darwinism and Five Fabians', *History of Political Thought*, 8(1987), 521.

century, as is suggested by the impact of Social Darwinism on the popular fiction of the period.[24] Greta Jones likewise refers to the 'ubiquity of Social Darwinism' in English thought, while the historian, Sternhell, has proposed that after Darwin's death, biology played a dominant role in the emerging sciences of man and society, with Social Darwinism virtually assuming the status of a religion.[25] The impression conveyed by these studies is that Social Darwinism was highly influential during the last few decades of the nineteenth and first four decades of the twentieth centuries, an influence that extended beyond the realms of social theory to encompass popular culture, literature and medicine.

This judgement, however, has come in for severe criticism. Several influential histories have downplayed the impact of Social Darwinism on the developing social sciences, claiming that the principal input into social evolutionism came from Lamarck or expressly social theorists rather than from Darwin.[26] Studies of individual countries have also concluded that the impact of Social Darwinism has been greatly exaggerated and that far from penetrating popular culture it in fact occupied a fairly marginal position in the country in question.[27] Moreover, revisionist historiography goes much further than simply denying an important role to Social Darwinism.[28] It often takes the additional step of claiming that far from reflecting an existential reality, 'Social Darwinism' is actually a construct of modern historians. For some revisionists the entire notion is a straw man, a myth – one which Hofstadter is often assigned a key role in manufacturing – concocted by reformers and critics of *laissez-faire* and individualism in order to

[24] Williams, 'Social Darwinism', 121, 126 *et seq.*
[25] Jones, *Social Darwinism*, viii; Z. Sternhell, *La Droite révolutionnaire* (Paris: Editions du Seuil, 1978), 146–7; Z. Sternhell, M. Sznajder and M. Asheri, *Naissance de l'idéologie fasciste* (Paris: Fayard, 1989), 23.
[26] Bock, 'Darwin and Social Theory', 124; R. A. Nisbet, *Social Change and History* (Oxford University Press, 1969), 161–2; A. Leeds, 'Darwinian and "Darwinian" Evolutionism in the Study of Society and Culture', in T. F. Glick, ed., *The Comparative Reception of Darwinism*, second edn (University of Chicago Press, 1988), 440–3; P. Bowler, *Evolution* (Berkeley: University of California Press, 1984), chap. 10; Bowler, *The Invention of Progress* (Oxford: Blackwell, 1989).
[27] This is the verdict of Bannister with regard to Britain and the USA in his *Social Darwinism* and 'The Survival of the Fittest'; of Kelly for Germany in *The Descent of Darwin*, 8, 109–10; and of L. Clark for France in her *Social Darwinism in France* (University of Alabama Press, 1984), chap. 6.
[28] The term 'revisionist' initially referred to the critics of Hofstadter who denied any evidence of a widespread endorsement of Social Darwinism among American businessmen. See J. A. Rogers, 'Darwinism and Social Darwinism', *Journal of the History of Ideas*, 33(1972), 267. It has since been extended to cover all opponents of the view that Social Darwinism was influential and widespread. See Jones, *Social Darwinism*, ix; Crook, *Darwinism, War and History*, 200–6.

discredit their opponents.[29] They contend that careful analysis reveals that figures who have been seen as paradigmatic Social Darwinists – for example Ernst Haeckel in Germany and William Graham Sumner in the USA – have in fact been misinterpreted and their alleged Social Darwinism blown out of proportion.[30]

There can be no question of the importance of revisionism to the study of Social Darwinism. Critical appraisal of earlier studies coupled with detailed investigations of individual thinkers or countries have shifted the burden of proof to those who believe Social Darwinism was significant and underlined the need for a more careful consideration of the subject matter and how it is to be investigated. Nevertheless, one of the purposes of the present study is to challenge the revisionists. In some instances their conclusions are an artefact of their conceptualisation of Social Darwinism. For example, Leeds defines Darwinism in terms of its *modern* theoretical content, purged of those original features that have been subsequently discarded or revised as well as its original philosophical underpinnings.[31] Small wonder, then, that he found little evidence of 'genuine' Darwinism in the social theories he examined. Bannister, who, as was noted earlier, defines Darwinism as a set of catchphrases, implies that apologists for US expansionism and imperialism cannot be described as Social Darwinists because they used the notion of struggle to justify national solidarity rather than remorseless individualistic competition.[32] This constitutes an arbitrary switch from a conceptualisation of Darwinism in terms of *content* to one in terms of *function* – in this case the defence of *laissez-faire* individualism. Here again is evidence of the need for an adequate definition of Social Darwinism before any realistic assessment of its influence and significance is possible. But quite apart from any methodological shortcomings in the work of the revisionists, recent research on key figures in the development of the social sciences in Europe and the USA renders the alleged marginality of Social Darwinism deeply implausible. It is impossible to give more than a cursory overview of this research here, and there is still a good deal of work to be done, but the results to date contradict the assertions of the revisionists.

[29] Kelly, *Descent*, 101; Bannister, *Social Darwinism*, 9, and 'Survival of the Fittest', 398. Crook, while critical of the revisionists, nevertheless agrees that 'There were no schools of Social Darwinists': *Darwinism, War and History*, 204.
[30] For Haeckel, see Kelly, *Descent*, 113; on Sumner, see R. Bannister, 'William Graham Sumner's Social Darwinism: A Reconsideration', *History of Political Economy*, 4(1973), 89–109.
[31] Leeds, 'Darwinian and "Darwinian" Evolutionism', 437–8.
[32] Bannister, *Social Darwinism*, 231.

Darwinism certainly played a formative role in the development of psychology.[33] Darwin's own attempts to derive human mental traits from an animal origin were an important influence on the work of the British psychologist George Romanes.[34] This influence is also evident in the social psychology of the American William James (1842–1910), who sought evolutionary explanations for such human instincts as acquisitiveness, fear, play and pugnacity, and repeatedly cited Darwin's authority.[35] The impact of Darwinism is equally discernible in the emerging disciplines of sexology, psychiatry and psychoanalysis. In the latter instance, one historian has described the work of Sigmund Freud (1856–1939) as a 'psychobiology of mind' in which Darwinism supplied a framework for the investigation not only of mental pathologies but also of the origins of morality and civilisation.[36]

It is more difficult to assess the legacy of Social Darwinism in anthropology, sociology and political science, due to the absence of detailed studies of certain key contributors. Some theorists were overtly hostile to Darwinism, like Gaetano Mosca (1858–1931), who, in his efforts to establish a science of politics, denied any role to natural selection and the struggle for existence.[37] Vilfredo Pareto (1848–1923) was likewise critical of Social Darwinism which, he believed, required 'considerable modification' if it was to be of service to the social sciences.[38] Nevertheless, Pareto accepted the existence of adaptation and the struggle for survival in social life, suggesting a more complex (and perhaps ambivalent) stance *vis-à-vis* Darwinism on his part which would repay closer investigation.[39]

The position of the German sociologist Max Weber (1864–1920) is also a complex one. Weber's inaugural address of 1895 at the University of Freiburg contained strong echoes of Social Darwinism. Referring to relations between Germans and Poles in East Prussia, Weber remarked that 'the free play of the forces of selection does not always operate in

[33] E. Boring, *A History of Experimental Psychology*, second edn (New York: Appleton-Century-Crofts, 1950), 743.
[34] See the comments by Romanes in the preface to his *Animal Intelligence*, sixth edn (London: Kegan Paul, Trench, Trübner, 1895), vi, xi.
[35] William James, *The Principles of Psychology*, 2 vols. [1890] (London: Constable and Co., 1950), especially II, chaps. 24–8.
[36] F. J. Sulloway, *Freud, Biologist of the Mind* (London: Fontana, 1980), 275 and chap. 10. See also C. Badcock, *Psycho-Darwinism* (London: HarperCollins, 1994).
[37] G. Mosca, *The Ruling Class*, tr. H. Kahn (New York: McGraw-Hill, 1939), 28–31, 121–3.
[38] S. E. Finer, ed., *Vilfredo Pareto: Sociological Writings*, tr. D. Mirfin (Oxford: Blackwell, 1966), 213.
[39] *Ibid.*, 102, 113–14. There is a discussion of the role of Social Darwinism in Pareto's work in T. Parsons, *The Structure of Social Action*, 2 vols. (London: Collier-Macmillan, 1968), I, 219–28.

favour of the nationality which is economically the more highly developed or better endowed'. He went on to attack optimists who imagined 'anything other than the hard struggle of man with man can create any elbow room in this earthly life', and urged acceptance of 'the *eternal struggle* to preserve and raise the quality of our national species'.[40] Yet Weber was subsequently to express considerable scepticism over the utility of Social Darwinism. He undoubtedly saw conflict as a constant and multi-dimensional facet of social reality, and occasionally made use of terms like 'the material struggle for existence'.[41] But he explicitly eschewed Darwinian accounts of the collapse of ancient civilisations and was critical of the transfer of the concept of adaptation from biology to sociology.[42] Weber perhaps furnishes an example of an attempt to emancipate sociology from the influence of pervasive biological models of social relationships.

This would certainly be a valid assessment of the work of the French sociologist, Emile Durkheim (1858–1917). In his first major publication in 1893 Durkheim explicitly made use of the struggle for existence among conspecifics to explain the high levels of occupational specialisation found in civilised societies.[43] This is no mere passing reference since Durkheim's argumentation made extensive use of Darwinism and relied upon parallels between the growth of the social division of labour and zoological processes.[44] But thereafter, while retaining an interest in evolutionary themes in his work on pedagogy and penal law, Durkheim did not make use of Darwinism. On the contrary, his remarks on Darwinism were dismissive and his attitude to Social Darwinists was invariably hostile.[45] This is not difficult to understand in the light of Durkheim's mission to establish sociology as an autonomous science, not to mention the sensitivity of a Jew and a Dreyfusard to the racialist possibilities of biological reductionism in the highly charged ideological

[40] M. Weber, 'The Nation State and Economic Policy', in Weber, *Political Writings*, ed. P. Lassman and R. Speirs (Cambridge University Press, 1994), 11, 14, 17, original emphasis. See Weikart, 'The Origins of Social Darwinism in Germany', 482; H. Gerth and C. Wright Mills, eds., 'Introduction' to *From Max Weber* (London: Routledge and Kegan Paul, 1948), 11.

[41] For example, in M. Weber, *The Methodology of the Social Sciences*, tr. E. Shils and H. A. Finch (New York: The Free Press, 1949), 26–7.

[42] M. Weber, *The Agrarian Sociology of Ancient Civilisations*, tr. R. Frank (London: NLB, 1976), 390, 408; Weber, *Methodology*, 25–6.

[43] E. Durkheim, *The Division of Labour in Society*, tr. W. Halls (London: Macmillan, 1984), Book II, chaps. 2–4.

[44] *Ibid.*, 277. There is a detailed analysis of Durkheim's use of Social Darwinism in this text in M. Hawkins, 'Durkheim, the Division of Labour and Social Darwinism', *History of European Ideas*, 22(1996) 19–31.

[45] Hawkins, *ibid.*

atmosphere of the Third Republic.[46] But the fact that even a theorist like Durkheim was tempted to make use of Social Darwinism is surely indicative of a pervasive and prestigious theoretical presence. That this presence also existed in the United States is evidenced by the work of the sociologist Lester Frank Ward (1841–1913). Ward was critical of the use made of Darwinism by apologists for *laissez-faire* and unrestrained economic competition, whom he accused of ignoring the role of invention in social evolution, the effect of which was 'the reduction of competition in the struggle for existence and the protection of the weaker members'.[47] Nevertheless, Ward's own theoretical writings made considerable use of Darwinism. Ward depicted the struggle for existence as acting primarily upon social structures rather than upon individuals, races or societies, although he believed racial struggle through warfare had played a vital role in progress.[48] Furthermore, Ward was one of the few social theorists to endorse sexual selection, which he used to account for the differentiation of the sexes and the subordination of women.[49]

I am not claiming that Pareto, Weber, Ward or Durkheim were Social Darwinists. But the fact that all of them utilised Darwinism at certain points in their careers surely suggests that Social Darwinism cannot be dismissed as marginal or as the construct of later historians and social critics. On the contrary, these examples indicate that Social Darwinism was an omnipresent reality for the practitioners of the social sciences during this period. Even when not adopting it as such, theorists sometimes found it difficult to avoid (or resist) the language of selection and survival of the fittest.[50] To designate Social Darwinism as a 'straw

---

[46] Although he repudiated biological reductionism, Durkheim remained ambivalent over the social significance of biology. This is apparent in his treatment of suicide and gender, and in his eventual endorsement of a *homo-duplex* model of human nature in which the psyche is divided between a pre-social and a social component. On the first point see H. Kushner, 'Suicide, Gender and the Fear of Modernity in Nineteenth Century Medical and Social Thought', *Journal of Social History*, 26(1993), 472; on the second, M. J. Hawkins, 'A Re-examination of Durkheim's Theory of Human Nature', *Sociological Review*, 25(1977), 229–52.

[47] L. F. Ward, 'Mind as a Social Factor', in D. A. Hollinger and C. Capper, eds., *The American Intellectual Tradition*, 2 vols., second edn (New York: Oxford University Press, 1993), II, 47.

[48] L. F. Ward, *Pure Sociology* (New York: Macmillan, 1903), 184, 238–40.

[49] *Ibid.*, 323 *et seq.* Ward's ambivalence towards Darwinism has been noted by Lewis Coser, 'American Trends', in T. Bottomore and R. A. Nisbet, eds., *A History of Sociological Analysis* (London: Heinemann, 1979), 298–300.

[50] This is the case with Edward Tylor, whose non-Darwinian stage-theory of social evolution occasionally referred to selection, struggle and survival of the fittest. See his *Anthropology* (London: Macmillan, 1892), 6, 55, 412–13, 427. The contexts suggest that Tylor largely confined struggle to primitive phases of evolution, to be replaced by 'peaceful and profitable intercourse' among civilised nations (286).

man' is, therefore, to misinterpret the intellectual context in which the social and psychological sciences were forged and developed.[51]

Social Darwinism and Darwin

Finally, to what extent, if at all, can Darwin himself be regarded as a Social Darwinist? Responses to this question constitute one of the most fiercely contested areas within Darwin scholarship. One response has been to present Darwin as a natural scientist concerned with discovering the principles of organic evolution by means of argument, experiment and observation. From this standpoint, Darwin's work must be sharply distinguished from the ideological perversions and vulgarisations which have been perpetrated under the rubric of Social Darwinism and for which the English naturalist was not responsible.[52] A variant of this position acknowledges the role of ideological currents in the formation of Darwin's theorising while still insisting on a distinction between this theorising and the products of Social Darwinism.[53] Adherents to both versions often seek to drive a wedge between Darwin and the work of Herbert Spencer, insisting that the latter's theories were devoid of a genuinely Darwinian content and would be more appropriately designated 'Social Lamarckism', or that Social Darwinism be renamed 'Social Spencerism'.[54]

This interpretation of Darwinism has been sharply opposed by readings which seek, albeit in a variety of ways, to contextualise Darwin's evolutionary writings within the philosophical, religious and ideological debates of his time. The aim of these studies is to demonstrate that Darwinism is quintessentially *social* and that to separate Darwinism as scientific theory and Darwinism as social theory leads to an impoverishment of our understanding of the historical context of Darwin's work in particular and of the interaction between science and society in

---

[51] This seems to be the conclusion of the detailed and scholarly overview by the American historian, Donald C. Bellomy: ' "Social Darwinism" Revisited', *Perspectives in American History*, new series, 1(1984), 1–129. Though evincing some sympathy with the revisionists (28) Bellomy concludes that 'every serious thinker had to come to terms with Darwinism and evolution' (128).

[52] For the assertion of radical differences between Darwin's theories and Social Darwinism, see Nisbet, *Social Change*, 161–4; K. Bock, 'Theories of Progress, Development, Evolution', in Bottomore and Nisbet, eds., *History of Sociological Analysis*, 70–2; For a recent forceful presentation of Darwinism as a pre-eminently scientific theory, see E. Mayr, *One Long Argument* (Harmondsworth: Penguin, 1993).

[53] Rogers, 'Darwinism and Social Darwinism', 268, 271, 280.

[54] Bock, 'Theories of Progress', 70; Leeds, 'Darwinian and "Darwinian" Evolutionism', 440–3; D. Freeman, 'The Evolutionary Theories of Charles Darwin and Herbert Spencer', *Current Anthropology*, 15(1974), 211–37; Bowler, *Evolution*, 225–6, 267, 272; Bowler, *Invention of Progress*, 157–8.

general.[55] They tend to emphasise the links between Darwin and Herbert Spencer, links consisting of a network of shared assumptions and viewpoints about God, nature, society and history which rendered Spencer a 'Darwinian before Darwin'.[56] On this reading, Darwin shared, in essential respects, the philosophical and ideological assumptions of one of the most salient Social Darwinists of the nineteenth century and must himself be included as a Social Darwinist.

The controversy over the extra-scientific connotations of Darwin's work extends to the issue of the Malthusian legacy in Darwinism. Darwin acknowledged the impact of Malthus on his own notion of the struggle for existence. Given the explicitly ideological motivations behind Malthus's original *Essay* of 1798 – to criticise the radical social theories of Godwin and Condorcet – this suggests a close connection between Darwinian biology and socio-political theory. Yet the nature of this connection has remained the subject of much debate. For Young, Malthus was 'the source of the view of nature which led to Social Darwinism – the social struggle for existence, the struggle for survival'.[57] Hirst, in contrast, insists on the qualitatively different theoretical contexts within which Malthus and Darwin deploy the notion of struggle.[58] Other writers argue that Malthus was primarily interested in the struggle between humans and their environment, and not with intrasocial manifestations of this struggle.[59] Yet Vorzimmer argues precisely the opposite thesis, namely that prior to reading Malthus, Darwin was already familiar with the idea of struggle between different species and between species and their environment: what Malthus

---

[55] Examples of this perspective can be found in J. C. Greene, *Science, Ideology and World View* (Berkeley, CA: University of Berkeley Press, 1981); R. M. Young, *Darwin's Metaphor* (Cambridge University Press, 1985); Young, 'Darwinism is Social', in D. Kohn, ed., *The Darwinian Heritage* (Princeton University Press, 1985), 609–38; G. Jones, 'The Social History of Darwin's *Descent of Man*', *Economy and Society*, 7(1978), 1–23. The most sustained effort to locate Darwin's work within his intellectual and social milieu is A. Desmond and J. Moore, *Darwin* (London: Faber and Faber, 1991).

[56] Greene, *Science, Ideology and World View*, 134, 140. See also Greene, *Darwin and the Modern World View* (Baton Rouge, LA: Mentor, 1963), 84–9.

[57] R. M. Young, 'Malthus and the Evolutionists: The Common Context of Biological and Social Theory', *Past and Present*, 43(1969), 111–12. See also B. Gale, 'Darwin and the Concept of Struggle for Existence: A Study in the Extrascientific Origins of Scientific Ideas', *Isis*, 63(1972), 321–44.

[58] P. Q. Hirst, *Social Evolution and Sociological Categories* (London: Allen and Unwin, 1976), 19–22.

[59] Bannister, *Social Darwinism*, 25; Crook, *Darwinism, War and History*, 17. Bowler maintains that while Malthus did focus on intrasocial struggle, he confined this to primitive rather than modern European societies. See P. Bowler, 'Malthus, Darwin, and the Concept of Struggle', *Journal of the History of Ideas*, 37(1976), 636.

allowed Darwin to see was 'the third and most important aspect of struggle – that between closely related members of the same species'.[60]

This last controversy is connected to the debates over the definition of Social Darwinism in that often disagreements derive from different understandings of the discursive entities under consideration – Darwinism, Malthusianism and Social Darwinism. Once again, it underscores the need for a conceptualisation of Darwinism which relates a notion like 'struggle for existence' to other components in the overall configuration. As I stated above, this procedure will not eliminate disagreement and different readings; but it will facilitate a fuller understanding of the configuration in question and the extent to which, if at all, its various elements are comparable to those contained in other discursive entities.

The present study

Given the disagreements and confusion surrounding the term 'Social Darwinism', the question inevitably arises: why bother retaining it? Why not, as Bowler has recommended, confine Darwinism to the realm of biological theory and avoid the expression Social Darwinism altogether?[61] The answer, quite simply, is: because the term refuses to go away. It occurs not only in scholarly texts on the histories of Europe and the USA during the late nineteenth and early twentieth centuries but is frequently used by journalists.[62] In the last twenty years it has figured prominently in the numerous controversies surrounding the discipline of sociobiology. In these circumstances it is tempting to adopt Darwinian terminology and to refer to the 'survival value' of Social Darwinism and its 'adaptation' to a variety of ideological and social contexts. It may be what Richard Dawkins has designated as a *meme*, the cultural analogue of the gene. This is a cultural unit such as an idea (or set of ideas), a fashion in clothes or a tune, which is capable of being replicated in diverse circumstances and enduring over lengthy time-periods.[63] For well over a century there has existed a body of ideas and images – albeit a shifting and contested one – subsumed, for better or worse, under the

---

[60] P. Vorzimmer, 'Darwin, Malthus and the Theory of Natural Selection', *Journal of the History of Ideas*, 30(1969), 540. See also S. Herbert, 'Darwin, Malthus and Selection', *Journal of the History of Biology*, 4(1971), 209–17.

[61] P. Bowler, 'Social Darwinism', *Sunday Correspondent*, 13 May 1990.

[62] The following examples, appearing in the British national press around the time Bowler published his comments, made extensive use of Darwinian terminology in the context of international economic competition and the policies of the Thatcher governments respectively: Guy de Jonquières, 'The Survival of the Fittest', *Financial Times*, 10 May 1990; Tony Cole, 'Surplice to Requirements', *New Statesman and Society*, 4 May 1990.

[63] R. Dawkins, *The Selfish Gene*, second edn (Oxford University Press, 1989), chap. 11.

term 'Social Darwinism'. This alone would furnish sufficient justification for seeking a better grasp of the ideas and images in question. But I have an additional reason: to show that the term is capable of being constructed and used in a way that is invaluable for an understanding of certain features of both historical and contemporary socio-political discourse.

The first step towards realising this goal is to conceptualise Social Darwinism. This is the task of the next chapter, which reconstructs the set of assumptions that underpinned Darwin's theory of evolution. My thesis is that this network represents a *world view* – an abstract configuration of interlinked ideas about time, nature, human nature and social reality. It is this world view, rather than a discrete ideology, which constitutes Social Darwinism, and Darwin himself was a major (though by no means the only) contributor to its elaboration and dissemination. The specific attributes of this world view are then illustrated through a comparison between it and Lamarckism, followed by an assessment of the historical uniqueness of Social Darwinism.

Of crucial importance to the development of my argument is the contention that, as a world view, Darwinism is a powerful *rhetorical* instrument. Its persuasive and flexible rhetorical resources derive from the existence of *indeterminacies* within the world view itself, i.e. open-endedness and even ambiguity over the precise meaning either of certain key terms or over how they are to be related to other terms. However, two series of events have consequences for these indeterminacies. The first comprises developments within the theory of organic evolution which 'close up' some of the original indeterminacies while at the same time opening up others. The second derives from the very processes of argumentation and ideological conflict through which the rhetorical and ideological limits of Social Darwinism are realised. Both processes interact to engender modifications of the original world view, in some instances leading to the emergence of different world views – something that happened, I shall argue, with certain versions of 'reform Darwinism'.

The work of the social psychologist Michael Billig and his collaborators on the rhetorical features of ideologies, and the inevitability of what they refer to as dilemmas, is very suggestive for exploring the rhetorical implications of Social Darwinism. Billig maintains that ideologies are never closed systems of thought but languages within which any proposition can be countered by contrary assertions, requiring deliberation and the assessment of competing values.[64] I have already proposed

[64] See M. Billig, *Arguing and Thinking* (Cambridge University Press, 1987). See also Billig *et al.*, *Ideological Dilemmas* (London: Sage, 1988), 23, 163.

that Social Darwinism contains a series of indeterminacies which provide a rich source for different rhetorical uses and interpretations. But these always take place within a specific ideological context: Social Darwinism, as a world view, was deployed as the background to different ideological positions. Now it is precisely at the intersections between the world view and the content of the ideology that some of the most interesting and important dilemmas were encountered. In particular, various ideologists discovered a persistent property of the world view, namely that nature was janiform. It could appear both as a model to be emulated by social practices and institutions and as a threat whose processes and laws were to be feared and counteracted by the appropriate actions. Of particular significance is the manner in which this dual aspect of nature was manifested not simply in the competing claims of rival ideologies or in different interpretations within the same ideology, but often within the ideas of the same thinker, and sometimes within the same text.

This janiform quality of Social Darwinist discourse will be explored in part II of this study through an examination of some of the pioneers in the construction, application and popularisation of the world view. Certain of these thinkers are well known and their ideas have been subjected to considerable scrutiny in the scholarly literature. My reason for including them is that the definition of Social Darwinism used here, and the focus upon the duality of nature as model and threat, allows these writers to be examined in a new light, uncovering implications and tensions that have received little or no attention in the historiography to date but which are, I shall argue, fundamental to an understanding of Social Darwinism. I shall also be including less well-known figures who either exerted considerable influence in their time or else exemplified features which typify in some manner a particular discursive tactic or structure.

Part III comprises a series of case studies intended to illustrate the role of Social Darwinism in different ideological contexts. The choice, in addition to being constrained by considerations of time and space, reflects a personal estimation about which of the many areas of social and political controversy during the last century or so are significant or interesting. Inevitably, not everybody will be satisfied with my selection, and some may feel that certain topics, such as Fascism, have already received a great deal of attention in the specialist literature. My purpose, however, in examining any particular topic, is to understand the role of Social Darwinism within it, and this is something which, though often assumed in the specialist literature, is rarely subjected to any detailed analysis.

The subject matter has been restricted in two ways. First, I have concentrated on social and political thought and have not explored the role of Social Darwinism in other contexts such as literature, the media or the popular culture of different social strata. This undertaking is beyond my resources and competence and, moreover, is dependent upon the exercise attempted in this study, namely the clarification of the nature and roles of Social Darwinism within its locus of origin – socio-political thought. Second, I have taken the bulk of my material from the period 1860–1945. These are the years during which Social Darwinism appeared and developed and probably enjoyed its most widespread appeal. Thereafter the topic would require a study in its own right, especially in the light of the transformations that occurred within the Darwinian theory of organic evolution, first with the 'Modern Synthesis' of the 1930s and 1940s and then with the discovery of the structure of DNA in 1953. There is, however, a concluding chapter on Social Darwinism and sociobiology. This is included partly in order to test the robustness of the conceptualisation of Social Darwinism in a very different historical context. But it also derives from the specific features of the controversies surrounding sociobiology which resonate some interesting continuities, as well as exhibiting some differences, with the earlier period. Again the hope is that this discussion of modern Social Darwinism will stimulate further inquiry.

It will be apparent from these comments that this is not a history of Social Darwinism in the conventional sense, i.e. it is not a narrative which traces in detail the trajectory of the world view step by step through time. In my view, this approach would be inappropriate at the present time. This study is both more limited and yet more comprehensive in scope. It is limited by its focus on a number of themes and thinkers because I consider it essential to grasp the character of Social Darwinism as a configuration of interlinked propositions and ideas and to examine how this configuration was used in ideological debate. This requires a detailed textual examination of the thinkers under discussion, and such detail precludes extending the analysis to cover all the relevant contributions. Some readers may well find the textual exegeses excessive. But the understanding of Social Darwinism has been obscured by the manner in which it has been treated in the majority of commentaries – a cursory definition accompanied by the occasional citation from a particular thinker. If the concern is with how ideas are interlinked and with how they function in discursive practice then a more detailed presentation of the texts under consideration is absolutely essential.

If this exercise necessitates a restriction of the number of texts under examination, then the comparative features of the study add a degree of breadth and generality to the conclusions which would be lacking had it been confined to a specific country. Drawing upon material from Europe and the USA opens up new possibilities for understanding and interpretation, and allows for a fuller appreciation of what Social Darwinism is and was, its different manifestations, and its importance in Western culture.

1 Defining Social Darwinism

The structure of social theory

Before proposing a conceptualisation of Social Darwinism, I need to make a detour by way of some brief observations on the structure of social and political theory. As will become evident during the course of this chapter, this digression is central to my argument about the nature of Social Darwinism.

Social and political theory in the West, from the Greeks until the present time, consists of two structural components, which I am going to label a *world view* and an *ideology*. The first component consists of a set of assumptions about the order of nature and of the place of humanity within it, and how this order relates to and is affected by the passage of time. It also usually contains a view of social reality and where this fits into the overall configuration of nature, human nature and time.

The second component comprises a theory of human interactions and how these are mediated by institutions. It will therefore contain a *descriptive* element that purports to explain some features of social and psychological existence; a *critique* of certain aspects of this existence, and probably of other theories as well; and a *prescription* for how the socio-political system ought to be organised. The ideological aspect of a theory thus contains both descriptive and evaluative features which often makes difficult the separation of the empirical and normative claims that are being made. Theories may vary according to the prevalence of one or other of these sorts of claims, but both are integral to their articulation.

In the light of the contested nature and overall dissensus about the meaning of the term 'ideology' among historians, social scientists and philosophers, I must emphasise that I am only using it for want of a better one. In this study, it simply refers to this second feature of socio-political theory and carries no pejorative connotations, i.e. as necessarily implying distortion or prejudice.

A world view, then, consists of a relatively abstract set of background assumptions which supply overall coherence to the ideology. Often these assumptions are implicit, becoming manifest only when needed to substantiate specific propositions. For example, a thinker arguing for the inevitability of conflict and competition in social life might legitimate this by reference to the ubiquity of competition throughout the natural world and argue that human relationships, as part of nature, are inescapably subject to the same mechanisms. The world view underpinning a particular ideology is not usually itself subjected to explicit discussion (although this sometimes occurs), but is nonetheless fundamental to the overall theoretical enterprise.

Among the various elements within a world view, the concept of human nature usually occupies a pivotal role. This concept purports to describe the fundamental motives which govern human conduct. The portrait of human nature is then located within a view of nature as a whole, and how both are affected, if at all, by temporal processes. It is also connected to the ideological aspects of the theory, since the way in which human drives and capabilities are conceptualised influences the manner in which the possibilities for social and political organisation are conceived. Thus a theory which posited the primacy of instincts and passions in human behaviour and which saw only a limited role for reason and self-discipline could infer the necessity for authoritative political, religious and moral direction as a universal feature of social life. In contrast, a theory in which people were depicted as inherently altruistic, rational and cooperative, but liable to corruption through the influence of vicious institutions and practices that warped their spontaneous proclivities, might recommend anarchism as the system most in harmony with human nature. In both instances, human nature acts as the reference point for specification of ideal but plausible modes of social and political organisation.

From the ancient world to the advent of modernity, human nature provided a conceptual bedrock for socio-political discourse. Though differing in their estimation of the attributes of this nature, theorists took for granted the existence of a permanent human essence that remained intact through both time and space. It was this essence which enabled thinkers to generalise about human conduct and to recommend the optimal social and ethical arrangements for the realisation of human welfare, however this was conceived.[1] It is the denial of this essence which constitutes one of the most striking claims of contemporary post-

[1]   See J. W. Burrow, *Evolution and Society* (Cambridge University Press, 1966), 98. There is an illuminating analysis of the role of models of human nature in Western thought in A. MacIntyre, *A Short History of Ethics* (London: Routledge, 1967).

modernism in its efforts to redefine the nature and purpose of socio-political theory.[2]

However, long before the advent of post-modernist thought the postulate of a universal human nature was under threat. By the mid-nineteenth century a series of developments had combined to render this postulate problematic. These developments cannot be discussed here,[3] but two are worthy of mention. The first was a growing awareness of the diversity of human values and behaviour. This was brought about through the expansion of trade and colonialism and the ensuing exposure of Westerners to non-European cultures, although a heightened consciousness of the cultural diversity *within* modern societies may also have been important. The second development derived from the challenge to the notion of nature as a divine creation which received impetus from different conceptions of the natural order that emerged during the nineteenth century.[4] The consequences of these changes were two-fold: first, they raised questions about the order of nature and the place of humanity within it; and second, they undermined confidence in the presumption of a set of motives or attributes common to mankind as a whole. Both consequences had ramifications for the construction of social and political theories in that they rendered problematic the conceptual foundations upon which the ideological components of these theories reposed. In particular, they called into question the validity of assuming a universal human nature, an assumption which, as we have seen, played a pivotal role in connecting world views to ideologies. If some of the key elements which comprised world views were problematic, then the descriptive, critical and prescriptive features of a theory were deprived of their legitimating and integrative grounding. The result was a crisis, and Burrow's characterisation of this crisis in Victorian Britain has a much wider relevance, when he writes of a need 'for ethical and political certainty, for ethical premises which should not be arbitrary and recommendations which should be more than tentative and piecemeal'.[5]

The distinction between world view and ideology is important to my argument in two ways. First, as I shall argue below, it enables the discursive nature and functions of Social Darwinism to be grasped. Second, it provides the basis for an understanding of the intellectual

---

[2]   See R. Rorty, *Contingency, Irony and Solidarity* (Cambridge University Press, 1989).

[3]   They are ably treated in Burrow, *Evolution and Society*.

[4]   Developments in what we would now regard as the biological sciences, and their implications for prevailing views of nature, are discussed in F. Jacob, *The Logic of Living Systems*, tr. B. E. Spillman (London: Allen Lane, 1974); D. R. Oldroyd, *Darwinian Impacts*, second edn (Milton Keynes: Open University Press, 1983).

[5]   Burrow, *Evolution and Society*, 93.

context in which Social Darwinism appeared. This was a situation in which generalisations and prescriptions about behaviour and institutions were made difficult by alterations to the ways in which people had traditionally perceived human nature in particular, and nature in general. Social Darwinism, I shall argue, represented both a contribution and a response to these difficulties.

Darwinism and Social Darwinism

Darwinism is a biological theory about how new species are formed and existing ones can become extinct. A species is 'a population of actually or potentially interbreeding organisms sharing a common gene pool'.[6] Darwinism holds that while heredity generally acts as a force for species continuity, minute variations are created within individual organisms through genetic mutations and the recombination of genetic material during sexual reproduction. If any of the variations engendered by mutation and recombination confer an advantage on certain organisms within a particular environment, then this will enhance their survival and/or their reproductive success. Their progeny inherit the advantageous trait, and their enhanced ability to reproduce ensures that the change will become widespread throughout the breeding population. This is the process of natural selection which, over time, results in the appearance of new species and the elimination of others. The role of natural selection in bringing about evolutionary change is aptly described by Dobzhansky as 'a deputy of the environment', ensuring that genetic changes produced by mutation and sexual reproduction are useful to the organism.[7]

This summary, however, is a description of *modern* Darwinism. Certain features of the original formulation have been excised in the light of subsequent advances in the biological sciences, while new elements have been incorporated, most notably from genetics. The modern version of Darwinism dates from the 'New Synthesis' which took place approximately between 1936 and 1947. During this period important advances in Mendelian genetics, population genetics and palaeontology during the 1920s and 1930s were synthesised with natural selection to produce an integrated evolutionary theory.[8] Until then, while evolution was widely accepted, Darwin's particular explanation of

---

[6]   S. J. Gould, *Ever Since Darwin* (Harmondsworth: Penguin, 1980), 232.

[7]   T. Dobzhansky, 'Species After Darwin', in S. A. Barnett, ed., *A Century of Darwin* (London: Mercury, 1960), 24.

[8]   J. Huxley, *Evolution: The Modern Synthesis*, third edn (London: Allen and Unwin, 1974); E. Mayr, 'Preface' to E. Mayr and W. B. Provine, eds., *The Evolutionary Synthesis* (Cambridge, MA: Harvard University Press, 1980), ix.

it had waned in popularity since the beginning of the twentieth century, leading to what some historians have described as an 'eclipse of Darwinism'.[9] There are, therefore, important differences between the original and the modern versions of Darwinism.[10] My intention is to reconstruct the original theory, including those elements that have since been dropped, and to include the framework of assumptions concerning time, nature and human nature which was essential to Darwin's reasoning. My method of inquiry, therefore, consists in identifying Darwinism through an investigation of Darwin's own writings. It is here that Darwinism was forged and from which it derived its name and its discursive identity.

Darwin's theory of evolution

In *On the Origin of Species* of 1859,[11] Charles Darwin (1809–82) endeavoured to account for 'the changing history of the organic world' (151). He did so by proposing 'one general law, leading to the advancement of all organic beings, namely multiply, vary, let the strongest live and the weakest die' (263). According to this law, minute variations in the organisation of an organism, induced largely through reproduction but to some extent also by the effects of use and disuse of organs and the action of the environment, were selected by nature if they gave the organism an advantage over others as measured by its survival and reproductive success. Darwin contended that useful variations would be inherited by descendants, and the cumulative effects of this process would enable the organisms involved to mutate into new varieties, species or even genera (170).

Selection took place through a struggle for existence. 'I should premise', Darwin wrote, 'that I use the term Struggle for Existence in a large and metaphorical sense, including dependence of one being on another, and including (which is more important) not only the life of the individual, but success in leaving progeny' (116). Darwin observed that although many organisms were capable of very high reproductive rates the numbers of any given species remained more or less stable over time. He concluded from this that organisms competed for available resources, success going to those possessing some advantage, however

---

[9] P. Bowler, *The Eclipse of Darwinism* (Baltimore: Johns Hopkins University Press, 1983). The expression was initially coined by Julian Huxley.
[10] There is an examination of the relationship between Darwin's theory and modern Darwinism in E. Sober, *The Nature of Selection* (Cambridge, MA: MIT Press, 1985), chap. 6.
[11] C. Darwin, *On the Origin of Species by Means of Natural Selection*, ed. J. W. Burrow (Harmondsworth: Penguin, 1968). Page references occur in the text.

slight, in this competition. This struggle for life occurred at three levels, 'either one individual with another of the same species, or with individuals of distinct species, or with the physical conditions of life' (117).

Of these three levels Darwin argued that 'the struggle almost invariably will be most severe between individuals of the same species, for they frequent the same districts, require the same food, and are exposed to the same dangers' (126). Although the struggle for life did not create the initial variations, it acted upon the probabilities affecting survival and reproduction and hence, in conjunction with heredity, supplied the dynamic of evolutionary change. In Darwin's own words: 'The theory of natural selection is grounded on the belief that each new variety, and ultimately each new species, is produced and maintained by having some advantage over those with which it comes into competition; and the consequent extinction of less favoured forms almost inevitably follows' (323).

It is important to be aware, however, of the role that Darwin assigned to mechanisms other than natural selection in the production of organic change. These were the use and disuse of organs, the inheritance of acquired characters and sexual selection. In the first edition of the *Origin* Darwin was highly sceptical about the direct action of the environment on plants and animals in bringing about change. He did, though, acknowledge a small role for the prolonged use or disuse of organs, although he thought that their effects had 'often been largely combined with, and sometimes overmastered by, the natural selection of innate differences' (182). From the fifth edition he ceded greater importance to the effects of use and disuse of organs and faculties, and even allowed a limited role for the inheritance of acquired characters. By the time of the publication of *The Descent of Man* in 1871, Darwin had moved even further in this direction.[12] Here he confessed that though he was unshaken in his conviction that natural selection played a primary role in evolution, he had perhaps attributed too much to the 'survival of the fittest' in his efforts to overthrow 'the dogma of separate creations'.[13] In subsequent correspondence he admitted 'the greatest error which I have committed, has been not allowing sufficient weight to the direct action of the environment, i.e. food, climate etc., independently of natural selection'. He justified this stance as follows: 'When I wrote the *Origin*, and for some years afterwards, I could find little evidence of the direct

---

[12] Greene, *Science, Ideology and World View*, 129; R. Korey, ed., *The Essential Darwin* (Boston: Little, Brown, 1984), 243–4; D. Rochowiak, 'Darwin's Psychological Theorising: Triangulating on Habit', *Studies in History and Philosophy of Science*, 19(1988), 238–9.

[13] C. Darwin, *The Descent of Man*, second edn (London: Murray, 1896), 91–2.

action of the environment; now there is a large body of evidence.'[14] This raises the issue of the relationship between the theories of Darwin and Lamarck, which I shall discuss in the next chapter. For the moment I simply want to make the point that any differentiation between the two theories must be based upon more than the presence or absence of the inheritance of acquired characters, since this mechanism occurs in both. For this reason it is quite inappropriate to classify a theory as non-Darwinian just because it accepts the inheritance of acquired characters. Not only did Darwin grant a role to this mechanism, but it was endorsed by many of his most fervent admirers, such as Ernst Haeckel in Germany. As Greene has argued, the 'Lamarckian' principle of the inheritance of acquired characters was not seen as a rival to natural selection, but rather as a complementary process in evolution.[15]

The theory of sexual selection was developed in the *Descent*. Here Darwin agreed that many physical and behavioural traits of humans and animals (such as the differences between races among the former) could not be adequately explained by natural selection. On the contrary, some features, like the ostentatious plumage of the peacock, would seem to reduce the survival probabilities of the organism in question. Equally, such traits were inexplicable by the direct action of the environment or the inherited effects of use and disuse. In order to account for such characteristics Darwin invoked another mechanism, sexual selection, or the competition for sexual partners and the opportunity for procreation.[16] This took place either through conflict between males for access to large numbers of females (e.g. among stags in deer herds), or else competition between males to attract females by means of display, courtship patterns, etc. (as in the case of the peacock). The most combative or attractive males, therefore, were able to reproduce at the expense of their less successful conspecifics.

Despite concessions to use and disuse and to the inheritance of acquired characters and his innovative model of sexual selection, Darwin continued to make natural selection the touchstone of his theory of evolution. This is evident in his treatment of human evolution. Darwin avoided this topic in the *Origin*, which concluded with the vague

---

[14] Darwin to M. Wagner, 13 October 1876, in F. Darwin, ed., *Charles Darwin*, second edn (London: Murray, 1902), 278.

[15] Greene, *Science, Ideology and World View*, 121. The accuracy of Greene's assessment is borne out by the example of scientists who saw no difficulty in synthesising natural selection and the inheritance of acquired characters. For a British example see Raphael Meldola, *Evolution: Darwinian and Spencerian* (Oxford: Clarendon Press, 1910), 31. For the USA, see L. H. Bailey, 'Neo-Lamarckism and Neo-Darwinism', *The American Naturalist*, 28(1894), 677–8.

[16] Darwin, *Descent*, 305–8. For a discussion of Darwin's notion of sexual selection see J. M. Smith, 'Sexual Selection' in Barnett, *Century of Darwin*, 231–44.

statement: 'Psychology will be based on a new foundation, that of the necessary acquirement of each mental power and capacity by gradation. Light will be thrown on the origin of man and his history' (458). But it is clear from Darwin's notebooks that from the earliest period of his theoretical development between 1836 and 1839 he had desired an understanding of human evolution. He excluded it from the *Origin* in order to avoid jeopardising the acceptance of his theory by dealing with such a controversial notion.[17] In a letter to the co-discoverer of natural selection, Alfred Russel Wallace (1823–1913), written just before the publication of the *Origin*, Darwin stated: 'You ask whether I shall discuss "man". I think I shall avoid the whole subject, as so surrounded with prejudices; though I fully admit it is the highest and most interesting problem for the naturalist.'[18]

This omission was rectified in the *Descent*, although by then a number of other theorists had already extended the principle of natural selection to human evolution. Still, from the very outset of this text, Darwin made explicit his conviction 'that man must be included with other organic beings in any general conclusion respecting his manner of appearance on this earth' (1). He contended that only arrogance and prejudice can sustain the belief in the separate creation of mankind, arguing that humans have descended from a non-human ancestry which they share with the apes. He insisted on the continuities between humans and animals, claiming that differences are quantitative rather than qualitative, and this not just with respect to physical traits but also with regard to language, reason, imagination and morality.[19]

The issue of the origin of the moral faculty was a very important one for Darwin, as indeed it has proved to be throughout the entire history of Darwinian theory. For many of his contemporaries morality was something unique to humans. Darwin argued that this was not so. The moral faculty derived from the 'social instincts', the most primitive manifestation of which was the parental instinct, which humans shared with other social creatures. Since man is a social animal, Darwin asserted, 'it is almost certain that he would inherit a tendency to be faithful to his comrades, and obedient to the leader of the tribe; for these qualities are common to most social animals' (167). Qualities such as altruism and courage, however, were problematic, for while individuals who pos-

---

[17] For Darwin's early interest in human evolution, see H. E. Gruber, *Darwin on Man* (New York: Dutton, 1974); Greene, *Science, Ideology and World View*, 97–101; Desmond and Moore, *Darwin*, chaps. 14–17.

[18] Darwin to Wallace, 1 May 1857, in F. Darwin, *Charles Darwin*, 183.

[19] The study of animal behaviour played an important part in Darwin's theory of human evolution. See R. W. Burkhardt, 'Darwin on Animal Behaviour and Evolution', in D. Kohn, *The Darwinian Heritage*, 327–65.

sessed these attributes would unquestionably benefit their tribe, they would expose themselves to increased risk of death. Hence they would be unlikely to reproduce themselves in sufficient numbers for their type to thrive (200). The difficulty here was one of explaining how a process – natural selection – that acted upon *individuals* produced an outcome with *collective* benefits in the form of moral sensibilities which were potentially lethal for the individuals who possessed them. Theoretically, survival and reproductive success should fall to cowards and egoists. Darwin provided two answers. The first – one now favoured by the majority of biologists – was to stress the self-regarding consequences of altruistic actions: helping others would increase the likelihood of aid to oneself in times of need. Darwin additionally stressed the importance to the individual of the praise and blame of neighbours in stimulating virtuous behaviour (201). But occasionally Darwin's language suggested a very different explanation, namely that selfless individual behaviour aided group survival. For example, he argued: 'A tribe including many members who, from possessing in a high degree the spirit of patriotism, fidelity, obedience, courage, and sympathy, were always ready to aid one another, and to sacrifice themselves for the common good, would be victorious over most other tribes; and this would be natural selection' (203).[20] I shall argue below that this ambiguity over group versus individual selection is an important component of Darwinism.

The above quotation does, though, indicate Darwin's conviction that natural selection operated in human evolution. Humans exhibited variations in body and mind and for him these 'variations are induced, either directly or indirectly, by the same general causes, and obey the same general laws, as with the lower animals'. As our early ancestors must at times have increased beyond their means of subsistence, 'they must, therefore, occasionally have been exposed to a struggle for existence, and consequently to the rigid law of natural selection' (70–1). Darwin believed that this struggle was mitigated within advanced civilised societies although there is some ambivalence in his evaluation of this. The growth of the instinct of sympathy had resulted in the proliferation of welfare and charity schemes which not only supported the mentally and physically incapable but enabled them to proliferate. The struggle for existence was thus attenuated in 'highly civilised nations', with the result that the biological value of their populations was in danger of being reduced (205–6). Yet we could not check this sympathy for the unfortunate 'without deterioration in the noblest part of our nature' (206), and Darwin assured his readers that there was

[20] For a discussion of the role of individual versus group selection in Darwin's thought, see M. Ruse, *The Darwinian Paradigm* (London: Routledge, 1989), 34–54.

reason to believe that far from diminishing, the social instincts and the virtues derived from them would be enhanced in the future (192). Nevertheless, the struggle for existence seemed only to be mitigated within civilised nations. The latter would, so Darwin argued, in the future exterminate 'the savage races throughout the world' as well as the 'anthropomorphous apes' (241–2). He was emphatic that without natural selection the heights of achievement exhibited by civilised nations would never have been attained. Indeed, Darwin even suggested that when one considered the vast tracts of fertile land populated only by wandering savages, one could not help but wonder whether the struggle for existence had been sufficiently severe (219).

The portrait of nature which emerges from Darwin's writings is thus one in which change is paramount. Though very gradual and requiring vast time scales for their realisation, selective pressures rendered unviable the notion that species were permanent. In the *Origin* Darwin wrote: 'I am fully convinced that species are not immutable' (69). He went on to suggest that the conceptual categories employed by taxonomists to identify species were matters of convention, the products of a consensus within the scientific community (104). Darwinism, therefore, represents another source of difficulty for the belief in 'species essentialism'[21] and hence, by implication, for the notion of a universal human nature. It contributed to the intellectual and moral crisis in mid-century Western culture already referred to; it also, as I will argue, could be employed as a means of resolving that crisis.

The Social Darwinist world view

On the basis of this sketch of Darwin's theory I want to propose the following: Darwin's theory of natural selection – the theory that forms the nub of the modern theory of evolution – was embedded within and formed part of a wider world view.[22] This world view was a configuration of assumptions concerning nature, time and human nature which gave natural selection its relevance and meaning. It consisted of the

[21] For a discussion of Darwin's rejection of species essentialism, see D. Hull, *Darwin and His Critics* (Cambridge, MA: Harvard University Press, 1973), 66–7; M. T. Ghiselin, *The Triumph of the Darwinian Method*, second edn (London: University of Chicago Press, 1984), 49–57, 60–1, 72–3; Sober, *Nature of Selection*, 159–65.

[22] In arguing this I have been influenced by Greene's thesis in *Science, Ideology and World View*, although I differ from Greene in my conception of the content and the durability of this world view. I want to emphasise that in referring to Darwinism as a world view I am in no way suggesting that evolution through natural selection fails to qualify as a genuine scientific theory, a thesis propounded at one time by Karl Popper. See his 'Darwinism as a Metaphysical Research Programme' in P. Schlipp, ed., *The Philosophy of Karl Popper* (La Salle, IL: Open Court, 1974).

following elements: (i) biological laws governed the whole of organic nature, including humans; (ii) the pressure of population growth on resources generated a struggle for existence among organisms; (iii) physical and mental traits conferring an advantage on their possessors in this struggle (or in sexual competition), could, through inheritance, spread through the population; (iv) the cumulative effects of selection and inheritance over time accounted for the emergence of new species and the elimination of others.

Now the first assumption is one of scientific determinism, and was a powerful organising assumption for Darwin (and many others) in his opposition to supernatural and teleological accounts of species formation. Social Darwinism, however, involves a crucial fifth assumption, namely that this determinism extends to not just the physical properties of humans but also to their social existence and to those psychological attributes that play a fundamental role in social life, e.g. reason, religion and morality. It is possible to endorse elements (i)–(iv) without adhering to the fifth, either on the grounds that such features are unique to mankind, which stands apart from the rest of nature as a divine creation; or, as was increasingly argued by social scientists, because humans are cultural creatures and culture cannot be reduced to biological principles. Social Darwinists, however, are of the view that many (if not all) aspects of culture – religion, ethics, political institutions, the rise and fall of empires and civilisations, in addition to many psychological and behavioural features – can be explained by the application of the first four elements to these domains. Social Darwinists, then, endorse two fundamental facts about human nature: that it is continuous with animal psychology, and that it has evolved through natural selection.

The five elements are interwoven in a particular way. There is, as it were, a *syntax* governing their relationships, although this term implies a more rigorous logical interconnection than is in fact the case.[23] Yet there is a hierarchy among the elements, with each one following sequentially, from laws of nature to evolution as an instance of such laws, then from the causes of evolution to its relevance to human psychological and social phenomena. Loose though it is, this sequence is important for the meaning and weighting of the individual components. Thus species formation and extinction are not presented as facts of nature in their own right, but are derived from the effects of selection and heredity.

---

[23] The theory of natural selection can, however, be reformulated as a deductive structure. See A. Flew, *Darwinian Evolution* (London: Paladin, 1984), 36–40. There is an illuminating presentation of Darwin's theory which underlines the looseness of its deductive inferences in M. Ruse, *Darwinism Defended* (Reading, MA: Addison-Wesley, 1982), 47, fig. 2.10.

Similarly, the struggle for existence is in turn predicated on the discrepant ratio of population growth to available resources. It is this total configuration and the relationship among its elements which is specific to Social Darwinism. The individual elements have a history of their own, independent of Social Darwinism. What constitutes the latter is the manner in which these elements are articulated and connected to form a striking conception of the causes and dynamics of social change.

By referring to Social Darwinism as a world view I am making a claim about its discursive role. This is that Social Darwinism is not, in itself, a social or political theory. Rather, it consists of a series of connected assumptions and propositions about nature, time and how humanity is situated within both. What it does not possess is any concrete specification of human social and mental development, nor any particular vision of the optimal conditions for human social and spiritual existence. In other words, the ideological component of a theory is absent from Social Darwinism. This is not to argue that Darwin himself was personally free of ideological interests or that these were unimportant to his formulation of the world view. What I am claiming is that the world view is separable from whatever religious, political or ethical perspectives Darwin may have professed. Indeed, the success of Social Darwinism lies in this very flexibility, in the possibilities it contained for transference to a whole spectrum of ideological positions.

Why this flexibility? The answer is to be found in a feature of the world view that has already been touched upon, namely the existence of a series of indeterminacies surrounding some of its elements – indeterminacies evidenced by Darwin's own hesitancies and ambiguities. Even in his own writings, 'Darwinism' was not a fixed entity, but more a set of models of evolutionary transformation which received different emphases at different points in his scientific career.[24] These indeterminacies are therefore crucial to an understanding of the different ideological contexts in which Social Darwinism could be deployed.

The first of these concerns the mechanisms of evolutionary change. Natural selection, use and disuse of organs, acquired characters, sexual selection – all of these formed part of the Darwinian lexicon, and different theorists could, and did, emphasise different ones. Sexual selection tended to fall into abeyance after Darwin, although it has been very much revised in modern versions, as I will show in the final chapter of this study. The inheritance of acquired characters was stressed by many eminent popularisers of Social Darwinism. This gave rise to another indeterminacy, namely the cause of organic and behavioural

[24] E. Mayr, 'Darwin's Five Theories of Evolution', in Kohn, *Darwinian Heritage*, 755–72; D. Hull, 'Darwinism as a Historical Entity', in Kohn, *Darwinian Heritage*, 810.

variations. Advocates of the inheritance of acquired characters could posit environmental changes as a source of such variations (rather than innate mutations), a position which could legitimate agendas of political and social reform. The compatibility of the inheritance of acquired characters with natural selection was, nonetheless, put into question by the work of the German biologist August Weismann (1834–1914). Weismann theorised the existence of a 'germ-plasm' which determined somatic traits. Whereas the latter could be influenced by environmental conditions, the germ-plasm could not be so influenced. The upshot of this was that any somatic modifications induced in an organism during its lifetime could not be transmitted to its offspring. This encouraged a neo-Darwinism which espoused a 'hard hereditarianism', insisting that natural selection of innate organic variations was the only mechanism of evolution. Yet although this version became increasingly widespread during the first half of the twentieth century, the inheritance of acquired characters continued to stimulate a great deal of research in biology between the 1870s and the 1920s.[25] It gradually lost favour during the period of the evolutionary synthesis, more as a result of becoming an unnecessary hypothesis through the general acceptance of natural selection than through falsification.[26] The struggle for existence was also a concept open to a number of interpretations by social theorists. It could be equated with violent struggle and warfare, or – in keeping with Darwin's suggestions about the attenuation of struggle in civilised nations – warfare could be confined to primitive stages of social evolution, to be replaced by industrial competition or perhaps the battle of ideas as civilisation progressed. Hence the possibility of being both a Social Darwinist and a pacifist. Another very important area of indeterminacy related to the *unit* of evolution upon which natural selection acted. We have noted how Darwin tended to see this as the individual organism but sometimes presented the group as the evolutionary unit. This opened up the possibility of variable interpretations of the unit of selection – individual, species, tribe, nation, race were some of the candidates that were put forward between 1860 and 1945 (compared to the 'selfish gene' of modern Darwinism). Hence the world

---

[25]   E. Mayr, 'Prologue' in Mayr and Provine, *Evolutionary Synthesis*, 15. It is interesting to note that Weismann himself came to admit the possibility that the germ-plasm could be directly affected by the environment. Cf. E. Mayr, *One Long Argument*, 125–6.

[26]   R. W. Burkhardt, 'Lamarckism in Britain and the United States', in Mayr and Provine, *Evolutionary Synthesis*, 347. The inheritance of acquired characters has never been completely abandoned by biologists. Some modern geneticists believe it possible for an organism to alter its genes through environmental modification of the DNA molecule, and to then transmit this alteration to its offspring. See N. Schoon, 'Genes "Heresy" May Revolutionise Evolutionary Theory', *The Independent*, 14 December 1989.

view possessed great flexibility over what units were engaged in the struggle for existence, in addition to flexibility with regard to how the struggle was conducted.

Two other indeterminacies relate to the rate and the direction of evolutionary change. First, Darwin saw the rate of change as inevitably gradual, building upon minute variations. It was, however, possible to be a Darwinist and believe change to be more uneven, with long periods of stability juxtaposed with periods of relatively dramatic change, a view held by one of Darwin's most formidable champions, T. H. Huxley (1825–95).[27] Second, the Darwinian world view did not entail a commitment to a particular direction for evolutionary change, and theories of degeneration were as prolific as theories of progress. Certainly many Social Darwinists did believe that evolution entailed progress, a view endorsed by Darwin himself, as I shall argue below. But belief in progress forms part of the ideological aspect of a theory, and the Darwinian world view was equally compatible with a quite antithetical perspective.

One final area of indeterminacy – and an extremely important one – derives not from the meaning of particular terms but from the articulation between the fifth element and the remainder of the world view. It was especially pronounced for those whose interest was in social evolution. Two broad strategies were available to theorists. They could be completely reductionist and argue that social evolution was dependent on the biological properties of humans, or they could argue that social evolution, while not reducible to biology, nonetheless took place through analogous processes of adaptation, selection and inheritance. In practice the two approaches were not always kept distinct, with some theorists adopting both. But whatever strategy was opted for, there was a need to show that the social order in some way mirrored the natural order. This created a potential for the production of a whole range of equivalences, analogies, images and metaphors: that societies are equivalent to biological organisms or that races represent biological species; individuals are akin to cells; that war is a manifestation of the struggle for existence; that women and children occupy the same position as 'savages' in the scale of evolution, and so on. Metaphors and images were thus central to any Social Darwinist enterprise, whatever its

[27] For Huxley's saltationism, see M. Di Gregorio, *T. H. Huxley's Place in Natural Science* (New Haven/London: Yale University Press, 1984), 66; A. Desmond, *Huxley* (London: Michael Joseph, 1994), 256, 262. A modern version is the theory of 'punctuated equilibrium' propounded by Stephen Jay Gould and his co-workers. This theory has, however, met with a great deal of criticism. For a critical overview of the literature see E. O. Wilson, *The Diversity of Life* (Harmondsworth: Penguin, 1994), 80–1, 344; J. M. Smith, *Did Darwin Get it Right?* (Harmondsworth: Penguin, 1993), chaps. 16–17.

scientific pretensions, necessitated by the need to link the first four elements of the world view with the fifth and to show how human culture was governed by inexorable laws of nature.

These indeterminacies do not mean that the world view was so abstract as to be indistinguishable from others, or so bland that it could go with anything. It embraces scientific materialism, the rejection of supernatural forces in natural explanation, and a view of humans as having evolved from non-human life-forms and as susceptible to change over time. As for its indeterminacies, these undoubtedly make for adaptability, but not ideological licence. Despite its flexibility and the depth of its rhetorical resources, there were boundaries to both. My point is that these boundaries cannot be arbitrarily specified but must be discovered by an examination of its actual discursive uses. From the fact of somebody being a Social Darwinist it is not possible – or rather, it would be extremely unwise – to deduce his or her position on warfare, capitalism, race, imperialism or the social status of women. The indeterminacies within the world view allow for the taking up of quite antithetical positions on all these, and other, issues.

There is, however, one feature of the world view – one that was to be discovered in the course of its deployment in ideological debates – which was to mark most of Social Darwinist theorising, irrespective of its ideological bent. This is the Janus-like picture of nature that it presents. Hints of this are discernible in Darwin's own writings, for example when he highlights the deleterious consequences of the diminution of the struggle for survival within civilised societies but then asserts the impossibility of counteracting these without violating some of our most exalted values. Here we see the laws of nature as both beneficent and malign, as something to be emulated and as a force to be feared, as both a model and a threat. If the indeterminacies within Social Darwinism provided a veritable quarry of rhetorical materials, then the janiform visage of nature it also contained constituted a source of dilemmas which at times threatened the coherence of the theories in question. But again, neither the rhetorical potential nor the dilemmatics of Social Darwinism can be identified prior to the investigation of the texts in which they appeared.

Darwin and Social Darwinism

Finally, where did Darwin stand in relation to Social Darwinism? On my reading he clearly was a Social Darwinist and, moreover, one of the major architects of the world view. In particular the crucial fifth assumption was one that he had made early on in his theoretical labours and very likely formed one of the motives behind his entire research effort. The *Origin* formulated the framework of evolutionary theory which books like the *Descent* and *The Expression of the Emotions in Man and Animals* (1872) then applied to psychological and behavioural propensities such as language, emotional expression, cognition, sexual attraction and morals. In the light of Darwin's quite explicit desire to apply evolutionary theory to these areas, as well as the continuing importance they have had in social thought, from sexology to contemporary sociobiology, it is both perverse and inaccurate to deny his status as a Social Darwinist. Darwinism *was* inherently social in that Darwin himself sought to apply evolutionary theory to mental and social phenomena.

What Darwin did not do was construct a complete social theory himself, i.e. he did not erect an ideology on the foundations of the world view he propounded. True, he adopted positions on the issues of his day which reveal his own preferences and prejudices. For example, despite his awareness of the problems of equating evolutionary change with progress, he nonetheless often made the connection. I have already drawn attention to his assertion in the *Descent* that moral development would continue to the point where 'the struggle between our higher and lower impulses will be less severe, and virtue will be triumphant' (192). But the *Origin* also concluded with the assurance that 'as natural selection works solely by and for the good of each being, all corporeal and mental endowments will tend to progress towards perfection' (459). Darwin also expressed conventional views on the superiority of the civilised 'Anglo-Saxon' nations over other countries and regarded 'savages' as examples of mankind arrested at its most primitive stage of development, while being convinced of the intellectual superiority of men over women.[28] At the same time he was a passionate opponent of slavery and highly critical of the conduct of the Portuguese and Spanish colonists towards negroes and the indigenous Indian populations in South America.[29] But Darwin never attempted to formulate his social

---

[28] These themes have been frequently remarked upon in studies already cited by Greene, Young and Desmond and Moore. Darwin's relationship to prevailing social values are also discussed in S. Strawbridge, 'Darwin and Victorian Social Values', in E. M. Sigsworth, ed., *In Search of Victorian Social Values* (Manchester University Press, 1988), 102–15. For Darwin's attitude towards women, see E. Richards, 'Darwin and the Descent of Woman', in D. R. Oldroyd and I. Langham, eds., *The Wider Domain of Evolutionary Thought* (Boston, MA: Reidel, 1983), 57–111.

[29] On slavery, see Darwin's letter to Lyell, 25 August 1845, in F. Darwin, *Charles Darwin*, 137. On the Spanish and Portuguese treatment of subject races, see C. Darwin, *A Naturalist's Voyage Round the World* (London: Murray, 1902), 19, 24 and chap. 4. In 1882 Darwin signed a petition protesting against the persecution of Jews in Russia; see W. J. Fishman, *East End Jewish Radicals, 1875–1914* (London: Duckworth, 1995), 69.

and political views in a systematic fashion. And even if he had, this would have been irrelevant to the question of whether or not he was a Social Darwinist.

Darwin's role in the formulation of the Social Darwinist world view was indisputable, therefore. But he was not the only contributor. The *Origin* is a highly original work which rationalised the first four components of the world view, but Alfred Russel Wallace had also grasped the workings of natural selection during the 1850s. Moreover, historians have uncovered close parallels between the assumptions about nature, time and human nature which underpinned the work of Wallace and Darwin and those found in the writings of Spencer, Lyell and Robert Chambers. There is also a close connection between Darwin's ideas and contemporary debates and developments within political economy, theology and the philosophy of science.[30]

Darwin's relationship to prevailing currents of thought is even more pronounced in the *Descent*. The *Origin* was, after all, largely based upon Darwin's own fieldwork, experiments and observations.[31] But as a number of commentators have remarked, and Darwin himself acknowledged, the *Descent* is a much more derivative item, heavily dependent on the observations and speculative endeavours of his contemporaries.[32] So, for example, his ideas on the habits and institutions of tribal peoples were influenced by the likes of Spencer and Bagehot (neither of whom had any practical fieldwork experience of such cultures). In fact, by the time he came to write the *Descent*, natural selection had been applied to human evolution by Royer in France, Bagehot, Spencer, Wallace and Galton in Britain, Haeckel in Germany, and Charles Loring Brace in the USA – all of whom, with the exception of Royer and Brace, Darwin drew upon.[33] The Social Darwinist world view was, therefore, elabo-

[30] See, *inter alia*, Greene, *Science, Ideology and World View*; Desmond and Moore, *Darwin*; R. M. Young, *Darwin's Metaphor* and 'Darwinism is Social', 609–38; D. Ospovat, 'God and Natural Selection', *Journal of the History of Biology*, 13(1980), 169–94; Ospovat, *The Development of Darwin's Theory* (Cambridge University Press, 1981); S. Schweber, 'Darwin and the Political Economists', *Journal of the History of Biology*, 13(1980), 195–289; Ruse, *Darwinian Paradigm*, 9–33.

[31] There is a discussion of the importance of fieldwork in the theoretical development of Darwin, Wallace and other creative naturalists of this period in G. Canguilhem, *Etudes d'histoire et philosophie des sciences*, second edn (Paris: Vrin, 1970), 99–110.

[32] Greene, *Science, Ideology and World View*; G. Jones, 'The Social History of Darwin's *The Descent of Man*'; Darwin, *Descent*: 'This work contains hardly any original facts in regard to man' (3).

[33] Bagehot, Royer, Spencer, Brace and Haeckel are dealt with at length later in this study. Francis Galton was Darwin's cousin who later coined the term 'eugenics'. He published a number of influential items during the 1860s, including 'Hereditary Talent and Character', *Macmillan's Magazine*, 12(1865), 157–66, 318–27, and *Hereditary Genius* (London: Macmillan, 1869). Wallace published his important 'The Origin of Human Races' in 1864, reproduced in M. Biddiss, ed., *Images of Race* (Leicester University

rated by a number of theorists interested in linking organic and human evolution, among whom Darwin was a seminal, but not the only, figure.

Press, 1979), 39–54. It is noteworthy, however, that by the end of the 1860s Wallace had renounced his earlier belief that natural selection was capable of accounting for 'the higher intellectual and spiritual nature of man', thereby distancing himself from the fifth element in the Social Darwinist world view: Wallace, cited in H. Clements, *Alfred Russel Wallace* (London: Hutchinson, 1983), xv. This shift of position is discussed in Desmond and Moore, *Darwin*, 569–70.

The Lamarckian world view

At this juncture I propose to explore the distinctiveness of Social Darwinism by comparing it, first, to the ideas of the French naturalist Lamarck, and second, to some earlier examples of evolutionary thought.

Jean Baptiste Lamarck (1744–1829) elaborated a systematic and influential account of evolution based upon a complex philosophy of life.[1] Although Darwin publicly acknowledged Lamarck's contribution to the theory of evolution, he privately dismissed the Frenchman's work, claiming he had derived nothing from it.[2] There may have been pragmatic reasons for repudiating Lamarck which will be considered below. Other contemporaries of Darwin certainly had a high opinion of Lamarck and I have already drawn attention to Darwin's own endorsement of 'Lamarckian' evolutionary mechanisms like the use and disuse of organs and the inheritance of acquired characters. Thus the relationship between the two theories is a matter of importance since some historians have suggested that what has been passed off as Social Darwinism would actually be far more accurately designated Social Lamarckism.

Lamarck's biological theory – he actually coined the word 'biology' in the early nineteenth century – was heavily influenced by the *idéologues*:

[1]   For critical accounts of Lamarck's ideas, see E. Boesiger, 'Evolutionary Theories After Lamarck and Darwin', in F. J. Alaya and T. Dobzhansky, eds., *Studies in the Philosophy of Biology* (London: Macmillan, 1974), 22–7; R. Burkhardt, 'Lamarckism in Britain and the United States'; L. Jordanova, *Lamarck* (Oxford University Press, 1984).

[2]   Darwin, letter to Lyell 12 March 1863, in F. Darwin, *Charles Darwin*, 257. Here Darwin mentions 'a wretched book' by Lamarck, presumably the latter's *Zoological Philosophy*. Darwin imputed to Lamarck the view that animals adapted to changing environments through acts of will, a common misinterpretation deriving from the misconstrual of *besoin* as 'want' whereas Lamarck intended 'need'. See Jordanova, *Lamarck*, 102; J. Burrow, 'Introduction' to *On the Origin of Species*, 32. Lyell defended Lamarck against this misinterpretation in a letter to Darwin, 3 October 1859 (F. Darwin, *Charles Darwin*, 207). The same error was committed by later theorists, e.g. J. Fiske, *Outlines of Cosmic Philosophy*, 2 vols. (London: Macmillan, 1874), II, 6–7; W. James, *The Principles of Psychology*, II, 678.

late eighteenth-century French philosophers dedicated to the creation of a science of mankind.[3] Lamarck extended their project by insisting that humans were part of nature and subject to its laws. Far from constituting a special creation, people differed only quantitatively from other creatures in that they possessed more complex faculties than animals but nothing uniquely human, including the ability to reason.

In his *Zoological Philosophy* of 1809,[4] Lamarck asserted the existence of an evolutionary progression from the simplest to the most complex forms of biological organisation. He observed that 'in ascending the animal scale, starting from the most imperfect animals, organisation gradually increases in complexity in an extremely remarkable manner' (1). This progression was a consequence of organic transformations impelled by environmental changes. Lamarck proposed as a general law that 'variations in the environment induce changes in the needs, habits and mode of life of living beings; and that these changes give rise to modifications or developments in their organs and the shape of their parts' (45). The impact of environmental change on the animal was not direct: rather, in striving to adapt to new conditions, an animal's needs were altered. If these became permanent then organic transformations were made possible either through the development of new organs or by the modification of existing structures (107). The features of the milieu considered critical in causing these modifications were climate, temperature, habits and 'the means of self-preservation, the mode of life and the methods of defence and multiplication' (114).

On the basis of these considerations Lamarck postulated two laws of development. The first asserted that in any animal that had 'not passed the limits of its development', increased frequency in the use of an organ or faculty would augment or enlarge it, while prolonged disuse would cause it to atrophy. The second claimed that any losses or acquisitions brought about by use or disuse or through adaptation to changing conditions would be 'preserved by reproduction to the new individuals which arise, provided that the acquired modifications are common to both sexes, or at least to the individuals which produce the young' (113). Lamarck concluded from these laws that new species evolved very slowly from existing species through the accretion of these modifications. Hence there were no fixed and immutable entities in nature, while species 'shade gradually into some other neighbouring species', making it difficult to establish clear-cut species boundaries (36–7).

These laws applied to humanity whose ancestors, having acquired the facility of standing and walking in an upright position, developed new

[3]   Jordanova, *Lamarck*, 77–80.
[4]   Tr. H. Elliot (London: Macmillan, 1914).

needs to which they adapted and thus not only left the other animals behind in terms of development, but gained mastery over them as well. With the extension of needs and ideas, the necessity for communication intensified, leading to the formation of the organs of speech and language (170–3).

This brief survey reveals some points in common between the theories of Lamarck and Darwin. In both there is an assertion of the universality of evolution which occurs gradually through the accumulation of small changes. Both consider species to be mutable, which makes possible the emergence of new species, although Lamarck's reference to 'limits of development' implies the existence of some constraints on this process. Both endorse the thesis that humans evolved from animal life-forms. Where Lamarck and Darwin differed was, first, in their characterisation of evolution, with Lamarck describing a linear process from the simple to the complex in contrast to Darwin's branching notion; and second, in their respective explanations of these transformations. Lamarck was certainly attuned to the existence of competition and predation throughout nature (including mankind), which has prompted some commentators to credit him with advocating the struggle for existence as a selective device.[5] Careful attention to the contexts in which his remarks on this topic are made show this not to be so.

Lamarck argued that the fecundity and rapid multiplication of organisms, particularly those low in the scale of complexity, posed a threat to the preservation and perfectibility of the higher species by crowding them out of existence. Predation corrected this imbalance and preserved the natural equilibrium:

The multiplication of the small species of animals is so great, and the succession of generations is so rapid, that these small species would render the globe uninhabitable to any others if nature had not set a limit to their prodigious multiplication. But since they serve as a prey to a multitude of other animals, and since the duration of their life is very short and they are killed by any fall of temperature, their numbers are always maintained in the proper proportions for the preservation of their own and other races.

As to the larger and stronger animals, they might well become dominant and have bad effects upon the preservation of many other races if they could multiply in too large proportions; but their races devour one another, and they only multiply slowly and a few at a time, and this maintains in their case also the kind of equilibrium that should exist (54).

Human beings might, at first glance, seem to be exceptions to this rule because their intelligence and other abilities protected them from the

---

[5]   For example, G. Himmelfarb, *Darwin and the Darwinian Revolution* (New York: Norton, 1962), 177–8.

predation of other animals. But nature had endowed humans with many passions and these, through the warfare they engendered, checked population growth. Thus mankind regulated itself through the unintended consequences of its powers and passions.

> By these wise precautions, everything is thus preserved in the established order; the continual changes and renewals which are observed in that order are kept within limits that they cannot pass; all the races of living bodies continue to exist in spite of their variations; none of the progress made towards perfection of organisation is lost; what appears to be disorder, confusion, anomaly, incessantly passes again into the general order, and even contributes to it; everywhere and always, the will of the Sublime Author of nature and of everything that exists is invariably carried out (55).

From these arguments and the language in which they are couched it is evident that Lamarck had a different view of nature to that exhibited in Darwin's writings. While they shared a number of assumptions, Darwin's advocacy of a creative role for struggle in bringing about organic change was very different from Lamarck's remarks about the effects of predation and warfare. For the French naturalist both were conservative principles, serving to maintain an equilibrium in the natural order. In this respect at least, Lamarck's philosophy of nature had its roots in eighteenth-century conceptions of nature as a system of harmony and perfectibility.[6]

Other differences over the nature of struggle are also discernible. In contrast to Darwin, who considered the battle for life to be most acute among conspecifics, Lamarck declared: 'individuals rarely eat others of the same race as themselves; they make war on different races' (54). For him predation was not a question of culling the weakest specimens within a species: on the contrary, 'ill-fed, suffering or sickly individuals' were capable of adaptation and modification and their descendants would therefore move up a rung on the evolutionary ladder (108). Jordanova has summarised the difference between the two naturalists thus: where Darwin saw animals and plants competing for survival, Lamarck saw a more harmonious process of mutual adaptation.[7]

Lamarckism, then, cannot be reduced to a belief in the inheritance of acquired characters as a mechanism of evolution. Rather it must be seen as a world view in its own right in which change takes place from below as inferior organisms strive to adapt, improve and progress. This conception of a self-improving natural order, mediated through the writings of the French anatomist Etienne Geoffroy Saint-Hilaire, was

---

[6]   There is a useful discussion of eighteenth-century conceptions of nature in B. Willey, *The Eighteenth Century Background* (London: Chatto and Windus, 1965).

[7]   Jordanova, *Lamarck*, 106.

deployed in both France and Britain as the philosophical foundation of early radical, republican and socialist political agendas. As Desmond has demonstrated, Lamarckism provided these movements with a powerful scientific rationale for doctrines of progress through 'development from below'. For the radicals: 'Nature and society were congruent. Both were improving and progressive: the moral evils of society were benevolent dispensations favouring working-class improvement, while in the animal kingdom the inferior organisms triumphantly progressed to escape their lowly station.'[8] These arguments appealed not only to radical and socialist agitators, but also to the non-establishment medical schools of Edinburgh and London that were challenging the hegemony of Oxbridge and the medical corporations. 'Clearly', writes Desmond, 'Lamarckism had some disreputable associations. It was being exploited by extremists promoting the dissolution of Church and aristocracy, and calling for a new economic system. These atheists and socialists supported a brand of evolution quite unlike Darwin's.'[9] He concludes that this ideological context helps explain Darwin's tardiness in publishing his own theory. Darwin had attended Edinburgh University for a time and had there met some of the foremost radical Lamarckians. He was terrified of becoming associated with the political uses to which they were putting their transformist ideas. For, like them, Darwin also perceived nature to be self-developing and courted the risk of having his own ideas pirated by the radicals, notwithstanding his Malthusian, anti-Lamarckian view of the causes of this development.[10] Fortunately for Darwin the routing of the radical Lamarckians during the late 1840s coupled with the relative political quiescence of the following decade enabled him to avoid the taint of radicalism, although his ideas did become part of the arsenal of anti-establishment figures like Huxley and Spencer.

Darwinism and Lamarckism, therefore, though sharing some assumptions, diverged widely on others. In particular, they proposed different explanations of organic change which in turn resonated discrepant conceptions of the natural order. For Darwin, evolution was brought about primarily through the selective consequences of struggle, an explanation that was alien to Lamarckism. Yet the differences are more than just a disagreement over the role of competition. This notion was integral to Darwinism, intimately linked to the configuration of assumptions comprising the world view as a whole. Its absence (as a creative

---

[8] A. Desmond, *The Politics of Evolution* (London: University of Chicago Press, 1989), 208.

[9] *Ibid.*, 4.

[10] *Ibid.*, 412. Desmond describes how working-class audiences during the 1860s interpreted Darwin for their own purposes in his *Huxley*, 292–3.

mechanism) in Lamarck likewise reflected the Frenchman's belief in adaptation from below as the driving force in evolution and of nature as a moving equilibrium. Darwinism additionally implied a much greater stress on heredity than did Lamarckism. In the latter perspective, heredity acts to ensure the transmission of successful adaptations, whereas in the former it is itself a source of variations (although Darwin was unsure how these occurred). Darwinism also contained the potential for depicting heredity as a much more autonomous force, relatively immune from environmental pressures, as in its Weismannian guise. Hence the Darwinian conception of heredity is one that potentially lends itself to a form of hereditarian determinism which is at odds with the environmentalist focus of Lamarckism.

This last consideration points to a need for care in analysing the writings of evolutionary thinkers who enlisted the inheritance of acquired characters within Social Darwinist frameworks. This is especially true of those who believed in progress. The inheritance of acquired characters could be used to explain cumulative mental or social improvement. But what clearly separates such theories from the Lamarckian view is that in the former this is invariably accompanied by a commitment to the struggle for survival made necessary for the elimination of the 'unfit' who are incapable of improvement because of their hereditary disposition. Here we encounter another example of the way in which specific terms need to be understood in the overall discursive context of which they are a part. Struggle and heredity play different roles and have different significations within the Darwinian and Lamarckian world views. And it was precisely because the former possessed a stress on heredity and on struggle that it could depict nature as at once both a model and a threat.

Pre-Darwinian theories of social change

Social Darwinism is a world view which explains social evolution. But how distinctive is it? After all, the notion that social change exhibited developmental patterns can be traced back to the ancient Greeks, who were also aware of heredity and the selective effects of breeding.[11] My answer is that Social Darwinism cannot be seen as simply a variation on these old themes except in the general sense of sharing a concern with social change. This is because the conception of nature expressed in the world view differs markedly from those of its predecessors. Certainly

[11] For accounts of theories of social change in Western thought, see A. D. Smith, *The Concept of Social Change* (London: Routledge and Kegan Paul, 1973); K. E. Bock, 'Theories of Progress, Development, Evolution'; Nisbet, *Social Change and History*.

'nature' represents a key reference point in previous theories because it comprises a central element in any world view. But there is an enormous difference between perceiving nature as a realm of eternal and un- changing essences or as a cycle of birth, maturation and death (two recurrent models in earlier thought) and the Darwinian picture of nature as an arena of continuous change extending backwards (and forwards) into barely imaginable time scales. Social theorists who embraced Darwinism were engaged in something more than the reiteration of an age-old preoccupation with nature and its rhythms. This was because the world view itself rendered problematic many of the certainties upon which social and political theories had been premissed – the fixity of human nature, or the harmony of nature, or nature as evidence of divine creation. Social Darwinism was a challenge to the viability of social theory itself as traditionally conceived and practised.

The separate elements of the world view are certainly discernible in earlier theories – the unity of humanity and nature; the importance of population growth in bringing about social change; adaptation; speciali- sation; the paramountcy of competition. But, as was stressed in the previous chapter, Social Darwinism was a fusion of these elements into a distinctive vision of the laws of natural and social change. What has to be considered in any estimation of the historical specificity of the world view, therefore, is not the existence of its elements but the appearance of the total configuration and the logic by which these elements are interconnected.

The importance of focusing upon the whole rather than its parts can be appreciated from a comparison between Social Darwinism and the world view underpinning the political theory of the seventeenth-century English philosopher, Thomas Hobbes (1588–1679). The portrayal of nature in Social Darwinism has frequently been depicted as a transfig- uration of Hobbes's 'state of nature'.[12] Yet while there are some important similarities, there are equally essential differences. Hobbes, in his *Leviathan* of 1651,[13] asserted that mankind was regulated by the same laws which governed nature at large, man being a machine and hence in constant motion (81). This applied equally to his mind which was driven by appetites and aversions. But though men were engines of a similar design, the objects of their appetites and aversions differed in

[12] For example, H. Stuart Hughes, *Consciousness and Society* (St Albans: Paladin, 1974), 38–9; M. Sahlins, *The Use and Abuse of Biology* (London: Tavistock, 1976), 101; S. Rose, R. Lewontin and L. Kamin, *Not in Our Genes* (Harmondsworth: Penguin, 1990), 241. This connection was often made in the nineteenth century as well, e.g. by Engels (see Sahlins, *The Use and Abuse of Biology*, 102–3), and by the anarchist Peter Kropotkin in his *Mutual Aid*, ed. P. Avritch (London: Allen Lane, 1972), 36, 84.
[13] Ed. C. B. McPherson (Harmondsworth: Penguin, 1968).

accordance with 'the constitution individuall, and particular education ' (83). Hobbes contended that humans were intrinsically egocentric and, given the scarcity of resources, inevitably rivalrous, engaged in competition for riches, honour and power. As the ability to secure good and avoid evil in the future depended, to a large degree, on the ability to control other people, Hobbes saw mankind engaged in a continuous struggle for power. This arose, not through the inherent insatiability of human wants, but through insecurity, because each person 'cannot assure the power and means to live well, which he hath present, without the acquisition of more' (161).

Hobbes's notorious state of nature is a hypothetical condition deduced from human nature. He invited his readers to contemplate a situation in which there was no government to enforce laws. Given the egoistic and competitive nature of man and the finitude of resources this would very quickly degenerate into violent anarchy in which each person lived in perpetual fear of his neighbour, while art, science and commerce would be rendered impossible. In other words 'they are in that condition which is called Warre; and such a warre, as is of every man, against every man' (185). Self-interest, activitated by the fear of death (the one evil to which everybody had an aversion because death stopped motion), would lead men to the realisation that the only way out of this predicament was by conferring all their rights and powers upon a Sovereign with absolute authority.

Hobbes's theory rests upon some assumptions equally visible in Social Darwinism, notably the unity of mankind and nature, the importance of competition, and social organisation as a reflection of innate human proclivities. On the other hand, the laws Hobbes believed regulated mankind and nature were those of mechanics rather than biology. Thus his model of human nature was a static one: though appetites and aversions supplied the dynamics of social interaction, the human machine remained the same through time and across space. It was not transformed in any substantive sense by membership in a political community – Leviathan constrained, but did not alter, human nature. In the Hobbesian scenario it was precisely because human nature was fixed that Leviathan held out the promise of peace. As for competition, there was no suggestion in Hobbes that this had any selective consequences in the form of the survival of the fittest. On the contrary, it is one of his most telling points that in a state of nature even the strongest may be killed by the weakest 'either by secret machination, or by confederacy with others ...' (183). This is a far cry from the Darwinian perspective of adaptation, selection and transmutation in which time is a dimension of impermanence.

During the eighteenth and nineteenth centuries several theories appeared which did stress the importance of social change, giving the impression of an anticipation of Social Darwinism. The remainder of this chapter examines some of these theories in order to draw attention to the varieties of evolutionary theory and underline the distinctive properties of Social Darwinism.

The Enlightenment and the stages of social change

During the second half of the eighteenth century, principally in France and Scotland, there emerged a genre of theory which sought to describe the successive stages of the development of civilisation. These conjectural histories were remarkable not only for their focus upon the role of population pressures on resources and space in inducing development, but also for their representation of the unity of mankind and nature – sometimes even speculating on the links between monkeys and humans.[14] They usually classified societies according to socio-economic criteria, establishing stages of social development according to the manner in which subsistence was produced. Some of the most important examples of this genre were more a narrative of the trials and eventual triumph of enlightened reason against the forces of obfuscation and oppression than a systematic account of social development.[15] But others succeeded in presenting a coherent theory of change, for example the French philosopher Claude-Arien Helvétius (1715–71).

His *De l'homme* of 1773[16] began from the postulate that man was an animal striving to preserve himself by shunning pain and seeking happiness – motives which encouraged cooperation with his fellows for the purposes of hunting and defence. 'Interest and need', according to Helvétius, 'are the principles of all sociability' (I, 112). But the primacy of hunting and warfare among early men had left their stamp on human nature. Nature offered a spectacle in which multitudes of beings devoured one another; man, who possessed the dentition and the

---

[14] On this last point, see R. Wokler, 'From *l'homme physique* to *l'homme moral* and Back', *History of the Human Sciences*, 6(1993), 121–38. For a discussion of the importance of population in eighteenth-century thought, see F. G. Whelan, 'Population and Ideology in the Enlightenment', *History of Political Thought*, 12(1991), 35–72.

[15] Such is the case with the *Esquisse d'un tableau des progrès de l'esprit humaine* (1795) by the mathematician and social theorist, the Marquis de Condorcet (1743–94). Whereas the first three of Condorcet's ten stages of development are based upon socio-economic criteria, the remainder consist of historical and cultural constructs, for example 'the Ancient Greeks' and the 'Crusades': see, for example, *Esquisse* (Paris: Editions Sociales, 1966), 99. The outcome is a highly heterogeneous series of stages. See R. L. Meek, *Social Science and the Ignoble Savage* (Cambridge University Press, 1976), 207.

[16] *De l'homme*, 2 vols. (London: Société Typographique, 1773).

mentality of a carnivore, was part of this carnage. Helvétius claimed that children were spontaneously cruel to animals and exhibited all the vices of mankind, proving that 'goodness and humanity cannot be the work of nature, but solely that of education' (II, 17). When population growth resulted in the diminution of game, early humans turned to pastoralism for their subsistence. Once again, population pressures displaced nomadism in favour of fixed agriculture, paving the way for the emergence of property rights, law and the achievements of civilisation (II, 350–2). But throughout this development man retained his destructive traits: 'Habituated to murder, he must be deaf to the cry of pity' (II, 17–18). Good people existed, but as the products of education, not of nature. 'Born among the Iroquois, these same men would have adopted their barbaric and cruel customs' (II, 20).

These arguments, however, do not derive from an embryonic Social Darwinism. If the unity of mankind and nature is a premiss of Helvétius' theory, there is no suggestion that the developmental history of the former is an instance of general laws relevant to all organisms. While population growth exerts pressure on resources, this encourages adaptation rather than selection through survival of the fittest. In any case, Helvétius was equivocal over the ramifications of population pressure, which he sometimes presented as causing a decline in the value of labour and the polarisation of society into rich and poor with a concomitant increase in oppression, vice and corruption (II, 81–7). Nor were aggression and predation converted into principles of development or certain nations described as winners and losers in this process. History showed 'to the contrary, that from Delhi to Petersburg all peoples have been successively foolish and enlightened; that in the same proportions, all nations . . . have the same laws, the same spirit . . .' (I, 130, note a).

This last statement betrays a supposition prevalent throughout *De l'homme* (and indeed, throughout Enlightenment social theory) that grounds the very possibility of a science of man, namely the presence of a universal human nature. This nature grew in complexity according to a developmental logic deriving partly from the workings of the mind itself as its operations expanded from their initial sensory foundations, and partly from the exigencies of social existence. The differences between nations, then, were explained by the opportunities afforded their inhabitants for the exercise of their faculties.

Despite some apparent similarities with Social Darwinism, Helvétius wrote with a very different set of background assumptions concerning nature, time and human nature. This is equally true of the Scots stage-theorists, whose conjectural histories charted the course of progress from the most savage to the most civilised societies. The work of Adam

Ferguson (1732–1816) is a case in point. His *Essay on the History of Civil Society* (1767)[17] narrated the transition from 'rude' to 'polished' societies. The latter were characterised by the refinement of the arts and lifestyles of their members; the former were divided into two sub-types. In 'savage' societies there was no private property and the inhabitants lived by hunting, fishing and gathering. In 'barbarian' societies there existed ownership of herds and lands and thence the distinction between rich and poor, servant and master. In both types war was endemic and was still important, in a modified form, in polished societies. This is because warfare is natural to both humans and animals. All animals derive pleasure from the exercise of their 'natural talents and forces'. They rehearse, in play, 'the conflicts they are doomed to sustain. Man too is disposed to opposition and to employ the forces of his nature against an equal antagonist' (24). Humans are innately social, but the obverse of this sociality is animosity to those outside their group. Ferguson believed this to be fortunate because it stimulated some of the finest features of human nature such as generosity and self-denial. He even invoked warfare as a cause of progress: 'The strength of nations consists in the wealth, the numbers and the character of their people. The history of their progress from a state of rudeness is, for the most part, a detail of the struggles they have maintained, and of the arts they have practised, to strengthen or to secure themselves' (232).

A closer examination of Ferguson's arguments, however, dispels any suggestion that he espoused Social Darwinism before the name. His main thesis was that development was an unintended consequence of the division of labour, which promoted civilisation and perfection in the 'arts of life' (180–2). But contrary to the implication of the above citation on war and progress, he was actually vague over the precise causes of specialisation, and he certainly made no mention of population growth as a factor. Indeed, alongside Ferguson's history of social change can be found the Enlightenment commitment to a universal human nature. He was adamant that the savage shared civilised men's follies and vices as well as sometimes excelling the latter in 'talents and virtues' (76). All men were motivated by 'similar dispositions', so that while societies changed, human nature remained fundamentally the same. Far from embodying an anticipation of Social Darwinism, Ferguson's work is more profitably considered within the context of the Enlightenment and perhaps even the much older mode of discourse, 'civic humanism', with its celebration of the republican virtues of individual autonomy coupled

---

[17] *Essay on the History of Civil Society* ed. D. Forbes (Edinburgh University Press, 1966).

with public-spiritedness.[18] Thus, notwithstanding his occasional praise for warfare, Ferguson's ultimate commitment was to the morality of community, anticipating a time when: 'The same maxim will apply throughout every part of nature. *To love is to enjoy pleasure: To hate is to be in pain*' (54, original emphasis).

Before leaving the eighteenth century it is useful to consider one of the most uncompromising critics of the Enlightenment, Thomas Malthus (1766–1834). His *An Essay on the Principle of Population* (1798),[19] which was to exert such an influence on both Wallace and Darwin, was directed against Enlightenment doctrines of progress and perfectibility. Malthus argued that population always increased at a much faster rate than food production and was held in check by natural disasters, plague and warfare, and (as he subsequently conceded) sexual temperance. His goal was to show that population growth, far from stimulating progress, actually made such progress impossible. He allowed that 'the goad of necessity' was certainly responsible for the improved conditions of modern civilisation (47), and he also acknowledged the possibility of improving animals and plants through selective breeding (53–4). But such could occur only within the limits imposed by the essential nature of the species concerned and these limits were particularly marked in the case of mankind. 'In human life', Malthus asserted, 'though there are great variations from different causes, it may be doubted whether, since the world began, any organic improvement whatever of the human frame can be clearly ascertained.' Small changes were no doubt possible in theory but, since they would necessitate the celibacy of 'all the bad specimens', extremely difficult to realise in practice (54). Although familiar with the stage-theory of development, Malthus regarded this as confirmation of the universality of his law of population and hence of the impossibility of any radical alteration in the quality of life for the majority of the population.[20]

Darwin and Wallace took over Malthus's thesis on the pressure exerted by fecundity on resources and deployed it within a very different outlook on nature and time – in fact as a cause of precisely those organic transmutations which Malthus had deemed to be ruled out by this thesis. Nevertheless, as will be evident in following chapters, the new

---

[18] Ferguson deplored the pursuit of private gain at the expense of the public weal in modern societies (19, 32–3, 86–7, 199). On civic humanism, see J. G. A. Pocock, *The Machiavellian Moment* (Princeton University Press, 1975); Pocock, *Politics, Language and Time* (London: Methuen, 1972), chaps. 3 and 4.

[19] Ed. D. Winch (Cambridge University Press, 1992). For a discussion of the political context of Malthus's theory, see D. Wells, 'Resurrecting the Dismal Parson: Malthus, Ecology and Political Thought', *Political Studies*, 30(1982), 1–15.

[20] On this point, see Meek, *Social Science*, 223.

world view of Social Darwinism could be enrolled in the same ideological cause as the original Malthusian doctrine, i.e. to support free markets and oppose doctrines of equality.

The nineteenth century

The nineteenth century was marked by a profound historical awareness among intellectuals which stimulated an interest in change in its various manifestations. The previous chapter has drawn attention to the implications of these developments for social theory, and how the consciousness of change and human diversity challenged the assumption of a timeless human essence. There was, in addition, a focus on conflict – not just as a feature of social life (as in Hobbes), but also as a cause of change. In these circumstances it is important that the theory in question be considered as a whole and that certain ideas and phrases are not singled out as indicative of Social Darwinism. The latter is but one among many possible approaches to the issues surrounding the place of humanity in history and nature and the role of conflict in social life, and it is vital to recognise this diversity, whatever the degree of overlap among some of the concepts involved.

The philosophy of the German G. W. F. Hegel (1770–1831) furnishes an example of how conflict and change could be depicted as creative processes within a discursive context very different to that of Social Darwinism. Hegel interpreted history as the growth of reason and reflexive consciousness achieved through the dialectical interplay and confrontation of opposing ideas and cultural forms. Within this frame-work he provided a philosophical rationale for war as an event that forced citizens of a state to rise above the limited horizons of self-interest and recognise the reciprocal obligations derived from membership in a political community. In fact, war sometimes acted as a pre-condition for the mutual self-recognition of the antagonistic states themselves.[21] But Hegel was hostile to the evolutionism of his time for trying to explain the higher in terms of the lower, whereas his methodology recommended the opposite procedure – explaining lower developmental forms in terms of the higher.[22]

---

[21] Hegel's *Elements of the Philosophy of Right*, ed. A. Wood, tr. H. Nisbet (Cambridge University Press, 1991) contains a discussion of war (360–5), in which Hegel claims that war prevents stagnation, raises citizens above mundane concerns and promotes internal strength and unity. For an overview of Hegel's position on this topic, see S. Walt, 'Hegel on War: Another Look', *History of Political Thought*, 10(1989), 113–24.

[22] This did not prevent the emergence of evolutionary theories inspired by Hegel's philosophy, for example among the British idealists during the end of the nineteenth and early twentieth centuries. See D. Boucher, 'Evolution and Politics: The

From the perspective of the present study, the writings of the French philosopher Auguste Comte (1798–1857) deserve consideration for providing a comprehensive and influential theory of evolution that represented an alternative to Social Darwinism.[23] Comte's ambition, realised in his massive *Cours de philosophie positive* and *Système de politique positive*,[24] was to forge a science of society – he coined the neologism 'sociology' – which was both linked to and a completion of the natural sciences. Biology was an important foundation for this project, partly for methodological reasons (e.g. the use of the comparative method) and partly because he believed humans and animals shared many biological attributes (*Cours*, III, 832–5). This was true even for human psychological propensities. Comte maintained 'that animals, at least in the higher part of the zoological scale, in reality manifest most of our affective and even intellectual faculties, with simple differences of degree' (*Cours*, III, 774). On no account, though, was sociology reducible to biology, because social existence involved the emergence of properties which were not to be found in the natural world. Societies existed in a temporal dimension which ensured that each generation was influenced by the culture of its predecessors. As society evolved, this cultural heritage expanded and played a correspondingly larger role in the shaping of the human mind and action.

Contrary to a misconception, widely held during his own lifetime as well as now, Comte did not ignore the subjective dimension of experience.[25] As he announced in the *Cours*, the history of society was 'above all else dominated by the history of the human mind' (IV, 649). Later, in the *Système*, he remarked: 'From the first rudiments of civilisation up to the present state of the most advanced peoples, the entire human spectacle shows the continuous development of order determined by the fundamental laws of human nature' (III, 620). The Law of the Three States represents different points in the evolution of human nature and different modes of equilibria between the affective

---

Naturalistic, Ethical and Spiritual Bases of Evolutionary Arguments', *Australian Journal of Political Science*, 27(1992), 95–102.

[23] Comte's influence extended not only to theories of social evolution, but also contributed to the development of structuralist models. See A. Kremer-Marietti, *Le Projet anthropologique d'Auguste Comte* (Paris: Société d'Edition d'Enseignement Supérieur, 1980); T. Bottomore and R. Nisbet, 'Structuralism', in Bottomore and Nisbet, *A History of Sociological Analysis*, 559–62; M. J. Hawkins, 'Comte, Durkheim, and the Sociology of Primitive Religion', *Sociological Review*, 27(1979), 429–46.

[24] Comte, *Cours de philosophie positive*, 6 vols. (Paris: Bachelier, 1830–42); Comte, *Système de politique positive*, 4 vols. (Paris: Mathias, Carilian-Goury et Delmont, 1851–4).

[25] For an investigation of Comte's theory of the mind and its evolution, see M. J. Hawkins, 'Comte's Theory of Mental Development', *Revue européenne des sciences sociales*, 22(1984), 71–90; Hawkins, 'Reason and Sense Perception in Comte's Theory of Mind', *History of European Ideas*, 5(1984), 149–63.

and the cognitive, the altruistic and the egoistic components of the psyche. To these correspond different relationships between the subject and the external world, as well as distinctive forms of social organisation. Equilibrium had to be attained between all these levels, making it both difficult to achieve and precarious to maintain. Comte summarised his theory of evolution as 'always consisting of the increasing ascendancy of our humanity over our animality, according to the double supremacy of our intelligence over our affective inclinations, and the sympathetic instinct over the personal instinct' (*Cours*, VI, 837).

Although ostensibly preoccupied with change, Comte held to the fixity of species (*Cours*, III, 560–9) and was critical of Lamarck's transformism for attributing too much variability to the organism and for exaggerating the importance of the environment 'as if the organism was at the same time purely passive and indefinitely modifiable ...' (*Cours*, VI, 287). New needs could never create new faculties, but only stimulate existing ones (*Cours*, III, 563–4). Even man, the most adaptable (because most complex) of all organisms, retained his essential characteristics throughout the evolutionary process despite the enormous environmental diversity encountered by the various races. Comte posited 'the essential tendency of living species to perpetuate themselves indefinitely with the same principal characters, despite the variations in their external conditions of existence' (*Cours*, III, 569). From his earliest writings Comte had insisted that what made social evolution a uniform process was its derivation from 'the fundamental laws of human organisation, which are common to all'.[26] Though eschewing a simple, linear sequence of development, on several occasions he repeated the point that all races possessed a shared mental constitution, and the differences among them had, therefore, to be explained by variable levels and rates of change rather than by innate differences in capabilities (*Cours*, V, 100; VI, 730; *Système*, I, 390).

To these quite striking differences between Comte's theory and Social Darwinism must be added Comte's vagueness over heredity. He suggested that actions, if constantly repeated, could become fixed in the organism and in the race at large, and thereafter reproduce themselves spontaneously without external stimulation (*Cours*, III, 786–7). But he did not explain how this happened and throughout his work the primary focus was not upon biological but upon cultural transmission through communication and socialisation. Even more significant is the absence of anything remotely analogous to the mechanism of natural selection and survival of the fittest in Comte's theory. He repudiated Malthus

[26] A. Comte, *Plan des travaux scientifiques nécessaires pour réorganiser la société* [1822] (Paris: Aubier-Montaigne, 1970), 90.

because technological advances enabled modern societies to cope with population increases, hence removing the latter as a cause of social conflict (*Cours*, IV, 645–6; *Système*, I, 143). As for warfare and other forms of conflict, these were anathema to Comte. War had played a positive role at early stages in human evolution, but the natural proclivities which had occasioned it were disciplined by the development of altruism, reason and social responsibility (*Cours*, VI, 65–7, 837). Modern warfare, colonial conquests, class conflict and untrammelled egoism were pathological, and Comte's philosophical labours were motivated by a search for a new moral consensus capable of eliminating them.

Comte's theory of evolution has its foundations in the Enlightenment, with its notions of population growth as a stimulus to specialisation and adaptation; a universal human nature capable of development through the interplay of its own internal operations with appropriate social conditions; and the augmentation of altruism and harmony at the expense of egoism and conflict. It thus stood in sharp contrast to Social Darwinism and constituted an influential alternative approach to social and psychological evolution.[27]

However, some theorists were willing to apply biological concepts to social phenomena, as is illustrated by an English insurance company actuary, Thomas Rowe Edmonds (1803–89), who published his *Practical, Moral and Political Economy* in 1828.[28] Edmonds described humans as animals upon whom Providence had bestowed superior faculties and powers augmented by an extensive social life. They possessed several 'innate passions or pains' in addition to innate faculties such as a sense of justice (172, 186). These inherent properties (bodily and mental) were originally habits which became fixed in the constitution of predecessors through constant usage and then transmitted though inheritance. 'The minds and bodies of animals', argued Edmonds, 'are capable of adapting themselves to circumstances. Every species of animal is continually acquiring those mental and bodily powers which are most conducive to its welfare' (185). Reproduction ensured the maintenance of the numbers of each species within boundaries determined by the availability of food: 'If the number of the population exceed this limit prescribed by nature, the excess is carried off by the increased mortality caused by semi-starvation.' This is a condition of 'natural pauperism', and for people such a state 'would be

[27] Schweber, however, has argued that Comte influenced Darwin's own thinking on evolution. See S. S. Schweber, 'The Origin of the *Origin* Revisited', *Journal of the History of Biology*, 10(1977), 219–316.
[28] London: Effingham Wilson, 1828.

similar to that suffered by all the lower animals, which are constantly pressing against the bounds of subsistence' (107).

For Edmonds: 'Nature has laid down laws for the perpetual improvement of the human race' (65), which it is 'not in the power of man to prevent' (283). One of these is 'the law of the strongest, or war' which, according to Edmonds, 'is one of the most benevolent institutions of Nature … Beneficent providence has so ordained it that the powerful are continually bringing the weak under their subjection' (199). This subordination of the weak to the strong was advantageous because knowledge equated to power and conquest disseminated knowledge through compulsion, the only method which enabled rapid advances to take place. Yet although subjected to inexorable laws of nature, Edmonds thought it possible to improve mankind through something very akin to eugenics. Signalling the way in which domestic breeds of animals and vegetables could be improved by 'selective culture', he suggested that such techniques could be applied to humans.

The bodies of a coming generation may be rendered superior in health, strength and activity to the bodies of a present generation, by selecting for the purposes of propagation the individuals of both sexes possessing the most healthy, vigorous and active bodies, and not suffering weak and diseased people to transmit their diseases and miseries to posterity. In similar manner, the minds of a people may be improved by selecting for propagation those people who excel in the most useful qualities of mind, as justice, judgement, imagination, benevolence, &c., and not permitting ideots [sic] or madmen, or people approaching to such, to propagate (269).

Striking though these passages are, Edmonds cannot be regarded as a proto-Social Darwinist for a number of reasons. First, he maintained that species were created and designed by God (34), who had likewise created the separate races of mankind. He denied that the mental differences between Europeans and negroes derived from accidental variations and considered them immutable (187). Such argumentation was inconsistent with any notion of the evolution of humans from ape-like ancestors. Second, although Edmonds believed that population growth was constrained by the availability of food supplies, he did not argue that such growth was a cause of adaptation and specialisation. He exempted mankind from this constraint anyway since all European nations were populated to a level far below that which they were capable of supporting (107–8). Although Edmonds sometimes adopted a Malthusian stance, as when he claimed that 'pauperism is caused by improvident propagation' (237), elsewhere he asserted pauperism to be the effect of private property and the division of society into rich and poor (107–8). Thus his 'law of the strongest' was not deduced from the ratio of population increase to food production as a general law of nature but derived from the lack of international justice due to the absence of regular concourse among nations (235). His support for conquest was couched in terms of the benefits to be gained from the diffusion of knowledge rather than as a means of winnowing the unfit. Third, Edmonds did not regard market competition as a selective device but rather as an obstacle to the advance of the division of labour in that it was not only injurious to the public interest but also to the firms involved (75). In no sense, therefore, does his focus on adaptation, selective breeding and the inheritance of acquired characters in a social context – interesting though they are – represent a formulation of the Social Darwinist world view.

The only likely case for a genuine formulation of Social Darwinism prior to Darwin that I have encountered is the writing of a Scots fruit farmer and aboriculturalist, Patrick Matthew (1790–1874), although the evidence is equivocal. In 1860 Matthew claimed to have discovered the principle of natural selection almost thirty years previously in his book *Naval Timber and Aboriculture*.[29] In an appendix to this text Matthew wrote of a 'law universal in nature':

> This law sustains the lion in his strength, the hare in her swiftness, and the fox in his wiles. As Nature, in all her modifications of life, has a power of increase far beyond what is needed to supply the place of what falls by Time's decay, those individuals who possess not the requisite strength, swiftness, hardihood, or cunning, fall prematurely without reproducing – either a prey to their natural devourers, or sinking under disease, generally induced by want of nourishment, their place being occupied by the more perfect of their kind, who are pressing on the means of subsistence (98).

This is a succinct statement of the selective impact of competition arising from the pressure of population on subsistence. Matthew stressed the 'extreme fecundity of nature' and argued that: 'As the field of existence is limited and preoccupied, it is only the hardier, more robust, better suited to circumstance individuals, who are able to struggle forward to maturity, these inhabiting only the situations to which they have superior adaptation and greater power of occupancy than any other kind; the weaker, less circumstance-suited, being prematurely destroyed' (107–8). He suggested that an examination of the fossil record on the

---

[29]   Edinburgh: Adam Black, 1831. The most pertinent comments were contained in an appendix which has been reproduced with other publications by Matthew in W. J. Dempster, *Patrick Matthew and Natural Selection* (Edinburgh: Paul Harris, 1983), from which the following exposition has been drawn. Darwin acknowledged Matthew's priority in subsequent editions of the *Origin*. See Matthew's letter to *The Gardeners' Chronicle and Agricultural Gazette*, 17 April 1860, and Darwin's letter to the same chronicle, 21 April 1860, in Dempster, *Patrick Matthew*, 112–17.

extinction and emergence of species left the naturalist with a clear choice
between belief in 'a repeated miraculous creation' or in 'a power of
change' in nature which had the effect of blurring the distinction
between varieties and species (106).

Matthew applied these arguments to social arrangements, insisting
that hereditary nobility and primogeniture were 'an outrage on this law
of nature' and a debasement of the racial stock, since all aristocracies
required renovation by 'regular married alliance with wilder stocks' (98).
He was critical of the English Poor Laws for discouraging self-reliance
and effort among the unemployed and compared this situation with the
one in Scotland, where the absence of parish relief fostered independence and a willingness to move to more promising circumstances
(103). Matthew was an ardent supporter of emigration and colonial
enterprise – his work on naval timber was motivated by the desire to
strengthen Britain's overseas power. He claimed that emigration
ensured that the mentally and physically ablest persons 'will be thrown
into their natural position as leaders' whereas the 'feebler or more
improvident varieties will generally sink under the incidental hardships'
(102). Faint hearts were a hindrance to successful overseas ventures:

Our milder moods, benevolence, gentleness, contemplation – our refinement in
sentiment ... have a negative weight on the balance of national strength. The
rougher excitement of hatred, ambition, pride, patriotism, and the more selfish
passions, is necessary to the full and strong development of our active powers.
That Britain is leaving the impress of her energy and morality on a considerable
portion of the world, is owing to her having first borne fire and sword over these
countries ... (103).

However, these sentiments were not consistently adhered to, for
elsewhere in the same text Matthew looked forward to the obliteration of
national distinctions which would reduce the reasons for warfare and
'bring the European family closer into amity' (110). He suggested that
war and conquest should be confined to the annexation of land
inhabited by non-Europeans. These ambivalences pose problems for the
interpretation of Matthew's ideas. Some historians have seen his work as
a complete anticipation of Darwinism and Social Darwinism, while
others have rejected this and located his ideas in an older, Providential
and catastrophist outlook.[30] Matthew himself seemed to have hesitated
over the universal application of natural selection, which is a fundamental assumption of the world view. Darwin's brother, Erasmus,

---

[30] For the first interpretation, see Dempster, *Patrick Matthew*; the second is argued in
K. D. Wells, 'The Historical Context of Natural Selection: The Case of Patrick
Matthew', *Journal of the History of Biology*, 6(1973), 225–58.

chided Matthew for this, suggesting that Charles 'is more faithful to your own original child than you are yourself'.[31]

In conclusion, then, it is evident that Social Darwinism did not emerge until after 1859. All of its separate components had certainly been articulated in one form or another as aspects of the natural and/or social realms. But the overall configuration, with its particular inter-connection of these various elements, was the work of Darwin and the other pioneers who forged the world view. It is to some of these pioneers that we now turn.

[31] Erasmus Darwin to Matthew, 21 November 1863, in Dempster, *Patrick Matthew*, 120.

Part II

Pioneers

3   The emergence of Social Darwinism

Introduction

Before Darwin published his *Descent* in 1871, Europeans and Americans
had already started to explore the social and psychological implications
of Darwinism. As a German enthusiast wrote: 'from the first appearance
of the Darwinian doctrine, every moderately logical thinker must have
regarded man as similarly modifiable, and as the result of the mutability
of species'.[1] Though exaggerating the acceptance of Darwinism this
statement accurately conveys the realisation by many intellectuals that
this was a theory rich in implications for the study of human society.
Within a quarter of a century of the appearance of the *Origin* there had
emerged a literature devoted to exploring these implications in a wide
range of contexts: social and psychological development, class, race and
gender, religion and morality, war and peace, crime and destitution.
Well before the label itself, Social Darwinism was established as a rich
and versatile theoretical resource.

These pioneering examples of Social Darwinism are the focus of this
and the next three chapters. The intention is not to provide a
comprehensive account of the emergence of Social Darwinism, but
rather to investigate the manner in which the world view was deployed in
a variety of discursive contexts. This chapter deals with several very early
examples which appeared in the 1860s and 1870s in Europe and the
USA.

Brace and the evolution of racial harmony

A popular and persistent interpretation of Social Darwinism associates it
with doctrines of racial hierarchy and conflict. It certainly was adapted
for these purposes at an early stage. In Germany, for instance, a
geologist, Friedrich Rolle, in a text published in 1866, emphasised the

---

[1]   O. Schmidt, *The Doctrine of Descent and Darwinism* (no. tr.) (London: King and Co.,
1875), 283.

role of struggle and selection in human history and drew attention to the 'struggle for space' between races.[2] In this struggle Rolle saw progress attained through the elimination of the lower races. But other applications were possible, as demonstrated by the work of the American, Charles Loring Brace (1826–90).

Brace published his theory of races in 1863, at the height of the American Civil War. A passionate opponent of slavery, which he described as an 'organised system of heathenism',[3] Brace sought to undermine existing ethnological arguments in support of negro inferiority. This study took over a decade, during which time Brace was heavily influenced by the *Origin*, which he read repeatedly.[4] He was convinced that if Darwin's theory was true, then 'the law of natural selection applies to all the moral history of mankind, as well as to the physical'.[5] *The Races of the Old World*[6] was an elaboration of this principle.

Using linguistic evidence, Brace posited a common origin for all races and argued that present racial differences were a consequence of the interaction between environmental conditions, natural selection, inheritance and variations. Although admitting to ignorance concerning the cause of variations, Brace argued that those conferring advantages in the form of 'the best chance of living and propagating' (351) would be selected and spread through a population. In this way, Brace saw no difficulty in 'accounting for the origin of the negro from the white man, or from the brown, or from some other race' (390).

Brace was careful to emphasise that races were varieties, not species. He insisted that there was no physiological evidence to support the latter thesis, and differences among individuals of the same race were as great as those between races on such measures (365). Furthermore, all races could inter-breed, and Brace emphatically rejected the claim that racial hybrids were infertile (376–7). In fact, Brace evinced a great deal of sympathy for mulattos, blacks and Red Indians in the United States, who he believed were dying out as the result of the destruction of their health and habitats by the rapaciousness of the white races rather than through any inherent inferiority (383–4). Negroes would benefit greatly from freedom and integration with whites, partly at least because all humans were capable of conscious, rational adaptation to new condi-

[2] F. Rolle, *Der Mensch, Seine Abstammung und Gesittung im Lichte der Darwin'ischen Lehre* (Frankfurt am Main: Germann'sche Verlagsbuchhandlung, 1866), 109.
[3] Brace, letter to *Washington Independent*, 12 September 1861, in Emma Brace, ed., *The Life of Charles Loring Brace Chiefly Told in His Own Letters* (London: Sampson, Low, Marston and Co., 1894), 243.
[4] Emma Brace, *Life*, 300.   [5] Brace, cited in Emma Brace, *Life*, 302.
[6] London: John Murray, 1863.

tions (372–4). This process was plainly in evidence among the European settlers in North America, who were changing physically from their ancestors. Initially this would result in the elimination of those who were weaker or unable to adapt to the new conditions, but the stronger would survive and pass their advantageous traits to their descendants 'until a new type is formed, adapted to the country and climate' (375). The lesson Brace drew from this was that the varieties of humanity were no more immutable than those found in nature at large. He concluded that 'we do not regard the Races of men now existing as permanent. Their lives converge into one another in the past, and they may meet again in the future or they may cease altogether' (399–400).

This text is of interest for several reasons. The first is Brace's use of Darwinism to attack belief in the fixity of racial differences. An example of this mode of thought is furnished by a book published with the explicit intent of demonstrating 'that the so-called slavery of the South was the Negro's normal or natural condition'.[7] The author, van Evrie, regarded the boundaries between species as 'absolutely impassable',[8] and the white and black races as separate species of vastly different capabilities. The blacks were hopelessly inferior to the whites, and nothing could alter this condition:

The organism of the race – the species – whether human or animal, never changes or varies from that eternal type fixed from the beginning by the hand of God; and men, therefore, are now, in their natural capacities, what they always have been and always will be, whatever the external circumstances that may control or modify the development of these capacities.[9]

The significance of this statement lies not in its creationism – for, as we will see, Brace saw no contradiction between Darwinism and a belief in God as creator – but in its static perception of species as immutable essences. From it van Evrie concluded, in sharp contrast to the position of Brace, that racial crossings were violations of nature and hence abominations, while slavery was the natural condition of negroes. To grant them independence was akin to forcing ten-year-old children to fend for themselves: the result would be the extermination of the negroes in America.[10]

The second notable feature of Brace's use of Darwinism consists in his refusal to erect a hierarchy of races. Races were not species, there were no insuperable boundaries between them, and their relationships could not be conceived in terms of inferiority and superiority. Indeed, he envisaged a time in the future when racial inter-mixture could result

---

[7] J. H. van Evrie, *White Supremacy and Negro Subordination*, second edn (New York: Van Evrie, Horton and Co., 1868), dedication to reader.
[8] *Ibid.*, 37.   [9] *Ibid.*, 126.   [10] *Ibid.*, 161, 309–10.

in a new and more perfect race (400). This contrasts not only with the perspective of van Evrie – who was not a Social Darwinist – but with other avowedly Darwinist accounts of race. Thus the German zoologist Oskar Schmidt (1826–86) argued that human progress, though a fact of history, was confined to a few nations only. Some inferior races, which were distinct species, were capable of advancement, but for many 'destruction in the struggle for existence as a consequence of their retardation ... is the natural course of things'.[11] While Brace believed that in certain circumstances races could degenerate (cf. *Races*, 368–72), he did not adhere to the doctrine of the inevitability of racial conflict and extermination. He depicted the struggle for existence as occurring between individuals and their environments rather than between different races.

Third, Brace – who was a church minister – denied any incommensurability between Darwinism and his religious beliefs. He wrote in 1866 that Darwinism 'furnishes what historians and philosophers have so long sought for, a law of progress', which would result in the triumph of good because good was a life-preserving force.[12] He insisted that there was no general tendency in nature to degeneration or imperfection, but only one 'towards higher forms of life. Natural selection is a means of arriving at the best.'[13] The social significance of this was clarified in a subsequent study, *The Dangerous Classes of New York*.[14] These classes consisted of destitute urban elements living in crime and vice. Brace admitted that while such traits could become hereditary there was little chance of this happening in New York. This was because geographical mobility and the American values of self-improvement and equality prevented the emergence of families with long criminal pedigrees, which in turn reduced the hereditability of crime (47). Additionally, the laws of nature worked in parallel fashion:

The action of the great law of 'Natural Selection', in regard to the human race, is always towards temperance and virtue. That is, vice and extreme indulgence weaken the physical powers and undermine the constitution; they impair the faculties by which man struggles with adverse conditions and gets beyond the reach of poverty and want. The vicious and sensual and drunken die earlier, or they have fewer children, or their children are carried off by diseases more frequently, or they themselves are unable to resist or prevent poverty and suffering. As a consequence, in the lowest class, the more self-controlled and virtuous tend constantly to survive, and to prevail in the 'struggle for existence',

---

[11] Schmidt, *Doctrine of Descent*, 298.
[12] Brace, letter to Lady Lyell, 23 December 1866, in Emma Brace, *Life*, 285.
[13] Brace, *Life*, 302.
[14] *The Dangerous Classes of New York and Twenty Years Work Among Them* (New York: Wynkoop and Hallenback, 1872).

over the vicious and ungoverned, and to transmit their progeny. The natural drift among the poor is towards virtue (44–5).

Even in the worst families, the superior hereditary qualities of earlier ancestors were latent within individuals, and could be nurtured by better food and conditions, regular work and, above all, religion, all of which would 'awaken these hidden tendencies to good' (45). The application of Christian principles of charity was thus in harmony 'with natural and economic laws' (441).

Finally, Brace's use of Darwinism contains tensions which are instructive for a more general understanding of Social Darwinism. As was noted above, the struggle for existence appears in his work as something which operates between individuals and their natural and social environments, but not between individuals themselves. As a consequence, Brace did not explore the full implications of Darwinism, namely that the struggle for life is at its most intense between members of the same species. His hesitation in this respect undoubtedly derived from his religious convictions and his commitment to racial integration and social reform. Moreover, his correspondence reveals his belief in Theism and in a Creator who could 'arrange forces on a general plan', coupled with an admission that it was nonetheless difficult to recognise the hand of God in the play of chance and natural selection.[15] Brace's writings, therefore, present nature as a model and evolution as an ultimately benign force working towards progress and human perfection. But they do so by playing down those features of Darwinism which could pose problems for this view of nature, i.e. intra-specific competition and scientific determinism. In this respect, the pioneering Social Darwinism of Brace is, as we shall see, paradigmatic.

Büchner and social equality

In Germany, the materialist and atheist philosopher Ludwig Büchner published a popular Darwinist tract in 1869 entitled *Man in the Past, Present and Future*.[16] Humans had evolved from an ape-like ancestor and this evolution, like all organic transmutations, had been brought about by the struggle for existence in conjunction with variability and inheritance (151). But this struggle had itself undergone a transformation from a material and violent to a peaceful social and mental process:

Whilst the struggle between peoples was formerly a contest of weapons, strength of body, courage and ferocity, it now consists in an emulation in good and useful

---

[15] See letters in Emma Brace, *Life*, 301, 303.
[16] Tr. W. S. Dallas (London: Asher and Co., 1872).

arts, in discoveries, contrivances and sciences. The time is past in which one people subjugated another or exterminated it to take its place; it is not by destruction but by peaceful competition that one can attain a superiority over the other (156).

The violent struggle for existence still occurred between 'backward' races, but Büchner was confident that those who survived this struggle would only be able to stand up to civilised races by adopting the culture of the latter (157). Here natural selection acted upon the brain, but this by no means entailed any relaxation of the struggle for existence, which rages in 'the domain of morals, to which it has been transferred, as violently and inexorably, as it formerly did on the physical field' (158).

For this struggle to be effective, however, required the equalisation of the conditions of existence for the majority of the members of modern societies. There was competition in name only when some people possessed many advantages while others had none: where the result of the contest was known in advance, then the very desire to compete was paralysed (176–7). Büchner advocated a number of radical measures aimed at altering this situation: the state ownership of land, communal education of children and care for the aged and indigent, and a more equal distribution of capital (177–9). He also proposed equal rights for women in order to bring them into the competition and out of their present situation of 'mitigated slavery' (201–2). This emancipation did not, however, extend to the granting of female suffrage for the moment (207).

Büchner perceived the state as an organ concerned with the welfare of all and he saw modern society as a vast organism in which individuals enjoyed a high degree of autonomy but, through the specialised division of labour, cooperated for the collective welfare. At the international level he foresaw the cessation of armed conflicts, the reduction of national hatreds, and a corresponding weakening of militarism (166–8). In the future, the struggle would be for 'the highest general well-being'. 'In other words', wrote Büchner, 'the struggle for the means of existence will be replaced by the struggle for existence, man by humanity at large, mutual conflict by universal harmony, personal misfortune by general happiness and general hatred by universal love' (162).

Büchner's insistence on a transformation of the struggle for existence from violent to peaceful modes of competition, the selective impact of which would be principally on the brain, was typical of radical and reformist uses of Social Darwinism. Equally typical were the difficulties implicit in the attempt to reconcile the language of struggle, selection and incessant change with the ideals of universal harmony and mutual cooperation. Büchner mobilised the rhetorical resources of Darwinism in the service of radical social and political change to considerable effect, as did Brace in the cause of racial integration and social reform. But these rhetorical resources were equivocal, and the portrait of nature they conveyed was not obviously compatible with their ideological goals. In the case of Büchner, this is evident in statements which contradicted his assertion that the struggle for existence is not mitigated but only transposed in the course of evolutionary progress. Thus he proposed that the task of humanity was to oppose nature, so that progress 'consists in the struggle *against* the struggle for existence, or in *the replacement of the power of nature by the power of reason ...*' (175–6, original emphases). The suggestion here – one that will be encountered often in this study – is that far from constituting an inspiration for social policy, nature and her laws are a constraint to be surmounted in order for progress to be attained to the full.

Bagehot on monarchs and masses

The French Revolution inaugurated a new phenomenon in politics – the entry of the 'masses' into the political arena, not as spectators, nor as spectral but marginal actors in a drama written primarily for others, but as a presence no longer ignorable in practice or in theory.[17] Throughout the nineteenth and early twentieth centuries, as first the middle and then the working classes formulated social and political demands, there occurred a whole series of debates about the masses. These took a variety of forms and were conducted in a number of different modes – in literature, journalism, religion, the social sciences, medicine and health, and in political polemics.[18] They had in common an interest in the nature of the masses, i.e. who they were, their physical, mental and moral characteristics and how they compared in these respects to other social groups. These themes were fundamental to the controversies surrounding socialism as an alternative socio-economic system to capitalism, and to arguments about individual versus collective responsibility for personal welfare. They were also central to questions about the viability (and desirability) of democracy; the political role of the masses in civil society; and the form and scope of the modern state.

An influential discussion of some of these questions is contained in the writings of the English banker and journalist, Walter Bagehot (1826–77). His *Physics and Politics*, first published as a series of articles during

[17] See H. Arendt, *On Revolution* (Harmondsworth: Penguin, 1973).
[18] For an analysis of attitudes to the masses that were prevalent among the literary intelligentsia of this period, see J. Carey, *The Intellectuals and the Masses* (London: Faber and Faber, 1992).

1867–8, was a seminal work in the application of Darwinism to politics, cited by Darwin himself and a number of other important thinkers, including the Americans Fiske and James.[19] The ostensible aim of this text was to explain progress, but additional intentions become apparent when it is viewed in the context of Bagehot's other writings.

Bagehot defined progress as 'an increase of adaptation of man to his environment, that is, of his internal powers and wishes to his external lot and life' (209). He was of the opinion that his contemporaries were inclined to take progress too much for granted when in fact it was confined to a very small number of societies which represented rare exceptions to the norm of stagnation (211). Bagehot sought an explanation for this situation.

Bagehot assumed that human history exhibited laws analogous to those found in natural history. In both instances, such laws derived from the action of heredity which (for reasons which were as yet not understood) produced both similarity and difference between successive generations. However, Bagehot did not believe that variations were random but were due to moral causes. It was through the exertion of will and effort that successful adaptations were achieved and, through the inheritance of acquired characters, transmitted to successive generations. In this way, inheritance acted as a 'continuous force which binds age to age, which enables each to begin with some improvement on the last, if the last did itself improve . . .' (8).

According to Bagehot, people in pre-historic times lacked any moral and intellectual discipline, as could be verified by observing the behaviour of modern savages. The main difference between savages and primitives was that the minds of the latter, lacking the impress of centuries of custom and superstition, were more flexible and receptive to learning than those of the former, but otherwise they both exhibited the same proclivities, which they also shared with children in civilised societies. This meant that, 'like savages they [i.e. pre-historic people] had strong passions and weak reason; that like savages they preferred short spasms of greedy pleasure to mild and equable enjoyment; that like savages, they could not postpone the present to the future; that like savages, their ingrained sense of morality was, to say the best of it, rudimentary and defective' (113). Driven by their instincts and passions,

---

[19] *Physics and Politics* originally appeared during 1867–8 in the *Fortnightly Review* before publication as a book in 1872. The edition used here was published in London by Kegan Paul, Trench, Trübner in 1903. Darwin read the article version which he cited several times in *Descent*, e.g. 179, 180, 200, 204, 284. See also Fiske, *Outlines of Cosmic Philosophy*, II, 269, 264, 270–1; W. James, 'Great Men and their Environment', [1880], in James, *The Will to Believe and Other Essays in Popular Philosophy* (New York: Dover, 1956), 232.

primitives and savages indulged in repellent practices such as lying and thieving, placed little value on human life, killed their aged kin and wallowed in sexual licence and 'communal marriage' (115–16, 122). In these circumstances, the pre-condition for any progress was law – 'rigid, concise, definite law' – and the incentive to acquire this was furnished by warfare. 'Whatever may be said against the principle of "natural selection" in other departments', wrote Bagehot, 'there is no doubt of its predominance in early human history. The strongest killed out the weakest as they could' (24). Considerable advantage was therefore conferred upon groups organised in permanent bands rather than in scattered families. This required binding rules that forced people to act in concert. Thus was initiated 'the cake of custom' which enforced the 'hereditary drill' essential for survival (27). This was achieved through unswerving obedience to an elite, blind acceptance of collective norms, and total submission to an oppressive and all-encompassing religion. 'Later are the ages of freedom: first are the ages of servitude' (30). These highly regimented communities prevailed against their less well-organised competitors, leading Bagehot to conclude that 'the most obedient, the tamest tribes are, at the first stage in the real struggle of life, the strongest and the conquerors' (51).

In this way there appeared the 'preliminary' stage of civilisation, or the 'fighting age' as Bagehot sometimes called it. It was facilitated by a universal trait of human nature particularly pronounced among primitives – imitation. This propensity encouraged primitives to follow their leaders, as was evident among savages: 'A savage tribe resembles a herd of gregarious beasts; where the leader goes they go too; they copy blindly his habits, and thus soon become that which he already is' (100–1). In this way, unconscious imitation selected approved habits and actions and discouraged those that were disliked, thereby moulding the character of the society's members (97).

The creation of government and custom to form the preliminary stage was a great step in the advance of civilisation, but the next was even more momentous. The very factors enabling tribes to survive during the fighting age had the ultimate effect of stultifying progress beyond a certain point. Imitation, custom and religious dogma all reinforced conformity and prevented the emergence of novel variations that provided the material for new developments. The result was the 'stationary state', arrested at a certain stage of progress and incapable of additional movement. The only societies capable of continued improvement were those 'happy cases where the force of legality has gone far enough to bind the nation together, but not far enough to kill out all varieties and destroy nature's perpetual tendency to change' (64).

Bagehot confessed he was unable to provide a full explanation for the existence of such cases, but one factor that played a major part in the maintenance of backwardness was insulation from the struggle for existence. This had been the fate of tribes inhabiting the interiors of Africa and Australia, whereas progress had been extensive and continuous in Europe where the struggle had been exceptionally prolonged and severe (82–3).

For whatever reason, at certain points in their evolution a few favoured nations succeeded in breaking the cake of custom. There emerged a social type within which government was conducted on the basis of rational discussion rather than upon imitation, coercion and conformity. This was best attained by means of an element of 'popular government'. Discussion demystified the workings of power, promoted the growth of intelligence and encouraged toleration, and in these ways reawakened 'the dormant inventiveness of men' (161–3, 221). Such societies were vastly superior to less advanced nations, even if one excluded from consideration the 'higher but undisputed region' of morals and religion. Not only were the English colonists cerebrally and technologically more advanced than the aboriginal populations they came into contact with, but their bodies were 'better machines' for evolutionary adaptation and progress, as evidenced by the fact that savages died from diseases which were not fatal to the colonists (48). Bagehot acknowledged that the 'savages' themselves might disagree with these criteria of superiority and progress, but he confidently assured his readers that 'we need not take account of the mistaken ideas of unfit men and beaten races' (209).

Bagehot's blasé assertions about the mentality and social life of 'savages' derived from a set of cultural attitudes and prejudices rather than from direct field experience. The political resonance of these sentiments can be illuminated by exploring the assumptions behind his celebrated work *The English Constitution*, published a little before *Physics and Politics*.[20] In the latter text, Bagehot had made plain his conviction that the mentality of primitives and savages was reproduced within the ranks of a civilised country like England, i.e. among the 'English poor' and 'servants': 'The lower classes in civilised countries, like all classes in uncivilised, are clearly wanting in the nicer part of those feelings which, taken together, we call the *sense* of morality' (117–18, original emphasis).

[20] *The English Constitution* was published in book form in 1867 but had appeared earlier as a series of articles. The edition used here is Glasgow: Fontana/Collins, 1963. Commentaries rarely highlight the connections between this and *Physics and Politics*. There is, for example, a perceptive analysis of both texts in K. C. Wheare, *Walter Bagehot* (London: Oxford University Press, 1974), but no examination of their interrelationship.

Evolution was an uneven process differentially affecting the various members of society so that: 'Civilised nations inherit the human nature which was victorious in barbarian ages, and that nature is, in many respects, not at all suited to civilised circumstances' (185). The implications of this were made explicit in the *English Constitution*, where Bagehot proclaimed: 'Great communities are like great mountains – they have in them the primary, secondary and tertiary strata of human progress; the characteristics of the lower regions resemble the life of old times rather than the present life of the higher regions' (63). These differences in development were reflected in the English class structure:

We have in a great community like England crowds of people scarcely more civilised than the majority of two thousand years ago; we have others, even more numerous, such as the best people were a thousand years since. The lower orders, the middle orders, are still, when tried by what is the standard of the educated 'ten thousand', narrow-minded, unintelligent, incurious. It is useless to pile up abstract words. Those who doubt should go out into their kitchens (62–3).

Bagehot went on to distinguish between the *dignified* and the *efficient* parts of the machinery of government. The former referred to those of its features 'which excite and preserve the reverence of the population' largely through the symbolic and ceremonial representation of authority, as exemplified by the monarchy and, for the most part, the House of Lords. The real work of government was carried on elsewhere, in the efficient parts of the constitution. Here, in the Commons, the Cabinet, and in some of the lesser-known activities of the Lords, the business of government was carried out quietly and effectively by unassuming men upon whom the administration of the nation's affairs depended.

Bagehot's purpose in drawing attention to these facts was not one of demystifying the workings of parliamentary government, despite his aspirations for a science of politics. On the contrary, he argued strongly for the retention of the dignified features of the constitution as fundamental to the stability of the entire system. Hence this text was not merely a treatise on the workings of the British political system but also a contribution to contemporary debates surrounding the extension of the suffrage. Statements about the various evolutionary strata implied that governance was in the hands of the 'educated ten thousand' who alone had reached the level of the 'age of discussion', but whose activities would appear dull and uninspiring to the remainder of the populace. These latter could, however, empathise with the dignified aspects of government: 'The best reason why Monarchy is a strong government is that it is an intelligible government. The mass of mankind understand it, and they hardly anywhere in the world understand any other' (82). Thus in England the masses mistook the symbolism of authority for the reality of power. 'The poorer and more ignorant classes ... really believe that the Queen governs' (241). Like savages and primitives, their rudimentary intellectual and moral faculties were incapable of attaining a more sophisticated understanding of politics. Hence: 'They defer to what we may call the *theatrical show* of society' (248, original emphasis).

The continuation of this deference required a mass which 'abdicates in favour of its elite, and consents to obey whoever that elite may confide in' (247). The theatrical aspects of the constitution secured the allegiance of the masses in a way that the efficient parts could not. But this allegiance, and the stability it ensured, was fragile, and Bagehot warned his audience that 'in communities where the masses are ignorant but respectful, if you once permit the ignorant class to begin to rule you may bid farewell to deference forever' (251). In the context of continuing pressure to extend the suffrage he took the opportunity of a second edition of the *English Constitution* in 1872 to underline this point. He maintained that 'it must be remembered that a political combination of the lower classes, as such, and for their own ends, is an evil of the first magnitude ... So long as they are not taught to act together, there is a chance of this being averted ...' (277). Constitutional government might be inscribed in the warp and woof of political evolution, but its maintenance required a restricted suffrage and the mystification of the majority of its subjects who, by virtue of their hereditary dispositions, were incapable of understanding or participating in it.

Bagehot's theory of evolution incorporated all the components of Social Darwinism to produce an account of the class structure of British society and its relationship to the functioning of constitutional government. But whereas natural selection worked well for explaining the evolution of early social formations or the relations between colonists and their subjects, it was less serviceable for dealing with the future of change *within* advanced societies. This is evident in Bagehot's treatment of the struggle for existence. During the preliminary age this took the form of war, and on occasions Bagehot explicitly made this a universal feature of social life: 'In every particular state of the world, those nations which are strongest tend to prevail over the others; and in certain marked peculiarities, the strongest tend to be the best.'[21] This was certainly consistent with his perception of the relationship between

---

[21] Bagehot, *Physics and Politics*, 43; also 215. In the light of Bagehot's stress on the selective role of warfare, particularly among 'savages', there seems no justification for Himmelfarb's claim that *Physics and Politics* was 'a travesty of Darwinism' which sought to repudiate the role of the struggle for existence during the early stage of human evolution. See Himmelfarb, *Darwin and the Darwinian Revolution*, 426–30.

colonialists and 'barbarians', with the latter reduced, through this conflict, to a point where they were 'no longer so much as vanquished competitors; they have ceased to compete at all'.[22] On other occasions, though, he described warfare as largely confined to the preliminary age and asserted that war had 'ceased to be a moving force in the world...'[23] This could reflect an evolutionary perspective on the struggle for existence, as for Büchner, but Bagehot did not elaborate upon this point or discuss alternative methods of selection.

This vagueness on the status of struggle and warfare among advanced nations was compounded by an implicit reinterpretation of struggle. For Bagehot did not derive this from the relationship between fecundity and resources. He was unquestionably aware of the overcrowding, poverty and vice typical of the large cities, which he attributed to population growth, and he explained this by the strength of the sexual instinct which was a residue of early human nature, moulded at a time when rapid multiplication was integral to military success. But he did not regard this as a permanent trait, since he believed that this instinct was weakened in proportion as the cerebral faculties grew. There was only so much energy available to each individual, and the expansion of certain activities had to be compensated by a contraction of others.[24] Bagehot did not suggest that population pressures engendered the struggle for existence among advanced nations, nor was it invoked as the cause of warfare at early stages of evolution. War and struggle, therefore, appear as facts of life in themselves, rather than as the effects of other processes. Furthermore, Bagehot only used struggle as an explanation for the formation of societies during the preliminary stage, attributing the break-up of the stationary state in ancient, mediaeval and modern times to the emergence of debate and a popular element in government.[25] It would be plausible to interpret discussion and argument as a mode of struggle transported to the realm of ideas, something argued by other Social Darwinists, but Bagehot did not do so. As a consequence, while all the elements of the Darwinist world view can be easily discerned in his writings, the interconnection between the elements was loosened and the struggle for existence became detached from the remaining elements to appear as part of the human condition, albeit a shadowy and problematic one beyond certain levels of evolution.

---

[22] Bagehot, *Physics and Politics*, 46.   [23] *Ibid.*, 78.

[24] *Ibid.*, 195, 199–200. It is significant that Bagehot wrote at a time when the birth-rate had not yet declined among the 'higher ranks' in a manner that was later to alarm the eugenicists.

[25] Bagehot, *Physics and Politics*, 158, 175, 185.

Lombroso and the semiotics of criminality

The British adventurer and novelist Winwood Reade, in his Darwinist-inspired *The Martyrdom of Man* of 1872, proposed that human anatomy held the key to human evolution. Referring to the body as a 'document' concerning man's origins, he wrote: 'There, in unmistakable characters, are inscribed the annals of his early life. These hieroglyphics are not to be fully deciphered without a special preparation for the task; the alphabet of anatomy must first be mastered, and the student must be expert in the language of all living and fossil forms.'[26] Here Reade was expressing a widespread belief during the nineteenth century that a person's mental and moral character could be inferred from certain facets of his or her appearance, and that physical and correlated behavioural traits were signs of an inherited moral disposition.

This belief informed much of the thinking on degeneration, as well as the aspiring sciences of phrenology and criminal and physical anthropology, even finding their way into the popular fiction of the period.[27] Moreover, physical traits were deemed not only to differentiate the morally and physically healthy from the unhealthy, but also demarcated social groups and races. Indeed, the vocabularies of morality, race and class were often interchangeable. The urban residuum was sometimes conceived to be a race apart from the rest of society. Thus Henry Mayhew, in the first volume of his *London Labour and the London Poor* (1861–2), referred to the street folk of London as wandering tribes or races, distinguishable from civilised races both physically and behaviourally.[28] The terms used to describe these nomads – prominent jaws and cheekbones, repugnance to continuous labour, lack of foresight, insensitivity to pain and love of sensual pleasure – were identical to those usually applied to 'born criminals', 'savages' and 'lower races'. When these assumptions were grafted on to evolutionary theory, physical and behavioural traits could be taken as signs not only of an individual's inner character, but also of his or her location in the evolutionary spectrum. An early exemplar of this thinking was the Italian criminologist, Lombroso, who depicted crime as the province of *homo criminalis*, a distinctive type belonging to an alien social group recruited primarily

---

[26] W. Reade, *The Martyrdom of Man* (London: Watts, 1945), 312–3. A similar ambition was expressed by Bagehot in *Physics and Politics*, 2–3.
[27] Pick, *Faces of Degeneration*; Jones, *Social Darwinism*, 103 *et seq.*; N. Rose, *The Psychological Complex* (London: Routledge and Kegan Paul, 1985), 57 *et seq.*
[28] See G. Himmelfarb, *The Idea of Poverty* (London: Faber and Faber, 1984), 324–5.

from the lower classes, especially, though not exclusively, in the towns and cities.[29]

Cesare Lombroso (1835–1909) held various chairs in forensic medicine, psychiatry and criminal anthropology at the universities of Pavia and then Turin. His book *L'Uomo Delinquente* ('The Criminal Man') reached a wide audience, expanding from 252 pages in its first edition of 1876 to 1,203 pages (in three volumes) by the fifth edition of 1895. Here Lombroso elaborated the concept of the 'born criminal', a man or woman who broke the law not through habit, or the pressure of circumstances or temporary passions – all of which played a part in the motives of other kinds of criminal – but by virtue of a hereditary predisposition to evil.

Towards the end of his career Lombroso recalled how, in 1870, he had been struck by the similarities between the skull of a brigand and those of the 'inferior invertebrates'. He concluded from these observations that 'the characteristics of primitive man and of inferior animals must be reproduced in our times'.[30] How did Lombroso arrive at these conclusions? In his *Crime: Its Causes and Consequences* he announced himself to be a disciple of Darwin, convinced that social life 'was governed by silent laws, which never fall into desuetude and rule society much more surely than the laws inscribed in the codes' (369). One such law was that 'the very progress of the organic world is entirely based upon the struggle for existence', which was equally applicable to human evolution (427). In pre-civilised stages of human development, this struggle took the form of warfare, which was the source of 'immense progress' by welding tribes into increasingly larger and more complex societies. This had the effect of imposing social discipline upon the naturally idle and capricious savage through the principles of hierarchy and subordination that were vital to civilised existence (441). War, however, was an evil when nations were civilised, although Lombroso did not specify how the struggle for existence manifested itself in these circumstances, despite his insistence on its omnipresence. Another natural law was heredity, about which Lombroso was also rather vague. He confidently asserted, nonetheless, that while heredity fixed the 'organic type', not all of its influences were apparent at any given moment in the life-history of an organism, but often remained latent

---

[29] For a discussion of *homo criminalis* see M. Foucault, *Discipline and Punish*, tr. A. Sheridan (Harmondsworth: Penguin, 1977), 101–2, 275–6.

[30] C. Lombroso, opening address to the Sixth Congress of Criminal Anthropology, Turin, April 1906. Cited by M. Parmelee, 'Introduction to the English Edition', of Lombroso, *Crime: Its Causes and Remedies*, tr. from the French edition by H. P. Horton (Boston: Little, Brown, 1911), xiv.

'and manifest themselves gradually throughout the whole period of development' (174).[31]

Society was therefore subjected to the laws of heredity and the struggle for survival, which interacted to cause evolutionary change. But progress was uneven, and modern societies contained many persons whose development was fixed at the level of savages or even animals. This was the case with the born criminal. The physical features of the born criminal were a low cranial capacity, retreating forehead, highly developed frontal sinuses, a thick skull, large ears, protruding lower jaw, tufted and crispy hair, and often included prominent canine teeth, prehensile feet and left-handedness for good measure. Psychologically, such a person was insensitive to pain, prone to sensual pleasures, capable of only blunted affections, lazy, impulsive and incapable of remorse. Since all of these attributes, physical and mental, were observable among savages, and even among the anthropoid apes, Lombroso's conclusion was that 'many of the characters presented by savage races are very often found among born criminals', and when a criminal 'lacks absolutely every trace of shame and pity', he 'may go back far beyond the savages, even to the brutes themselves' (365–8). The born criminal – responsible, according to Lombroso, for as much as 40 per cent of modern crime – was an atavistic throwback to the savage and even animal ancestry of modern man, an alien and menacing presence in the very interstices of a civilisation to which he was innately inimical. This atavism was evident in many of the practices of born criminals, for example tattooing (which was typical of savages) and the use of slang: 'They talk differently from us because they do not feel in the same way; they talk like savages because they are veritable savages in the midst of this brilliant European civilisation.'[32]

For Lombroso the physical traits of born criminals signifying their innate criminality could be deciphered by someone with the appropriate training. He gave several examples of the deployment of his own expertise for this purpose. When six men were accused of violating a three-and-a-half-year-old girl by the victim's mother – all of whom denied the offence – Lombroso was called upon to interrogate the suspects, and reported: 'I picked out immediately one among them who had obscene tattooing upon his arm, a sinister physiognomy, irregularities of the field of vision, and also traces of a recent attack of syphilis. Later this individual confessed his crime' (437).

[31] For Lombroso's knowledge of heredity, see Parmelee, 'Introduction', xxx. Parmelee thinks it probable that Lombroso upheld the inheritance of acquired characters, xxxi.
[32] Lombroso, *L'Homme criminel*, 3 vols. (Paris: 1895), I, 497. Cited by Parmelee, 'Introduction', xx.

Lombroso took his analysis beyond a comparison between the savage and the born criminal. He conceptualised a syndrome of physical and mental pathologies which brought within a common frame of reference not only criminals, but 'moral imbeciles' and epileptics. In *Criminal Man* he announced: 'The perversion of the affective sphere, the hate, exaggerated and without motive, the absence or insufficiency of all restraint, the multiple hereditary tendencies, are the source of irresistible impulses in the moral imbecile as well as the born criminal and the epileptic.'[33] What linked these afflictions was their hereditary basis and their primitive origins, that is, their derivation from the earliest phases of the physical and mental evolution of humanity. In these periods, the savage had existed in circumstances in which hatred and violence, unrestrained passion and indifference to suffering, whether in himself in or in others, were normal daily experiences, which explained the proclivity of the modern savage for such practices as cannibalism and infanticide. Civilisation removed these circumstances and repressed the proclivities, but the latter reappeared in the psyche of the born criminal and the 'instinctive animalism' of the epileptic.

A glimpse of this primitive heritage was afforded by observing children. Lombroso was convinced that 'the most horrible crimes have their origin in those animal instincts of which childhood gives us a pale reflection'.[34] In *The Female Offender*[35] written by Lombroso and his colleague Ferrero, criminal women were likened to children because in the former 'their moral sense is deficient . . . they are revengeful, jealous, inclined to vengeances of a refined cruelty' (151). The authors speculated about the enormous potential for crime possessed by children, only prevented from effective expression by their physical weakness and undeveloped intelligence (152). In this manner, Lombroso combined evolution, recapitulation and heredity to construct a developmental continuum. Pre-historic humans and modern savages were closest to our animal forebears; criminals, lunatics and epileptics were cases of arrested development – individuals stuck on the lowest rungs of a phyletic ladder which every 'normal' child traversed in the course of maturation. Or rather, every normal male child, since Lombroso believed that women were at a considerably lower stage of evolution than men.

In their study of women offenders Lombroso and Ferrero argued that female born criminals were, like their male counterparts, typified by a series of physical abnormalities reflecting their atavistic natures:

---

[33] *L'Homme criminel*, II, 125. Cited by Parmelee, 'Introduction', xxiii.
[34] Lombroso, *Crime*, 368.
[35] C. Lombroso and W. Ferrero (no tr.), *The Female Offender* (London: Owen, 1959).

The criminal being only a reversion to the primitive type of his species, the female criminal necessarily offers the two most salient characteristics of primordial woman, namely, precocity and a minor degree of differentiation from the male – this lesser differentiation manifesting itself in the stature, cranium, brain, and in the muscular strength which she possesses to a degree so far in advance of the modern female (112–13).

Here the authors ran into difficulties. Female born criminals were supposed to be more masculine than non-delinquent women. Yet their data actually revealed that delinquent females displayed significantly less physical anomalies than their male counterparts, so much so that female offenders seemed 'almost normal' in comparison to male criminals (107). But if females were closer to the evolutionary origins of the species than were males, then women offenders should exhibit more anomalous features than men. Lombroso and Ferrero appealed to a number of factors to explain this seeming contradiction. First, they insisted that women were inherently more conservative than men, the primary cause of which was 'the immobility of the ovule compared with the zoosperm'. Second, the demands of childrearing exposed women to less varied conditions of existence. Among vertebrates and even more so among savages, the struggle for life devolved principally upon males, and this caused variations and 'peculiar adaptations in functions and organs'. For this reason, women were less exposed to 'transformation and deformation'. These causes were reinforced, finally, by sexual selection: 'Man not only refused to *marry* a deformed female, but ate her, while, on the other hand, preserving for his enjoyment the handsome woman who gratified his peculiar instincts. In those days he was the stronger, and the choice rested with him' (109, original emphasis). These arguments combined popular perceptions (or, rather, misperceptions) of savage societies, sexual stereotypes, recapitulation theory and Social Darwinism in an account of the criminal psyche which, well before the endorsement of germ-plasm theory, was heavily reductionist.

It has been suggested that in the latter part of his career Lombroso came to place more stress on social determinants of criminal behaviour.[36] If this was indeed the case he always assigned a preponderant role to atavism in the cause of crime, even to the extent of attributing tattooing and the use of slang to inheritance. His biological determinism was clearly in evidence, for example, in his discussion of alcoholism, when he wrote: 'The progeny of the alcoholic are blind, paralytic, impotent. Even if they begin life with wealth, they must necessarily become poor. If they are poor, they are incapable of working.' The criminal was likewise driven to act as he did by innate predispositions

[36] Parmelee, 'Introduction', xxviii.

over which he had no control. Thus Lombroso saw in the criminal 'a savage and at the same time a sick man'.[37] Despite this, Lombroso cautioned against any undue sympathy for *homo criminalis*. If crime was an inescapable feature of social life, so was punishment, for it was pointless to try and reform the born criminal: the death penalty was part of the incessant struggle for existence and was therefore 'inscribed in the book of nature'. Lombroso reasoned: 'The fact that there exist such beings as born criminals, organically fitted for evil, atavistic reproductions, not simply of savage men but even of the fiercest animals, far from making us more compassionate towards them ... steels us against all pity.' But Lombroso opposed the indiscriminate use of the death penalty, preferring instead the isolation of born criminals to prevent them reproducing, and he even toyed with the possibility of turning their instincts to good use: 'If we try to apply the Darwinian law (according to which only those organisms survive which have utility for the species) to the fact that crime does not cease to increase ... we are driven to believe that it must have, if not a function, at least a social utility.' So instead of repressing criminals, the state should seek to harness their behaviour to socially useful ends, and he recommended the army for murderers and the police force or journalism for swindlers.[38]

Lombroso's methodology, which relied upon anthropometric measurements for its data base, had come under increasing attack by the beginning of the twentieth century. Nevertheless, the concept of the born criminal was to remain an important one in debates about criminality, especially in those emanating from eugenics and racial hygiene. This held true even among persons possessing a sophisticated knowledge of genetics, as is aptly illustrated by the eugenicist and professor of racial hygiene, Fritz Lenz (1887–1976), writing in Germany half a century after the Italian had first propounded his views. Lenz even embraced a similar semiotic approach, claiming it possible to infer mental constitution from physical traits. He argued:

there are close relationships between race and crime. I am inclined to think that there is even a certain amount of truth in the doctrine formulated a good many years ago by Lombroso, that the 'born criminal' belongs to a special and primitive racial stock. Criminals very often exhibit characters which remind us of Neanderthal man or of other primitive races, having prominent and massive jaws, receding foreheads, etc.[39]

---

[37] Lombroso, *Crime*, 89; Lombroso, *L'Homme criminel*, II, 135, cited by Parmelee, 'Introduction', xxiv.

[38] Lombroso, *Crime*, 426, 427, 440, 447.

[39] F. Lenz, 'The Inheritance of Intellectual Gifts', in E. Bauer, E. Fischer and F. Lenz, *Human Heredity*, tr. E. and C. Paul (London: Allen and Unwin, 1931), 681. This is a translation of the third edition (1927) of the important textbook *Grundriss der*

Lenz speculated that when these early races had been extirpated some of their blood had been preserved through inter-mixture with other races, with the result that vestiges of early man probably 'remain scattered here and there in the European population of today, and ... the carriers of this primitive hereditary equipment are peculiarly apt to come into conflict with the demands of modern civilised life'.[40] In the case of Lenz and his co-authors, familiarity with advances in modern genetics was utilised to reconfirm the theory of criminal atavism advanced by the 'Italian' school of criminal anthropology, with, ultimately, inhuman consequences, as will be shown in the chapter on Nazism.

Although I have pointed to the continuity between Lombroso's notion of the born criminal and the ideas of Lenz and his co-authors, it would be facile to interpret the Italian's work as a form of proto-Nazism. Gould has emphasised the reformist and even socialist proclivities of many of the leaders of criminal anthropology, who were committed to a more rational order.[41] As Pick has shown, Lombroso's criminal science was part of an attempt to understand the foundations of political instability and social stagnation in the post-unification era in Italy, and he was 'typically perceived at the time as a progressive figure ...'.[42] To see criminality and other forms of 'anti-social' behaviour as having a hereditary basis was commonplace at this time. What Lombroso and his co-workers did was to posit an explanation for crime that was to become an important model of Social Darwinist reasoning even after its methodological foundations had been undermined.

Conclusion

The theorists discussed in this chapter were by no means the only notable pioneers in the application of Darwinism to social and political subjects. Clémence Royer in France, Ernst Haeckel in Germany, and Herbert Spencer in England were all creative and influential participants in this development, and their contributions will be surveyed in later chapters.[43] From these early examples, however, it is possible to arrive at

---

menschlichen Erblichkeitslehre und Rassenhygiene. The second edition (1923) of this text was apparently read by Hitler during his imprisonment in Landsberg fortress. See R. Lerner, *Final Solutions* (Pennsylvania State University Press, 1992), 70.

[40] Lenz, 'Inheritance', 681.   [41] Gould, *Ever Since Darwin*, 227.

[42] Pick, *Faces of Degeneration*, 122. Chapter 5 of Pick's study provides a detailed assessment of Lombroso's work and its context.

[43] The quality of these pioneering efforts makes it impossible to concur with D. Bellomy's assertion that the 'earliest applications of Darwinism by social scientists were cavalier and imprecise': '"Social Darwinism" Revisited', 39. The writings of Brace, Royer and Spencer were highly detailed and imaginative applications of Darwinism, as was Bagehot's contribution, even if his Darwinism was looser than that of the others.

some general inferences concerning the nature and discursive functions of Social Darwinism.

First, the writings of Bagehot and Lombroso established a set of identities and differences located along an evolutionary continuum in which the presumed attributes of pre-historic people designated the starting point of evolution. Various other categories could then be equated with primitive people if they were deemed to exhibit these characteristics. Modern 'savages', children, women, criminals, the insane, epileptics – sometimes even entire classes in the case of Bagehot – could be assigned inferior positions and substituted for one another on the evolutionary ladder. This tactic did not originate with Social Darwinism, as was pointed out above. But Social Darwinism increased its plausibility and provide the value judgements implicit in these categorisations with a scientific mantle. As the example of Lenz indicates, and subsequent chapters will confirm, it is a constantly recurring feature of much Social Darwinist theorising.

Second, the theorists discussed above already indicate the flexibility of Social Darwinism, which underwrote the conservatism of Bagehot, the atheistic materialism and political radicalism of Büchner, the Christian humanism of Brace and the criminal anthropology of Lombroso. In all instances the elements comprising the world view were clearly discernible, though in some cases their interconnections were modified. Finally, all the writers displayed ambiguities and tensions in their use of Social Darwinism. These aporias derive from the dilemmas exposed by the rhetorical appropriation of Social Darwinism: they occur even in theorists dedicated to the construction of a comprehensive evolutionary philosophy of nature and society, such as Herbert Spencer, the subject of the next chapter.

4   Herbert Spencer and cosmic evolution

Introduction

For many people the name of the English philosopher Herbert Spencer (1820–1903) would be virtually synonymous with Social Darwinism. Not only did Spencer coin the expression 'the survival of the fittest' and apply it to social evolution, he was also instrumental in popularising the term 'evolution' in its modern sense.[1] Although his influence waned in the twentieth century, during the last three decades of the nineteenth century he enjoyed a world-wide reputation: his books were translated into many languages and at times there were over a million copies in print.[2] Spencer appears to be not only a quintessential Social Darwinist, therefore, but also a highly influential one.

As was noted in the introduction, however, this identification of Spencer with Social Darwinism has been questioned by modern historians who have denied the existence of specifically Darwinian elements in Spencer's thought.[3] Some commentators have gone so far as to suggest that to interpret Spencer as a Social Darwinist is to misrepresent and even to caricature his work.[4] Others focus upon Spencer's political theory and pay less attention to his evolutionary arguments.[5] Contrary to both these tendencies, I am going to argue, first, that Spencer *was* a Social Darwinist; and second, that the relation-

---

[1] P. J. Bowler, 'The Changing Meaning of Evolution', *Journal of the History of Ideas*, 36(1975), 106–9.

[2] R. M. Young, 'Herbert Spencer and Inevitable Progress', *History Today*, 37(1987), 18. It is important not to exaggerate Spencer's decline for he continued to exert an influence throughout the twentieth century. See, for example, C. W. Saleeby, *Evolution, the Master Key* (London: Harper, 1906), which hints at 'hero-worship' (v); Meldola, *Evolution*; Sir E. Benn, *The State the Enemy* (London: Benn, 1953).

[3] J. D. Y. Peel, *Herbert Spencer: The Evolution of a Sociologist* (London: Heinemann, 1971), 147; Bannister, *Social Darwinism*, 55; P. J. Bowler, *Evolution*, 267–72.

[4] J. H. Turner, *Herbert Spencer: A Renewed Appreciation* (Beverly Hills/London: Sage, 1985), 11.

[5] For examples, see W. L. Miller, 'Herbert Spencer's Theory of Welfare and Public Policy', *History of Political Economy*, 4(1972), 207–31; and the essays devoted to Spencer's political ideas in *History of Political Thought*, 2(1981).

ship between Spencer's evolutionary and political thought is fundamental for an understanding of this latter aspect of his work.[6]

At the age of sixteen, Spencer published a defence of the new Poor
Laws in which he invoked scriptural authority for his assertion that the
idle and improvident should not be allowed to prosper at the expense of
the thrifty and diligent.[7] This stance reflected the values of radical
individualism and self-help which Spencer had imbibed from his
family.[8] During his subsequent career as a railway engineer, journalist
and writer, his allegiance to these values was unwavering; what was to
change was the basis upon which they were validated. As an adult,
Spencer abandoned religion in favour of an all-embracing Synthetic
Philosophy, the central tenet of which was the idea of 'cosmic evolution'.

Cosmic evolution

Spencer's notion of evolution was derived from the principle of the
conservation of energy or, as he preferred, the 'persistence of force'.
Throughout the universe, matter and motion were constantly redistrib-
uted. Evolutionary change consisted in the simultaneous integration of
matter and dissipation of motion, whereas dissolution involved the
disintegration of matter and the absorption of motion. Nature was in a
state of constant evolution because of the 'instability of the homogeneous'; the differential impact of persistent force on a homogeneous
body induced changes within it, hence the progressive development of
all phenomena from simple and incoherent states to conditions of
structural complexity through the differentiation and integration of
parts. 'Not only is all progress from the homogeneous to the heterogeneous, but, at the same time, it is from the indefinite to the definite.'[9]

[6] A recent study has argued that, starting from a conception that was neither Darwinian
nor Lamarckian, Spencer sought to synthesise features of both biological theories. See
M. Taylor, *Men Versus the State* (Oxford: Clarendon Press, 1992), chaps. 2 and 3.
Although providing an excellent contextualisation of Spencer's thought and an
illuminating account of his evolutionary ideas, I believe Taylor underplays the
congruence between Darwin and Spencer. The same charge could be levelled against
Spencer's American disciple and populariser, E. L. Youmans, who insisted that, unlike
Spencer, Darwin was not concerned with elucidating 'the general laws of Evolution'.
See his 'Herbert Spencer and the Doctrine of Evolution' (1874), in J. Fiske, *Life and
Letters of Edward Livingstone Youmans* (London: Chapman and Hall, 1894), 526–43.

[7] Reproduced in J. Offer, ed., *Herbert Spencer: Political Writings* (Cambridge University
Press, 1994). See D. Wiltshire, *The Social and Political Thought of Herbert Spencer*
(Oxford University Press, 1978), 21 *et seq.*

[8] See Spencer's description of the character traits of his father and uncles in his
Autobiography, 2 vols. (London: Williams and Norgate, 1904), I, 42; II, 441.

[9] Herbert Spencer, 'The Social Organism', in Spencer, *The Man Versus the State, with
Four Essays on Politics and Society*, ed. D. Macrae (Harmondsworth: Penguin, 1969),
215. Spencer's general theory of evolution was set out in 1860 in his *First Principles,*

With regard to organic nature, Spencer claimed that each organism struggled to maintain an equilibrium between itself and its environment. Because the latter was constantly changing, adjustments were also continuous, producing moving equilibria until the organism either failed to adapt or eventually succumbed to the processes of dissolution and death. Spencer distinguished two forms of 'equilibration'. The first he named 'direct equilibration' consisting of 'certain changes of function and structure that are directly consequent on changes in the incident forces – inner changes by which the outer changes are balanced and the equilibrium restored'.[10] This direct adaptation by the organism to its environment was accompanied by 'indirect equilibration' in the form of natural selection, or survival of the fittest, a process which 'has always been going on, is going on now, and must ever continue to go on'.[11] There were, however, two facets of natural selection. The first he designated as a self-evident truth, namely that 'the average vigour of any race would be diminished did the diseased and feeble habitually survive and propagate; and that the destruction of such, through failure to fulfil some of the conditions to life, leaves behind those who are able to fulfil the conditions to life, and thus keeps up the average fitness to the conditions of life . . .'[12] This aspect of the survival of the fittest Spencer regarded as well established, having himself drawn attention to its role in maintaining the average fitness of a population in 1852.[13] What Spencer did not recognise until the publication of the work of Darwin and Wallace was the part played by natural selection in *producing* fitness through its action on the variations which occurred between organisms.[14] He wrote in his *Autobiography*: 'At that time I ascribed all modifications to direct adaptation to changing conditions; and was unconscious that in the absence of that indirect adaptation effected by the natural selection of favourable variations, the explanation left the large part of the facts unaccounted for.'[15] It was Darwin's achievement to have discovered and demonstrated this process.

sixth edn (London: Williams and Norgate, 1922), Part II. For a detailed account of this theory, see Taylor, *Men Versus the State*, 76–85.

[10] Spencer, *Principles of Biology*, 2 vols., revised edn (New York: Appleton and Co., 1898), I, 528.

[11] *Ibid.*, I, 531.

[12] *Ibid.* By 'race' Spencer here means a biological sub-species or variety.

[13] Spencer, 'A Theory of Population Deduced from the General Law of Animal Fertility', *Westminster Review*, 1(1852), 468–501. Spencer was correct to insist on the widespread acceptance of this notion of selection, which had often been employed by naturalists as evidence of the *impossibility* of evolutionary transmutation. See S. J. Gould, *An Urchin in the Storm* (Harmondsworth: Penguin, 1990), chap. 3.

[14] Spencer, *Principles of Biology*, I, 532–3.

[15] Spencer, *Autobiography*, I, 502. See also II, 50.

The stimulus to the struggle for existence was provided by population pressure, which had always been the 'proximate cause of progress'.[16] This struggle was both inter- and intra-specific. The relationship between predators and prey was an incessant cause of mutual adaptation which produced improvements in senses and organs.[17] Successful modifications were inherited by subsequent generations, leading to cumulative and progressive development.[18] This struggle was augmented by another which occurred within each species. 'The stronger often carries off by force the prey which the weaker has caught. Monopolising certain hunting grounds, the more ferocious drive others of their kind into less favourable places. With plant-eating animals, too, the like holds.'[19] The struggle for resources was thus a ubiquitous selective process: 'Placed in competition with members of its own species and in antagonism with members of other species, it [the organism] dwindles and gets killed off, or thrives and propagates, according as it is ill-endowed or well-endowed.'[20] Moreover, Spencer deemed rivalry over resources to occur even *within* each individual organism. Organs appropriated blood and nutrients from a common stock: 'So that though the welfare of each is indirectly bound up with that of the rest; yet directly, each is antagonistic to the rest.' This inter-organic competition stimulated the growth and development of organs.[21]

Like all organisms, humans were governed by the mechanisms of direct and indirect equilibration. Despite their relatively low rate of reproduction, humans were subjected to an ineluctable pressure of population on the means of subsistence, stimulating their faculties and engendering competition. Families and races which failed to adapt to this pressure were liable to extinction. This harsh discipline had enabled humanity to advance to its present level of development, thus ensuring 'a constant progress towards a higher degree of skill, intelligence, and self-regulation – a better coordination of actions – a more complete life'.[22]

Warfare was the human analogue of predation, and produced similar consequences: 'Warfare among men, like warfare among animals, has had a large share in raising their organisations to a higher stage.' Warfare produced the survival of the fittest groups whose successful traits would

[16] Spencer, *Principles of Biology*, II, 536.
[17] Spencer, *Principles of Sociology*, abridged, ed. S. Andreski (London: Macmillan, 1969), 176–7; Spencer, *The Study of Sociology*, seventh edn (London: Kegan Paul, 1878), 192.
[18] Spencer, *Man Versus the State*, 133.
[19] Spencer, *The Data of Ethics* (London: Williams and Norgate, 1879), 17.
[20] Spencer, *Man Versus the State*, 137.   [21] Spencer, *Principles of Sociology*, 75–6.
[22] Spencer, *Principles of Biology*, II, 526–8.

be inherited by their offspring, thereby ensuring the continual progress of humanity. 'The killing off of relatively feeble tribes, or tribes relatively wanting in endurance, or courage, or sagacity, or power of cooperation, must have tended ever to maintain, and occasionally to increase, the amounts of life-preserving powers possessed by men.'[23]

These predatory relations among different societies were accompanied by conflicts *within* societies, necessarily so 'since the nature which prompts international aggression prompts aggression of individuals on one another'.[24] But warfare and aggression were not permanent features of human relationships because the struggle for existence itself underwent an evolution from violent to peaceful forms. As humanity became more rational and altruistic it became correspondingly more peaceful and warfare was eradicated.[25] This did not mean that the survival of the fittest was likewise eliminated, only that it changed its form from warfare to the forces of market competition: 'After this stage has been reached, the purifying process, continuing still an important one, remains to be carried on by industrial war – by a competition of societies during which the best, physically, emotionally, and intellectually, spread most, and leave the least capable to disappear gradually, from failing to leave a sufficiently numerous posterity.'[26]

Industrial competition not only governed inter-social relations, but also produced a 'peaceful struggle for existence in societies ever growing more crowded and more complicated'. The selective consequences of this struggle stimulated the growth in the size and complexity of the brain.[27] Competition also caused the elimination of unfit individuals and for Spencer it was imperative that this process was not inhibited by misguided charity for the 'unworthy': 'Living and working within the restraints imposed by one another's presence, justice requires that individuals shall severally take the consequences of their conduct, neither increased nor decreased. The superior shall have the good of his superiority; and the inferior the evil of his inferiority.'[28] Spencer assured his readers that recognition of this principle by no means required that 'the struggle for life and the survival of the fittest must be left to work out their effects without mitigation'. Private charity was fully consistent with evolutionary progress so long as it remained within limits, i.e. did not encourage the procreation of the unworthy.[29]

Before proceeding to examine Spencer's views on socio-political evolution I want to draw two inferences from this exegesis of his general

---

[23] Spencer, *Study of Sociology*, 193.   [24] Spencer, *Data of Ethics*, 19.
[25] Spencer, *Principles of Sociology*, 177–8.
[27] Spencer, *Principles of Biology*, II, 529.   [26] Spencer, *Study of Sociology*, 199.
[29] Spencer, *Principles of Biology*, II, 533.   [28] Spencer, *Principles of Sociology*, 541.

theory. The first is that Spencer endorsed all the components of the Social Darwinist world view, even if he arrived at his position by a route different to that travelled by Darwin. Furthermore, although Spencer conceived evolution in cosmic terms and sought to incorporate natural selection within his universal framework, it was organic evolution which received the greatest emphasis in his numerous writings.[30] He constantly employed organic analogies and metaphors while consistently seeking the antecedents of human faculties and behaviour in the animal kingdom.[31]

The second point concerns Spencer's alleged Lamarckism. Spencer unquestionably assigned greater importance to direct adaptation and the inheritance of acquired characters than Darwin, as he frequently pointed out.[32] Nor was this differential emphasis the only disagreement between the two men. Spencer considered the analogy between natural and artificial selection to be misleading because the former could isolate specific traits whereas the latter acted upon 'individuals which are, by the *aggregate* of their traits, best fitted for living'.[33] More importantly, Spencer believed that the significance of natural selection declined as organisms became more advanced and therefore more self-directed:

Natural selection, or survival of the fittest, is almost exclusively operative throughout the vegetal world or throughout the lower animal world, characterised by relative passivity. But with the ascent to higher types of animals, its effects are in increasing degrees involved with those produced by inheritance of acquired characters; until, in animals of complex structures, inheritance of acquired characters becomes an important, if not the chief, cause of evolution.[34]

In humans, especially *vis-à-vis* the development of their intellectual and moral faculties, direct adaptation was preponderant.[35] Before construing these remarks as 'Lamarckian', however, it is necessary to recall Spencer's distinction between the dual aspect of natural selection. The comments just cited refer to the role of this mechanism in selecting innate variations; the *culling* action of natural selection remained as a fundamental evolutionary force. Furthermore – and contrary to the pre-Darwinian view of selection – Spencer insisted that the survival of the fittest and direct adaptation were *integrated* processes, combining to produce the *dynamics* of development: 'There must be a natural selection of functionally acquired peculiarities, as well as of spontaneously

[30] Spencer maintained that the interpretation of organic nature constituted the most important part of his Synthetic Philosophy. See 'Preface' to *First Principles*, xii.
[31] This strategy is employed throughout the *Data of Ethics*, for example.
[32] Spencer, *Principles of Biology*, I, 560; Spencer, *The Inadequacy of Natural Selection* (London: Williams and Norgate, 1893), 41–2.
[33] Spencer, *Inadequacy*, 11, emphasis added.   [34] *Ibid.*, 45.
[35] Spencer, *Principles of Biology*, I, 552–3, 560.

acquired peculiarities', the changes accruing from the former being speeded up through natural selection. Spencer concluded: 'The survival of the fittest must nearly always further the production of modifications which produce fitness, *whether they be incidental modifications, or modifications caused by direct adaptation.*'[36]

There is nothing Lamarckian about these arguments or the world view they express. Spencer's notion of equilibrium entailed a competitive dynamic both between and within species which was antithetical to the Lamarckian perspective. To depict this competition as simply a stimulus to effort is seriously to misrepresent Spencer's argument.[37] The contrast between a Social Darwinist perspective and one consistent with a Lamarckian position is strikingly apparent from a comparison between Spencer's thesis on the survival of the fittest and Samuel Smiles' perception of advance through self-cultivation and improvement. For Smiles, even the poorest labourers were capable of raising themselves as a class, 'not by pulling down others, but by levelling them up to a higher and still advancing standard of religion, intelligence, and virtue'.[38] But for Spencer, evolutionary progress entailed the continuous purging of the unfit; he had no vision of these latter improving their position and moving up the evolutionary ladder.

Spencer's goal was a synthesis of natural selection and the Lamarckian focus upon direct adaptation: the result was an evolutionary theory which was much closer to Darwin's theory than to the French naturalist's conception of the self-advancement of the lowly, a conception also in evidence in the self-help philosophy of Smiles. Unlike the essay on population of 1852, Spencer's later writings wedded the winnowing effects of selection to the notion of *evolutionary change*. Furthermore, Spencer always insisted both on the centrality of natural selection in his theory and of the importance of direct adaptation in Darwin's work, defending what he considered to be the true Darwinian heritage against Weismann and his disciples.[39] Given the indeterminacy over the mechanisms of evolutionary change within Darwin's theory, Spencer's claim, viewed historically, was quite plausible.[40]

[36] *Ibid.*, 540, emphasis added.   [37] This is the argument of Bowler, *Evolution*, 267, 272.

[38] S. Smiles, *Self-Help*, revised edn (London: Murray, 1897), 294. On this point, see my 'The Struggle for Existence in Nineteenth Century Social Theory: Three Case Studies', *History of the Human Sciences*, 8(1995), 53–4.

[39] See Spencer's comments in *Principles of Biology*, I, chap. XIVa; Spencer, *Inadequacy*, 41.

[40] Spencer was closely linked to the Darwinian circle through his friendship with Huxley and his membership of the X Club. (See Spencer's comments in *Autobiography*, I, 402–4; II, 115–16). The interchange of ideas is apparent in Darwin's own work, quite apart form the borrowing of the phrase 'survival of the fittest'. In his autobiography Darwin acknowledged Spencer's abilities but confessed to neither liking him nor finding his

From militant to industrial society

Spencer's theory of evolution was not only part of an architectonic philosophical scheme; it also grounded his political thought. This consisted of a liberalism which extolled the virtues of individualism and decried the evils of an interventionist state. By the last quarter of the century this creed – known as 'Individualism' – was deployed by the opponents of the 'New Liberalism'. Supporters of the latter were prepared to countenance a democratic interventionist state as a vehicle for social reform. The Individualists fought to reassert what they saw as the essence of liberalism – negative freedom and *laissez-faire* – and Spencer was their most prestigious advocate.[41]

Spencer's political ideas reposed upon and were legitimated by his theory of socio-political evolution. Evolution acted both upon individuals (as organisms) and upon societies as a whole. To lend credence to this second claim Spencer argued that social and biological organisms exhibited many similarities: 'Societies slowly augment in mass; they progress in complexity of structure; at the same time their parts become more mutually dependent; their living units are removed and replaced without destroying their integrity; and the extents to which they display these peculiarities are proportionate to their vital activities. These are traits that societies have in common with organic bodies.'[42] Social and natural bodies displayed differences as well, the most important being that whereas natural bodies possessed a single centre of consciousness, in societies there were as many such centres as there were individual members. Hence there was no separate corporate consciousness independent of and superior to that of the individuals who comprised the social organism. From this Spencer derived an important methodological conclusion, namely that societies consisted of aggregates of individuals. Since the nature of aggregates – at least in regard to their essential as opposed to inessential characteristics – was determined by the traits of their constituent parts, it followed 'that the properties of the

---

speculative methods and generalisations congenial: C. Darwin and T. H. Huxley, *Autobiographies*, ed. G. de Beer (Oxford University Press, 1983), 64. Yet in the *Descent* Darwin referred to Spencer as 'our great philosopher' (189) and cited him seven times, compared to eleven references to Haeckel and seventeen to Huxley.

[41] For an analysis of these developments, see A. Vincent, 'Classical Liberalism and its Crisis of Identity', *History of Political Thought*, 11(1990), 143–61; E. Bristow, 'The Liberty and Property Defence League and Individualism', *The Historical Journal*, 18(1975), 761–89; Taylor, *Men Versus the State*. On the growth of welfare legislation during this period, see D. Fraser, *The Evolution of the British Welfare State* (London: Macmillan, 1973).

[42] Spencer, 'The Social Organism', 206.

units determine the properties of the whole they make up', a proposition that Spencer insisted held true 'of societies as of other things'.[43]

Spencer did not consistently adhere to this reductionism and sometimes proposed a more dialectical conception of the relation of part to whole.[44] But the individual remained the primary focus of his account of social evolution, enabling him to reassert the significance of 'human nature' in sociological analysis:

> Society is made up of individuals; all that is done in society is done by the combined actions of individuals; and therefore in individual actions only can be found the solutions of social phenomena. But the actions of individuals depend on the laws of their nature; and their actions cannot be understood until these laws are understood. These laws, however, when reduced to their simplest expressions, prove to be corollaries from the laws of body and mind in general. Hence it follows, that biology and psychology are indispensable as interpreters of sociology.[45]

Human nature was not static: as with all of nature, it changed over time, albeit very slowly and in accordance with evolutionary laws. Spencer eschewed the notions of either a fixed or a malleable human nature in favour of a 'conception of human nature that is changed in the slow succession of generations by discipline'.[46] Now a society was a system of cooperative interactions which allowed members to increase their welfare and adapt and compete more effectively than was possible through their unaided efforts. But the ability of people to cooperate, and hence the mode of cooperation adopted, depended upon their level of intellectual and moral development.[47] The evolution of human nature, therefore, held the key to social evolution, and this was the sense in which Spencer's approach can be described as individualistic. Despite his deference to the dialectic of whole/part interactions, human nature provided the ultimate explanation of social change.

Spencer constructed two models of social organisation – the militant and industrial – which expressed two very different modes of cooperation that in turn derived from different stages of the evolution of human nature. The militant type was typical of the earliest phases of evolution, and evidence for the intellectual and moral proclivities of people during these phases could be derived from a number of sources. One was the institutions and behaviour of the members of contemporary hunter–

[43] Spencer, *The Study of Sociology*, 51.
[44] For example, *Principles of Psychology*, 2 vols., third edn (London: Williams and Norgate, 1890), II, 535; Spencer, *Facts and Comments* (London: Williams and Norgate, 1902), 94–6; Spencer, *Data of Ethics*, 3; Spencer, *Study of Sociology*, 337.
[45] Spencer, *Education: Intellectual, Moral and Physical* (London: Williams and Norgate, 1906), 44.
[46] Spencer, *Study of Sociology*, 145.   [47] Spencer, *Principles of Psychology*, II, 508.

gatherer societies, or 'savages'. Another was those members of advanced societies who, like savages, remained fixed at primitive evolutionary levels, such as the 'less cultivated', especially women from 'inferior ranks'.[48] Finally, because he endorsed a 'recapitulation' theory of human development according to which advanced organisms reproduced the various stages of their evolutionary ancestry during their maturation,[49] Spencer was able to deduce the physical and behavioural traits of primitive people from the corresponding traits of modern children, a deduction that was equally unflattering to both:

> During early childhood every civilised man passes through that phase of character exhibited by the barbarous race from which he is descended. As the child's features – flat nose, forward-opening nostrils, large lips, wide-apart eyes, absent frontal sinus, etc. – resemble those of the savage, so too, do his instincts. Hence the tendency to cruelty, to thieving, to lying, so general among children.[50]

Due to their rudimentary moral and intellectual capabilities primitives had no foresight or ability to provide for contingencies. Beliefs were rigidly adhered to but abstract ideas were impossible, including any conception of truth, while the imagination was but poorly developed.[51] As was evident from the behaviour of savages, primitives were capricious, possessing an 'impulsive nature incapable of patient inquiry', in addition to which they were aggressive and devoid of any notions of morality.[52] Given these traits, any system of social relationships based upon rational, voluntary cooperation was impossible. This was why the militant social type was the first organised form of social cooperation. Cooperation was enforced, producing a regimented and authoritarian system in which the individual was totally subordinated to the community. 'His life is not his own, but is at the disposal of his society.' Centralisation of power and hierarchy were complete, with intermediate organisations either prohibited or else closely regulated by the state, with the position of this latter institution reinforced by a dogmatic religion from which deviations were severely repressed.[53] In these communities,

[48] *Ibid.*, II, 537–8. Although he placed women at a lower stage of evolution than men in civilised societies, Spencer believed that the differences between the sexes would diminish in the future; *Study of Sociology*, 377–9.
[49] Spencer, *Principles of Psychology*, II, 220–1. Spencer was here adopting a perspective of the German school of *naturphilosophie*. On this, and for an illuminating discussion of Spencer's theory of psychological evolution, see C. U. M. Smith, 'Evolution and the Problem of Mind: Part I. Herbert Spencer', *Journal of the History of Biology*, 15(1982), 55–88.
[50] Spencer, *Education: Intellectual, Moral and Physical*, 163.
[51] Spencer, *Principles of Psychology*, II, 523, 527–33.
[52] Spencer, *Study of Sociology*, 116, 174; *Principles of Psychology*, II, 601.
[53] Spencer, *Principles of Sociology*, 502–4.

virtue was synonymous with bravery and bodily vigour and martial prowess much admired. The only form of justice was revenge, which encouraged an ethos conducive to the 'survival of the unforgiving', while people took pleasure in acts of violence and cruelty and scorned non-military activities such as trade and productive labour. Throughout the entire society there existed great deference and loyalty to the authorities and a corresponding faith and confidence in 'governmental agency'.[54]

The struggle for existence between neighbouring tribes was responsible for the emergence of the militant type, which provided the seedbed for all future cooperation. Warfare motivated the first specialisation within the primitive horde when a permanent chieftain and his warrior elite established relations of subordination and domination. Thus was initiated a vital step in the structural differentiation and functional specialisation of parts which, for Spencer, constituted the essence of cosmic evolution.[55]

There were a number of additional ways in which warfare had contributed to progress. First, as we have already noted, warfare raised the average level of ability among humans by killing off inferior individuals and tribes. Second, war facilitated the creation of ever larger social units through conquest and slavery. Force alone was responsible for the welding of small nomadic groups into large tribes and the latter into small, and then large, nations. Increased social mass augmented both the need and the opportunity for greater occupational specialisation. Spencer argued that among the larger social aggregates hostilities became less frequent and were punctuated by increasingly lengthy periods of peace, providing an additional stimulus to productive activities. The unintended consequence of warfare, then, was to nurture 'a social aggregation which furthers that industrial state at variance with war; and yet nothing but war could bring about this social aggregation'.[56] Third, militant society had the seemingly paradoxical effect of fostering the qualities conducive to *voluntary* cooperation, namely a rational and imaginative perception of the relationship between present efforts and future consequences. Militant social systems encouraged 'the power of continuous application, the willingness to act under direction (now no longer coercive but agreed to under contract) and the habit of achieving large results by organisations'.[57] These developments were accompanied by an expansion of morality, the growth of altruism, and a corresponding decline in aggression, deceit and cruelty. In this way, militant society was gradually superseded by industrial society. Individual autonomy expanded and private associations proliferated while the

---

[54] *Ibid.*, 523–9.   [55] Spencer, *Study of Sociology*, 60   [56] *Ibid.*, 195.
[57] Spencer, *Man Versus the State*, 186.

domain and the authority of the state gradually contracted. 'Under the industrial *régime* the citizen's individuality, instead of being sacrificed by the society, has to be defended by the society. Defence of his individuality becomes the society's essential duty.'[58]

Attention has already been drawn to Spencer's thesis that warfare declined with the predominance of industrial organisation. Indeed, beyond a certain point, warfare ceased to have any beneficial impact on either social structure or individual character. This was because in modern societies only the healthiest and most capable males were conscripted and exposed to slaughter, 'leaving behind the physically inferior to propagate the race ... War, therefore, after a certain stage of progress, instead of furthering bodily development and the development of certain mental powers, becomes a cause of retrogression.'[59] Altruism and voluntary cooperation were hindered by bellicosity since 'only when the struggle for existence has ceased to go on under the form of war, can these highest social sentiments attain their full development'.[60] From this point on the struggle for existence took the form of industrial competition.

The relevance of this theory of individual and social evolution to Spencer's defence of a limited state and economic *laissez-faire* is not difficult to perceive. Central to his account of this process was the claim that the state receded in size and scope with the advance of civilisation. To substantiate this he constructed an elaborate analogy between the state and the brain. With development, the brain became more specialised, focusing on the organism's relationships with the external world. Industrial activities, in contrast, were analogous to the internal, alimentary activities of an organism and these gradually acquired independence from the central regulatory mechanism as evolution progressed. 'Digestion and circulation', proclaimed Spencer, 'go on very well in lunatics and idiots, though the higher nervous centres are either deranged or partly absent. The vital functions proceed properly during sleep, though less actively than when the brain is at work.' A parallel process took place within the social body: 'The production and interchange by which the national life is maintained, go on as well while Parliament is not sitting as while it is sitting.' The reduction in the activities of the state, therefore, was a natural consequence of evolutionary progress.[61] The specialised tasks to which government was suited were those implied by 'negative regulation', which consisted of preventing people from violating the rights of other persons and

---

[58] Spencer, *Principles of Sociology*, 539.   [59] Spencer, *Study of Sociology*, 197.
[60] Spencer, *Principles of Psychology*, II, 577.
[61] Spencer, 'Specialised Administration', in *Man Versus the State*, 290, 292, 308.

defending the society from foreign aggression. If confined to these spheres, Spencer believed that representative government was not only the most competent form of government but also the one most conducive to the preservation of liberty.[62] But when governments in industrial societies exceeded these functions and attempted to regulate market transactions, promote individual welfare, or aid the sick, the poor and the unemployed, then they not only invaded personal liberty but posed a grave threat to future progress.

Spencer was skating on thin ice with these arguments and critics exploited the weaknesses of his analogy between the brain and the state. Spencer arbitrarily equated the state in advanced societies with the dispersed nervous systems of invertebrates whereas with progression up the evolutionary ladder the brain became, in Huxley's phrase, the 'sovereign power of the body' which it ruled with a 'rod of iron'.[63] The relevant inference to be drawn from the evolution of the brain, therefore, was the opposite of Spencer's assertion of the contraction of the scope and authority of the state. This places a question mark over the coherency of his model of the social organism and its suitability for a defence of liberalism, an issue that has been the subject of considerable debate.[64] The point I wish to emphasise has a more general import, namely that a world view tends to be dominated by the ideological structure it supports, something which will be very evident throughout this study. The ideological components of the theory 'drive' the various elements of the world view, as is clearly the case with Spencer, whose liberalism preceded his Social Darwinism by many years. Given his lifelong commitment to radical individualism and his antipathy to state power, it is hardly surprising that he invoked a brain/state analogy and a theory of socio-political development which coincided with these preferences. The social order mirrored the order of nature in that both were under the governance of inexorable laws – evolution through direct and indirect equilibrations – which could not be thwarted without courting

---

[62] Spencer, 'Specialised Administration', 288–90; Spencer, 'Representative Government: What is it Good For?', *Man Versus the State*, 265–70.

[63] T. H. Huxley, *Critiques and Addresses* (London: Macmillan, 1873), 18–19. See also D. G. Ritchie, *The Principles of State Interference* (London: Swan Sonnenschein, 1891), 17–27.

[64] W. M. Simon, 'Herbert Spencer and the Social Organism', *Journal of the History of Ideas*, 21(1960), 294–9; E. F. Paul, 'Herbert Spencer: The Historicist as Failed Prophet', *Journal of the History of Ideas*, 44(1983), 619–38; T. S. Gray, 'Herbert Spencer: Individualist or Organicist?', *Political Studies*, 33(1985), 236–53; E. F. Paul, 'Liberalism, Unintended Orders and Evolutionism', *Political Studies*, 36(1988), 251–72; M. Taylor, 'The Errors of an Evolutionist', *Political Studies*, 37(1989), 436–42; E. F. Paul, 'Herbert Spencer – Second Thoughts', *Political Studies*, 37(1989), 445–8; Taylor, *Men Versus the State*, chap. 4.

the risk of extinction. One of the tasks of sociology was to expose the folly of political intervention in the working of natural laws by shattering the widespread and dangerous illusion that 'societies arise by manufacture, instead of arising, as they do, by evolution'.[65]

It is important to bear in mind precisely what *was* Social Darwinian in Spencer's arguments. He was vehemently opposed to publicly funded welfare schemes because he believed them to have the effect of preserving – indeed, often multiplying – the numbers of the unfit. His attitude to the latter is graphically displayed in the following description of London's 'undeserving poor':

'They have no work', you say. Say rather that they either refuse work or quickly turn themselves out of it. They are simply good-for-nothings, who in one way or another live on the good-for-somethings – vagrants and sots, criminals and those on the way to crime, youths who are burdens on hard-worked parents, men who appropriate the wages of their wives, fellows who share the gains of prostitutes; and then less visible and less numerous, there is a corresponding class of women.[66]

This condemnation was not of itself a product of Social Darwinism but reproduced a common attitude toward the underclass in Victorian society. J. S. Mill (certainly no Social Darwinist) expressed similar views and wrote scathingly about the evils of misdirected charity, which relieved its recipients of responsibility and shielded them 'from the disagreeable consequences of their own acts ...'[67] Spencer's Social Darwinism was exhibited in the *explanation* he gave for this underclass and in his *interpretation* of its likely impact on future evolution. As to the first, he maintained that for generations the English had supported the 'dissolute and idle' who used 'lying and servility' to delude those in authority. Consequently the race had for centuries been bred from the improvident. Liberal spleen against the old Poor Laws was here wedded to a hereditarian account of their outcomes. As to the second, Spencer predicted that collective welfare would reduce self-control by mitigating the effects of having large numbers of children. Through the artificial preservation of these unfit offspring, society imposed an unnecessary burden on its successful members, who had to support the profligate and their progeny as well as their own families. Thus not only were the unfit no longer exposed to the rigours of the survival of the fittest, but their increasing numbers would swamp the superior individuals. The result would be the impoverishment of the stock, and society's eventual

[65] Spencer, *Study of Sociology*, 122.   [66] Spencer, *Man Versus the State*, 82.
[67] J. S. Mill, *The Subjection of Women* (London: Dent, 1985), 304. For a discussion of Victorian attitudes to the urban underclass, see Himmelfarb, *The Idea of Poverty*, chaps. 14 and 15.

annihilation by its competitors.[68] Liberal regimes facilitated progress because they unequivocally located responsibility for personal welfare in the individual, leaving those unequal to the task to be eliminated in the struggle for survival. Unlike many later supporters of eugenics, Spencer desired this elimination of the unfit through their failure to reproduce themselves rather than through state intervention to secure their physical annihilation.[69] But the 'survival of the unfit' represented an evolutionary blasphemy by removing 'nature's' punishment for those too idle or improvident to adapt. 'Is it not manifest', asked Spencer, 'that there must exist in our midst an immense amount of misery which is the normal result of misconduct and ought not to be dissociated from it? . . . To separate pain from ill-doing is to fight against the constitution of things, and will be followed by more pain.'[70] He concluded that 'social arrangements which retard the multiplication of the mentally best, and facilitate the multiplication of the mentally worst, must be extremely injurious'. To foster the 'good-for-nothings' at the expense of the industrious and talented members of society was to engage in 'a deliberate storing up of miseries for future generations. There is no greater curse to posterity than that of bequeathing them an increasing population of imbeciles and idlers and criminals.' It was, accordingly, extremely dangerous to interfere with 'that natural process of elimination by which a society continually purifies itself'.[71]

These arguments were integral to Spencer's entire theory of organic evolution and cannot be dismissed as aberrations or lapses on his part, as has sometimes been suggested.[72] In them Spencer appealed to the winnowing aspect of natural selection as a mechanism for facilitating continuous adaptation. The inevitability of the social manifestation of this mechanism was presented as a deduction from the general principles of evolution and the survival of the fittest. This belief was vigorously asserted throughout Spencer's evolutionary writings and its later instances did not differ in substance or in tone from earlier versions. 'True' liberals, therefore, were furnished with additional reasons for resisting the incursions of state power. Not only did this encroachment reduce the scope of individual freedom and subvert the 'natural' principles regulating the economic order, it also contravened the general laws of evolution of which both the freedom and the principles were reflections.

---

[68] Spencer, *Study of Sociology*, 369–71.
[69] Although Spencer did contemplate the design of a euthanasia machine for 'criminals of an extremely degraded type': see *Facts and Comments*, 162–3.
[70] Spencer, *Man Versus the State*, 83.   [71] Spencer, *Study of Sociology*, 344–5, 346.
[72] Bannister, *Social Darwinism*, 10, 50; Bellomy, ' "Social Darwinism" Revisited', 41. Taylor, *Men Versus the State*, 86–8.

In his critique of the reform movements of his day Spencer relied heavily upon the 'scientific' conception of human nature afforded by a knowledge of evolution. Reformers – particularly socialists – had an unwarranted and naive faith in the efficacy of political action. They ignored the fact that the condition of society was determined by the evolutionary level of human nature, and that the latter was transformed very slowly in accordance with natural laws refractory to legislative fiat. 'The machinery of Communism, like existing social machinery, has to be framed out of existing human nature; and the defects of existing human nature will generate in the one the same evils as in the other.' The defects in question were love of power, selfishness, injustice and untruthfulness, all of which had been inculcated during the militant phase of development and their 'effects accumulated from generation to generation'.[73] Failure to recognise this prevented trade unionists from realising how their proposals for the reform of industrial relations were rendered impractical by 'the imperfections of existing human nature, moral and intellectual', and that contemporary evils 'are not due to any special injustice of the employing class, and can be remedied only as fast as men in general advance'.[74]

Spencer did not confine himself to conservative apologetics, and at times mobilised the Social Darwinist world view against various facets of the status quo. For example, he attacked organised religion as an anachronistic institution and lambasted imperialism as a 'new barbarism', warning against the motives of people who contended that in the interests of humanity 'the inferior races should be exterminated and their place occupied by the superior races'. Evolution was not for export and the oppression of colonial peoples would result in the brutalisation of the colonising nation rather than any increase in civilisation.[75] His negative evaluation of the mental and moral features of militant societies was often a thinly veiled critique of the mores of the landed aristocracy of his own time and place.[76] Nor was Spencer oblivious to the corruption and injustices often found in contemporary commercial activities, or to the deleterious effects of overwork on the prospects for happiness of whole classes of people.[77] His situation reflects that of

---

[73] Spencer, *Man Versus the State*, 108–9.   [74] Spencer, *Study of Sociology*, 250, 253.

[75] Spencer, *Man Versus the State*, 143; *Study of Sociology*, 213; see also Spencer's essays 'Imperialism and Slavery', 'Re-Barbarisation' and 'Regimentation' in *Facts and Comments*.

[76] Spencer's critique of militarism was utilised by the anti-war feminists in Britain in their opposition to the First World War. See M. S. Florence, C. Marshall and C. K. Ogden, *Militarism Versus Feminism*, ed. M. Kemester and J. Vellacott (London: Virago, 1987), 85, 105–6. (I am grateful to Phylomena Badsey for providing me with this reference.)

[77] See, for example, Spencer's criticism of certain features of capitalism in 'From

liberalism generally, fighting a battle on two fronts – against aristocratic privilege on the one hand and the demands of the organised working class on the other. For Spencer, to modify liberalism in order to accommodate the latter was tantamount to a betrayal of the historic mission of liberalism. Hence: 'The function of Liberalism in the past was that of putting a limit to the power of kings. The function of true Liberalism in the future will be that of putting a limit to the powers of Parliament.'[78] In the light of the recrudescence of neo-liberalism and support for *laissez-faire* in Britain and the USA in the 1970s, this prediction has proved remarkably prescient.

Spencer's Social Darwinism

The significance of Spencer as a Social Darwinist resides in two features of his thought. The first has already been remarked upon: his world-wide popularity and influence. The second consists of the detail with which Spencer worked out his philosophy, and its intended comprehensive explanatory scope. This detail and comprehensiveness bring into relief certain features of his use of Social Darwinism which have a more general relevance to an understanding of the world view.

Of crucial importance to Spencer's theory of social evolution was his notion of primitive humans. The 'primitive' was conceptualised as the point of departure for social evolution, the meeting point of animality and humanity, with the presumed attributes of the former usually predominating although these were wedded to distinctly human vices such as mendacity and lust. Spencer needed to portray primitives as immoral, irrational and aggressive in order to show how individuality, freedom and morality emerged during the process of evolution through a logic of differentiation, specialisation and individuation. It enabled him to construct an evolutionary continuum and, by means of his recapitulation perspective, to substitute a number of contemporary social categories for those at the lowest point of the continuum. Thus children, women, inferior social ranks and tribal social cultures could all be substituted for pre-historic man, depending on the context in question.

The primary purpose of this conceptualisation was to establish a series of identities and differences within modern societies and to facilitate judgements about the various social groups in question – or, more accurately, to legitimate prior judgements arising from Spencer's

Freedom to Bondage', in *Man Versus the State*, 314–16, which also contains references to earlier publications on this topic. On overworking see *Data of Ethics*, 94.
[78] Spencer, *Man Versus the State*, 183.

political standpoint. To repeat a point made earlier in regard to Spencer's political and moral convictions, these judgements do not constitute Social Darwinism. The latter consists of a configuration of images and metaphors about nature, time and humanity that impart both drama and credence to his otherwise quite conventional representations of savages, paupers, women, children and the lower social orders. By integrating these representations with Social Darwinism, Spencer invested them with additional bite and moral portent. It was a tactic that would be adopted by many other Social Darwinists albeit – as we have already established with Bagehot and Lombroso – often for quite different ideological purposes.

There are a number of elements to this repertoire of images. First, there is a series of analogies between biological organisms and social systems, with interactions within each realm under the empire of the same principle, the struggle for existence, which induces the imperatives of adaptation, survival and reproduction. Second, there is an analogy between human history and organic evolution, since both are created through the struggle for survival, thereby facilitating a narrative of the destruction and extinction of some groups and individuals as the inevitable corollary of the survival and improvement of others. Time appears as a dimension of winners and losers, and change is not only accretional and directional, but progressive in some implicitly moral sense of this term. Finally, development is made possible through the action of heredity. Operating throughout nature, this mechanism makes possible the narration of history as progress by producing the traits – physical, psychological, behavioural – whose visible manifestations constitute the signs by which winners and losers, fit and unfit, superior and inferior, can be detected and differentiated. In Spencer's work heredity appears as a conservative force, functioning to preserve successful traits induced by adaptive pressures. But the reverse side of this coin is that the unfit are biologically worthless and no amount of charity, exhortation or compulsion can alter their hereditarian legacy or evolutionary fate. Spencer's position here stands in sharp contrast to that of Brace who believed that meliorative social policies complemented the workings of nature's laws.

Social Darwinism furnished Spencer with a powerful rhetorical device which laid claim to the mantle of scientific authenticity. But, as I argued in chapter 1, Social Darwinism also possessed considerable potential for the creation of dilemmas and aporias, particularly at its intersections with the ideological elements of a theory. This is undoubtedly the case with Spencer's system which contains problems which are once again instructive for an understanding of the history of Social Darwinism.

The first of these problems relates to Spencer's portrayal of primitive humans as vicious, immoral, violent and intellectually weak. As noted above, this portrait was crucial to Spencer's rendition of evolution as the development of reason, morality, foresight and voluntary cooperation. Spencer constructed this model of primitive mentality from the alleged attributes of contemporary 'savages'. Not only was this model highly questionable but Spencer himself had accumulated material on hunter–gatherer communities which would have permitted him to paint a very different picture.[79] Now at times Spencer *did* conceptualise 'savage' mental and social life differently. For example, he instanced certain tribal communities in contemporary India and North America that were characterised by the absence of centralisation, despotism and hierarchy. Their members possessed a strong sense of freedom, including respect for the liberty of their fellows and for the rights of women and children.[80]

Thus free from the coercive rule which warlike activities necessitate, and without the sentiment which makes the needful subordination possible – thus maintaining their own claims while respecting the like claims of others – thus devoid of the vengeful feelings which aggressions without or within the tribe generate; these peoples, instead of the bloodthirstiness, the cruelty, the selfish trampling upon inferiors, characterising militant tribes and societies, display, in unusual degrees, the humane sentiments.[81]

On occasions Spencer went as far as to argue that the inhabitants of these pre-militant communities sometimes surpassed civilised people in their possession of virtues such as truthfulness, honesty, justice and generosity.[82] What then, has become of the aggressive, immoral, capricious savage, or, for that matter, of evolution? In this scenario, militant society appears as an interregnum between the peaceful, industrious, law-abiding social systems of pre-militant times and the industrial regimes of today, an impression confirmed in such statements as 'with diminution of warfare and growth of trade, voluntary cooperation more and more replaces compulsory cooperation, and the carrying on of social life by exchange under agreement, *partially suspended for a time, gradually re-establishes itself*; its re-establishment makes possible that vast elaborate industrial organisation by which a great nation is sustained.'[83]

These passages conflict with others in which the earliest stages of social existence are depicted as polar opposites, both temporally and

[79] Peel, *Herbert Spencer*, 20.   [80] Spencer, *Principles of Sociology*, 546–8, 559–63.
[81] *Ibid.*, 561.
[82] *Ibid.*, 563; Spencer, *Study of Sociology*, 210; *Man Versus the State*, 112.
[83] Spencer, *Man Versus the State*, 175, emphasis added.

substantively, to industrial systems. Thus Spencer claimed of the evolution of social types: 'At one extreme we have that small and simple type of society which a wandering horde of savages presents. This is a type almost wholly predatory in its organisation. It consists of little else than a cooperative structure for carrying on warfare – the industrial part is almost absent, being represented only by the women.'[84] Elsewhere he observed that the nature required for this type of existence was radically different from that appropriate to industrial social life, 'and long continued pains have to be passed through in re-moulding the one into the other'.[85]

This inconsistency poses difficulties for Spencer's account of the dynamics of evolution, for if the psychological and behavioural traits conducive to industrialism could be found in early social systems then the roles of population pressure and the struggle for life in inducing adaptation become problematic. There is an implication that rational self-interest alone suffices to ensure progress and that, far from emerging during the course of evolution, it is an innate feature of human nature. Indeed, it was present in the earliest humans, providing the incentive for them to enter into social relationships in the first place.[86] These assertions imply an essentialism on Spencer's part: despite his insistence on the slow modification of human nature, he nonetheless posits the existence of attributes that are constitutive of human nature, merely expanding in strength and scope over time. It is possible, of course, for an evolutionist to assert that some species have, for a variety of reasons, retained their structural and behavioural properties over millennia, without at the same time adhering to essentialism. That Spencer did slip into essentialism is, I believe, suggested by the fact that this assumption is closely connected to the inconsistent account of primitives/savages noted above.[87]

Spencer's treatment of natural selection was also highly significant for the subsequent development of Social Darwinism. We saw that Spencer distinguished between the creative and the winnowing aspects of selection. Darwin undoubtedly perceived natural selection as creative for its ability to generate new varieties and even species. Yet his own language quite often emphasised the culling aspect. This is apparent not only in some of the statements cited in chapter 1 (e.g. his summary of nature's injunction to multiply, vary, let the strongest live and the

---

[84] Spencer, 'Specialised Administration', 285.
[85] Spencer, 'From Freedom to Bondage', 333.
[86] Spencer, *Man Versus the State*, 174.
[87] For an analysis of essentialism in Spencer and other nineteenth-century Social Darwinists, see my 'The Struggle for Existence in Nineteenth Century Social Thought', 47–67.

weakest die), but in the very sub-title of the *Origin* on the preservation of favoured races. Indeed, Darwin toyed with the idea of replacing 'natural selection' with 'natural preservation'. Spencer's work exacerbated this ambiguity and induced yet another indeterminacy, this time over the meaning of selection itself. As we shall see, this tension between the creative and preservative functions of the survival of the fittest was typical of later adaptations of Social Darwinism.

Underlying these different accounts of human nature, primitive mentality, and social evolution, lies a deeper ambivalence concerning nature itself. This can be discerned in Spencer's treatment of ethics, which he perceived as a facet of the evolution of conduct in general. Defining conduct as the adjustment of acts to ends, he described two types of conduct: self-maintaining and race-maintaining (the care of offspring by the previous generations). Both evolved simultaneously in the context of the struggle for existence, which meant that successful adjustments by one organism entailed adverse effects on others, either directly, as in the case of predation, or indirectly, as when stronger individuals acquired more resources than weaker members of the same group. Spencer contemplated a higher form of conduct in which adjustments did not involve perverse consequences for others, some-thing which could only occur in 'permanently peaceful societies', i.e. communities not engaged in violent activities, either internally or externally.[88] In these conditions a yet more elevated form of conduct would appear in which individuals not only refrained from obstructing the adjustments of their neighbours, but actively assisted them through industrial cooperation or voluntary aid.[89] This suggests a future in which the struggle for existence is mitigated, which was occasionally hinted at by Spencer when he speculated about a time when population growth declined with a corresponding reduction of pressure on resources. This was possible because Spencer proclaimed an inverse ratio between 'individuation' and 'genesis'. The more individuated a creature became, the more energy was expended on self-maintenance leaving less available for reproduction, thereby reducing fecundity.[90]

These arguments point to a time when social relations would be governed by peace, cooperation and mutual concern. They contrast with others in which such outcomes seem impossible, or at least so distant as to be virtually irrelevant. For instance, Spencer insisted that population was growing and that its pressures 'cannot be eluded'.[91] Consistent with this was the additional claim that: 'Always there must have been, and always there must continue to be, a survival of the fittest; natural

[88] Spencer, *Data of Ethics*, 17–19.   [89] *Ibid.*, 19.
[90] Spencer, *Principles of Biology*, II, 487–504.   [91] *Ibid.*, II, 526.

selection must have been in operation at the outset, and can never cease to operate.'[92] In his writing on ethics Spencer vacillated between describing concern for others as the apex of moral evolution, and warnings about the dire consequences of pushing this concern too far and for the need to recognise the truth 'that egoism comes before altruism'.[93] Earlier in this chapter I remarked on his thesis that there was competition within biological organisms. This was also true of social organisms, and necessitated boundaries to altruistic behaviour if evolutionary progress was to continue: 'Not only does this struggle for existence involve the necessity that personal ends must be pursued with little regard to the evils entailed on unsuccessful competitors; but it also involves the necessity that there shall not be too keen a sympathy with that diffused suffering inevitably accompanying this industrial battle.'[94] Yet moral evolution was presented elsewhere as a development in which not only did this zero-sum feature of existence diminish, but was accompanied by aid to alleviate the lot of the less fortunate.

Spencer's equivocation over the implications of social evolution reflects a deep-seated ambivalence towards the natural order itself. The discipline generated by the pressure of population on subsistence and the consequential struggle for survival were, on the one hand, beneficent because they caused adaptation, the elimination of the unfit, and progress. But if these were inexorable laws of nature, then what of the quest for happiness, peace, the elevation of individual character, and the concern for the condition of others which have traditionally motivated liberals?[95] As we have seen, there are moments in Spencer's writings when these considerations come to the forefront: but when they do, they carry the implication that the full realisation of a liberal social order requires *emancipation* from the laws that govern the natural order.

These ambiguities and aporias in Spencer are partly consequences of his particular attempt to couple Social Darwinism with liberalism. But they also inhere in the world view itself, from a perception of nature which carried within it disturbing implications when applied to psychology and sociology. These implications were uncovered in the ideological appropriation of Social Darwinism, particularly when, as with Brace, Büchner and Spencer, the goals pursued were those of cooperation and harmony.

[92] *Ibid.*, I, 552.
[93] Spencer, *Data of Ethics*, 187.
[94] Spencer, *Principles of Psychology*, II, 611.
[95] There is an illuminating discussion of the notion of 'character' in Victorian sociopolitical thought in R. Bellamy, *Liberalism and Modern Society* (Oxford: Polity Press, 1992), 1–57.

5 Social Darwinism in the USA

Introduction

When Darwin published the *Origin* Americans were preoccupied with slavery, the future of their nation, and the likelihood of war: indeed, the Civil War may have impeded the reception of Darwinism during the 1860s. By this time, however, the United States was experiencing many of the social and political problems besetting Britain, in addition to the divisive issue of slavery, which made race a more immediate domestic concern and one, moreover, that was to be constantly fuelled by successive waves of immigration. This provided a fertile context for 'scientific' approaches to and resolutions of these problems, and Darwinism was soon enlisted to these ends, as is evident from Brace's writings on race and class.

Thanks to the efforts of Darwin's supporters, Darwinism had become well established by the 1870s, although not all American scientists were prepared to endorse natural selection fully, and neo-Lamarckism remained influential throughout the century.[1] The position of the distinguished palaeontologist Edward Drinker Cope (1840–97) exemplifies both the continued hold of Lamarck on American naturalists and the powerful fascination exercised by Darwinism. Cope conceded that natural selection performed a culling action upon organic variations but insisted it was unable to account for the variations themselves. These he explained as the consequence of growth forces which increasingly came under the control of 'intelligent choice' as one ascended the animal scale.[2] Despite this refusal to grant natural selection a wider role, Cope was profoundly affected by Darwinism. Prior to the publication of the

---

[1] See E. J. Pfeifer, 'The United States', in Glick, *Comparative Reception*. Pfeifer (199) estimates that neo-Lamarckians outnumbered Darwinists among American scientists by the end of the century.

[2] E. D. Cope, *The Origin of the Fittest: Essays on Evolution* (London/New York: Macmillan, 1887), 16, 40; Cope, 'The Energy of Evolution', *American Naturalist*, 18(1894), 205–19.

Ascent he had signalled his hostility to natural selection as a cause of progress while simultaneously perceiving the relevance of Darwinism to human evolution. He accepted the simian ancestry of humans, endorsed a racial hierarchy defined by 'greater or less approximation to the apes', speculated about the evolution of human intelligence, speech, morality and social organisation, and described sexual differences as the products of evolution.[3] He also indulged in a tortured attempt to reconcile these positions with divine creation and biblical accounts of human development – an attempt which he subsequently admitted was unsuccessful.[4] Even for a convinced neo-Lamarckian like Cope, then, Social Darwinism constituted an authoritative – not to say seductive – body of ideas.

Spencer's writings furnished another influential source of evolutionary theory. In a series of articles published in the *New York Herald* in 1870 – the same year she declared her intention of standing for the Presidency – the feminist Victoria Woodhull (1838–1927) reinterpreted the history of civilisation in evolutionary terms. Although these essays did not make use of natural selection and the survival of the fittest, they did insist on the relevance of biological evolution to the study of society, declaring: 'The same laws that govern the growth and multiply the plant also govern society and multiply it. The same laws that bring fruit to perfection and dissolution perfect and dissolve societies. The same laws that produce and control the units of the animal kingdom produce and control the units of society.'[5] In later years this assumption would underpin Woodhull's campaigns for eugenics and the elimination of the unfit.[6]

Woodhull's essays exhibit the influence of Spencer's doctrine that evolution and dissolution were derivatives of the persistence of force. In this she typified the tremendous popularity among Americans enjoyed by Spencer during the nineteenth century.[7] The enthusiasm for Spencer is captured in a letter to the Englishman by one of his most fervent admirers and popularisers in the United States, Edward Livingstone Youmans (1821–87). Youmans wrote: 'I am an ultra and thoroughgoing American. I believe there is great work to be done here for civilisation. What we want are ideas – large, organising ideas – and I believe there is

---

[3] Cope, *On the Hypothesis of Evolution: Physical and Metaphysical* (New Haven: Chatfield and Co., 1870), 29, 31, 35, 54–5.

[4] *Ibid.*, 33–4, 63–70. For the admission that this reconciliation was unsuccessful see the Preface to *Origin of the Fittest*, vii. Cope still included an amended version of this essay in this volume.

[5] V. Woodhull, *The Origin, Tendencies and Principles of Government* (New York: Woodhull, Claflin, 1871), 48.

[6] Woodhull's eugenics are discussed below in chapter 9.

[7] Hofstadter, *Social Darwinism*, 33–5.

no other man whose thoughts are so valuable to our needs as yours are.'[8] Though not himself an original thinker, Youmans zealously publicised Spencer's philosophy in the United States. According to Fiske, in Youmans Spencer found someone always alert to 'the slightest chances to promote his interests and those of his system of thought'.[9] But however congenial American Social Darwinists found Spencer, they were never slavish imitators or uncritical disciples, and they modified his ideas to suit their own intellectual and ideological requirements. The Social Darwinist world view remained intact throughout these modifications and constituted a significant factor not only in the political controversies of the nineteenth century, but also in the development of the social sciences and philosophy. This significance requires emphasis because revisionist historiography has contributed to a serious misrepresentation of the role of Social Darwinism in American thought.

This chapter focuses upon the work of three leading American intellectuals: Sumner, James and Fiske. The latter, with Youmans, was one of the most important early American popularisers of Darwin and Spencer, and his philosophy graphically illustrates both the potential and the dilemmas contained in Social Darwinism.

The cosmic philosophy of Fiske

The philosopher and historian John Fiske (1842–1901) published his *Outlines of Cosmic Philosophy* in 1874.[10] The first volume dealt with abstract matters of knowledge, causation, the persistence of force, evolution and dissolution. It concluded by rejecting the doctrine of special creations in favour of the evolutionary theories of Darwin, Huxley and Haeckel (I, 440–9). This theme provided the point of departure for the second volume, which commenced with an explanation of natural selection and the survival of the fittest. Fiske maintained that natural selection was the chief, but not the sole, agency of organic evolution, and insisted on a role for direct adaptations. However, he was equally adamant that irrespective of whether variations were internal to the organism or derived from direct adaptations, they were always subject to the action of natural selection (II, 61).

Although Fiske depicted natural selection as a 'prodigious' and 'unceasing' slaughter (II, 11, 12), when he came to describe human

---

[8] Youmans to Spencer, 14 December 1863, in Fiske, *Life and Letters*, 169–70.
[9] Fiske, *Life and Letters*, 115.
[10] Fiske had published what was to become a chapter of *Outlines* as early as 1866, and other portions had been delivered as lectures at Harvard in 1869. See Fiske's comments in *Life and Letters*, 203, and *Outlines* (I, vii).

evolution he did so with pronounced optimism. He informed his readers that 'progress has been on the whole the most constant and prominent feature of the history of a considerable and important portion of mankind' (II, 193). Not all social change was progressive, and only a few societies had attained the heights of civilisation, but nonetheless progress was *the* law of history (II, 196). For Fiske sociology was a branch of psychology because social change was governed by psychic developments, which he summarised as 'a gradual supplanting of *egoism* by *altruism*' (II, 201, original emphasis). Altruism originated within conjugal and parental relations which owed their permanence to the prolonged helplessness of the human infant and thus furnished the basis of moral evolution (II, 360).[11] Hostility, warfare and aggression dominated the primitive condition but gradually sympathetic feelings were extended to the tribe as a whole. With the increased size and complexity of societies came an extension of altruism to the point where shared humanity alone became the focus of obligations to others (II, 207). The individual replaced the family as the fundamental unit of society, and his or her requirements predominated over those of the aggregate as a whole (II, 223). Fiske envisaged a future in which individuals existed in perfect harmony with their fellows, united in a World Federation (II, 228). He embraced a 'Cosmic Theism' in which God was equated with Spencer's Unknowable and was therefore accorded a scientific validation (II, 412–15). In a later essay Fiske asserted that although the evolution of a complex organism was due to the aggregation of minute circumstances, the theist could still believe that these changes were 'an immediate manifestation of the creative action of God'.[12]

Fiske's optimistic vision included a time – one he considered not too far distant – when warfare would become extinct (II, 252). He referred to natural selection as rigorous and constant – 'like a power that slumbers not nor sleeps'.[13] What form, then, would natural selection take in this period of peace and mutual harmony, and how would progress continue? Not only did Fiske provide no answer to these questions, but sometimes his own arguments implicitly contradicted the possibility of this future condition. For example, when Fiske addressed the issue of why progress was confined to the European Aryans, he concluded that the reason was to be found in the rigorous selective pressures to which Aryans had been exposed. Certainly natural selection

---

[11] Fiske was to develop this argument at length in his *The Meaning of Infancy* (Boston: Houghton Mifflin, 1909).

[12] Fiske, *Darwinism and Other Essays* (New York: Macmillan, 1879), 7.

[13] *Ibid.*, 15.

was mitigated within complex societies, where the advanced division of labour allowed the less fit to fill a niche and hence survive: 'But while natural selection among individuals grows somewhat less rigorous, its effects upon rival or antagonistic societies are in no wise diminished in their beneficent severity. The attributes which tend to make a society strong and durable with reference to surrounding societies are the attributes which natural selection will chiefly preserve' (II, 259). The attributes in question were self-restraint and intelligent foresight and their stimulation resulted in an increased military capacity and efficiency. Natural selection had eliminated the threat of invasion by uncivilised and barbaric peoples and concentrated the power of war on a 'grand scale' in societies in which 'predatory activity is at a minimum and industrial activity at the maximum' (II, 264). In these communities, the possibility of invasion and military humiliation, rather than their actuality, motivated investment in military strength (II, 260).

According to this reasoning, progress entailed a reduction of the struggle for existence within civilised societies accompanied by the maintenance of potentially hostile relations among them which acted as a selective pressure. But what then of the World Federation, the eradication of warfare, and universal harmony and altruism?[14] Fiske's philosophy alternated between a description of an evolutionary outcome (peace and harmony) in which the laws of nature (and hence of evolution) were suspended, and another in which these laws continued to operate in ways that made the first outcome highly improbable. The ceaseless 'beneficent severity' of natural selection sits awkwardly with the predicted obligations owed to persons simply by virtue of a shared humanity. Here, once again, we encounter the dilemma which the determinism and universalism of Social Darwinism posed for thinkers like Fiske who believed in moral progress and the triumph of civilisation. These could be shown to be the work of natural laws such as the struggle for existence. But the complete realisation of these ideals implied a future state in which the laws of nature were no longer applicable to humans. And unless these laws were suspended, the harmonious ideal appeared unrealisable.

Sumner and the 'iron spur' of competition

Although he believed in progress, Fiske shared Spencer's mistrust of social engineering. The European Aryans had progressed precisely

---

[14] Fiske continued to take this idea of federation seriously, later proposing it as an 'Anglo-Saxon' mission which would bring peace and prosperity to the entire world. On this, see Hofstadter, *Social Darwinism*, 176–8.

because their cultures were flexible, containing an inbuilt tendency to variation which allowed for innovation without revolution (II, 272–9). Fiske objected to the 'Jacobin' for failing to appreciate the resistance of habits to rapid change. Habits were the outcome of adaptations and were fixed through heredity; change could come only through new adaptations. Societies could not be made, but rather they grew in accordance with the laws of nature. Thus 'men cannot be *taught* a higher state of civilisation, but can only be *bred* into it' (II, 489, original emphasis).

William Graham Sumner (1840–1910) made this conservatism the explicit message of his sociology. Like Fiske, Sumner (a professor of political economy at Yale) was influenced by Spencer during the 1870s. But in contrast to both Fiske and Spencer, Sumner eschewed optimism and was considerably less sanguine about either the fact or the inevitability of progress. The foundation of his work, from his essays during the 1880s to the publication of his study of folkways in 1906, was the assumption that Darwinism was as relevant to an understanding of social life as it was to the organic world. Because Sumner's Social Darwinism has been downplayed by revisionist historians,[15] there is a need to establish in detail the nature and role of the Darwinist world view in his theories.

Sumner's essay 'Sociology', published in 1881,[16] contained a comprehensive statement of his social philosophy. It began with an explicit linkage between sociology and biology:

We have already become familiar, in biology, with the transcendent importance of the fact that life on earth must be maintained by a struggle against nature and also by a competition with other forms of life. In the latter fact biology and sociology touch. Sociology is a science which deals with one range of phenomena produced by the struggle for existence, while biology deals with another. The forces are the same, acting on different fields and under different conditions (14).

The cause of the struggle against nature was population growth which placed pressure on resources. This produced considerable social distress, but also the impetus for development, especially when coupled with another law, that of the diminishing returns on labour. According to Sumner, progress had meaning only in relation to these two laws: 'The laws of population and the diminishing return, in their combination, are the iron spur which has driven the race on to all which it has

---

15 Cf. Bannister, 'William Graham Sumner's Social Darwinism'.
16 Reprinted in S. Persons, ed., *Social Darwinism: Selected Essays of William Graham Sumner* (Englewood Cliffs: Prentice-Hall, 1963). This collection also contains the essay 'War' which is considered below.

ever achieved ...' (16). The advance from the sexual division of labour within the family to complex systems of specialisation and exchange was due, like developments in the arts, to the struggle these laws generated.

At this juncture Sumner introduced what for him was a crucial distinction between two facets of struggle. 'There is first the struggle of individuals to win the means of subsistence from nature, and secondly there is the competition of man with man in the effort to win a limited supply' (16). The first – the 'struggle for existence' – involved a relationship between each person and nature; the second – the 'competition for life' – was a social relationship. Both were exacerbated by population growth and neither should be mitigated by social reforms. 'The law of the survival of the fittest', wrote Sumner, 'was not made by man and cannot be abrogated by man. We can only, by interfering with it, produce the survival of the unfittest' (17).

In another essay Sumner applied this distinction to an analysis of warfare. Contrary to most of the popular anthropology of the period, he did not regard warfare as endemic to primitive societies because war arose out of the competition for life, not from the struggle for existence (35). In the latter struggle, members of a primitive tribe cooperated with one another, and while potentially hostile to other tribes their small numbers placed little pressure on land and resources, which reduced the seriousness of conflict. Population growth led to territorial expansion and bloodshed. 'Real warfare comes with the collisions of more developed societies' (30).

Hostile inter-group relations produced two moral codes – one for inside the group and another for outsiders. Sumner referred to these two sentiments as 'industrialism' and 'militancy' respectively, and averred that 'Industrialism builds up; militancy wastes' (50). Yet he insisted on the benefits of militancy in terms of the development of social organisation and cohesion, discipline, cooperation, fortitude and patience (40). Sumner counselled the avoidance of war if possible and disapproved of its use as a deliberate policy instrument (56). But by his own arguments, war was ultimately unavoidable, and there was no reason to believe in the possibility of universal peace (56). 'It is the competition for life ... which makes war, and that is why war has always existed and always will. It is in the conditions of human existence' (36).

In these essays, then, Sumner forcefully elaborated all the elements of the Social Darwinist world view. In his commentaries on the social and political issues of the times he drew upon this world view to support his arguments against socialism, collective welfare and state interference. It is his spirited defence of individualism and *laissez-faire* which has earned

Sumner notoriety as a Social Darwinist. But, as I shall argue later, this world view was still very much in evidence in his overtly academic publications.

In *What Social Classes Owe to Each Other*, published in 1883,[17] Sumner tackled the question of public welfare. The question resolved into this: was there any class which had the right to formulate demands on another class, or to get the latter to fight the battle of life on its behalf? Sumner responded by appealing to the order of nature: 'We cannot get a revision of the laws of human life. We are absolutely shut up to the need and duty, if we would learn how to live happily, of investigating the laws of Nature, and deducing the laws of right living in the world as it is' (14). The first requirement was to distinguish hardships which derived from faulty social and political institutions from those which flowed from the struggle for existence. The first were modifiable through collective effort: the second could only be faced manfully (18). All adult individuals were responsible for their welfare and the welfare of their dependants in the struggle with nature, and hence entitled to reap the rewards of their efforts. This, for Sumner, was a permanent feature of the human condition: 'There can be no rights against Nature, except to get out of her whatever we can, which is only the fact of the struggle for existence stated over again' (135).

Politically enforced charity violated this precept and distorted nature's laws by shifting the burden of the struggle from some classes on to others. Paupers were consumers, not producers, and Sumner objected to the use of emotive but ill-defined expressions such as 'poor' and 'weak', which camouflaged their parasitism. What he thought about such people is evident from the following statement: 'Under the names of the poor and the weak, the negligent, shiftless, inefficient, silly and imprudent are fastened upon the industrious and prudent as a responsibility and a duty' (21). This moral condemnation of paupers was accompanied by a celebration of the 'Forgotten Man' – the frugal, unassuming, industrious man (and woman) who, without being consulted, was forced to support the improvident (123, 132–3, 145–9). In another publication, Sumner wrote: 'The Forgotten Man is weighted down with the cost and burden of the schemes for making everybody happy, with the cost of public beneficence, with the support of all the loafers, with the loss of all the economic quackery, with the cost of all the jobs.' He proposed that the Forgotten Man was therefore someone more worthy of pity than the 'good-for-nothing'.[18]

---

[17] New York: Harper.
[18] 'The Forgotten Man' in Persons, *Social Darwinism*, 133.

In the text on classes, Sumner maintained that unskilled workers in the United States were in a favourable position due to the shortage of labour, needing only to be freed from the parasites who lived off them. Freedom was in fact an essential condition, and being 'an affair of laws and institutions which bring rights and duties into equilibrium', it was a consequence of modern social developments (33). Liberty, then, had nothing to do with issues such as democracy and universal suffrage. History disclosed 'a tiresome repetition of one story', namely the appropriation of the state by a class for the purpose of living in luxury. The causes of this lay deep in human nature and were not peculiar to any particular class, so irrespective of which class governed, there was a need to protect individuals from the abuse of state power (30–2). Civil liberty consisted of '*a status created for the individual by laws and institutions, the effect of which is that each man is guaranteed the use of all his own powers exclusively for all his own welfare*' (34, original emphasis). Equality was incompatible with liberty (16), and any interference in society and economy through political engineering was doomed to be counter-productive:

Whatever we gain . . . will be by growth, never in the world by any reconstruction of society on the plan of some enthusiastic social architect. The latter is only repeating the old error over again and postponing all our real chances of real improvement. Society needs first of all to be freed from these medlars [*sic*] – that is, to be left alone. Here we are, then, once more back at the old doctrine – *Laissez-faire*. Let us translate it into blunt English, and it will read, Mind your own business (120).

Sumner was adamant that the appearance of capital – which was simply stored and accumulated labour, i.e. human energy (62) – represented a great advance for civilisation by providing people with some insurance against the 'sport of Nature' (59). Capitalism, based upon private property, civil liberty and contract, he described as a 'great social cooperation. It is automatic and instinctive in its operation' (66). This spontaneity should not be subverted by socialistic schemes for redistributing property which failed to understand that the irksome necessity of labour was induced by the struggle for existence, not by the machinations of capitalists. Sumner certainly considered 'plutocracy' – the domination of the state by capitalists – to be a real danger in the United States (106–7). Nor was he opposed to trade unions: although critical of the abuses to which they were liable (94, 130) he considered them quite legitimate instruments in the conflict between employers and labourers, and even urged that they should assume responsibility for the industrial regulatory functions currently exercised by government (93–5). What Sumner desired was that no class should be able to use the state to despoil another. Good government was confined to the provision of 'peace, order, liberty, security, justice, and equality before the law'.[19] These activities established the social framework within which industrial activities could flourish; thereafter, it was the responsibility of each individual to provide for his or her wants. 'The State gives equal rights and equal chances just because it does not mean to give anything else' (41). In other texts Sumner concluded that conservatism was the only sound political position, which he defined as the belief that 'the only possible good for society must come of evolution not of revolution'.[20] This being so, then it was 'a matter of patriotism and civic duty to resist the extension of State interference'.[21]

In his assault on collective welfare Sumner did not level the charge made by Spencer, i.e. that it represented an evolutionary regression to the militant type of society. For Sumner, militancy and industrialism were psychological propensities arising from outgroup aggression and ingroup solidarity respectively. He tended to conceptualise the extremes of evolutionary development in terms of 'barbarism' and 'civilisation', but, like the English philosopher, he believed that the advance from one state to the other had been very uneven. Not only did mankind represent every grade of civilisation, from the most barbarous to the most advanced, but these levels were reproduced *within* the most civilised states. As Sumner pointed out in his essay on classes, this was especially true of large cities 'where the highest triumphs of culture' coexisted with 'survival of every form of barbarism and lower civilisation' (70). Civil liberty and *laissez-faire* therefore constituted the foundations for future development by placing the onus of adaptation exclusively on the individual: 'The penalty of ceasing an aggressive behaviour towards the hardships of life on the part of mankind is, that we go backward. We cannot stand still' (73). Sumner's evolutionary sociology thus exhibited many of the features of Spencer's theory: development as a consequence of unceasing struggle which, being a law of nature, was ineluctable; an uneven social advance from a primitive to a civilised condition, with the distinct possibility of stagnation if current political trends were not reversed; the construction of a category of the unfit, largely on the basis of a moral evaluation ('loafers', the 'silly', etc.) whose parasitic behaviour threatened future evolution; and *laissez-faire* elevated to the status of a natural law, creating the appropriate social milieu within which selection could occur.

[19] Sumner, *Collected Essays in Political and Social Science* (New York: Henry Holt, 1885), 99.
[20] 'The New Social Issue', in Persons, *Social Darwinism*, 163.
[21] 'State Interference', in Persons, *Social Darwinism*, 108.

Sumner's sociology differed from that of Spencer, however, on a number of points.[22] For example, Sumner made far less use of analogies from the animal kingdom, and was sceptical about the alleged inheritance of instincts from an animal ancestry.[23] Even more significant is their different interpretations of militancy and warfare. Spencer's evolutionary perspective on the impact of natural selection on human societies allowed for a transformation of the struggle from violent to peaceful means. Sumner's position was more static: ingroup selection was peaceful, but militancy remained important between states. Universal peace was impossible because war derived from the competition for life and was therefore an inevitable feature of the human condition. This argument expresses Sumner's qualified acceptance of progress. Societies became larger and more complex through time, leading to increased specialisation, advances in the arts and sciences and in economic productivity, and the emergence of civil liberty. But the optimism of both Spencer and Fiske was absent from the pages of Sumner's publications. The very circumstances of advancement appear to coexist with an unalterable condition of effort and abstinence: 'Labour and self-denial, to work yet abstain from enjoying, to earn a product yet work on as if one possessed nothing, have been the condition of advance for the human race from the beginning, and they continue to be such still.'[24] This struggle for welfare 'constitutes history, or the life of the human race on earth'.[25] Nature for Sumner unquestionably acted as a model for social relations, as for Spencer and Fiske. But it was a much harsher one in that, unlike the other two men, Sumner did not seek to soften what he saw as the realities of the natural order by erecting a vision of a future world in which these realities were transcended or even mitigated. He approved of peace and repudiated militancy and violence, yet the laws of nature indicated no possibility of mankind's emancipation from either. Spencer and Fiske counselled patience in the face of the laws of progress; Sumner offered stoical acceptance of the need for ceaseless struggle.

---

[22] These differences, and their significance, render inappropriate the description of Sumner's sociology as 'Spencerianism in American dress'. See the essay of that title by H. E. Barnes in Barnes, ed., *An Introduction to the History of Sociology*, abridged edn (London: University of Chicago Press, 1966), chap. 17.

[23] Sumner, in *Folkways* (New York: Ginn, 1906), argued that this inheritance was possible but unproven (2). Later he drew parallels between human and organic heredity and variation but insisted that these had no value (84). Sumner was not consistent in this, however, and occasionally likened humans to 'other animals' (4).

[24] Sumner, *Collected Essays*, 40.

[25] Sumner, 'Sociology', 24.

Sumner's science of society

Sumner's pungent critiques of state interventionism and his celebrations of individualism and *laissez-faire* have become fused with Social Darwinism in the popular mind. Like Spencer, Sumner has come to exemplify the ruthless advocacy of the survival of the fittest with a concomitant disregard for the impact of the struggle for existence on the losers. This last judgement is, in my view, apt: both men utilised Social Darwinism as a weapon against state intervention on behalf of people whom they stigmatised as evolutionary (and moral) failures. The evidence for this is overwhelming and I see no purpose in denying it or explaining it away, particularly in view of the ubiquity of this attitude towards the underclass at that time. What I do object to is the conflation of this particular ideological position with Social Darwinism *per se*. In the case of Sumner, this can result in an underplaying of the role of Social Darwinism in his *Folkways*, which formed part of a more comprehensive project of a science of society.[26] Although published almost fifty years after Darwin's *Origin*, therefore, *Folkways* is important for an appreciation of Sumner. An examination of this text not only underscores the continuity of Sumner's Social Darwinism over time, but also helps elucidate some of its ideological resonances which are easily passed over by concentrating on the *laissez-faire* aspects of his earlier writings.

Folkways emerged through need, and in primitive times the only guides to effort were pleasure and pain. 'Thus ways of doing things were selected, which were expedient. They answered the purpose better than other ways, or with less toil and pain. Along the course on which efforts were compelled to go, habit, routine, and skill were developed' (2). This was how folkways emerged in primitive societies – overwhelmingly unconscious, uniform, invariable and imperative modes of thought and practice which became the cultural heritage of the group (2–4).

Once again, Sumner invoked a distinction between the struggle for existence, which took place between the individual and nature, and the competition of life. The latter comprised 'the rivalry, antagonism, and mutual displacement in which the individual is involved with other organisms by his efforts to carry on the struggle for existence for himself.

---

[26] It has been alleged that after the mid-1880s Sumner avoided the expression 'survival of the fittest'. Cf. Bannister, 'William Graham Sumner's Social Darwinism', 102; Bellomy, ' "Social Darwinism" Revisited', 37. But in *Folkways* (265) Sumner explicitly referred to slavery and forced labour as consequences of the survival of the fittest. L. Coser highlights other continuities between *Folkways* and Sumner's earlier work in 'American Trends', in Bottomore and Nisbet, eds., *A History of Sociological Analysis*, 295–7.

It is, therefore, the competition of life which is the societal element, and which produces societal organisation' (16). The struggle with other organisms thus engendered cooperation as well as competition (17).

Commentators are quite right to point out that the distinction between the struggle for existence and the competition of life was not always easy to discern in Sumner's arguments.[27] He ascribed industrial organisation to the struggle for existence (157), defined aristocracies as groups who were superior in this struggle (183), and derived slavery from the tendency of stronger groups to exploit weaker ones in the struggle for existence (265). In all these instances, but certainly in the case of aristocracy and slavery, one might have expected these phenomena to derive from 'rivalry and antagonism' and hence from the competition of life. But what is important to the present study is the fact that Sumner assigned struggle, however conceived, a preponderant role in the evolution of folkways. In a remarkable anticipation of the views of some modern sociobiologists on intra-familial antagonisms, he described the conjugal bond as a cooperative union between the sexes brought about by the struggle for existence, but containing within it conflicting interests (between males and females and between parents and children) which all folkways sought (never with complete success) to resolve (345–7, 310).

Selection acted upon variations: what were the sources of variations if folkways induced uniformity and invariability? Sumner's answer was partly prefigured in his earlier essays in which he had argued that the masses were governed by their passions and instincts, and only in the elite were conscience and reason sufficiently elevated to curb these primitive tendencies.[28] In *Folkways* this argument was developed more fully. Sumner distinguished between 'classes' (sub-divisions of society) and the 'masses'. The latter were the conservative core of society, dominated by the folkways. Classes were the sources of variation, introducing changes which the masses then imitated (45). Thus: 'It is the classes who produce variation; it is the masses who carry forward the traditional mores' (47). Sumner's concept of social structure is explicated in the following statement:

Every civilised society has to carry below the lowest section of the masses a dead weight of ignorance, poverty, crime, and disease. Every such society has, in the great central section of the masses, a great body which is neutral in all the policy of society. It lives by routine and tradition. It is not brutal, but it is shallow,

[27] Persons, 'Introduction', *Social Darwinism*, 3; Bannister, 'William Graham Sumner's Social Darwinism', 97.
[28] Sumner, *What Social Classes Owe To Each Other*, 75.

narrow-minded, and prejudiced. Nevertheless it is harmless. It lacks initiative and cannot give an impulse for good or bad. It produces few criminals. It can sometimes be moved by appeals to its fixed ideas and prejudices. It is affected in its mores by contagion from the classes above it (50).

As this citation makes plain, the masses initiated nothing: creativity was the prerogative of the few. 'Only the elite of any society, in any age, think . . .' (206).

Sumner repeated his earlier conviction that no class could be trusted to rule society impartially and hence the task of constitutional govern-ment was to devise means for preventing the abuse of state power. At the same time, he was convinced of the inevitability of a ruling class. 'In every societal system or order', affirmed Sumner, 'there must be a ruling class or classes; in other words, a class gets control of any society and determines its political form or system. The ruling class, therefore, has the power' (169). This meant that ultimately all controversies over rights were resolved by force, although he used this latter term in a broad sense. 'Nothing but might has ever made right, and if we include in might (as we ought to) elections and the decisions of courts, nothing but might makes right now' (65). All disputes have to end, and they are terminated by force: the aggrieved parties invariably complain of violated rights, but they are ultimately 'overborne by force of some kind. Therefore might has made all the right which ever has existed or exists now' (66).

In *Folkways*, then, Social Darwinism functions as an organising narrative. In the earlier essays, while this function was discernible it was secondary to the rhetorical use of Darwinian concepts to support Sumner's political and moral views. This use appears in the later text as well, for instance in Sumner's strictures on the notion of wage-slavery (178–9). But the main thrust of this book was to catalogue various folkways and to show how they arose through and were modified by the struggle for existence and the competition of life. Indeed, by focusing upon the sources of social variation and by including a chapter on 'Societal Selection', Sumner was more strictly Social Darwinist in *Folkways* than in his earlier publications. In this he may have been influenced by the uncompromising versions of Social Darwinism associated with European theorists such as Westermarck, Vacher de Lapouge, Ratzel, Gumplowicz, Ammon and Galton, who appear in his notes and bibliography. Yet Sumner did not explicitly assign a preponderant role to heredity as did many of these authors; for him, social evolution was *analogous* to, rather than derivative from, organic evolution, and he sought to explicate the sources of variation and conservation and the cultural mechanisms through which competition and selection took place. He was thus a determinist because for him evolutionary laws were inexorable and unavoidable, but he was not a biological reductionist in that the laws in question operated in and through social beliefs, practices and institutions.

James and genius

Spencer, Fiske and Sumner shared a perception of science as the domain of certainty. Scientific laws, for them, were deterministic, and their discovery and formulation in the realm of human behaviour constituted the goals of psychology and sociology. During the 1870s this understanding of science was challenged by American philosophers in ways which were to lead to innovative conceptions of scientific method and hence of the nature and content of the social sciences. The new philosophy was 'pragmatism' and its leading practitioners were Charles Sanders Peirce, William James and John Dewey. Darwinism was to play a crucial role in the formation and development of pragmatism.[29]

Peirce (1839–1914) pioneered the pragmatic view of scientific method in an essay of 1877 entitled 'The Fixation of Belief'. Peirce grasped the revolutionary import of Darwin's approach to evolution in his assertion that: 'Mr Darwin proposed to apply the statistical method to biology.' This had already been successfully achieved in the theory of gases, which could not predict the movement of any particular gas molecule but made probabilistic statements about collections of molecules. 'In like manner, Darwin, while unable to say what the operation of variation and natural selection in every individual case will be, demonstrates that in the long run they will adapt animals to their circumstances.'[30]

This appreciation of the probabilistic nature of science in general, and Darwinism in particular, was central to James's attack on the deterministic conception of science as popularised by Spencer and his disciples. For James, science was concerned with statements of probabilities and lacked the certitude ascribed to it by Spencer. As James argued in his *The Will to Believe* (1897), failure to understand the true nature of science was responsible for the misconstrued relationship between science and faith. Far from being mutually opposed they were in fact connected, since scientific knowledge reposed upon faith in the validity of science as a source of knowledge. James urged his readers to resist

[29] See P. Wiener, *Evolution and the Founders of Pragmatism* (Cambridge, MA: Harvard University Press, 1949).

[30] Peirce, 'The Fixation of Belief', in Hollinger and Capper, eds., *The American Intellectual Tradition* (New York: Oxford University Press, 1993), II, 15. For a discussion of Peirce's theory of science and its impact on James, see P. J. Croce, 'William James' Scientific Education', *History of the Human Sciences*, 8(1995), 9–27.

what he saw as the tyranny of science, arguing that it had never actually demonstrated the invalidity of religious belief.[31] He suggested a Darwinist interpretation of the various religious creeds and their histories, claiming that 'the freest competition of the various faiths with one another, and their openest application to life by their several champions, are the most favourable conditions under which the survival of the fittest can proceed'.[32]

An illustration of James's exploration of the social implications of Darwinism is afforded by his essay of 1880 on 'Great Men and Their Environment'.[33] Although this text commenced with the assertion of a 'remarkable parallel' between the facts of social evolution and the facts of zoological evolution as propounded by Darwin, it repudiated Spencer's interpretation of both processes. The Englishman was accused of making change exogenous to the individual by locating its sources in the environment or in ancestral conditions (218). James posed the question of the social equivalent of the accidental variations upon which natural selection acted. His answer was that these variations took the form of 'great men' – creative and imaginative individuals whose genius generated the raw material which the environment then selected (226). It was precisely this 'fermentative influence of geniuses' which caused social evolution to take one direction rather than another (229).

Thus social evolution is a resultant of the interaction of two wholly distinct factors, – the individual, deriving his peculiar gifts from the play of physiological and infra-social forces, but bearing all the power of initiative and origination in his hands; and second, the social environment, with its power of adopting or rejecting both him and his gifts. Both factors are essential to change. The community stagnates without the impulse of the individual. The impulse dies away without the sympathy of the community (232).

Darwin's distinction between the sources of variation and the selective action of the environment could also be fruitfully applied to the production and subsequent fate of mental phenomena. According to James, the lower strata of the mind generated variations in the form of 'random images, fancies, accidental out-births of spontaneous variation in the fundamental activity of the excessively instable human brain, which the outer environment simply confirms or refutes, adopts or rejects, preserves or destroys, – selects, in short, just as it selects morphological and social variations due to molecular accidents of an analogous sort' (247).

---

[31] James, *The Will to Believe and Other Essays in Popular Philosophy* (New York: Dover Publications, 1956).
[32] *Ibid.*, 'Preface', xii.   [33] Reproduced in James, *The Will to Believe*, 216–54.

What is striking about this formulation is the combination of accident and causation in its characterisation of organic, mental and social evolution, reflecting James's conception of the probabilistic form of scientific method. It is additionally noteworthy for its description of genius. James was opposed to Spencer's rejection of 'Great Men' approaches to historical explanation (232–4), and his celebration of the importance of genius could easily be construed as a reaffirmation of an elitist approach to the analysis of social change. But for James, genius was an accident. Contrary to the prevailing hereditarian intrepretations of genius as a property confined to outstanding families, James seems much closer to modern views of creative genius as something which, even if containing a hereditary component, is randomly distributed within a population.[34]

James published this essay at the same time that Sumner was developing his own version of social evolution. Referring to it as a Social Darwinist tract might appear preposterous to those accustomed to equate this body of ideas with the rhetorical uses to which it was assigned by Sumner and Spencer. But even a casual inspection of James's essay reveals the world view in its entirety. The difference lies in his interpretation of some of its components. Selection was given a much wider connotation than elimination through war or industrial competition and included the selection of ideas and arguments as perhaps the most important mechanism of social change. The role of chance was emphasised in the production of variation. Above all, James's statistical understanding of scientific laws allowed him to place a particular construction on the fifth element of the world view: the application of evolution to mental and social phenomena. Contingency and probability combined to open up a space for human action, to establish a social environment with room for reason *and* faith, causality *and* will. The pragmatist evaluation of Darwinism and its social implications were central to the construction of this theoretical perspective.

Conclusion

By the beginning of the 1880s Darwinism had been put to a variety of theoretical usages by American intellectuals. Brace made it the basis of a science of racial development; Fiske and Sumner employed it to show

---

[34] The sociobiologist Wilson proclaims that the combination of genes responsible for any particular gifted person is unlikely to appear in the same family more than once. 'So if genius is to any extent hereditary, it winks on and off through the gene pool in a way that would be difficult to measure or predict.' E. O. Wilson, *On Human Nature* (London: Harvard University Press, 1978), 198.

that social change was refractory to political and legislative engineering; James extolled the evolutionary significance of genius. Sumner's adaptations achieved the greatest notoriety and his name, along with Spencer's, has become synonymous with Social Darwinism. But Brace and James were every bit as committed to the world view as Sumner and Spencer, as indeed they were to the idea of individual liberty. Having different conceptions of how the latter was realised, and different evaluations of the status quo with respect to this realisation, Brace and James differed from Sumner and Spencer on the ideological implications of Darwinism. Moreover, James re-interpreted the world view itself. But the components of the world view and their interconnections were clearly discernible in all these instances.

The American situation affords a vivid illustration of both the diversity of contexts in which Social Darwinism could be employed and the impossibility of deducing a theorist's ideological position from the fact of being a Social Darwinist. Brace and Fiske both believed Darwinism to substantiate progress as a historical law; Sumner was at best sceptical about the existence of any such law. Brace, Fiske and James explicitly argued for the compatibility of Darwinism and religious belief, while Sumner's views on warfare differed from those of Fiske (at least when the latter was in his optimist mode). In all instances, nature was assigned normative status as a guide for the social sciences and/or as a model for social action. The world view itself, however, with its indeterminacies, allowed for radically different perceptions of nature and its laws. It also promoted hesitancies, ambivalences and inconsistencies within the same thinker as he sought to come to terms with the social ramifications of these laws.

This feature has already been commented upon in the work of Fiske and Sumner, but it is also evident in James's writings. For example, in his book on psychology James dismissed the claim that habits were inherited. Habit undoubtedly represented the 'enormous flywheel of society, its most precious conservative agent'.[35] But its heritage was social rather than biological, since it was not inscribed in the constitution of the mind. It was precisely because habits were not inherited in this way that men could think anew, recombine ideas and innovate. This is why man was, above all, 'the *educable* animal'.[36] Instincts, on the other hand, were inherited, and James sometimes depicted their influences in ways which contradicted his strictures against scientific certainty as well as placing severe limits on the educability of humans. Aggression and warfare, deriving from the circumstances of primitive tribal existence,

---

[35] James, *Principles of Psychology*, I, 121.   [36] *Ibid.*, II, 368, original emphasis.

were instances of the instinctive heritage of human nature. 'If evolution and the survival of the fittest be true at all, the destruction of prey and of human rivals *must* have been among the most important of man's primitive functions, the fighting and the chasing instincts *must* have become ingrained.'[37] Whatever pacific virtues men professed, these 'smouldering and sinister traits' remained part of their psychological make-up. 'It is just because human bloodthirstiness is such a primitive part of us', continued James, 'that it is so hard to eradicate, especially where a fight or a hunt is promised as part of the fun.'[38] Likewise with women: totally formed in character by the age of twenty, they possessed brains that were less efficient than those of men, rendering them unreceptive to thoughts that were inaccessible to their 'direct intuition'.[39]

These claims were highly deterministic and placed boundaries to the efficacy of education. In making them James appears to be guilty of espousing the rigid determinism of which he was elsewhere so critical. What they reflect, in part at least, is the ambivalence of someone who on the one hand wished to develop a science of psychology along Darwinist lines, which involved the linking of human and animal behaviour via the doctrine of descent, and on the other wanted to acknowledge the importance of individual creativity and freedom. Social Darwinism served both causes, but not in ways that were always commensurable.

[37] *Ibid.*, II, 412, original emphases.   [38] *Ibid.*   [39] *Ibid.*, II, 368–9.

6   Social Darwinism in France and Germany

Introduction

When Darwin published the *Origin*, France and Germany were in the throes of socio-economic change and political conflict. In France the legacy of the Revolution was one of cleavage and political confrontation expressed in the episodes of insurrection, restoration and coup which occurred until the formation of the Third Republic. Born from the trauma of military defeat and civil war, the Republic was itself a precarious compromise that was to be riven by crises during its seventy-year history. Class divisions, provincial loyalties and the dislocative impacts of rapid industrialisation and urbanisation were compounded by an embittered antagonism between the Catholic Church and the forces of anti-clericalism. Small wonder, then, that French philosophers and social theorists were continually preoccupied with what Comte had designated the 'seventh science': *la morale*. Their aim, whatever their political predilections, was to discover an authoritative body of beliefs capable of uniting the nation around an ethical consensus. The achievements of the natural sciences ensured that many theorists would seek to emulate these disciplines in the search for models and methods that could assist in the construction of this moral concordance.

After the abortive revolution of 1848, Germany also experienced political division against a background of brisk economic growth and social change. After national unification under Bismarck, the new Reich was fraught with continuing regional differences and enmities, compounded by hostility between Protestants and a sizeable Catholic minority. Abrasive class divisions were reflected in the emergence of the largest socialist party in Europe, in addition to a sharp differentiation between rural/agrarian and urban/industrial sub-cultures. Tensions with rival nationalities added to these difficulties, and in the neighbouring Austro-Hungarian Empire these tensions between Germans and other ethnic groups were such as to encourage some of the former to contemplate an expansion of the Reich that would include all German nationals within its boundaries. To the pressures wrought by industria-lisation, urbanisation, nationalism and democratisation were added conflicts between religious orthodoxy and a critical and rationalist temper exemplified by a new spirit of biblical criticism and the growth of science, particularly in the field of biology.

Both national contexts, therefore, provided fertile conditions for the reception and development of the Social Darwinist world view. As we have seen in the cases of Britain and the USA, the world view offered the promise of new certainties that could be inferred from the processes which regulated both history and human nature, namely adaptation, selection and heredity. The theorists who represent the main focus of this chapter – Clémence Royer and Ernst Haeckel – were quick to exploit this promise in France and Germany respectively.

Royer and the semiotics of nature

Historians of science agree that, for a variety of reasons, Darwinism had a limited impact on French biology.[1] In the realm of social theory, however, Darwin found an early champion in the person of Clémence-Auguste Royer (1830–1902), who produced a translation of the *Origin* in 1862 and was a staunch advocate of Darwinian and evolutionary ideas in the *Société d'Anthropologie de Paris*, of which she was for many years the only female member.[2] Royer hailed from a monarchist and religious background but became an ardent convert to republicanism and anti-clericalism. Prior to her translation of the *Origin* she had absorbed the evolutionary views of Lamarck as well as the teachings of political economy. Both influences were evident in her prize-winning study on taxation in which she described nature as a 'work of perpetual transition', as a series of gradual changes. She likened society to a biological organism and cautioned against the twin dangers of seeking to prevent change and trying to proceed too rapidly. Royer also insisted that the laws of supply and demand were as immutable and universal as

---

[1]   For the reception of Darwinism in France see C. Limoges, 'A Second Glance at Evolutionary Biology in France', in Mayr and Provine, *The Evolutionary Synthesis*; R. Stebbins, 'France' in Glick, *Comparative Reception*; Y. Conry, *L'Introduction du darwinisme en France au dix-neuvième siècle* (Paris: Vrin, 1974).

[2]   See J. Harvey, 'Evolutionism Transformed: Positivists and Materialists in the *Société d'Anthropologie de Paris* from Second Empire to Third Republic', in Oldroyd and Langham, *The Wider Domain of Evolutionary Thought*; Harvey, ' "Doubly Revolutionary": Clémence Royer Before the Société d'Anthropologie de Paris', *Proceedings of the Sixteenth International Congress For the History of Science*, Symposium B, 1981, 250–7. There are valuable discussions of Royer in L. Clark, *Social Darwinism in France*, 12–16, 25–7, 34–7, 72–3; and Clark, 'Le Darwinisme social en France', *La Recherche*, 19(1988), 193, 194.

the laws of biology and physiology, drawing a parallel between the growth of physical organs and the progressive elaboration of political institutions from primitive times to the present. Progress was a fact of the natural world affecting all species and from which it was vital to draw the relevant moral and political conclusions. Inequality she considered to be natural and the foundation of the social division of labour, though this was no warrant for consolidating differences into a caste system through unjust legislation. Inequalities also marked the relationships among the various human races and, as in the animal kingdom, 'the higher races seem destined to supplant the lower races and to make them disappear or slowly assimilate them.'[3] Dedicated to all 'free men', the book extolled the virtues of individualism, economic freedom and competition, themes that were to be prominent in her subsequent publications.

In the long and provocative preface to her translation of the *Origin*,[4] Royer not only embraced an unequivocally Darwinist perspective, but chided the English naturalist for failing to draw the necessary conclusions about political and moral evolution from his inquiries (xxxix, lxii). She was excited by the comprehensiveness of Darwinism and by its potential relevance to so many areas. Every so often, claimed Royer, a work appeared which synthesised the achievements of an entire era, constituting a cosmogony, a theology and a sociology. Darwin's book was just such a work, capable of integrating the study of nature, morals, politics and international relations (xii).[5] Royer foresaw the possibility of a semiotics of nature because for her nature was a text, a system of signs, and it was the task of the philosopher to 'decipher the meaning of the often incoherent signs that it delivers to our interpretation, like the scattered fragments of an inscription for which we sometimes do not even know the language' (xiv). Her main contribution to this project was a study of human evolution, which appeared in 1870, a year before Darwin's *Descent*.[6] Royer deserves recognition, therefore, as one of the earliest pioneers, not only in the dissemination of Social Darwinism, but also in its formulation and application to social and political phenomena.

In her *Origine de l'homme et des sociétés*, Royer rejected creationist

---

[3]   Royer, *Théorie de l'impôt, ou la dîme sociale*, 2 vols. (Paris: Guillaumin, 1862), I, x–xi, 5, 20, 66–7, 141.

[4]   Royer, 'Préface' to Darwin, *De l'origine des espèces, ou des lois du progrès chez les êtres organisés*, tr. Royer (Paris: Guillaumin, 1862),

[5]   In her foreword to the second edition of her translation, Royer equated Darwin's work to a 'revolution'. Royer, 'Avant Propos', *De l'origine des espèces par sélection naturelle, ou des lois de transformation des êtres organisés*, second edn (Paris: Guillaumin, 1866), vi.

[6]   Royer, *Origine de l'homme et des sociétés* (Paris: Guillaumin, 1870).

accounts of human origins, arguing that all living things evolved from an anterior state in accordance with the two biological laws of heredity and variability. These laws were complemented by two others: the struggle for life, which arose out of the pressure exerted by population growth on resources, and natural selection (6–14). The result was the survival of the fittest, and Royer was emphatic in her portrayal of the ubiquity and relentlessness of its effects, insisting that 'struggle, war and not peace, is the inescapable law of life. Species struggle against other species, varieties against other varieties, and within each variety, in the social group, the tribe, the family itself, individuals struggle against other individuals' (520). Human beings had evolved from ape-like ancestors, as reflected in the fact that all the allegedly human attributes, such as language, cognition, intelligence and moral faculties, were to be found in the animal kingdom, albeit in rudimentary form (55–8, 85–6, 136). There was, therefore, nothing unique about the mental and physical constitution of humans: what they had evolved were greater variety and complexity of instincts, sentiments and faculties which enabled them to attain superiority over other animals (95).

The continuity between humans and animals was graphically illustrated by savages, among whom the struggle for existence was especially acute. Royer dismissed Rousseau's portrait of the state of nature as a peaceful and benign condition. She argued that 'man in a savage state, at universal war with nature and his fellow men, is placed in conditions of life common to animals; he must, therefore, have all their instincts and passions ...' (222). To be gentle and good in these circumstances would have been disastrous, which is why savages were driven by ferocious and degrading passions which made theft, murder, rapine, mendacity and violence normal features of their lives. Royer qualified this account somewhat by agreeing with Rousseau that a savage was capable of empathising with another's suffering. But she insisted that this deeply rooted sentiment did not suffice to offset the other features of primitive mentality and render savage existence an age of innocence and gold (230–2, 248).

Progress from this primitive condition took place through adaptation, selection and the inheritance of acquired characters. Individuals who adapted passed their successful traits to their offspring, thereby enhancing the chances of the latter in the struggle for life. Modern people had inherited the mental make-up of the savage, but the passions of the former were more complex and diversified, and accompanied by new ones, for example the passion for truth, justice and beauty. This made modern men more individualistic than savages, and more modifiable (169, 215–7, 270–2). Hence the evolution of humanity was progressive, showing a gradual improvement over time. Darwinism, wrote Royer in the 'Préface', had made necessary a clear choice between the doctrine of progress and the dismal dogma of the Fall, and she left her readers in no doubt of her own choice on this issue: 'I believe in progress.'[7] Yet in her book she warned against any complacent belief in the inevitability of progress as arrests and reversals had happened throughout history and could happen again (274). Furthermore, the sanguinary instincts and passions of the savage still lurked in the breasts of modern man, as exemplified by the hunter, the absolute monarch intoxicated with power, and the 'popular masses' (250).

Royer was adamant that continued progress depended upon the existence of inequalities. Differences were the raw material on which selection operated, and throughout nature those species with a marked tendency to variability enjoyed an advantage in the struggle for life, since some of these variations would be useful. Competition and selection took place at all levels, from the individual to the species: 'The struggle between individuals produces the selection of individuals. The struggle between varieties decides their future. The struggle between species has as its consequence the triumph of some, the disappearance or emigration of others' (14). Among humans the same processes were at work, both within societies, and between societies and races.

Within advanced societies, inequalities were biologically grounded. Occasionally, admitted Royer, these inequalities outlived their usefulness and, becoming ossified in outmoded customs and institutions, were the cause of resentment and conflict. But she felt confident enough to propose a general law to the effect that every social inequality originated in a 'natural' inequality and only persisted if it corresponded to a social need (545–6). 'Men', proclaimed Royer, 'are by nature unequal', a principle she extended to the different races in the conviction that the higher races were destined to supplant the lower in the course of evolution. Since the resources of the planet were finite then it was both necessary and right that their usage should fall to the races most capable of utilising them. This made warfare between the Aryans and inferior races legitimate, although the former could still allow the latter to exist if their labour was made essential by climatic conditions. Sometimes it might even be beneficial to allow racial inter-mixing to create varieties, though in general Royer considered 'the mixing of blood between higher and lower races' to be 'immoral'.[8] Within and between advanced societies warfare was to be condemned, and Royer evidently saw

---

[7] Royer, 'Préface', lxiv.   [8] Royer, 'Préface, lxi; *Origine*, 531–2.

competition here taking a peaceful form, although she did not elaborate on this point.

Royer, therefore, endorsed all the elements of the Darwinist world view, which she applied to questions concerning the origins and development of humans and their social arrangements. She also forcefully raised what she saw to be the political and ethical implications of this world view.

Liberty, equality and the status of women

Royer's preface to her translation of the *Origin* possessed the tenor and the challenge of a manifesto. It opened with a resounding declaration of faith in human reason: 'Yes, I believe in revelation, but in a permanent revelation of man to himself and by himself, in a rational revelation which is only the result of the progress of modern science and awareness...' (v). This proclamation reflected her lifelong adherence to the ideals enshrined in the eighteenth-century Enlightenment – ideals that celebrated reason, liberty and progress (xi).[9] This stance was accompanied by a pungent anti-clericalism. What distinguished Darwinism from other revelatory modes was the former's bases in induction and Cartesian doubt and its freedom from prejudice. Christianity, in contrast, was a stifling and debilitating dogma, a sign of sickness and decrepitude, an obstacle to freedom and progress (viii–ix, xiii–xiv).

Darwinism also controverted the notion that human nature possessed a fixed and immutable essence which, in one form or other, provided the intellectual scaffolding of platonism, Christianity and socialism. These doctrines attempted to restrict individual liberty in the name of this timeless essence. Darwinism showed that no such permanent qualities existed, that human nature, as with all of nature, was subject to change over time (xviii–xix). For Royer, this entailed a commitment to freedom as an essential prerequisite, in modern conditions, for experiment, innovation, and for the proliferation of variations which would then be exposed to competition in order that the most beneficial would be selected and progress maintained. She hailed Darwin's work as a great weapon for the 'liberal and progressive party' because it justified a political regime dedicated to the principles of unlimited personal liberty and free competition (xx, lxii). In the *Origine* she expressed her ideal as liberty 'without limit, with its struggles and perils ... without any civil restraint [*règle-morale*] other than respect for the equal rights of others' (580). But this equality of liberty was the only form of equality consistent

---

9   See Royer's defiant reassertion of these views in her 'Avant Propos' of 1866, vii.

with evolution. Since nature had decreed the unequal value of individuals, liberty allowed each one to realise his or her own worth, and competition weeded out the unsuccessful. Egalitarian policies stifled initiative and reduced the rewards accruing to effort and success (583–4). 'The formula for the highest social prosperity is therefore equality of initial liberty for each member of the national group, and the free play of individual capabilities [*forces*] and initiatives' (585). One of the objectives of science must be the exposure of the absurdity of egalitarian creeds and the demonstration that 'equality of liberty and progress through inequality is the law of equity and the road to happiness for all . . .' (587).

Royer looked to Darwinism to provide a naturalist foundation for ethics. In her view, it established an absolute criterion for distinguishing between right and wrong because 'the moral rule for every species is that which tends to its conservation, to its multiplication, to its progress, relative to place and time'.[10] This was the rationale for Royer's swingeing attack on misguided public and private charity, i.e. charity which, by evolutionary standards, had the consequence of sacrificing the good to the bad:

What is the result of this exclusive and unintelligent protection accorded to the weak, the infirm, the incurable, the wicked, to all those who are ill-favoured by nature? It is that the ills which have afflicted them tend to be perpetuated and multiplied indefinitely; that evil is increased instead of diminishing, and tends to grow at the expense of good.[11]

The targets of this diatribe were the losers in the struggle for existence whose hereditary defects would be perpetuated and increased by charitable actions aimed at their protection and welfare. In the light of these sentiments it is ironic (or perhaps poetic justice) that Royer, although achieving some belated public recognition and financial security by the end of her life, at one time fell into indigence and was obliged to enter a retirement home.[12]

We have already encountered Royer's assertion that social inequalities invariably had a biological foundation. There was, though, an exception to this rule: the subordinate position of women in modern societies. This arose with the appearance of warrior societies which provided the opportunity for male domination to replace the equal relationships between the sexes that had prevailed hitherto. Royer repudiated the idea that patriarchal relations had any natural or biological foundation. She considered them to be an interregnum in the otherwise co-equal development of the sexes, and responsible for an unbalanced evolution

[10] Royer, 'Préface', lxiii. Royer developed her ideas on ethics in her *Le Bien et la loi morale* (Paris: Guillaumin, 1881).
[11] *Ibid.*, lvi.   [12] Harvey, ' "Doubly Revolutionary" ', 256.

of the mental faculties and social roles of men and women. Hence 'it follows from these considerations that there is nothing inevitable, nothing absolute, about the differences in aptitudes and functions which exist today among the two halves of humanity'. Races which failed to recognise this and adapt to modern conditions by allowing women freedom to participate in intellectual progress would succumb to more enlightened rivals in the struggle for life, and vanish from the face of the earth.[13]

Royer was in a good position to appreciate the workings of patriarchalism, since her failure to secure an academic post was probably a result of her gender. Her feminism, therefore, resonated her experiences as well as her convictions, and was conveyed with passion in her writings. Yet its relationship to her hereditarian determinism is highly problematic, and it is difficult to resist the impression of intellectual and political opportunism in her insistence that the position of females represented an exception to the general rule that social inequalities reflected biological differences. To argue for the social determination of sex roles is therefore an aporia in her writings, a switch in the mode of argumentation stemming from certain ideological motives that led her to contradict the assumptions that grounded her work.

In assessing Royer's Social Darwinism it is tempting to focus on those facets of her 'Préface' which had so shocked her contemporaries, i.e. her feminism, anti-clericalism and her critique of charity for the 'unfit'. But to do so would be to understate in some respects the importance of her ideas. She never achieved the readership and popularity of Haeckel and Spencer, but her projected 'semiotics of nature' should be seen as one of the earliest attempts to locate Darwinism within a wider philosophical framework – one that was systematically formulated and explicitly linked to socio-political issues. It was a framework proposed as an alternative to religion through a comprehensive account of humanity – its origins, its history, its relationship to the rest of nature, and its future. It was, in short, an attempt to discover a naturalistic basis for *la morale* – one that was capable of dealing with the inescapable fact of humanity's location in time and hence with the historicity and seeming contingency of its institutions and beliefs, of those very attributes by which it had, in various cultural contexts, defined itself as human. Royer's efforts confronted these issues by elaborating what she took to be the

[13]   Royer, *Origine*, 391; 'Préface', lx. For discussions of Royer's feminism, see Harvey, ' "Doubly Revolutionary" '; and Harvey, ' "Strangers to Each Other": Male and Female Relationships in the Life and Work of Clémence Royer', in P. Abir-Am and D. Outra, eds., *Uneasy Careers and Intimate Lives* (New Brunswick: Rutgers University Press, 1987).

philosophical, ethical and political implications of the Darwinian revolution in biological science.

Royer was not alone in France in her efforts to enlist Darwinism in the service of liberalism. A Belgian-born economist, Gustave de Molinari (b. 1818), was a prolific publicist of the doctrines of political economy which he readily assimilated to Darwinism. His *L'Evolution économique*,[14] for example, applied Darwinian concepts to the development of what he designated as the modern 'economic state', i.e. an international system of production and exchange. This state, and its continual progress, comprised a regime of 'unlimited competition' in which the penalty for remaining stationary for industries and nations was inevitable destruction (77). Molinari distinguished between *la petite industrie* in which production was principally achieved through physical labour, and *la grande industrie* where mechanical force dominated production. Since the birth of civilisation (i.e. the appearance of agriculture), the second type had gradually superseded the first, while the individual entrepreneur had in turn given way to industrial society and the current international system (43). Throughout this development, the motor of change was the struggle for existence.

In early phases of this evolution, struggle took the form of warfare. War, or its threat, encouraged invention, eliminated the least capable individuals and nations, and constrained the winners to cultivate their powers in order to maintain their dominance (86–8). But with the development of industry, war ceased to be advantageous in the struggle, and was replaced by economic competition. This Molinari considered to be even more effective as a goad to progress than warfare because whereas the latter was confined to the ruling classes, the former was universal in its scope (88). Competition eliminated the less intelligent, industrious and moral races. Within each society, evolution raised the general level of ability, and the least capable individuals slipped to the bottom of the social hierarchy, although even here there was no refuge from the brutal selective pressure of competition (94). Nor could one look forward to a golden age of repose in the future: 'No! competition is struggle, it is the civilised form of war, which it is destined to abolish . . .' (85).

Like Royer, Molinari was fervently opposed to either monarchical reaction or socialistic utopianism (136). He was aware that coincident with the production of great wealth there had occurred an equally great multiplication of pauperism which neither public nor private charity seemed capable of reducing (102). This he ascribed to the transitional status of modern societies and to defects in human nature: moral and

---

[14] G. de Molinari, *L'Evolution économique du dix-neuvième siècle: théorie du progrès* (Paris: Reinwald, 1880).

intellectual evolution had not kept pace with economic change. The solution was not to be found in social reconstruction, but in moral progress as a precondition for increased wealth and its more equitable distribution (125, 134). Here one detects an ambivalence on Molinari's part with regard to the implication of economic evolution. On the one hand, the trend was towards an equilibrium between production and consumption which represented 'an evolution towards order and justice' (84). On the other hand, competition was inescapable and entailed the expropriation and eventual destruction of the weak by the strong (90, 94). Molinari did not explain how moral evolution of any sort could overcome this dilemma.

Ernst Haeckel and *Darwinismus*

In contrast to France, Darwinism was rapidly endorsed by German biologists. The reception was uneven, certainly, and some leading naturalists were unconvinced, including the translator of the *Origin*, which was published in German in 1860.[15] But many scientists not only endorsed Darwinism, but succeeded in popularising it widely among the German public. This popularisation also extended to the social applications of Darwinism which gained credence from the fact that they were executed by established and, in some instances very eminent, natural scientists. The elaboration of Social Darwinism was in full flow by the mid-1860s, with German intellectuals quick to realise the implications of Darwin's work.

Social Darwinists made clear to their audiences that, as in the animal and plant kingdoms, human modification took place through natural selection. The 'struggle for existence' rapidly became a popular catchphrase, described by the naturalist Schmidt as 'a badge and common property of our age'.[16] This opinion was shared by the most famous and effective populariser of them all, a gifted zoologist from the University of Jena, Ernst Haeckel (1834–1919), who referred to struggle as 'a watchword of the day'. This accorded with Haeckel's wishes because he was determined that Darwinism should not remain the preserve of a privileged caste, but should 'become the common property of all mankind'.[17] Recent scholarship has demonstrated the predominantly liberal orientation of early Social Darwinism in Germany; only subse-

---

[15] For the history of Darwinism in Germany, see W. M. Montgomery, 'Germany' in Glick, *Comparative Reception*.
[16] Schmidt, *The Doctrine of Descent and Darwinism*, 140.
[17] E. Haeckel, *The History of Creation*, 2 vols., tr. E. R. Lankester (London: King, 1876), I, 161; I, 4.

quently did it become appropriated by racists and militarists, and then never exclusively so.[18] But German liberalism differed from Spencerian individualism in that while it extolled the virtues of private property, economic competition, freedom of speech and association, and secular education, it also endorsed a strong nation-state and the vigorous assertion of German national interests.[19] These features of German liberalism are important to an understanding of the work of Ernst Haeckel.

Haeckel was not only a creative naturalist in his own right but an indefatigable advocate for evolutionary theory in particular and for scientific education in general. His popular studies went through numerous editions and were translated into several languages.[20] For Haeckel and his followers, commitment to a scientific appreciation of man and nature carried with it the responsibility of challenging supernatural explanations, and they accused religious authorities – especially the Roman Catholic Church – of obfuscating the pursuit of scientific knowledge and perverting education. These attacks made Haeckel a controversial figure during the nineteenth century, and this continues to be the case in the present day, for modern scholars disagree over how his work should be interpreted. Some regard him as a thorough-going Social Darwinist, eugenicist, Aryan supremacist and anti-Semite who recommended racial and national conflicts as essential to progress. In these respects, Haeckel is deemed to be a forerunner of and contributor to National Socialism, all the more influential because his scientific credentials lent authenticity to his racism and bellicosity.[21] Other historians have argued that the incidence of Social Darwinism in Haeckel's writings has been greatly exaggerated and have objected to

---

[18] P. J. Weindling, *Darwinism and Social Darwinism in Imperial Germany* (Stuttgart: Gustav Fischer, 1991), 16. See also R. Weikart, 'The Origins of Social Darwinism in Germany'; T. Benton, 'Social Darwinism and Socialist Darwinism in Germany: 1860–1900', *Rivista di Filosofia*, 73(1982), 79–121.

[19] For a discussion of German liberalism in the context of social theory, see W. D. Smith, *Politics and the Science of Culture in Germany, 1840–1920* (Oxford University Press, 1991). There is an illuminating discussion of the different political contexts of Darwinism in Britain and Germany in Weindling, *Darwinism and Social Darwinism*, chap. 1.

[20] Kelly, *The Descent of Darwin*, 25, describes *The History of Creation* (1868) as the chief source for Darwinism in Germany until 1900, by which time it had gone through nine editions. Another book, *The Riddle of the Universe* (1899) was translated into twenty languages and by 1914 had sold over 300,000 copies in Germany alone. See H.-G. Zmarlik, 'Social Darwinism in Germany Seen as a Historical Problem', in H. Holborn, ed., *Republic to Reich: The Making of the Nazi Revolution*, tr. R. Manheim (New York: Pantheon, 1972), 452.

[21] D. Gasman, *The Scientific Origins of National Socialism* (London: Macdonald, 1970); J. Moore, 'Varieties of Social Darwinism'; G. J. Stein, 'Biological Science and the Roots of Nazism', *American Scientist*, 76(1988), 50–8; Lerner, *Final Solutions*, chap. 2.

treating his ideas as a 'theoretical rehearsal for Nazism', and instead located the German populariser within a secular and rationalist critical tradition.[22] The following account is not directly concerned with the relationship between Haeckel's ideas and those of National Socialism, but in evaluating the extent to which his ideas can be legitimately described as Social Darwinist it is possible to arrive at an assessment of their ideological import.

Haeckel perceived a close relationship between philosophy and science. For him, the former was a synthesising activity which interpreted the results of science and coordinated all knowledge into 'one grand and harmonious whole'.[23] Haeckel's own philosophical system was 'monism', which asserted 'the unity of all nature, the animating of all matter, the inseparability of mental power and corporeal substance'. Monism repudiated supernatural or teleological explanations on the grounds that 'all phenomena are due solely to mechanical or efficient causes ...'[24] Nature in its entirety must be approached from the standpoint of a unified descriptive and explanatory framework.

The framework in question was evolution. Organisms, arising from inorganic matter by 'spontaneous generation', underwent a continuous process of diversification and perfection. This was the 'law of progressive development', according to which species were modified over time to produce new species. Evidence for this development and the descent of all living beings from earlier life-forms was furnished by embryology: 'The history of the foetus is a recapitulation of the human race.' This was encapsulated in Haeckel's famous Biogenetic Law to the effect that ontogeny recapitulated philogeny.[25]

Haeckel was a devotee of the principle of the inheritance of acquired characters, dismissing Weismann's theory of the germ-plasm as mere metaphysical speculation. In this he considered himself to be faithful to the heritage of Lamarck and Darwin, insisting that the transmission of acquired characters was attested to by an enormous body of evidence and was 'an indispensable foundation of the theory of evolution'.[26] Darwin's specific contribution to evolutionary science was his theory of natural selection. The Englishman's meticulous marshalling of evidence revealed the struggle for life to be the impersonal regulator of the

---

[22] Kelly, *Descent of Darwin*, 8, 101, 114. Kelly maintains (113) that any hints of Social Darwinism in Haeckel's popular writings 'are minor asides and do not affect the general tone or substance of his work'.

[23] Haeckel, *Freedom in Science and Teaching* (no tr.) (London: Kegan Paul, 1879), 79; *History of Creation*, II, 349.

[24] Haeckel, *History of Creation*, I, 22; Haeckel, *The Evolution of Man*, tr. J. McCabe, 2 vols. (London: Watts, 1910), II, 748.

[25] Haeckel, *Evolution of Man*, I, 4.   [26] *Ibid.*, II, 736.

'reciprocal action of heredity and adaptation in the gradual transformation of species'. Nature did not unfold in accordance with God's design,
for its changes were 'merely the inevitable outcome of the struggle for
existence, the blind controller ...'[27] Haeckel preferred the expression
'competition for the means of subsistence' to 'struggle for existence',[28]
but his portrayal of this process was graphic and he was uncompromising
in the inferences he drew from its universality. The objective contemplation of nature, he argued, gave no warrant for any belief in peaceful
coexistence:

We shall rather find everywhere a pitiless, most embittered *Struggle of All against
All*. Nowhere in nature, no matter where we turn our eyes, does that idyllic
peace, celebrated by the poets, exist; we find everywhere a struggle and a striving
to annihilate neighbours and competitors. Passion and selfishness – conscious or
unconscious – is everywhere the motive force of life ... Man in this respect
certainly forms no exception to the rest of the animal world.[29]

There was no justification for crediting nature with a moral order. 'We
can only see a "moral order" and "design" in it when we ignore the
triumph of immoral force and the aimless features of the organism.
Might goes before right as long as organic life exists.'[30] Yet it was
through this 'purposeless drama' that progress occurred. The struggle
for existence, particularly among organisms closely resembling one
another, engendered adaptive pressures which induced specialisation,
diversification and perfection. These benefits were equally apparent in
the free competition of labourers: 'The greater or more general the
competition, the more quickly improvements are made in the branch of
labour, and the higher is the grade of perfection of the labourers
themselves.'[31] Haeckel was somewhat vague, however, on *why* this
struggle took place, and did not deduce its necessity from the ratio
between population growth and resources. The competition for the
means of subsistence appears as an existential datum, an inescapable
feature of nature and of society.[32]

Haeckel tirelessly reminded his readers that human beings were
governed by the same laws that ruled the rest of the natural order. He
castigated the anthropocentric claim that man was the centre of the
universe, insisting that 'as our mother-earth is a mere speck in the
sunbeam of the illimitable universe, so man himself is but a grain of

---

[27] Haeckel, *The Riddle of the Universe*, tr. J. McCabe (London: Watts, 1900), 269, 275.
[28] Haeckel, *History of Creation*, I, 161.   [29] *Ibid.*, I, 19–20, original emphasis.
[30] Haeckel, *Evolution of Man*, I, 72.   [31] Haeckel, *History of Creation*, I, 164.
[32] Such is also the case with a popular account of human evolution published by Haeckel's
disciple, Boelsche, which omits any mention of population in its discussion of natural
selection. Cf. W. Boelsche, *The Descent of Man* (no. tr.) (London: Simpkin, Marshall,
1926), 86–91.

protoplasm in the perishable framework of organic nature'.[33] Because humans were merely highly developed vertebrates, all of their characteristics were prefigured in the animal kingdom. Indeed, it was apparent in the ontogenesis of each individual that the first few weeks in the womb recapitulated a genealogy reaching beyond our vertebrate ancestry to even more primitive life-forms.[34] In order to combat Christian pride in the uniqueness of humanity – which he saw as an obstacle to scientific progress – Haeckel was particularly fond of stressing the continuity between humans and the primates. Every organ in the human body had been inherited from the apes, and the same was true of mental faculties, with the differences between man and the apes being quantitative rather than qualitative in nature. Even the maternal instinct stemmed from 'the instinct which is found in its extreme form in the exaggerated tenderness of the mother-ape'. Neither speech nor reason could be legitimately regarded as the exclusive prerogative of man, while social duties 'are merely higher evolutionary stages of the social instincts which we find in all social animals . . .'[35]

Haeckel's insistence on human subordination to the empire of natural laws often assumed the form of biological reductionism. For example, he claimed: 'We can only arrive at a correct knowledge of the social body, the State, through a scientific knowledge of the structure and life of the individuals who compose it, and the cells of which they are in turn composed.'[36] Likewise, he referred to social phenomena as the outcome of the laws of inheritance, adaptation and natural selection, from which had evolved the social division of labour, just as specialisation and differentiation had occurred in plants and animals. In fact, it was precisely due to the operation of these laws that progress was made possible, that 'the history of man is the history of his *progressive development*'.[37] The struggle for existence was very much a feature of this development. 'The ferocious conflict of interests in human society', observed Haeckel, 'is only a feeble image of the existence of the combat, incessant and cruel, which reigns throughout the living world.'[38] He concluded that the 'whole history of nations, or what is called "Universal History", must therefore be explicable by means of "natural selection" –

[33] Haeckel, *Riddle of the Universe*, 15. Cf. Haeckel, *History of Creation*, II, 264.
[34] Haeckel, *History of Creation*, I, 170; Haeckel, *Evolution of Man*, II, 404.
[35] Haeckel, *Evolution of Man*, II, 738; Haeckel, *Riddle of the Universe*, 51, 128, 359. There are similarities here with Darwin's comparison between humans and apes. See Desmond and Moore, *Darwin*, 244.
[36] Haeckel, *Riddle of the Universe*, 8.
[37] Haeckel, *History of Creation*, I, 271–9, 282, original emphasis.
[38] Haeckel, *Le Monisme: lien entre la religion et la science*, tr. G. Vacher de Lapouge (Paris: Schleicher, 1902), 33.

must be a physico-chemical process, depending on the action of Adaptation and Inheritance in the struggle for life. And this is actually the case.'[39] Thus the fate of nations and races 'is determined by the same "eternal laws of iron" as the history of the whole organic world', while the destiny of individuals was likewise governed 'with an iron necessity' by mechanical causes.[40] These facts occasionally prompted Haeckel to deny the existence of free will: 'The will of the animal, as well as that of man, is never free.' This assertion, made in Haeckel's first popular book, was repeated over three decades later: 'The human will has no more freedom than that of the higher animals, from which it differs only in degree, not in kind.'[41] There is a tension at the heart of Haeckel's system between this reductionism and determinism on the one hand, and his commitment to ethical values and ideals on the other. This commitment was plainly articulated in Haeckel's insistence that scientific materialism did not imply ethical materialism, which he rejected for its ascription of no other motive to human conduct than sensory gratification and for ignoring the role of ethical forces in human conduct.[42]

Before examining the ideological implications of Haeckel's *Darwinismus*, it is pertinent to underline the fact that Haeckel quite clearly *was* a Social Darwinist. All the components of the Darwinian world view were articulated in his writings and their relevance to the study of humans steadfastly maintained. Haeckel also went further than merely proposing the relevance of Darwinism to the study of humans, by insisting that nature supplied humans with a model capable of guiding moral and political actions. Although he described natural selection as a 'blind controller', Haeckel did not perceive history as a dimension of chance and accident or the future as unpredictable. Despite his objections to arguments from design and Creation, he still perceived the existence of an order in nature and advocated 'a complete and honest return to Nature and to natural relations'. The order in question consisted of biological laws and people must recognise their subjection to these laws and the need to live in conformity with them. This recognition would facilitate the rearrangement of social institutions such as the family and the state 'not according to the laws of distant centuries, but according to the rational principles deduced from knowledge of nature. Politics, morals, and the principles of justice, which are still drawn from all possible sources, will have to be formed in accordance with natural laws only.'[43]

[39] Haeckel, *History of Creation*, I, 170.   [40] Haeckel, *Riddle of the Universe*, 277–8.
[41] Haeckel, *History of Creation*, I, 237; Haeckel, *Riddle of the Universe*, 133.
[42] Haeckel, *History of Creation*, I, 36–7.   [43] *Ibid.*, II, 368.

Haeckel was not only a highly influential populariser of Social Darwinism, but wrote at a time when the application of Darwinism to psychological and social phenomena was still in its infancy. Furthermore, although Haeckel once warned of the dangers inherent in the unqualified transfer of scientific theories to the political domain, and described his own occasional ventures in this area as of 'no objective value',[44] he was a vigorous polemicist on behalf of secularism and educational reform, in addition to other causes. As he pointed out in the very text in which he made this disclaimer: 'Every great and comprehensive theory which affects the foundations of human science, and which, consequently, influences the systems of philosophy, will, in the first place not only further our theoretical view of the universe, but will also react on practical philosophy, ethics, and the correlated provinces of religion and politics.'[45] It is precisely Haeckel's adventures in these 'correlated provinces' which are the basis of controversies over the ideological import of his ideas. What was this ideological import, and how did it relate to Haeckel's Social Darwinism?

Darwinismus, inequality and religion

One of the documents invariably cited in any discussion of Haeckel's ideology is his response to an accusation made by the eminent German cytologist and liberal politician, Rudolf Virchow, to the effect that Darwinism implied socialism and was therefore politically subversive. To this charge Haeckel's riposte was that socialism and Darwinism were 'about as compatible as fire and water'. The equality of rights, duties and possessions advocated by socialism was invalidated by biology, which demonstrated how 'in the constitutionally organised communities of men, as of the lower animals, neither rights nor duties, neither possessions nor enjoyments have ever been equal for all the members alike, nor ever can be'. The more complex and highly organised a society became, the more pronounced was the division of labour, producing a variety of tasks, with concomitant discrepancies in the skills required of, and the rewards commanded by, the individuals who performed them. Such facts rendered socialist egalitarianism 'a fathomless absurdity'.[46] Any political tendency to be inferred from Darwinism – 'as is, no doubt, possible' – was unlikely to accord with the doctrine of equality:

The cruel and merciless struggle for existence which rages throughout all living nature, and in the course of nature *must* rage, this unceasing and inexorable

---

[44] Haeckel, *Freedom in Science*, 94–5.   [45] *Ibid.*, 88.   [46] *Ibid.*, 90–2.

competition of all living creatures, is an incontestable fact; only the picked minority of the qualified 'fittest' is in a position to resist it successfully, while the great majority of the competitors must necessarily perish miserably ... The selection, the picking out of these 'chosen ones', is inevitably connected with the arrest and destruction of the remaining majority At any rate, this principle of selection is nothing less than democratic, on the contrary, it is aristocratic in the strictest sense of the word.[47]

Some commentators have seen these remarks as typifying Haeckel's elitism and authoritarianism; for others, they were delivered during the heat of a polemical exchange and should not be taken too seriously.[48] By relating these comments to Haeckel's overall philosophical and ideological system rather than considering them in isolation, it is possible to evaluate their significance.

The first point to note is that the anti-democratic and anti-socialist features of this statement were not *ad hoc* but belonged to a series of arguments about the general impact of differentiation and selection on all social organisms, including humans, and I have already shown how such arguments were integral to Haeckel's evolutionary philosophy. Second, anti-egalitarian assertions appear throughout Haeckel's writings. *The History of Creation*, his first popular book, emphasised individual inequalities and posited a law 'that all organic individuals from the commencement of their individual existence are unequal, though often very much alike'. These original differences became exacerbated during the life-cycle due to adaptation, and acquired differences were then transmitted to the individual's progeny, thus producing progressively greater degrees of differentiation through time. This was why the members of the 'lowest tribes' were so much alike that they could scarcely be distinguished, in contrast to the highly individuated appearances of the English and Germans.[49]

As this last statement suggests, the dynamics of evolution created inequalities between races as well as within societies. Haeckel divided humanity into twelve species and thirty-six races on the basis of differences in speech and hair-type, which he regarded as the most reliable indices of race. These species and races could be arranged in a hierarchy according to their degree of proximity to the apes. The most primitive peoples were almost indistinguishable from the latter, eating wild fruit and living in herds containing no trace of marriage and family life which, to Haeckel, were the building blocks of civilisation. He

---

[47] *Ibid.*, 93, original emphasis.
[48] Bannister (*Social Darwinism*, 267) claims Haeckel made these statements tongue in cheek.
[49] Haeckel, *History of Creation*, I, 228, 232, 281.

affirmed that all 'woolly-haired' peoples 'are on the whole at a much lower stage of development, and more like apes' than straight-haired races. The former were 'incapable of a true inner culture and a higher mental development' even when they inhabited a civilised milieu like the USA. The Mediterranean species, in contrast, had always been the most physically and mentally advanced type, and, with the exception of the Mongolians, the only one with a history and a civilisation. The English and Germans were the best representatives of this species, and were laying the basis for a new era of even higher mental development.[50] His views on inequality were summed up as follows: 'The most primitive races, such as the Veddahs of Ceylon, or the Australian natives, are very little above the mental life of the anthropoid apes. From the highest savages we pass by a complete gradation of stages to the most civilised races. But what a gulf there is, even here, between the genius of a Goethe, a Darwin, or a Lamarck, and an ordinary philistine or a third-rate official.'[51]

Haeckel believed racial inequalities to be biologically determined, and he denied any possibility of reducing them through education or other 'artificial methods'. It was futile to try and civilise the lower races because the necessary precondition for human culture, 'the perfecting of the brain', had not taken place; any contact with civilisation accelerated their extinction rather than their improvement. Haeckel was adamant that all the inferior races 'will sooner or later completely succumb in the struggle for existence to the superiority of the Mediterranean races'.[52] While the Europeans were destined to spread across the globe, the lower races were doomed to perish. 'Even if these races were to propagate more abundantly than the white Europeans', proclaimed Haeckel, 'yet they would sooner or later succumb to the latter in the struggle for life.'[53]

The anti-egalitarian sentiments expressed in Haeckel's defence of Darwinism against the charge of socialism were not, therefore, off-the-cuff remarks but part of a system of beliefs about the unequal value of human beings brought about by the operation of biological laws. Closely connected to these beliefs were others that anticipated the eugenic programmes of some later Social Darwinists. Haeckel approved of the elimination of weak and sickly infants among the ancient Spartans and the American Indians, and lamented the preservation of inferior babies at the expense of strong and healthy children in modern states. He

---

[50] *Ibid.*, II, 303–10, 321–3, 332.
[51] Haeckel, *Last Words on Evolution: A Popular Retrospect and Summary*, tr. J. McCabe (London: Owen, 1906), 100–1.
[52] Haeckel, *History of Creation*, II, 363, 325.   [53] *Ibid.*, I, 256.

accused militarists of proposing to squander the best of the younger generation in needless wars, leaving the unfit and infirm safe at home to breed, thus perpetuating their disabilities and diluting the biological value of the population. This value was additionally under threat from medical practitioners who kept alive the chronically sick and insane long enough for them to reproduce, and by a judicial failure to make adequate use of the death penalty. The latter sanction was required not just in the interests of justice, but for 'weeding out' incorrigible criminals among the population. This weeding process eased the struggle for existence among 'the better portion of mankind' and prevented the transmission of criminality to the offspring of these 'degenerate outcasts'. He warned that these examples of 'artificial selection' were responsible for the currently poor mental and physical condition of most individuals and the scarcity of healthy and 'free and independent spirits'.[54]

In spite of these degenerative tendencies, Haeckel remained confident that their effects would ultimately be counteracted by the irresistible action of natural selection in maintaining and enhancing the progress of civilisation:

The result of the struggle for life is that, in the long run, that which is better, because more perfect, conquers that which is weaker and more imperfect. In human life, however, this struggle for life will ever become more and more of an intellectual struggle, not a struggle with weapons of murder. The organ which, above all others, in man becomes more perfect by the ennobling influence of natural selection is the *brain*. The man with the most perfect understanding, not the man with the best revolver, will in the long run be victorious; he will transmit to his descendants the qualities of the brain which assisted him in the victory. Thus then we may justly hope, in spite of all the efforts of the retrograde forces, that the progress of mankind towards freedom, and thus to the utmost perfection, will, by the happy influence of natural selection, become more and more certain.[55]

Haeckel's disparaging assessment of the intellectual capabilities of non-whites and his dismissal of their cultures, his attitude to the sick and the insane and his desire to weed out criminals, appear to lend credence to the thesis of his complicity in the elaboration of a proto-Nazi ideology. The fact is, as will become only too evident in subsequent chapters, these ideas were quite unexceptional by the standards of the time and were widespread throughout European and American society. We have already encountered similar notions in the work of Darwin, Spencer, Royer and Sumner, who were all liberals. Furthermore, Haeckel, like these thinkers, was equally ready to utilise Social Darwinism to attack established institutions and traditions as well as to uphold existing

[54] *Ibid.*, I, 170–1, 173–4, 172.   [55] *Ibid.*, I, 174, original emphasis.

conventions and values. He bemoaned the lack of biological and anthropological training among judges and politicians, which he held responsible for their numerous blunders and inadequacies. He derided the political and cultural pretensions of the hereditary nobility, whose inbreeding, aloofness and 'unnatural' education he despised. He was critical of conservative governments and political reactionaries in Germany who aligned themselves with repressive clerical forces in order to curtail the spread of science and enlightenment and stifle academic freedom.[56] Above all, Haeckel condemned the prevailing German educational system for its excessive focus on the classics and religious indoctrination at the expense of science. 'If the modern state gives every citizen a vote', reasoned Haeckel, 'it should also give him the means of developing his reason by a proper education, in order to make a rational use of his vote for the common weal.'[57]

What connected these disparate themes in Haeckel's discourse was their location within an allegedly scientific account of the world and of human nature. For him these political positions were matters of fact and reason, not of faith or utopian idealism. The main obstacles to the public recognition of this were the Church (especially the Roman Catholic Church) and Christianity in general. They represented rival systems of knowledge and thus were the prime targets of his polemical use of Social Darwinism. Haeckel insisted that all public issues were secondary to the question of the relationship between the state and organised religion: 'Whether a Monarchy or Republic be preferable, whether the constitution should be aristocratic or democratic, are subordinate questions in comparison with the supreme question: Shall the modern civilised state be spiritual or secular?'[58] It is worth exploring Haeckel's anti-clericalism in more detail, for it reveals the major ideological thrust of his writings and illuminates the role played by Social Darwinism in his arguments.

Haeckel pronounced an irreconcilable antagonism between science and religion: 'Where faith commences, science ends.'[59] This was because they reposed upon incompatible claims to knowledge; respectively, reason and revelation. Only knowledge of nature could constitute genuine revelation, and this was founded on rational, scientific methods. The obtuseness of religious authorities on the thesis of man's ape-like ancestry was typical of the way in which religion impeded scientific knowledge. In language reminiscent of that used by Huxley in his famous encounter with Bishop Wilberforce, Haeckel declared it prefer-

[56] Haeckel, *Riddle of the Universe*, 6–9; Haeckel, *History of Creation*, I, 181; Haeckel, *Last Words*, 102–3, 110.
[57] Haeckel, *Riddle of the Universe*, 372.   [58] *Ibid.*, 9.
[59] Haeckel, *History of Creation*, I, 9.

able to be the 'advanced offspring of a simian ancestor' who had evolved through struggle 'than the degenerate descendant of a god-like being, made from a clod, and fallen, for his sins, and an Eve created from one of his ribs'.[60] This led Haeckel into an often impassioned denunciation of religious influences in German culture. He despised what he saw as the narrow-mindedness and bigotry of German Catholicism and excoriated the 'eel-like sophistry' of the Jesuits in the belief that 'the charlatan of the Vatican is the deadly enemy of free science and free teaching'. The practices of priestly celibacy, confession and the sale of indulgences he stigmatised as immoral and/or prejudicial to family life. Haeckel's most intemperate invective, however, was directed against the Papacy, which he referred to as 'the greatest swindle the world has ever submitted to', while its doctrines were 'an unscrupulous tissue of lying and deceit' employed in the service of 'mental despotism and secular power'.[61]

Haeckel's objections to religion went beyond Catholicism to the fundamentals of Christianity itself. The truly valuable part of Christian teaching – the Golden Rule to love one's neighbour – was as old as civilisation and had its roots in the social practices of many animals. The same was also true of the kernel of Christianity adopted by monism, i.e. love, the equality of men before God, charitable conduct towards the poor and the wretched, all of which were 'merely higher evolutionary stages of the social instincts, which we find in all higher social animals...'[62] Other features of Christianity were totally objectionable. Its anthropocentrism encouraged a disdainful contempt towards the rest of nature, whereas Darwinism, by demonstrating man's links with the animals, taught us to regard the latter as our brothers, though Haeckel evidently did not wish to extend this fraternity to the 'lower' races. Christ reinforced the Asian undervaluation of women who were stigmatised as unclean, whereas in reality 'men and women are two different organisms, equal in worth, each having its characteristic virtues and defects'. Even the injunction to love one's neighbour was exaggerated by Christians to the detriment of egoism, a vital factor in self-preservation and creativity in the advance of civilisation. Its extension to one's enemies was downright unnatural, implying that the theft of a German colony by the English should be met by the renunciation of the remainder of Germany's overseas possessions.[63] Finally, to this catalogue of sins must be added the doctrine of the immortality of the soul.

[60] Haeckel, *Evolution of Man*, II, 742.
[61] Haeckel, *Last Words*, 43, 47, 106, 125; Haeckel, *Riddle of the Universe*, 333.
[62] Haeckel, *Riddle of the Universe*, 358–60, 359. See also Haeckel, *Freedom in Science*, 96.
[63] Haeckel, *Riddle of the Universe*, 361–6.

'Death puts an end, in man as in any other Vertebrate, to the physiological function of the cerebral neurone, the countless microscopic ganglionic cells, the collective activity of which is known as the "soul".'[64]

Convicted of so many egregious violations of the discoveries of evolutionary science, Christianity had to be replaced by a new religion: monism. This was pantheistic, upholding the existence of an impersonal God resident in every atom.[65] Haeckel often waxed lyrical on the religious dimension of monism: 'The will of God is at work in every falling drop of rain and every growing crystal, in the scent of the rose and the spirit of man.'[66] God and the world were one, since God was equivalent to nature or substance, which meant that, as far as Haeckel was concerned *'pantheism is the world system of the modern scientist'.*[67] Haeckel's professed scientific materialism was juxtaposed with a mystical adulation of nature derived from the influence of German *Naturphilosophie* on his thought.[68] But Haeckel quite plainly regarded monism and Christianity as competing belief-systems, equally comprehensive in scope but based upon incompatible knowledge claims, and Social Darwinism was central to his attempt to buttress the authority of the former and undermine that of the latter.

Haeckel's Social Darwinism, therefore, acted as a comprehensive framework within which the mysteries of nature and society could be investigated. Contemporary German society might be conflictual and fragmented, but political difficulties, like scientific problems, were resolvable through the application of reason and science and by the realisation of a philosophical project which revealed the interconnection of all these different areas and their governance by universal laws of nature.

Haeckel's personal political trajectory mirrored the development of German liberalism in general, which had lost its revolutionary and emancipatory character by the end of the nineteenth century and assumed a more stridently nationalist and authoritarian posture.[69] Notwithstanding his polemics against the establishment and Prussian militarism, Haeckel admired the authoritarian Bismarck as a 'great

---

[64] Haeckel, *Evolution of Man*, II, 578.   [65] Haeckel, *Le Monisme*, 34–5.
[66] Haeckel, *Last Words*, 112.
[67] Haeckel, *Riddle of the Universe*, 296, original emphasis.
[68] For the impact of *Naturphilosophie* on Haeckel, see Gasman, *Scientific Origins*, xvii–xx; Kelly, *Descent of Darwin*, 24, 28.
[69] There are excellent assessments of the influence and political direction of Haeckel's work in P. Corsi and P. Weindling, 'Darwinism in Germany, France and Italy', in Kohn, *Darwinian Heritage*, 685–98, and Weindling, *Health, Race and German Politics Between Unification and Nazism, 1870–1945* (Cambridge University Press, 1989), 40–8.

statesman'.[70] Becoming disillusioned with Germany's political leadership in his later years, he joined ultra-nationalist organisations such as
the Pan German League, which contributed to the political culture in
which National Socialism was spawned. As with German liberalism, too,
he upheld an organic rather than an atomistic conception of social
reality, believing that in complex systems the individual parts were, 'like
good citizens', subordinated to the welfare of the whole.[71] All of these
features of his thought are commensurable with the content and
development of liberalism in Germany, and it is to this context that
Haeckel should be assigned rather than some form of proto-Nazism.

Haeckel directed his polemical energies and rhetorical skills primarily
against the opponents of evolutionism, secularisation and scientific
freedom. At the same time, the significance of his views on inequality,
race and eugenics should not be minimised. Their importance does not
consist in their links with Nazism, but rather in their wide acceptance
among the European and American intelligentsia. Haeckel's denigration
of 'lower races', paupers, criminals and people suffering from congenital
mental and physical illness did not differ from the views expressed by
Royer and Spencer. All thinkers buttressed these opinions with Social
Darwinism: but Haeckel's views surely derived an added authenticity
from his status as a gifted and eminent naturalist.

Conclusion

It is now appropriate to make some general observations about the
pioneering examples examined in the last four chapters. First, all of the
theorists examined so far made selection, adaptation and heredity
fundamental processes in their accounts of social and psychological
change. Competition was the cause of adaptation and eliminated the
unfit. It occurred both within and between societies, in peaceful and
violent manifestations, although the majority of thinkers upheld an
evolution of struggle itself, from warfare to industrial competition or the
selection of ideas. This proved to be a troublesome concept, however,
with Sumner and Fiske equivocating over the future of warfare, and

---

[70] Haeckel, *Riddle of the Universe*, 342. See Gasman, *Scientific Origins*, 128. For an analysis
of the Pan German League and its relationship to the German right, see G. Eley,
Reshaping the German Right (London: Yale University Press, 1980); R. Chickering, *We
Men Who Feel Most German* (London: Allen and Unwin, 1984).

[71] Haeckel, *Freedom in Science*, 58. On this aspect of Haeckel's thought, see P. Weindling,
'Theories of the Cell State in Imperial Germany', in C. Webster, ed., *Biology, Medicine
and Society 1840–1940* (Cambridge University Press, 1981), 119. On the coexistence of
individualism and collectivism in German liberalism, see Weikart, 'The Origins of
Social Darwinism in Germany', 471.

Royer and Haeckel approving of bellicose relationships between races at different stages of evolution. The overwhelming tendency was to depict the struggle for existence as taking place between individuals *and* groups, although the German geologist Rolle focused almost exclusively on the latter, while Brace focused on the former. An important consequence of this treatment of competition was that social conflict (at least in certain guises) could be presented, not as a symptom of social instability and decline, but as the motor of progress.

Progress was a second salient feature of these pioneering efforts, although here Sumner would constitute an exception. This does not mean that these theorists were oblivious to the possibility of stagnation or even regression. Even Spencer, who is normally perceived as an unwavering apostle of progress, was fully aware of these possibilities.[72] With this qualification in mind, it is still true that evolution was on the whole progressive and humanity was the highest point of development. Regression was always possible and vigilance was required to ensure that the laws of nature were not infringed by ignorant politicians and reformers. In addition, even the most advanced societies contained survivals from previous evolutionary phases which were responsible for social pathologies. But all thinkers seemed confident that Western civilisation would continue to advance in the future.

A third facet of these pioneering theorists was their deterministic conception of natural law. None adopted Peirce's probabilistic representation of natural selection except James, and even he failed to do so consistently in his text on psychology. Dewey's characterisation of eighteenth-century social thought is thus equally applicable to the theories studied so far: 'Change was working on the side of man but only because of *fixed* laws which governed the changes that take place. There was hope in change just because the laws that govern it do not change. The locus of the immutable was shifted to scientific natural law ...'[73] This made for excellent rhetoric when attacking misguided policies but was inherently problematic, as we have seen, when a theorist came to make positive policy proposals, some of which implied the emancipation of humanity from the inexorability of natural laws.

Fourth, the theorists so far studied upheld biological reductionism to varying degrees. Culture certainly acted as an environment to which individuals must adapt, but usually successful adaptations became hereditary. This position possessed considerable rhetorical potential for

---

[72] R. Nye, 'Sociology and Degeneration: The Irony of Progress', in Chamberlin and Gilman, eds., *Degeneration*, 55–9.

[73] J. Dewey, 'Time and Individuality', in *John Dewey: The Essential Writings*, ed. D. Sidorsky (New York: Harper Torchbooks, 1977), 136, original emphasis.

the defence of inequalities or for denigrating attempts at social engineering, but encountered difficulties if the theorists wished to modify behaviour or institutions, which, since they were predominantly liberal in outlook, they sometimes wished to do. As we noted with Royer and her stance on the subordination of women, this required recourse to cultural rather than biological explanations. More generally, theorists elaborated a notion of 'social selection', describing social practices and values which had a selective impact upon members of society. Sometimes social selection worked in conjunction with its natural counterpart; more often it was perceived to run counter to the requirements of the 'natural order'. This argumentation was discernible in Darwin's *Descent* and was evident in the work of Spencer, Royer, Lombroso, Haeckel and Sumner and assumed considerable importance in later Social Darwinist theories, as we shall see. Social selection represents *social* processes which, particularly if opposed to the workings of natural selection, are very powerful. Their existence poses problems for biological determinism – how are they to be explained? – as well as to the health and potential survival of the societies in which they occur. Thus nature provided the social scientist with a means of explaining the structures and dynamics of social systems, but it also acted as a normative reference point, an ideal to be emulated, when these systems were threatened by 'unnatural' cultural forces.

Fifth, there emerges from Social Darwinist discourse a rather nebulous but ubiquitous category: the 'unfit'. It includes the indigent, the sick, criminals, the urban underclass and varying ethnic and racial groups. This category is not an artefact of Social Darwinism but derives from social and political values and prejudices that pre-exist the world view. Nor is the substitutability of these groups, i.e. the extent to which the description of one can be transferred to another, a product of Social Darwinism. Race, class and, as we shall see, sometimes gender as well, furnished a reservoir of interchangeable judgements, concepts and metaphors. What Social Darwinists did was locate these judgements, concepts and metaphors within an evolutionary continuum which explained, through selection and heredity, why the persons to whom they were applied were losers in the battle for life. In this way, not only the categorisation, but also the treatment of these persons was validated by science.

Sixth, the ideological orientation of pioneering Social Darwinism was overwhelmingly liberal when due consideration is given to the differing national connotations of this term.[74] Early European Social Darwinists,

---

[74] These connotations are explored in detail by Bellamy in *Liberalism and Modern Society*.

therefore, were never conservative in the sense that they were uncritical champions of the status quo. Like all liberals, they faced a double challenge from the entrenched forces of reaction and the reformist and sometimes revolutionary demands of the underprivileged. That is why their arguments sometimes appear as emancipatory (e.g. when opposing militarism, clericalism and aristocratic privilege), sometimes as conservative (e.g. when opposing welfare legislation). The United States lacked a feudal legacy and hence this Janus-faced aspect of liberalism is less evident there. But the liberal orientation of American Social Darwinists seems quite evident. Sumner, though a vociferous opponent of increased democratisation and welfare schemes, was an equally pungent critic of plutocracy and a supporter of trade unions. Brace, one of the earliest pioneers in the use of Social Darwinism, held progressive views on race and devoted his life to improving the conditions and educating the minds of the 'dangerous classes'. One major difference between European and American Social Darwinists, however, concerns religion. Spencer, Huxley, Büchner, Haeckel and Royer were ardently anti-clerical in sentiment, whereas Americans like Brace, Fiske and James perceived Darwinism and religion to be commensurable. A liberal disposition, then, provides no basis for inferring a thinker's position on specific issues: Spencer opposed imperialism, Royer endorsed colonial expansion.

The pioneers discussed so far disseminated the world view and explored some of its social implications. Their efforts are instructive because they highlight problems implicit in the world view which were to figure markedly in the subsequent history of Social Darwinism. But this history is one in which the world view was to be enlisted in other causes, some of which were antithetical to the liberal values endorsed by the majority of the pioneers.

Part III

Case studies

7   Reform Darwinism

Introduction

There is a sense in which many of the theorists discussed thus far could be regarded as 'reform Darwinists'. A. R. Wallace was a socialist; Lombroso, Brace, Haeckel, Royer and Büchner advocated considerable social and political change; and even Spencer and Sumner could be highly critical of contemporary values and institutions. With the extension of democracy during the nineteenth and early twentieth centuries, though, there came an intensification of debates over universal suffrage, equality, the emancipation of women, welfare provision and international fraternity. Darwinism was enlisted by protagonists on all sides of these debates: the concern of this chapter is with theorists supportive of socio-political change in the direction of greater equality, public welfare, and democracy. They ranged from Marxist revolution-aries through to democratic socialists and 'New Liberals' – all sharing a commitment to the use of state power in order to achieve their goals – but also included anarchists desirous of radical change but opposed to the state in any form.

The purpose of this examination is two-fold. The first is to argue that although there was a genre of reformist and socialist Darwinism, some of what has been subsumed under this label was actually opposed to Darwinism as defined in this study. The second aim is to explore the discursive limits of the world view. No matter how polysemous the elements of Social Darwinism were, their integration into a systematic whole acted as a constraint upon their appropriation by any and every ideological and theoretical enterprise. We have already encountered examples of how such constraints generated tensions within theories which presented peaceful cooperation as an ultimate social objective. The investigation of reform Darwinism allows for a richer analysis of such constraints and tensions.

Socialism and Darwinism

One association in need of clarification is the relationship between Darwinism and the theories of Marx and Engels. Karl Marx (1818–83) and Frederick Engels (1820–95) were both of the opinion that Darwin's theory of evolution was a major scientific achievement. In his speech at the graveside of Marx in 1883, Engels asserted: 'Just as Darwin discovered the law of development of organic nature, so Marx discovered the law of development of human history . . .'[1] This admiration aside, Marx and Engels did not perceive the struggle for existence replicated in social relations in the guise of class conflict. The remainder of Engels' graveside peroration made plain that the law of social development accredited to Marx was the latter's theory of the production of material necessities as the foundation of social relations, and the theory of surplus value as the 'law of motion' specific to the capitalist mode of production.[2]

The fathers of revolutionary socialism were acutely aware of the reality of the struggle for existence in contemporary society; but for Marx and Engels this struggle, far from being an inescapable feature of the human condition, was determined by socio-historical conditions. The capitalist mode of production generated competition which became intensified and universalised through the expansion of modern industry and the creation of world markets. Engels described this situation as 'the Darwinian struggle of the individual for existence transferred from Nature to society with intensified violence'.[3] But the prevalence and virulence of the struggle for life in capitalism was caused by the capitalist mode of production and would be transcended with the overthrow of capitalism and the establishment of socialism.

This raises an important point about the discursive limits of Social Darwinism. Resort to Darwinism would hardly constitute an acceptable methodological tactic for theorists who wished to construct a science of society with its own principles of explanation. Marx and Engels believed

---

[1]   K. Marx and F. Engels, *Selected Works* (London: Lawrence and Wishart, 1968), 435. Engels celebrated Darwin's achievements in biology on several occasions, e.g. 'Introduction' to *The Dialectics of Nature* (1875–6), in Marx and Engels, *Selected Works*, 350; *The Origin of the Family, Private Property and the State* (1884), *Selected Works*, 465; 'Ludwig Fuerbach and the End of Classical German Philosophy' (1886), *Selected Works*, 621.

[2]   For discussions of the relationship between Marx and Engels and Darwinism, see G. Runkle, 'Marxism and Charles Darwin', *Journal of Politics*, 23(1961), 108–26; Jones, *Social Darwinism*, 63–9. There is also a detailed discussion of Engels' later writings and their relation to Darwinism in Benton, 'Social Darwinism and Socialist Darwinism in Germany', 110–20.

[3]   Engels, *Socialism: Utopian and Scientific* (1880), *Selected Works*, 423.

their socialism was scientific, not because it borrowed the principles and explanations of the natural sciences, but because, like these sciences, it established general laws from the analysis of the relevant data. In human history the most important data consisted in the relationships of production and exchange arising from the necessity for people to provide the material conditions of their existence. The study of these relationships revealed the laws governing social change in general as well as those pertinent to specific modes of production.

Marxism expressed a world view very different to that of Social Darwinism. Both aspired to an explanation of their subject matter by general laws and rejected teleological and supernatural accounts, but Marx and Engels were adamant that the laws relevant to the animal and plant kingdoms were not pertinent to the study of human history. Social structures, social transformations and human nature itself had to be understood in the context of a materialist conception of social and historical reality.[4] Men made themselves, indirectly and – invariably – unconsciously, through the activities and relationships involved in producing their means of subsistence. From this 'first premise' of the 'materialist method' it followed that social phenomena were not to be explained as the effects of universal features of human nature, nor as the expression of biological laws. So Marx and Engels were implacably hostile to Malthus and his theory of population. For them, population increases could be accommodated by technological advances and enhanced productivity; any struggle for existence was the outcome of the exploitative class relationships characteristic of capitalism rather than the manifestation of some putative universal 'natural' law.

In addition to its methodological incompatibility with Social Darwinism, Marxism's vision of a future in which – with the socialisation of the means of production, the eradication of classes and the withering away of the state – social relationships would be more meaningfully and harmoniously constituted, was very much at odds with the proclamation of an ineluctable struggle for survival. Marx envisaged the possibility of the creation of abundance and an end to the crippling constraints on individual development imposed by the specialised division of labour. Contrary to the views of many Social Darwinists (and social evolutionists in general), Marx did not regard increasing specialisation as the concomitant of an expansion of individuation and autonomy, but as their nemesis. His speculations concerning the possibility of being shepherd, hunter and critic while not exclusively occupying any of these roles was a repudiation of the presumed correlation between specialisa-

---

[4] For an elucidation of this position, see K. Marx, *The German Ideology*, Part I (London: Lawrence and Wishart, 1970), 42.

tion and individual fulfilment. In its original formulation, Marxism, whether conceived as a method of inquiry or as a social and political ideology, was incommensurable with Social Darwinism.

However, as the history of Social Darwinism attests, originators of ideas are unable to control the careers of their theories, and Marxism was no exception in this respect. The theory itself contained a series of indeterminacies providing ample opportunity for the formulation of different, even antithetical, interpretations which, in turn, were translated into divergent political strategies. These included the viability of and necessity for proletarian revolution; the role of conscious human agency in historical change; and the nature and functions of the state in capitalism. Even theorists claiming the mantle of orthodoxy had ample scope for innovation; synthesising Marxism and Darwinism was one such possibility.

One of the most influential of these syntheses was produced by August Bebel (1840–1913), a founder of the German Social Democratic Party. His *Die Frau und der Sozialismus*, which argued in favour of sexual equality, first appeared in 1879 and had gone through fifty editions in several languages by 1911.[5] Bebel's position was that 'civilization is governed by immanent laws; and it is the task of the historian to discover these laws and under their guidance to shew how existing evils may be removed, and conditions brought into harmony with nature' (57). The laws in question were those of growth, heredity and adaptation (69). But though he endorsed Darwinism, Bebel was condemnatory of the manner in which this theory had been used by the bourgeoisie to legitimate anti-egalitarian and reactionary policies, insisting that 'Darwinism, like every real science, is eminently democratic ...' (127).

Bebel's response was to acknowledge both that the whole of nature was governed by the struggle for existence and that this struggle was currently fiercer than ever before in modern society, engulfing individuals, classes and the sexes (156). But he was adamant that this was the last great social struggle – one which would result in the realisation of socialism. He reasoned that the struggle for existence could not be automatically transferred to humanity because, unlike animals, people were capable of thought and reason. As they evolved they became increasingly influenced by rational considerations rather than by the blind struggle for existence in which the stronger organisms supplanted the weaker (127, 129, 253). With socialisation of the means of pro-

---

[5]   A. Bebel, *Woman in the Past, Present and Future* (London: Zwan, 1988). The original 1879 edition was followed by a new, improved edition in 1883. See the 'Introduction' to the 1988 edition by M. Donald, i; Benton, 'Social Darwinism', 98; Weindling, *Health, Race and German Politics*, 94.

duction, the end of exploitation and poverty, and the realisation of equality, human history would move on to a different plane in which conflict and the desire for dominance would be eradicated from human nature. The Malthusian thesis that struggle was endemic due to the ever-present threat of over-population Bebel dismissed as true for capitalism but not for socialism. The latter would be able to produce more efficiently and make productive use of the vast tracts of wilderness in the Americas and Africa (241, 248). Fecundity was regulated by social conditions, which for Bebel proved that 'relationships of supremacy, character and bodily peculiarities of individuals as well as of whole classes and nations depend primarily on the *physical conditions of existence, in other words, on the social and economic distribution of power*' (127, original emphasis). This environmentalist position was predicated on the action of the inheritance of acquired characters as the principal mechanism for producing and transmitting adaptive traits.

At the heart of Bebel's theory, however, there was an ambivalent attitude to nature. Although arguing that reflexivity and rationality separated humans from organic nature, rendering inadmissible the transfer of the laws regulating the latter realm to the sphere of human relations, Bebel sometimes advocated nature as a model for social relationships. In fact, part of Bebel's indictment of the bourgeois social and economic order was that it had deviated from the path of nature. The innate desires of both sexes were suppressed and distorted resulting in lunacy and suicide. 'Neither sex', he asserted, 'can overstep natural boundaries, as it would destroy its proper purpose in doing so ...' (122). Modern society was responsible for a contradiction between people as 'natural' and sexual beings on the one hand and their membership of society on the other, thereby creating social and psychological pathologies. It was because socialists looked to nature for their model of a healthy social order that their theories were genuinely scientific: 'Nature is everywhere our instructress, and if we abide by her teaching, the final victory must be ours' (264). Bebel's text thus contained a tension between the social and the biological, alternating between interpreting social relationships as culturally determined on the one hand, and seeing them as the outcome of the laws of struggle, adaptation and inheritance on the other. In addition, it contained an ambivalence over nature itself, vacillating between a vision of nature as something to be overcome *and* as a model to be emulated. These contradictory positions derived from Bebel's desire to integrate revolutionary, egalitarian socialism with the Social Darwinist world view, which required him to steer a difficult course between cultural and biological modes of explanation. Like liberals who anticipated a future in which cooperation and peace were the norm, socialists and other radicals encountered difficulties with universal laws of struggle and survival of the fittest when they attempted to specify their ideal socio-political systems. Hence the shift between biological and cultural explanations which marked the theory of Bebel and which we can expect to discern in other socialists and reformists.

This expectation is confirmed in the work of Enrico Ferri (1856–1929), an Italian criminologist and a deputy in the national parliament between 1886 and 1924. Ferri was originally a Radical, converting to socialism in 1893, although he subsequently supported Mussolini and flirted with Fascism.[6] In 1894 he published his influential *Socialism and Positive Science*,[7] in which he set himself the daunting task of synthesising Marx, Spencer and Darwin (xi).

Ferri was particularly concerned to refute the charge made by Haeckel and others that Darwinism was incommensurate with socialism. To do this he employed a number of arguments. First, he acknowledged innate inequalities between people (including 'natural' inequalities between the sexes) that could not be eradicated by social reform. The goal of socialism was to equalise the conditions and opportunities for all individuals and to prevent 'parasites' such as 'bankers and public speculators' from living off the efforts of others. But people varied in their capabilities, and socialists simply required that each should work according to his or her ability. He used a biological analogy to justify this: 'In the biological organism no living cell remains inactive, and it is only nourished by mutual exchanges in proportion to its work; in the social organism no individual ought to live without working, whatever may be the form of his work' (15).

Second, Ferri agreed with his opponents 'that the struggle for existence is a law inherent in humanity as in all living beings, although its forms are continually changing and though it gets weaker' (25). This proviso was crucial, for although the struggle 'tyrannically' regulated all organisms and was a 'law inseparable from life', among humans it was itself subject to an evolutionary transformation from its primitive violent form to one in which intellectual rather than physical force was decisive. 'The successive changes in the extent, or the ideals of the struggle for existence, are accompanied by a progressive mitigation of the methods of the struggle; violent and muscular at first, they become more and more peaceful and intellectual ...' (28). Despite occasional relapses, this process of amelioration would continue, although Ferri acknowl-

---

[6]   Pick, *Faces of Degeneration*, 145–7.
[7]   Originally published in Rome in 1894. The edition I have used was translated from the French edition of 1896 by E. Harvey (London: Independent Labour Party, 1905).

edged the continuation of the struggle for existence in some form, however attenuated, under socialism.

Third, while Ferri equated the struggle for existence with class struggles in societies, he drew attention to 'another law of natural and social Darwinism' – that of mutual cooperation and solidarity, which became 'progressively more efficacious in social evolution'. This was an argument often deployed in the service of social and political reform, and Ferri cited the work of one of its leading proponents, Peter Kropotkin, who will be considered below. Ferri's view was that the law of increasing social solidarity would become even more preponderant in social evolution with the collectivisation of property and the elimination of class exploitation and divisions (35–7).

Finally, Ferri insisted that 'fitness' was relative to the circumstances in which organisms were placed. In modern societies, those who survived did so in corrupted conditions which distorted the workings of natural selection. Ferri attacked the dysgenic consequences of military conscription and war as well as marriage conventions which enabled rich but degenerate women to secure husbands while poor but robust females had to choose between celibacy or prostitution. He criticised capitalism as an economic system favouring the unscrupulous while condemning the proletariat to debilitating working and living conditions. All this would be rectified by socialism:

In freeing society of all the corruptions with which an unbridled economic individualism pollutes it, socialism will necessarily correct the effects of natural and social selection. In a society physically and morally healthy, the best adapted, those who will consequently survive, will be healthy.

In the struggle for existence, victory will belong to him who possesses the greatest and most fruitful physical and moral energies (44).

Socialism, declared Ferri, would only abolish the evils of the current system, while preserving its real achievements in the arts, sciences and technology, and in the cultivation of personal liberty. Everything, in society as in nature, progressed through often imperceptible changes. When evolution reached a certain threshold, then a revolution took place which completed the process of transformation. Like Bernstein in Germany and the Fabians in Britain, Ferri advocated the gradual conquest of political power and the winning of concessions by the proletariat, so that a point would be reached when the final socialist 'revolution' would be bloodless (120–4, 134–5).

Ferri's difficulty in accommodating revolutionary praxis to the notion of the gradual processes of evolutionary change prompted him to opt for a reformist and democratic brand of socialism. But Ferri conceded a great deal to hereditarian thinking in his views on women, inequality and criminality, blurring the boundaries between sociological and biological explanations in a way which compromised the coherence of his theory of social change. For example, he defended the concept of the 'born criminal', arguing that while socialism would eliminate crimes caused by miserable social conditions and poverty, it would be unable to eradicate those deriving from the abnormal organic constitution of the criminal. Thus 'what will not disappear are outrages on chastity through sexual pathological inversion, murders committed by epileptics, robberies caused by psycho-pathological degeneracy, etc.' (33).[8] His debt to biological determinism was equally evident in the thesis that mutual aid and cooperation were laws of nature. As with Bebel, explanation shifted from biological to sociological causes and back again without any theoretical rationale for the change, although there was, of course, a transparent ideological reason for the shift. But Ferri's text attests to the hold of biological and hereditarian thinking on socialist intellectuals.

This hold is graphically illustrated by a very different synthesis of socialism and Darwinism undertaken by the German, Ludwig Woltmann (1871–1907), a holder of doctorates in philosophy and medicine and a Social Democratic Party activist during the 1890s.[9] Woltmann eschewed revolution in favour of the gradual evolution of socialism advocated by his compatriot Eduard Bernstein (1850–1932) in the latter's *Evolutionary Socialism* of 1899.[10] However, Woltmann was also convinced of the superiority of the Aryan race and started a journal, *Politische-Anthropologische Revue*, for the promulgation of racial theories. For him, anthropology demonstrated that the 'intellectual power of the white races is without doubt higher than that of all the other races'.[11] Because organic transformations took place over a very long period, the characteristics of the different races had remained unchanged throughout human history and pre-history.

Woltmann contended that the emergence of human culture had transformed the struggle for existence from one hitherto directed

---

[8]   These arguments were not uncommon among socialists of the period. See, for example, Lawrence Small, *Darwinism and Socialism* (London: Independent Labour Party, 1907/ 8). The author argued that the social and moral instincts had been fixed by natural selection, and proposed eugenics programmes to check the propagation of the diseased, deformed and criminal (12–13).

[9]   For details of Woltmann's background and political views, see Weindling, *Health, Race and German Politics*, 119–20, 129–30.

[10]   Although Bernstein was influenced by the British Fabians, several of whom embraced Social Darwinism, there is no evidence of Darwinism in this text, despite its title. See E. Bernstein, *Evolutionary Socialism* (New York: Shocken, 1961).

[11]   L. Woltmann, *Die Darwinische Theorie und der Sozialismus* (Düsseldorf: Michels, 1899), 305.

primarily against natural conditions and other creatures into a racial conflict over territory, food and power: 'New and more violent conflicts of interest arose in mankind's struggle amongst themselves. Races trampled on one another as if they were different species. The process of selection was repeated on a narrower but higher sphere of existence, in the struggle of man against man.'[12] Arguing that society itself was an organic entity, Woltmann attempted to convince German workers that they would benefit from national solidarity in the struggle for existence against other nations. In this context, socialism for Woltmann signified increased possibilities for technical and intellectual advance brought about through domestic cooperation. It entailed substituting conscious control and direction for the laws of fate and chance, emancipation from the superstitions and myths of religion, and a healthy enjoyment of work and earthly existence. This required a genuine harmonisation with 'Mother Nature', and hence, as with Bebel, nature afforded a model to be emulated by a healthy social organism: 'In this respect, socialism is a true return to nature.'[13]

In the race theory proposed by Woltmann, the extensiveness of evolutionary time was invoked as a justification for what amounted to a form of essentialism. Human nature varied in accordance with race, but racial characteristics remained unchanged for millennia and could be taken as fixed. For Woltmann, evolutionary time, far from problema-tising the idea of a fixed human nature, allowed for a differentiation of mankind into races, the various attributes of which were stable; having been formed very gradually they were refractory to any rapid transmuta-tions, save through miscegenation.

The British Fabians

In Britain, intellectuals associated with the Fabian Society played an important role in disseminating a socialism which eschewed violent change in favour of the gradual assumption of power through education, the ballot and administrative reform. Some historians discern a close connection between the Fabians, eugenics and Social Darwinism, while others, though acknowledging this connection, dispute its closeness and significance.[14] While a comprehensive investigation of this relationship

---

[12] *Ibid.*, 301.   [13] *Ibid.*, 397.

[14] 'Social Darwinism, eugenics and Fabianism could have been made for each other.' This is the verdict of Shaw in 'Eliminating the Yahoo', 43. In contrast, Searle, pointing to the environmentalism inherent in Fabianism, describes its relationship to eugenics as a flirtation. G. R. Searle, 'Eugenics and Class' in Webster, *Biology, Medicine and Society*, 231 and 240–2.

is beyond the scope of this study, it is possible to analyse the use of Social Darwinism by some Fabian theorists.

An important figure during the formative years of Fabianism was the philosopher David. G. Ritchie (1853–1903), who was a member of the Fabian Society from 1889 to 1893. His *Darwinism and Politics*,[15] published in 1889, sought to dissociate Darwinism from what Ritchie alleged was its monopoly by conservative apologists, while admitting that the language of natural selection did lend itself to the legitimation of *laissez-faire* and racial, sexual and class inequalities (12).

Ritchie endorsed an objective elucidation of the laws governing social relations, but argued that once established, these laws, being simply generalisation from experience, had no claims 'upon our reverence' (33). In his view, social evolution showed how conscious and deliberate adaptation among humans was analogous to the 'spontaneous variation' among animals and plants in the struggle for existence, although he appreciated the difficulty of deciding the boundaries between biological inheritance and cultural transmission in human affairs (40–1, 53). Ritchie described war as the 'primitive form of the struggle between races and nations' (29) but, *contra* Spencer, he designated economic competition as more primitive still, as 'only a phase of the oldest form of the struggle for existence – the struggle between individuals for subsistence, and that ... therefore belongs to a lower type than the struggles between organised communities, where a strict organisation mitigates the internal strife' (45).

Complementing this social evolution was another in which inherited instincts were gradually replaced by imitation and education in intelligent behaviour, facilitated by the greater size of the brain and the prolongation of infancy in humans. For Ritchie this showed human inheritance to be more a matter of moral and intellectual culture than of biology. His conclusion was:

From the fact that human societies, like natural organisms, grow and are not made, we have certainly to learn that every evil cannot be remedied in a day. But from the other, at least equally important fact, that human societies do not merely grow but are consciously altered by human effort, we have also to learn that every evil is not to be accepted as inevitable (68).

Ritchie applied this reasoning to a number of contemporary issues. He recognised a real danger of population growth outstripping food supplies and proposed birth control as a remedy. This measure would reduce excess population, especially among those who were currently going overseas with missionary and colonial zeal and enslaving, demoralising

[15] London: Swan Sonnenschein.

and destroying the 'lower races' (96–7). Fewer children would mean healthier children, but birth control was intimately linked to the position of women in society, and Ritchie was strongly in favour of equality for women and their full participation in political and economic life instead of their restriction to maternal and domestic roles (99). He rejected patriarchy and its rationalisation in terms of the presumed inferiority of women, which – assuming it to have any basis in fact at all – he believed would be eliminated in the course of evolution once equality was instigated (82). Like J. S. Mill before him, he argued that womanhood was largely a social construct, and concluded: 'It is hypocritical to deny the political capacity of women, simply because their political *in*capacity has through long centuries been so diligently cultivated . . . ' (86, original emphasis).

If these arguments hinted at a limited commitment to Social Darwinism, this impression was dispelled by a second edition.[16] In two additional chapters Ritchie attacked the claim by A. R. Wallace that natural selection was incapable of explaining the emergence and development of cognitive, moral and aesthetic properties. In doing so he clarified his views on the evolution of the struggle for existence: 'Natural selection operates in the highest types of human society as well as in the rest of the organic realm; but it passes into a higher form of itself, in which the conflict of ideas and institutions takes the place of the struggle for existence between individuals and races' (106). Thus struggle evolved from one between individuals to a conflict between aggregates of individuals in the form of races and nations, and then to the conflict of ideas. It was this progression which made socialism a realistic prospect and at the same time enabled Ritchie to reaffirm his allegiance to Social Darwinism: 'Progress comes only by struggle, though the struggle in its highest form may go on within the individual soul and may cause no death but the death of partial truths that have become errors and of customs that have outlived their use' (141). Moreover, as he had reminded his readers in the first edition, there was always one aspect of this struggle which could never be eliminated, i.e. 'the struggle *against* nature, including the blind forces of human passion' (100, original emphasis). With these arguments Ritchie both affirmed the importance of cultural and social conditions in human development, and retained the struggle for existence as the principle of change. This type of synthesis of Social Darwinism and socialism was to prove popular among the Fabians. However, as is apparent from Ritchie's thesis that social reforms would rapidly produce organic transformations in

[16] London: Swan Sonnenschein, 1891.

women, it was one which subordinated biological to sociological explanation to such a degree that the former was virtually eliminated as a factor in social change.

There is an equally discernible hesitancy over the respective roles of heredity and environment in the publications of Graham Wallas (1858–1932) who, in the application of Darwinism to the investigation of human nature, sought a means of strengthening democracy by providing the latter with a scientific foundation. Wallas, one of the original members of the Fabian Society, became disillusioned with the elitism and authoritarianism of some of its leaders, notably the Webbs.[17] For him, democracy was not simply a matter of environmental engineering, but involved active citizenship and the living of a 'good' life.

Wallas came to the conclusion that any vision of the good life must, in the manner of Aristotle, concern itself with the nature of those who were to live it, a concern he found to be lamentably absent in contemporary political thinking. The theories of human nature found in current – particularly liberal and utilitarian – discourses were woefully impoverished, with their over-intellectualised conceptions of people as rational, calculating, self-interested beings. The solution was to turn to scientific psychology for an understanding of human nature, and here Wallas believed Darwin had provided a critical direction with his investigations of human descent. Darwinism allowed for the possibility of an objective grasp of human psychology within a comparative framework that included animals; this would facilitate a more realistic basis for democratic theory and practice. As Wallas observed: 'Unless he is prepared to study undismayed the nature of man as evolution has for the moment left it, the reformer who is also a politician will find his life one of constant and cruel disillusion.'[18]

In his *Human Nature and Politics* (1908) and subsequent publications, Wallas sketched the main features of human psychology. In the slow course of evolution people had, through adaptation and selection, come to possess an inherited constitution which exhibited little variation from the Stone Age to the present day.[19] Of paramount importance were inherited predispositions, or instincts, the products of an interaction between individual and environment established through natural selection. Biologically speaking, human nature was, to all intents and

[17] Wallas contributed an essay on 'Property Under Socialism' to the *Fabian Essays* of 1889. For details of Wallas's break with the Fabians, see M. J. Wiener, *Between Two Worlds* (Oxford: Clarendon Press, 1971), 52–3; T. H. Qualter, *Graham Wallas and the Great Society* (London: Macmillan, 1980), chap. 2.

[18] G. Wallas, 'Darwinism and Social Motive' (1906), in Wallas, *Men and Ideas* (London: Allen and Unwin, 1940), 93.

[19] G. Wallas, *Human Nature in Politics*, third edn (London: Constable, 1927), 25.

purposes, fixed. Wallas was an anti-Lamarckian, believing that the results of personal experience and achievements, while they could modify the habits and proclivities of individuals (as was apparent even among animals), could not be inherited. Each new generation started 'not where their fathers left off, but where their fathers began'.[20] Furthermore, this instinctual apparatus was a very powerful factor in shaping a person's behaviour: 'Things that are nearer sense, nearer to our more ancient evolutionary past, produce a readier inference as well as a more compelling impulse.'[21] Wallas developed an analysis of the way in which images and symbols in election campaigns were used to appeal to this ancient instinctual apparatus, which included affection, inquisitiveness, self-preservation, competitiveness, fear and curiosity. Intelligence was also an inherited disposition, and it was to this that Wallas looked in order to guide personal conduct and social organisation. 'Thought', he argued, 'may be late in evolution, it may be deplorably weak in driving power, but without its guidance no man or organisation can find a safe path amid the vast impersonal complexities of the universe as we have learnt to see it.'[22] Although the different dispositions of the human psyche could be analysed separately, in actuality they were all part of a complex and interrelated whole: 'The mind of man is like a harp, all of whose strings throb together; so that emotion, impulse, inference, and the special kind of inference called reasoning, are often simultaneous and intermingled aspects of a single mental experience.'[23]

If human psychology was largely the product of natural selection, what role did the struggle for existence play in the modern world? Here Wallas was vague. He accused those believing that war and imperial conflict were manifestations of the struggle for survival of misunderstanding the doctrine of natural selection. Darwinism demonstrated that the human race was a biological whole, and that we should have 'love for that infinitely varying multitude'. It was a great 'intellectual tragedy' of the nineteenth century 'that the discovery of organic evolution, instead of stimulating such a general love of humanity, seemed at first to show that it was forever impossible'. Modern warfare was completely dysgenic in its consequences, and Wallas was convinced of the need to destroy the belief that progress was only possible through conflict between peoples.[24] He pointed out that individualists such as Spencer had once

---

[20] G. Wallas, *The Great Society* (New York: Macmillan, 1920), 8.
[21] Wallas, *Human Nature*, 106.   [22] Wallas, *Great Society*, 45.
[23] Wallas, *Human Nature*, 99.
[24] Wallas, *Human Nature*, 286–92; Wallas, *Great Society*, 164–5. Wallas, 'Comment on Dr Jack's Article "The Peacefulness of Being at War"', *Men and Ideas*, 96–8.

considered social progress to be possible only through a 'beneficent private war' within societies. This view had now been abandoned, and Wallas anticipated a similar rejection of the doctrine of inter-ethnic struggle:

The evolutionists of our own time tell us that the improvement of the biological inheritance of any community is to be hoped for, not from the encouragement of individual conflict, but from the stimulation of the higher social impulses under the guidance of the science of eugenics; and the emotional effect of this new conception is already seen in the almost complete disappearance from industrial politics of that unwillingly brutal 'individualism' which afflicted kindly English-men in the eighteen-sixties. An international science of eugenics might in the same way indicate that the various races should aim, not at exterminating each other, but at encouraging the improvement by each of its own racial type.[25]

Wallas apparently believed that eugenics should *replace* natural selection as the source of biological progress. But he was of the opinion that in the meantime much could be done to improve the environment. The need for this meliorism was intensified by the vast industrial and urban networks, with their international connections that together made up the modern Great Society. This Society was inconsistent with a mental apparatus developed ages ago. 'Why', asked Wallas, 'should we expect a social organisation to endure, which has been formed in a moment of time by human beings, whose bodies and minds are the result of age-long selection under far different conditions?'[26] Modern civilisation was threatened by war, by egoism and by the ignorance of the masses who were manipulated by ruthless entrepreneurs and politicians, one of the potential dangers inherent in representative democracy.[27] Yet unlike many of his contemporaries, Wallas did not turn his back on democracy. He believed in the power of reason and education to provide people with an understanding of their evolutionary heritage, and to appreciate the need to control their destinies by becoming enlightened and participatory citizens. He remained dedicated to attaining greater social equality, including female suffrage,[28] and propounded a vision of humanity in which he hoped that science would 'suggest a kinder pity for all the bewildered beings who hand on from generation to generation the torch of conscious life'.[29] While for Wallas evolution showed human nature had not changed for millennia and must be taken as fixed by the aspiring politician, he used this as a rationale for social reform and environmental meliorism rather than as an alibi for the status quo.

Yet the work of Wallas exhibited many of the difficulties already identified in the work of reform Darwinists. His notion of the human

[25] Wallas, *Human Nature*, 292–3.   [26] Wallas, *Great Society*, 8.   [27] *Ibid.*, 301–2.
[28] *Ibid.*, 345.   [29] Wallas, *Human Nature*, 296.

psyche as a complex of predispositions unaltered for millennia established the parameters of social and political action. However, Wallas never really confronted the limits heredity posed to the efficacy of educational and social reform. That he believed in the existence of such limits is evident from his assertion that: 'If, indeed, a man's "nurture" has not corresponded to his "nature", the possibility of anything like complete Happiness may have been destroyed for him before he is thirty.'[30] But the implications of this strong hereditarianism for the programmes he endorsed were unexplored. Wallas did not analyse the ways in which deeply seated impulses and instincts could be repressed or moderated or redirected by cultural processes in order to achieve harmony between an individual's nature and his or her milieu. Nor did he perceive the threats to individuality and liberty inherent in such efforts, or in eugenics, and could even propose 'deliberately placing the males and females of hopelessly backward tribes on different islands' in order to prevent their propagation.[31] Throughout his writings there is an unresolved tension between the project of grounding a scientific psychology in Darwinian principles and the desire to employ this psychology in the service of democracy and social equality. This results in a contradiction between, on the one hand, his view that individuals were governed by natural forces, and on the other, his strong commitment to rationally informed voluntarist political action.

Some Fabians did not shrink from the authoritarian implications of eugenics programmes. In 1889 the Fabians published an important and influential statement of the movement's ideas and aims in the form of a collection of essays which went to five editions by 1948.[32] A dominant theme was evolution, both of society in general and of socialism in particular, one which was especially pronounced in the contribution by Sidney Webb (1859–1947). Webb underlined the organic nature of society and the duty of individuals to work for the continuation of the community. Individual actions inimical to collective welfare 'must sooner or later be checked by the whole, lest the whole perish through the error of its member' (53). The rationale for the priority of collective over individual needs was a Social Darwinist one: 'We know now that in natural selection at the stage of development where the existence of civilised mankind is at stake, the units selected from are not individuals, but societies' (53). Among animals, physical strength or agility were the selected attributes; among men it was cerebral power which, at a certain stage of development, was in turn superseded by social organisation. Webb concluded that man must use his sociological knowledge to

---

[30] Wallas, *Great Society*, 362.   [31] Wallas, *Human Nature*, 294.
[32] G. B. Shaw, ed., *Fabian Essays* (London: Allen and Unwin, 1948).

achieve mastery over his destiny by consciously adapting to these new conditions, and he made it quite clear that the claims of the individual were very much secondary to those of the social organism:

If we desire to hand on to the afterworld our direct influence, and not merely the memory of our existence, we must take even more care to improve the social organism of which we form part, than to perfect our own individual development. Or rather, the perfect and fitting development of each individual is not necessarily the utmost and highest cultivation of his own personality, but the filling, in the best possible way, of his humble function in the great social machine (54).

This entailed the eradication of individualistic competition within the community, 'for the free struggle for existence among ourselves menaces our survival as a healthy and permanent social organism'. Conscious control and coordination of the various parts of the social system were now necessary, and this was the reason for what Webb perceived as an 'irresistible glide into collectivist Socialism' (56). These themes were to remain integral to Webb's brand of elitist and technocratic socialism, including a commitment to eugenics and the elimination of undesirable elements in the population, all in the cause of national efficiency. These policies were linked to reforms in public administration, health, education, housing and employment in order to produce a healthy and vigorous population capable of responding to the challenges of the modern world. Social Darwinism enabled Webb to connect domestic reform to national efficiency in the service of imperialism, for he, like some other Fabians, was obsessed with the ability of Britain to survive in the competitive struggle with other powers for colonies, markets and raw materials.[33]

Were Fabianism and Social Darwinism, then, always so closely entwined? Examination of the texts of other Fabians reveals this not to be so. The playwright George Bernard Shaw (1856–1950) is a case in point. He was a self-avowed evolutionist and 'neo-biologist', but he was a pungent critic of Darwinism, which he believed to be fundamentally in error because of its explanatory reliance on blind, objective forces. 'There is', he observed of Darwinism in the Preface to his play *Back to Methuselah*,[34] 'a hideous fatalism about it ...' (xl). Improvement was possible only 'through some senseless accident' (xvi), while every act of

---

[33] See Olivier's contribution on moral evolution in the same collection of essays. The author (who was governor of Jamaica 1907–13) wrote of societies perishing 'as societies organically weak among stronger competitors have done and will do' (102). For an early Fabian statement of the problem of Britain's survival as a great power see G. B. Shaw, ed., *Fabianism and the Empire: A Manifesto of the Fabian Society* (London: Grant Richards, 1900), especially 3–4.

[34] London: Constable, 1931.

pity or fellowship was interpreted as 'a vain and mischievous attempt to lessen the severity of the struggle and preserve inferior varieties from the efforts of Nature to weed them out' (li).

Shaw described his own theory of evolution as Lamarckian, although this designation is of questionable accuracy. He called it a 'new vitalism' and 'creative evolution', stressing the role of will and striving in producing novel evolutionary forms. Lamarck had realised how 'living organisms changed because they wanted to'. There was no question of the survival of the fittest, but the acquisition of new habits through volition and effort (xxii–xxiii). Shaw was convinced that the 'will to power', the desire to achieve, was the driving force of evolutionary change (lii): 'If you can turn a pedestrian into a cyclist, and a cyclist into a pianist or a violinist, without the intervention of Circumstantial Selection, you can turn an amoeba into a man, or a man into a superman, without it' (xxii).

This 'Lamarckism' did not prevent Shaw from supporting eugenics or the reduction in the numbers of the unfit through birth control, for he believed that certain categories of the unfit owed their situations to hereditary defects rather than to social circumstances. In his retrospective 'Sixty Years of Fabianism',[35] Shaw wrote: 'There are in our asylums idiots whose existence is a horror, lumps of flesh barely capable of breathing and swallowing; and we waste human lives in enabling these half-created things to live instead of sensibly and mercifully killing them' (225). The same fate was advocated for 'incurably mischievous criminals'. 'If criminals can be reformed, reform them', advised Shaw, adding that we should discover how this could be achieved through scientific psychology. 'Meanwhile they should not be punished: they cannot help being what they are. But they should be painlessly liquidated, not caged' (227–8). He also proposed a 'democratic aristocracy' in which the people would choose their leaders from the 'naturally qualified five per cent' of the population, the 'born managers, statesmen, artists and philosophers' supplied by Nature, 'guaranteed and empanelled as such by the best available anthropometric methods' (221, 223–4).

In his focus on conscious needs and volitions in bringing about evolutionary change, Shaw not only misunderstood Lamarck, but advocated a version of evolutionism and eugenics that clearly was not Social Darwinist. Shaw shared some of the ideological preoccupations of the Webbs, including their hereditarian and authoritarian attitudes to the 'unfit'. But he totally rejected the notion of the struggle for survival, especially between members of the same species, as a mechanism for

---

[35] Published in the 1948 edition of *Fabian Essays*.

evolutionary progress. Thus the relationship between Social Darwinism and Fabianism was a complex one defying any straightforward general-isation. In the case of Webb, Ritchie and Graham Wallas the relationship was close and the world view undoubtedly furnished the scaffolding for their political ideals and policy proposals. It must be recognised, though, that these proposals varied considerably between, for instance, those of the technocratic and elitist Webb and the much more democratic Ritchie and Wallas. In the case of Shaw, the connection was absent, while in some other one-time Fabians it was highly complex.[36]

Liberty, equality and democracy

The appalling conditions created by industrialisation and urbanisation, coupled with the growing political demands of the masses, generated heated controversies over whether personal welfare was the responsibility of the individual or of the community. Some liberals, like Spencer and Sumner, continued to believe that this responsibility was entirely an individual matter; others came to accept the case for public intervention on behalf of people who were unable to fend for themselves.

An influential advocate of the second position was one of the original standard-bearers of Darwinism, T. H. Huxley, whose later writings took up the question of the moral implications of the struggle for existence.[37] There is a long-standing tradition in Darwinian historiography of taking Huxley at his word when he declared the discontinuity between the spheres of nature and ethics.[38] In fact, nothing could be further from the reality of Huxley's own writings on ethics.

Huxley argued that the struggle for existence was a 'cosmic process', but social life, while part of nature in the broad sense of this expression,

---

[36] For example, H. G. Wells (1866–1946). Wells has been linked with Social Darwinism and eugenics by Shaw, 'Eliminating the Yahoo'; Carey, *The Intellectuals and the Masses*, chaps. 6, 7; M. Coren, *The Invisible Man* (London: Bloomsbury, 1993). However, Wells' relationship to Social Darwinism was complex (a point recognised in Carey's study), as demonstrated by Bellomy, ' "Social Darwinism" Revisited', 81–5.

[37] T. H. Huxley, 'The Struggle for Existence: A Programme', *The Nineteenth Century*, 23(1888), 161–80; Huxley, *Evolution and Ethics* (London: Macmillan, 1893). Although Huxley has the reputation of being Darwin's bulldog it is noteworthy that his early interventions on behalf of Darwinism avoided mention of selection and struggle. Cf. Huxley, *Man's Place in Nature and Other Essays* [1863] (London: Dent, 1906). For a detailed study of Huxley's scientific and political positions, see di Gregorio, *Huxley's Place in Natural Science*.

[38] For an example of this interpretation, see D. Raphael, 'Darwinism and Ethics', in Barnett, *A Century of Darwinism*, 347. Other instances are cited in Helfand, 'T. H. Huxley's "Evolution and Ethics": The Politics of Evolution and the Evolution of Politics', 159, note 1. This interpretation still persists: see Boucher, 'Evolution and Politics', 94; Bowler, *Evolution*, 230–1; Ruse, *Darwinism Defended*, 267–8.

differed from other aspects of nature in that it was created by man. Social life gradually evolved an 'ethical man' opposed to 'natural man' because the former lived at peace with his neighbours, thereby circumscribing the struggle for existence. Because of the discrepancy between population growth and resources, however, this struggle reappeared in the industrial and commercial relations between nations. Huxley insisted that 'so long as the natural man increases and multiplies without restraint, so long will peace and industry not only permit, but they will necessitate, a struggle for existence as sharp as any that ever went on under the *régime* of war'.[39]

Huxley, however, was perturbed by the urban poverty and squalor accompanying industrial competition. He advocated the provision of urban amenities and leisure facilities and in particular a programme of public education, as methods both of ensuring social stability and increasing competitiveness in international markets: 'Under such circumstances an education rate is, in fact, a war tax, levied for the purposes of defence.'[40] He acknowledged that raising the incomes of working people would make the nation's goods more expensive and less competitive. But he rather lamely side-stepped this problem by asserting that a stable society composed of healthy and vigorous persons would be unlikely 'to be troubled with many competitors of the same character, and they may be safely trusted to find ways of holding their own'.[41]

Far from constituting a refutation of Social Darwinism as is sometimes claimed, these arguments were an attempt to enlist the world view in a political cause, one equally opposed to the radical individualism of Spencer and the socialism of Wallace and other reformers.[42] In this attempt Huxley fluctuated between claiming social relations were outside of the struggle for existence, and placing them under the governance of this law due to the pressure of population on food supplies. Thus sometimes morality was seen as a triumph over nature, (of 'ethical man' over 'natural man'), and at others as part of nature, as when he discerned a rudimentary 'ethical process' in the social systems of birds and animals which formed the starting point for moral evolution.[43] Even here, Huxley was ambivalent over the implications of this evolution. On the one hand this was a story of moral progress in which concern for others was nurtured and developed, while on the other Huxley warned his audience that retrogression was as likely as progression, and that human nature could be changed only on condition that we 'cast aside the notion that the escape from pain and sorrow is the

[39] Huxley, 'Struggle for Existence', 168.   [40] *Ibid.*, 177.   [41] *Ibid.*, 172.
[42] Helfand, 'T. H. Huxley's "Evolution and Ethics"'.
[43] Huxley, *Evolution and Ethics*, 56–7.

proper object of life'.[44] This ambivalence should not be read as symptomatic of confusion on Huxley's part, for it has already been encountered at the very heart of other reform-oriented uses of Darwinism, with their fluctuating images of nature as model and threat.

Huxley tried to show that the struggle for existence between nations made necessary the provision of some publicly funded welfare. The critic, journalist and historian of ideas, Leslie Stephen (1832–1904) drew the opposite conclusion from this struggle. Stephen had produced a book on the 'science of ethics' which was heavily influenced by Darwin.[45] Like Spencer, he attempted to synthesise utilitarianism with evolutionary theory,[46] which in this instance resulted in a radical revision of classical utilitarianism. Stephen argued that society was not an aggregate of individuals but an 'organic growth' governed by the same laws of nature as those regulating the development of natural organisms, i.e. adaptation through a struggle for existence induced by the pressure of population on resources (118, 120–1, 165). There was, however, one very important difference between animal and human evolution in that adaptive changes in the latter consisted of *social* transformations rather than modifications to the individual. Moral evolution reflected this fact. The growth of reason facilitated a recognition of the distinction between *morality* – 'the sum of the preservative instincts of a society' devoted to its collective welfare – and *prudence*, which was confined to the welfare of the individual (208). Progress entailed the triumph of morality over prudence as individuals gradually became capable of preferring the good of society to their own happiness. Hence collective utility was not equivalent to the sum of individual utilities because the two could be antagonistic. When they were, collective welfare had priority over individual welfare.

In an essay on 'Ethics and the Struggle for Existence', Stephen enlisted his theory of moral evolution to attack redistributive welfare schemes, including those proposed by Huxley.[47] Such schemes undermined the sense of social obligation which for Stephen was the hallmark of ethical progress: 'A system which should equalise the advantages of the energetic and the helpless would begin by demoralising, and would very soon lead to an unprecedented intensification of the struggle for

---

[44] Huxley, 'Struggle for Existence', 163; Huxley, *Evolution and Ethics*, 27.

[45] L. Stephen, *The Science of Ethics* [1882] (London: Murray, 1907). For an account of Stephen and his work, see L. Annan, *Leslie Stephen: The Godless Victorian*, revised edn (London: Weidenfeld and Nicolson, 1984).

[46] For Spencer's synthesis of evolution and utilitarianism, see D. Weinstein, 'Equal Freedom, Rights and Utility in Spencer's Moral Philosophy', *History of Political Thought*, 11(1990), 119–42.

[47] L. Stephen, 'Ethics and the Struggle for Existence', *Contemporary Review*, 64(1893).

existence' (170). Additionally, these schemes ignored the inevitability of the struggle for survival. Stephen did envisage a future society in which self-interested motives had completely disappeared and where 'every man worked for the good of society as energetically as for his own'. 'That day is probably distant, but even upon that hypothesis the struggle for existence would still be with us, and there would be the same necessity for preserving the fittest and suppressing, as gently as might be, those who were unfit' (170). This was because the struggle derived from the pressure of population upon the finite resources of the earth and hence could never be transcended, no matter how humanised a form it took. Thus although they drew politically antagonistic conclusions from Darwinism, both Huxley and Stephen wished to present human evolution as a story of moral progress, while remaining haunted by the implications of the naturalistic process that had made this evolution possible – selection. This conundrum is also in evidence in the work of the next theorist to be examined.

Benjamin Kidd (1858–1916) was a clerk and autodidact who achieved fame with the publication of *Social Evolution*.[48] Even more so than Huxley, Kidd was supportive of the New Liberalism and welcomed the coming to power of the masses, 'gradually emerging from the long silence of social and political serfdom' (10). Though hostile to socialism, Kidd believed that equality of opportunity, state welfare, democracy and the emancipation of women were engraved in the process of evolution.[49]

Kidd was convinced that Darwinism provided an opportunity 'for the biologist to advance over the frontier and carry the methods of his science boldly into human society' (28). Weismann's theory of the germ-plasm conclusively demonstrated that the only way for progress to occur was through the inheritance of 'congenital variations' above the average for the race as a whole, and the elimination through competition of those variations below this average. The battle for life was indispensable to this process: all organisms reproduced at a rate above that supportable by present resources, and without competition specimens below the norm for the species would multiply and obliterate the superior organisms. In being subject to this law, man demonstrated its cosmic necessity (18).

Early humans – like modern 'savages' – engaged in 'ceaseless armed struggle' and lived in societies organised along military lines. Among the

[48] London: Macmillan, 1894. Kidd's Social Darwinism has sometimes been misconstrued. See C. Brinton, *English Political Thought in the Nineteenth Century* (London: Benn, 1933), 6, where Kidd is associated with the racist theories of Ammon and Lapouge. For Kidd's repudiation of racism and nationalism, see Crook, *Benjamin Kidd*, 66, 24.
[49] Crook, *Benjamin Kidd*, 318.

most advanced nations this type had been replaced by an industrial mode of organisation. This transformation was neither complete nor inevitable: the vast majority of societies were either eliminated by rivals or became arrested at a certain point in their development. Those that did reach the industrial phase were engaged in two forms of competition. The first of these was external, i.e. with other nations, for markets and resources. According to Kidd, nations exhibiting the greatest degree of 'social efficiency' triumphed in this struggle, and this in turn depended upon whether a nation was inhabited by a race with the requisite qualities. These had nothing to do with intellectual capabilities, skin colour or descent, but comprised 'strength and energy of character, humanity, probity and integrity, and simple-minded devotion to conceptions of duty ... ' (325). It was the Anglo-Saxon race, particularly as represented by the English-speaking peoples, which best exemplified these traits, which explained its international pre-eminence.

Of equal evolutionary importance was a second mode of struggle occurring within nations. Although non-violent, consisting of competition for jobs, rewards and status, it was absolutely crucial to the maintenance of social efficiency and the virility and energy of the citizenry. The political emancipation of the masses played an important part in enhancing this rivalry by allowing a larger proportion of the population to participate in the struggle, thereby intensifying it and augmenting efficiency. Political liberty and its associated stress on personal obligation had transported this form of the struggle for existence to every aspect of social life in the advanced societies of Western civilisation: 'In our families, our homes, our pleasures, in the supreme moments of our lives, how to obtain success or to avoid failure for ourselves, or for those nearest to us, is a question of the first importance' (53).

Kidd regarded current proposals for an eight-hour working day, graduated taxation, revision of the right to inherit wealth, and state provision of education, as indicative of this emancipation. This was not socialism, because equalising opportunities allowed working people to compete more effectively and hence drew more people into the struggle for existence (234, 238). This was why the democratisation of society should be applauded rather than deplored, and why there was nothing to fear from the emergent political power of the masses (10).

Despite this optimism, Kidd felt that Western civilisation had reached an important evolutionary threshold because threats to future progress would not come from rival races but from *within* the advanced nations as a result of their own evolutionary dynamics. Humans brought to the drama of evolution two attributes: reason and social organisation. Both had evolved to the point where they were potentially antagonistic. The progress of intellectual ability was an individualising process: the growth of reason encouraged the cultivation of individual personality and the expression of self-interest. The increase in social efficiency, however, might entail the sacrifice of personal interests for the good of society as a whole. Utilitarianism and other ethical systems which believed that individual and collective interests could be spontaneously harmonised were profoundly wrong, as was any attempt to secure a scientific, naturalistic foundation for personal morality (80, 290).

This was why increasingly large numbers of working people were attracted to socialism. The goal of socialism was 'the final suspension of that personal struggle for existence which has been waged, not only from the beginning of society, but, in one form or another, from the beginning of life' (207–8). From the standpoint of rational self-interest, it was irrational to sacrifice present personal well-being to the welfare of unborn generations: in this sense, socialist doctrines were 'unanswerable' (209). The problem was that from the wider perspective of evolution, the suspension of internal rivalry would be disastrous for the nation, eventually resulting in the atrophy of the traits responsible for social efficiency, and producing degeneration. Nobody worked hard, achieved or innovated unless compelled to do so by circumstances. If, then, a people restricted population increase and eliminated the stress of competition and selection, 'they would indubitably receive short shrift when confronted with the vigorous and aggressive life of societies where, other things being equal, selection and the stress and rivalry of existence were still continued' (210).

For Kidd, the contending doctrines of individualism and socialism were equally unrealistic as responses to 'the complex rivalry of life' (327). His solution was to point to the growth of altruism complementing the expansion of self-interest and individualism, as manifested in public welfare programmes, the widespread concern with injustice and suffering, and the benign treatment accorded to the natives of India and Egypt by the British. These activities were not attributable to the development of enlightenment and intelligence, which were individuating traits. Rather, they were consequential upon 'the immense fund of altruistic feeling with which our Western societies have become equipped ... ' (165). This feeling was, in turn, a product of religion. Kidd disagreed with the condemnation of religion as a mere anachronism, a survival from more primitive and less rational stages of evolution. He argued that all religions, from those of the most primitive to those of the most advanced societies, furnished a rationale for socially significant conduct by endowing the relevant actions with moral approbation. 'A religion', maintained Kidd, 'is a form of belief providing an ultra-rational sanction for that large class of conduct in the individual where his interest and the interest of the social organism are antagonistic, and by which the former are rendered subordinate to the latter in the general interests of the evolution which the race is undergoing' (103). In this way religion made available something which could not be established by reason – a 'super-rational' sanction for actions which might require the sacrifice of personal to collective interests. Hence religious sentiments afforded an essential complement to reason. They would be selected by the pressure of competition because they gave an advantage to nations possessing large numbers of people prepared to subordinate the present interests of the individual to the future interests of society. 'Natural selection seems, in short, to be steadily evolving in the race that type of character upon which these forces act most readily and efficiently; that is to say, it is evolving religious character in the first instance, and intellectual character only as a secondary product in association with it' (286).

Like Stephen and Huxley, Kidd denied the possibility of deriving moral imperatives from the workings of evolution, even though the cogency of his defence of religion depended upon its alleged foundations in an inexorable growth of altruism in the West. As with Wallas and other reformers, his writings reflect a tension between the ambition of uncovering the laws of social change and the desire to promote voluntarist political action. A similar tension dogs his reliance upon a non-rational mechanism – religion – to underpin a rationalist position that counselled both political intervention, and forbearance in not taking this intervention beyond certain limits. Small wonder, then, that in his later publications Kidd came to regard evolution as a purposive rather than a random process and to believe that man, through reason and ethics, could transcend his origins and place evolution on a new footing. Indeed, by the end of his life, Kidd indicted Darwinism as one of the forces responsible for threatening the breakdown of Western civilisation.[50]

The theories discussed above possess a number of common themes. The first is the moral priority of collective over individual welfare. The second is the interest in altruism and the difficulty of accommodating it to strict selectionism. The third is the representation of evolutionary dynamics – whether biological or social – as determinist and inexorable. This last feature paves the way for another, the attempt to derive ethical lessons from the putative course of social and moral evolution or even

---

[50] *Ibid.*, 116, 146, 342–3, 350–1.

directly from nature. The overt denial of the legitimacy of such derivations usually constituted the prolegomena to the construction of a moral ontology, as we saw with Huxley, Stephen and Kidd.

The interpretation of Darwinism by the American philosopher, John Dewey, offers a sharp contrast to these theories. Though explicitly interested in Darwinism,[51] Dewey would probably not be regarded as a Social Darwinist by most commentators. In my view he was, and even in texts where his Darwinism was not particularly salient it provided a set of crucial background assumptions. Since Dewey's understanding of Darwinism differed in important respects from that of most of his contemporaries, it is interesting to explore the moral and political conclusions he derived from it.

Dewey proposed that 'the evolution of living and thinking beings out of a state of things in which life and thought were not found is a fact which must be recognised in any metaphysical inquiry into the irreducible traits of the world. For evolution appears to be just one of those traits.'[52] Dewey accepted the Darwinian account of evolution through selection of adaptive variations in the struggle for existence, but he departed from conventional representations of Darwinism in a number of ways.

First, following Peirce, Dewey perceived the law of natural selection to be statistical in form and thus incapable of making statements about individuals. Hence: 'Laws do not "govern" the activity of individuals. They are a formulation of the frequency distributions of the behaviour of large number [sic] of individuals engaged in interactions with one another.'[53] Second, nature was variable, changing, the site of accident and the unforeseen. The implication of this was that:

It is the fate of a living creature ... that it cannot secure what belongs to it without an adventure in a world that as a whole it does not own and to which it has no native title. Whenever the organic impulse exceeds the limit of the body, it finds itself in a strange world and commits in some measure the fortune of the self to external circumstance.[54]

This notion of the 'fortune of the self' was a central feature of Dewey's thinking about human existence. 'Man', he wrote, 'lives in an aleatory world; his existence involves, to put it baldly, a gamble. The world is a scene of risk; it is uncertain, unstable, uncannily unstable. Its dangers are irregular, inconstant, not to be counted upon as to their times and seasons. Although persistent, they are sporadic, episodic.'[55]

---

[51] There is an illuminating analysis of Dewey's interest in Darwinism in David Sidorsky's 'Introduction' to *John Dewey: The Essential Writings*, xx–xxviii.
[52] Dewey, *John Dewey: The Essential Writings*, 109.   [53] *Ibid.*, 143.
[54] *Ibid.*, 267.
[55] Dewey, *Experience and Nature* [1925] (La Salle, IL: Open Court, 1971), 38.

Third, Dewey was adamant that morals must commence with the recognition that humans were part of nature, thereby linking 'ethics with physics and biology'.[56] Plainly, Dewey believed that the study of nature was a foundation for ethics. But because he perceived nature as a realm of change and chance as well as uniformity and necessity, he concluded that human nature was not fixed. In fact, human instincts were alterable whereas social institutions and practices were invariably resistant to change.[57] What interested Dewey, then, was not the persistence of some human essence through time, but the interactions between a changing human nature on the one hand, and social values and practices on the other.

Human existence – as with all organic life – took place within an environment which could be favourable or unfavourable to life activities. Humans were therefore obliged to struggle in order to enlist the support of the environment and effect changes to it.[58] Any interactive equilibrium between organism and environment was inclined to be short-lived on account of the changes emanating from the latter. Furthermore, these changes were:

so opposed in direction that we must choose. We must take the risk of casting in our lot with one movement or the other. Nothing can eliminate all risk, all adventure; the one thing doomed to failure is to try to keep even with the whole environment at once – that is to say, to maintain the happy moment when all things go our way.[59]

Knowledge played a fundamental role in this process by assisting individuals to cope with the crises of life and to adapt to change. But for knowledge to be instrumental required creative rather than routine intelligence, an ability which Dewey insisted was available to all people and 'not an aesthetic appreciation carried on by a refined class or a capitalistic possession of a few learned specialists, whether men of science or of philosophy'.[60]

Dewey was highly critical of *laissez-faire* individualism for identifying liberty with the actions of the entrepreneur, and was also aware of the ways in which Darwinism had been used to justify these and other exploitative actions.[61] He advocated instead 'humane liberalism', committed to radical reform of the prevailing social system and its inequalities, though a reform which was achieved democratically and not through coercion. This required the acceptance of two principles. The first was that individuality is 'nothing fixed, given, ready-made', but an achievement made possible by and through social institutions and

---

[56] Dewey, *Human Nature and Conduct* (London: Allen and Unwin, 1922), 12.
[57] *Ibid.*, 106–9.   [58] Dewey, *Essential Writings*, 72.   [59] *Ibid.*, 73.
[60] *Ibid.*, 93.   [61] *Ibid.*, 200; Dewey, *Human Nature*, 301.

interactions.[62] The second was that of 'historic relativity', i.e. that the content and meaning of individuality and freedom changed over time. 'Time signifies change' affirmed Dewey, and it was this feature of human existence which the enemies of freedom negated. Dictatorships and totalitarian states were 'ways of denying the realities of time and the creativeness of the individual. Freedom of thought and of expression are not mere rights to be claimed. They have their roots deep in the existence of individuals as developing careers in time.'[63]

Here Dewey utilised a distinctive conception of nature in order to authorise his ethical and political vision. What is of interest is the conception of nature itself, in which 'qualities and relations, individualities and conformities, finalities and efficacies, contingencies and necessities are inextricably bound together'.[64] This view, with its stress on change, contingency and choice, represented an interpretation of Darwinism which was unusual for its time and, as we shall see, still contrasts sharply with the reductionism and determinism typical of modern versions of Social Darwinism. It enabled Dewey to advocate liberty, democracy and rational political action as practices that were in tune with the realities of nature as well as pre-conditions for future evolutionary progress.

The evolution of social solidarity

The idea that cooperation was at least as important as natural selection in evolution – especially human evolution – appeared early in the history of Social Darwinism. As early as 1880 the French anarchist Emile Gautier published a tract entitled *Le Darwinisme social* in which he argued that the struggle for existence diminished in importance when human faculties and social institutions reached a certain level of development. Mutual assistance and social solidarity assumed increasing significance in human progress, and actually represented the genuine content of Social Darwinism rather than a misplaced focus on struggle.[65]

Proponents of this thesis (including Gautier) argued that Darwin himself had recognised the importance of group solidarity in the evolution of moral faculties and how the refinement of the latter reduced the importance of the struggle for existence. This was also the opinion of the Russian anarchist, Peter Kropotkin (1842–1921), whose *Mutual Aid*, published in book form in 1902, but appearing as articles in English

---

[62] Dewey, *Essential Writings*, 205.   [63] *Ibid.*, 147.
[64] Dewey, *Experience and Nature*, 340.
[65] See Clark, *Social Darwinism in France*, 76–7.

during the early 1890s, was an impressive and influential example of this genre.[66] As a naturalist Kropotkin was well aware of the severity of the struggle of animals to survive in the harsh conditions imposed by nature, but his own observations had failed to find evidence of any struggle between animals of the same species. Furthermore, the struggle against nature was so exhausting that he questioned whether this could act as an impetus for *progressive* change. What he did find was the widespread existence of mutual assistance and cooperation among the social animals. From this he concluded not only that mutual aid was 'as much a law of animal life as mutual struggle', but that the former was of more importance than the latter for the 'maintenance and further development of the species' (30–1). Kropotkin admitted that struggle was a fact of life in which the fittest survived, but he denied that convincing evidence had been adduced to support the actuality of intra-species competition, and he emphasised instead the significance of mutual aid in eliminating struggle and promoting progress.

'Don't compete! – competition is always injurious to the species, and you have plenty of resources to avoid it!' That is the *tendency* of nature, not always realised in full, but always present. That is the watchword which comes to us from the bush, the forest, the river, the ocean. 'Therefore combine – practice mutual aid! That is the surest means for giving to each and to all the greatest safety, the best guarantee of existence and progress, bodily, intellectual and moral' (81–2, original emphasis).

Kropotkin proposed an alternative model of nature in which mutual aid was a biological law. 'Man is no exception in nature. He also is subject to the great principle of Mutual Aid which grants the best chances of survival to those who best support each other in the struggle for life' (113). Evolution occurred through cooperation: intra-species conflict – the form Darwin considered the most intensive – was denied altogether. Kropotkin admitted that primitive tribesmen fought with other tribes, and that military aggression was a feature of the modern centralised state, but he depicted these as abnormal situations, the importance of which should not be exaggerated. In any case, warfare was largely confined to warriors and priests who massacred one another while ordinary people got on with their daily lives (112). The main form taken by the struggle for existence was between organisms and nature, and this necessitated cooperation and solidarity.

Is this view of the world Darwinist? The continuity between human beings and the social animals was stressed, as well as the universality of natural laws and the reality of evolution. But the cause of the latter was

---

[66]   The edition used here was edited by P. Avrich (London: Allen Lane, 1972).

not natural selection. For Kropotkin, struggle was relegated to the wings of evolution, responsible for exhaustion and waste rather than for cumulative change. Mutual aid rather than struggle provided the impetus for change and progress. True, the often adverse conditions imposed by nature were an incentive for solidarity and cooperation, but the battle of life had only a minor part in the drama of evolution. Kropotkin was not oblivious to the pernicious influences of militarism, exploitation, and unbridled individualism in modern societies, but against these he drew attention to cooperatives, friendly societies and trade unions in the towns, and the prevalence of village communities among millions of European country folk. The reality of mutual solidarity in the daily lives of ordinary people was unsurprising, 'because this feeling has been nurtured by thousands of years of human social life and hundreds of thousands of years of pre-human life in societies' (234).

The biological determinism in Kropotkin's analysis posed problems for the coherence of his theory. Some social phenomena – those involving solidarity – were derived from innate tendencies, while others – war, exploitation, political oppression – were attributed to perverse social conditions. But the outcome was hardly a synthesis of anarchism and Social Darwinism. Many Social Darwinists recognised the significance of group solidarity in social evolution, but they did so in order to accentuate its function in the struggle for survival against other groups. As an anarcho-communist Kropotkin rejected the notion of a 'cosmic code' of inevitable inter-group competition, and in his effort to demonstrate the reality of solidarity and mutualism he propounded a world view that differed on crucial details from Social Darwinism. Mutual aid was not, for him, a consequence of natural selection as it was for the Darwinists, but an independent process constituting the principal force behind evolutionary progress.

The appellation 'reform Darwinism' is equally problematic when applied to the French solidarity movement of the late nineteenth and early twentieth centuries. This doctrine attempted to synthesise individualism and collectivism by a programme of legislation aimed at ameliorating the condition of the urban proletariat while still respecting the claims of private property and avoiding the implementation of state socialism. Its most influential spokesman was the Radical deputy and minister, Léon Bourgeois (1851–1925), whose book, *Solidarité* (1896) achieved a remarkable degree of popularity and influence.[67]

---

[67] L. Bourgeois, *Solidarité* (Paris: Armand Colin, 1896). On Bourgeois and solidarism, see J. A. Scott, *Republican Ideas and the Liberal Tradition in France, 1870–1914* (New York: Octagon, 1966); J. E. S. Hayward, 'Solidarity: The Social History of an Idea in Nineteenth Century France', *International Review of Social History*, 4(1959), 261–84;

Bourgeois asserted that morality must be grounded in truth, which in turn was established by science. Economic and social phenomena, like physical, chemical and biological phenomena, obeyed ineluctable causal laws ascertainable through scientific inquiry. Biology showed that man was the product of a continuing evolution. The struggle for existence, undoubtedly a fact of life, coexisted with another biological law, solidarity. Just as each person was composed of mutually interacting elements, so was he or she inextricably linked with other members of society, both spatially and temporally. Individuals were culturally bound to their predecessors, and through specialisation and the division of labour, to their contemporaries. 'The laws of the species – laws of heredity, adaptation, selection, the laws of integration and disintegration – are only diverse aspects of the same general law of reciprocal dependence, that is to say, solidarity, of the elements of universal life' (45).

Mutual reciprocity did not contradict, but complemented, the struggle for existence. The latter was undoubtedly essential to evolutionary progress, but if left unchecked it would lead to harmful consequences for the social body as well as for the individual. The components of the social organism had to be organised, as did the multiple cells comprising each organism. This was achieved by force in authoritarian regimes and by consent in regimes founded upon liberty. Bourgeois argued that the brutal struggle for existence was the point of departure for human evolution (in contrast to the peaceful state of nature hypothesised by Rousseau), and that as mankind developed intelligence and morality the idea of voluntary association gradually became paramount. This paved the way for a pacific contractual social system which replaced the former state of war. Bourgeois regarded liberty – the opportunity for individuals to realise their full potential – as the primary condition of this form of social organisation. But people were not isolated beings and, accordingly, had to recognise a social debt, the fulfilment of which enabled society to ameliorate inequalities which arose, not from natural differences in aptitudes, but from adverse social circumstances and injustices (114).

This thesis portrayed solidarity as less the complement of the struggle for existence than its replacement as society evolved greater levels of harmony and reciprocity. Hence Bourgeois and Kropotkin both proposed models of social organisation which they claimed were validated by principles of biological science but in which natural selection played a minimal role. The biological models upon which they both drew – and

Hayward, 'The Official Social Philosophy of the French Third Republic: Léon Bourgeois and Solidarism', *International Review of Social History*, 6(1961), 19–48.

there were a number of such models in contemporary French thought[68] – depicted organisms as mutually harmonious systems, the multiple parts of which were interdependent and equilibrated. While this perspective on organic structure was compatible with Darwinist accounts of organic change, it could also be, and was, deployed as a counterweight to the Darwinian stress on competition in nature.[69] Rather than being labelled as examples of 'reform Darwinism', then, the theories of Kropotkin and Bourgeois should be seen as critiques of Social Darwinism which perceived nature as a model for social relations but drew upon alternative theories of nature and evolution. Nor was this simply a case of exploiting the indeterminate and ambiguous features of the Darwinian world view; for though these theorists tried to legitimate their position by invoking the authority of Darwin, they in fact proposed a totally different account of change in which natural selection was either minimised or eradicated.

A better candidate for the designation of reform Darwinist would be the Frenchman J.-L. de Lanessan (1843–1919), a theorist of French republicanism and a politician – he was for many years a deputy to the National Assembly and governor-general of Indo-China from 1891 to 1895. In 1881 Lanessan published a short tract on Darwinism which showed a firm grasp of the theory of natural selection.[70] Lanessan took issue with Darwin, though, on the role of the struggle for existence between the organism and its milieu, which he considered to play a negligible role in selection. The most important forms of struggle were between organisms and others of a different nature, and with conspecifics. The first led to the emergence of cooperation and association among animals, which often enabled weaker individuals to survive; the second (along with sexual selection) did produce the survival of the fittest and was the primary cause of the progressive development and transmutation of species (45–6).

Lanessan then argued that the struggle for existence applied equally to humans (66). As in the animal kingdom, the struggle between people and their milieu did not make for progressive selection but its opposite, since it was often the hardiest and ablest individuals who bore the brunt of environmentally imposed hardships (68). The struggle against other creatures motivated human association and cooperation, which in turn stimulated intelligence. But the growth of both society and intelligence had implications for the struggle for existence. Among animals, the

[68] See W. Schneider, *Quality and Quantity* (Cambridge University Press, 1990), 28–32.
[69] In Germany the concept of the cell-state was used in this manner. See Weindling, *Darwinism and Social Darwinism in Germany*.
[70] J.-L. Lanessan, *Etude sur la doctrine du Darwin* (Paris: Octave Doin, 1881).

struggle with conspecifics produced the survival of the fittest. Within human societies, 'this struggle has created kings, nobles, priests, exploiters of all kinds' and stifled the growth of intelligence through war and poverty (78–9). Similarly, sexual selection did not make for progress because the existence of inequalities of wealth encouraged women to sell themselves to the richest men (who were often the weakest), and ensured their maintenance in conditions of ignorance and servitude (79).

Lanessan was highly critical of theorists who used Darwinism to present social inequalities as reflections of the survival of the fittest. Like Kidd, he proposed the equalisation of rights, universal education and the abolition of hereditary wealth, in order to make the struggle for existence within society congruent with the 'true' nature of the struggle for existence and sexual selection (80), themes which were to be developed in his subsequent publications.[71] In their attempt to harmonise the struggle of conspecifics in society with its counterpart in nature, Lanessan's publications represent a genuine effort to construct a reform Darwinism, geared to the support of French republicanism.

Conclusion

This analysis of reform Darwinism has highlighted a number of contradictory features that are important for an appreciation of the discursive boundaries of Social Darwinism. These features are connected to the goals pursued by the majority of socialists, anarchists and liberal reformers, namely social harmony, individual fulfilment and the eradication of poverty and oppression. The logic of reformism involved ascribing conflict and inequality to social conditions that could be altered through appropriate policies. But if struggle and selection were ineluctable laws of nature, then the relationship between the natural and social orders could prove problematic. One response was to deny the relevance of biology to an understanding of society, and assert the methodological autonomy of the social sciences – the strategy adopted by Marx and Durkheim.[72] Another was to reinterpret the struggle for

---

[71] See J.-L. Lanessan, *La Lutte pour l'existence et l'évolution des sociétés* (Paris: Alcan, 1903); Lanessan, *La Concurrence sociale et les devoirs sociaux* (Paris: Alcan, 1904).

[72] Although, as argued in the introduction, Durkheim never fully emancipated his sociology from biologically grounded assumptions. Even theorists who explicitly denounced biological reductionism, therefore, sometimes succumbed to it. This is noticeable in Anton Pannakoek's *Marxism and Darwinism*, tr. N. Weiser (Chicago: Kerr, 1912; German edition, 1909). After claiming that Darwinism and Marxism were separate sciences (35), the author went on to depict cooperation and altruism as laws governing all social animals (36–42).

existence in order to consign violent struggle to the evolutionary past and portray market competition, or the conflict of ideas, as the social analogues of the struggle for existence. This strategy was adopted by a number of liberals and socialists, but the resultant theories were not always coherent, often containing an ambivalent representation of nature. Nature could appear both as a remorseless, impersonal process of change and destruction *and* as a benign force – often personified as a female, as in Bebel's image of nature as an instructress – which was paradigmatic for the future organisation of society. One way out of this dilemma – the one followed by Dewey – was to insist on the statistical character of scientific laws and to stress the aleatory features of the Darwinian view of nature, thereby opening up the possibility of a rationally inspired democratic politics. This mode of Social Darwinist theorising has not, however, found many disciples.

Another strategy consisted of elevating mutual aid to the status of a natural law, and marginalising or denying the importance of the struggle for existence. These theories, although invariably insisting upon their Darwinian lineage, were actually *opposed* to Social Darwinism. They amounted to an alternative interpretation, a different world view that rejected the Darwinian explanatory focus on adaptation through struggle. Biologically inspired theories of this ilk were influential. For example, they helped substantiate a significant form of pacifism which Crook has termed 'peace biology'.[73] Their existence attests to the persisting importance of biological models in social and political thought, but the model of nature they espoused was antithetical to that contained in Social Darwinism.

[73] Crook, *Darwinism, War and History*, which contains an extensive analysis of such theories. Examples are W. Trotter, *Instincts of the Herd in Peace and War* (London: Fisher Unwin, 1916); J. Novicow, 'The Mechanism and Limits of Human Association: The Foundations of a Sociology of Peace', tr. S. H. Otis, *American Journal of Sociology*, 23(1917), 289–349.

8 Races, nations and the struggle for existence

Introduction

Although several reform Darwinists were pacifists opposed to international armed conflict, most of them still believed that some form of competition – usually economic – would continue to govern inter-state relationships. What distinguishes the thinkers to be examined in this chapter is that, first, they made conflict between nations and races the *central* focus of their publications, and second, they regarded this conflict as ultimately violent, carrying the threat of national or racial extermination. Given the salience of the notion of 'race' in these texts, it is necessary to examine briefly some of its connotations.

Race was a widely used concept by the middle of the nineteenth century. It could designate an organic sub-species or variety, as in the sub-title of the *Origin*, or a human group. In instances of the second usage, it could be applied to humanity as a whole or to a combination of nationalities (e.g. the 'European race'), or to an individual nation (e.g. the 'English race'). Additionally, race was used to describe a group characterised by distinctive physical (and, invariably, psychological) traits, as in 'Celtic' 'Aryan' or 'Negroid' races. Such groups were often hierarchically arranged according to a scale of physical, mental or moral value. In some theories, those forming the subject of this chapter, the 'fact' that certain races were superior to others meant that relations between races assumed vital importance to an understanding of history and culture. In many cases, theorists tended to use the terms 'nation' and 'race' as broadly interchangeable, or to regard nations as embodiments of distinctive racial (i.e. physical and psychological) attributes.

For example, the Scots physician and anatomist, Robert Knox (1793–1862), published a systematic treatise on race in 1850 entitled *The Races of Man*.[1] Knox, while sympathetic to the 'darker races' and critical of

[1] This is the Robert Knox associated with the Burke and Hare bodysnatching scandal of 1828. For an account of the life and work of Knox, see H. Lonsdale, *A Sketch of the Life and Writings of Robert Knox the Anatomist* (London: Macmillan, 1870).

colonialism, argued that racial inter-breeding led to the corruption and collapse of civilisations.[2] This theme was the central argument of the Frenchman, Arthur de Gobineau (1816–82) in his four-volume *Essay on the Inequality of the Human Races* (1853–5), in which he foretold the future of humanity in terms of 'its waning and inevitable decline' through miscegenation.[3] The Aryans, of whom the Germanic peoples were the last remnants, were creators of modern civilisation but had become enfeebled through inter-breeding with inferior races and were threatened by extinction. This thesis received its most comprehensive elaboration by a Germanised Briton, Houston Stewart Chamberlain (1855–1927) in his famous *The Foundations of the Nineteenth Century* (1899). Chamberlain portrayed the history of the West as an incessant conflict between the spiritual and culture-creating Aryans and the mercenary and materialistic Jews. Western civilisation had declined, although Chamberlain believed the situation could be retrieved by decisive intervention, and came to regard Hitler as a potential saviour.[4]

None of these theorists drew upon Darwinism for their arguments. The work of Knox preceded Darwinism, and de Gobineau was hostile to Darwin, whom he accused of plagiarising his ideas.[5] Chamberlain has been associated with Social Darwinism, but although he was familiar with the biological thought of his day, he repudiated natural selection and embraced a vitalist conception of organic growth.[6] The relevance of these thinkers to an understanding of Social Darwinism lies in their popularisations of the idea that racial struggle was fundamental to a 'scientific' understanding of history and culture. Their theories made explicit something that was implicit in much racial thinking, i.e. that race was an intrinsically hierarchical and evaluative term, mingling phenomenological description with moral judgement. In this it was similar to the concept of class: indeed, descriptions and judgements were often interchanged between the two notions.[7]

---

[2] See S. Collinson, 'Robert Knox Anatomy of Race', *History Today*, 40(1990), 44–9.
[3] De Gobineau, *Essay*, in M. Biddiss, ed., *Gobineau: Selected Political Writings* (London: Jonathan Cape, 1970), 175.
[4] For an analysis of Chamberlain's ideas in *The Foundations*, see G. Field, *Evangelist of Race* (New York: Columbia University Press, 1981), chap. 5; R. Stackelberg, *Idealism Debased* (Ohio: Kent University Press, 1981), Part III.
[5] De Gobineau, foreword to second edition of *Essay*, *Selected Political Writings*, 232.
[6] M. Burleigh and W. Wipperman charge Chamberlain with fusing Social Darwinism with anti-Semitism in *The Racial State* (Cambridge University Press, 1991), 36. For an analysis of Chamberlain's racial ideas which stresses their anti-Darwinian orientation, see M. Woodroffe, 'Racial Theories of History and Politics: the Example of Houston Stewart Chamberlain', in P. Kennedy and A. Nicholls, eds., *Nationalist and Racist Movements in Britain and Germany Before 1914* (London: Macmillan, 1981), 143–53.
[7] D. Lorimer, *Colour, Class and the Victorians* (Leicester University Press, 1978), 60–2, 77, 80–1.

In Darwinism it was possible to conceive groups as the units of evolutionary change. In the light of the importance of both race and nationalism in nineteenth-century social thought, it is understandable why Darwinists very quickly showed interest in racial attributes and inter-ethnic relationships. Both A. R. Wallace and Charles Loring Brace produced evolutionary accounts of racial differences, while Haeckel, Royer, Rolle and Bagehot made racial and/or national conflict an important factor in social evolution. The theorists discussed below went further than this in making national and racial struggles the primary focus of their interpretations of socio-historical change.

Le Bon and the psychology of race

Gustave Le Bon (1841–1931) is best remembered for his studies on crowd and racial psychology.[8] Much less well known, but crucial to an understanding of the intellectual underpinnings of his work, is his two-volume *L'Homme et les sociétés*, published in 1881.[9] Here he explicitly endorsed all the components of the Darwinian world view. He embraced uniformitarianism and repudiated creationism, arguing for a condition of constant flux in nature wrought by the accretion of imperceptible changes leading to the increasing complexity of all phenomena (I, 1–11). In the realm of organic nature this process of perfection was brought about through the natural selection of favourable variations. Selection itself stemmed from a struggle for existence deriving from the super-fecundity of living beings (I, 124–5), a struggle that was at its most intense between organisms belonging to the same species (I, 131). For Le Bon, the source of variations was the acquisition of characters through adaptation which were then transmitted to subsequent genera-tions (I, 126–7). Natural selection ensured that inherited variations were useful and was responsible for all modification, whether to form, structure or character: 'It is the struggle for existence which has made beings more and more divergent' (I, 135).

This process was equally at work in human evolution, although less actively so because social organisation tended to protect the weak and allow them to procreate. Fortunately, such practices did not annul natural selection so much as transform it: 'In all living beings, from insect to man, the selection that results from the combat for existence

---

[8]   G. Le Bon, *Psychologie des foules* (Paris: Alcan, 1895); tr. *The Crowd: A Study of the Popular Mind* (London: Fisher Unwin, 1896); Le Bon, *Les Lois psychologiques de l'évolution des peuples* (Paris: Alcan, 1894).

[9]   G. Le Bon, *L'Homme et les sociétés: leurs origines et leur histoire*, 2 vols. (Paris: Rothschild, 1881).

will always remain the essential condition of progress. In human societies, this struggle takes several names, notably that of competition; but, beneath its diverse appellations, its results always remain the same, that is to say, the triumph of the fittest and the elimination of the less well-adapted' (I, 196–7).

Selection had formed the different races of mankind, which for Le Bon represented distinct species distinguished by physical characteristics and different mental traits and capabilities. He argued that whereas crossings between superior races were usually beneficial, those between an inferior and a superior race were disastrous, resulting in the elimination of the latter. If miscegenation did not take place it was the lower race that succumbed and was annihilated in the case of prolonged contact between the two. To Le Bon, nature was aristocratic, and mercilessly punished impure blood (I, 199–200).

It was because social evolution was subsumed under the same laws as evolution in general that a science of society was possible. Given the complexity of social reality this science could have a limited but still useful impact on social evolution, much as the knowledge of the physician had a small but nonetheless significant effect on the march of illness (II, 24–5). Social science could also play an important role in exploding various myths about former ages of gold and the noble savage (I, 12, 17–18). Anthropology revealed the struggle for survival to be more intense among men than among animals, with war representing one of man's principal preoccupations: 'Equally among the savage and the civilised man, the state of war against his fellows is the natural state, and the struggle is all the more cruel, by the number of victims that it brings about and the price that it exacts, when the people among whom it rages have attained a higher degree of civilisation' (II, 88). All that civilisation did was to shorten the length of wars on account of their enormous destructiveness. Furthermore, armed conflict was not the only guise in which the struggle for existence was manifested, and Le Bon mentioned commercial and industrial competition as a particularly acute form (II, 89). The sentiments of hostility and ferocity induced by struggle – and for Le Bon, it was sentiments which were the primary form of motivation among individuals and races – were fixed by heredity to such an extent that civilisation had proved impotent against them. But Le Bon was adamant that struggle and the miseries it occasioned were the determinants of progress, and when struggle was relaxed progress ceased and regression took place. 'The history of peoples', he wrote, 'is in reality only a narrative of facts resulting from their efforts to surpass their neighbours in military strength' (II, 95).

Le Bon was consequently perturbed by philanthropic efforts to curb the effects of struggle, efforts which sowed the seeds of future racial decadence by preventing the elimination of the unfit (II, 96). It was always the inferior specimens in a society which bred prolifically and threatened the quality of the race, for it was quality rather than mere numbers which enabled a race to be successful (II, 105). Le Bon was completely reductionist in his estimation of the relative roles of nature and nurture in moulding racial and personal character: 'Energy, fore-sight, perseverance, the taste for work, self control, initiative, the sentiment of family are all qualities that heredity can give but which no institution can create' (II, 137). It was for this reason that Le Bon excoriated the efforts by women to achieve equality with men. Evolution demonstrated the progressive differentiation of men and women through time and no education could alter this (II, 156). He warned that the day when women abandoned the 'inferior occupations' allotted them by nature and engaged in masculine activities there would commence 'a social revolution' that would destroy 'the sacred bonds of family' (II, 159).

This argument highlights a notable feature of Le Bon's use of Social Darwinism, one already encountered in other theorists. Throughout his writings Le Bon constantly reiterated the point that nature was in constant flux, and in human civilisation variability rather than fixity was the norm.[10] Yet these statements were juxtaposed with others which conveyed exactly the opposite impression, i.e. that certain aspects of human nature, particularly those characters and sentiments which were the major determinants of racial and sexual identities, were refractory to change. Thus he proclaimed the existence of two tiers to the anatomical and mental structures of any species – a small number of irreducible elements around which were grouped secondary traits. The latter were modifiable, the former much less so.[11] With human races, these irreducible elements were those comprising 'character', such as the sentiments of perseverance, energy, will, etc. Character governed the history of a people, and it was the incompatibility of different racial characters that brought about inter-racial conflicts.[12] Character was resistant to change through education, but it could rapidly atrophy if peace led to the death of the military virtues in favour of the pursuit of wealth and an untrammelled egoism.[13] Thus Le Bon posited the existence of a human nature which sometimes appeared resistant to 'artificial' change and had remained fixed for six millennia, and at other times was portrayed as fragile, susceptible to precisely those cultural transformations which were elsewhere dismissed as powerless against

[10] For example, Le Bon, *Les Lois psychologiques*, 20; Le Bon, *Psychologie des foules*, 73–4.
[11] Le Bon, *Les Lois psychologiques*, 21.   [12] *Ibid.*, 32, 34.   [13] *Ibid.*, 152–4.

heredity and natural selection. This opportunism was undoubtedly prompted by his desire to demonstrate that the policies proposed by feminists and socialists were futile because unrealistic, or else harmful because they promoted degeneracy. As a result, Le Bon sometimes denied the possibility of any genuine moral transformations, bringing him close to an implicit essentialism despite his express commitment to the protocols of Darwinism:

we must recognise, as a matter of daily observation, that human laws have been utterly powerless to modify the laws of nature, and that the latter continue to determine the relations of one people with another. All theories of right and justice are futile. International relations are today what they have been since the beginning of the world ... Right and justice have never played any part in the relations of nations of unequal strength.[14]

Or, more briefly put: 'History always turns in the same circle.'[15]

One other point about Le Bon's use of Social Darwinism deserves mention, namely his presentation of evolution as a force acting for the benefit of the species rather than the individual. Argued Le Bon: 'Nature is neither cruel nor kind. She thinks only of the species, and remains indifferent – formidably indifferent – to the individual.'[16] The species – or its human counterpart, the race – became the reference point against which the progressive or the degenerative potential of change was to be judged. The outcome was to derive harder, harsher consequences from Social Darwinism. Darwin, Royer, Haeckel and Spencer had all warned against the indiscriminate spread of charity and altruism but all had, nevertheless, esteemed both to be important and desirable expressions of the development of human character. Not so Le Bon, who unequivocally repudiated such foolishness: 'The term solidarity signifies merely association, and by no means charity or altruism. Charity is a noxious and anti-social sentiment; altruism is an artificial and impotent sentiment.'[17] Unlike the first pioneers for whom Social Darwinism implied moral perfection in the long run, Le Bon portrayed such perfection as not only chimerical but, should anyone attempt to realise it, as detrimental to the future of racial progress. Le Bon's theories, then, mark an important development in Social Darwinism due to their insistence on the permanence of hereditary traits and their advocacy of public policies based upon recognition of this fact.

There are similarities between Le Bon's linkage of inevitable racial conflict to a denial of moral progress with the theories of the Austrian sociologist, Ludwig Gumplowicz (1838–1909). In his *Outlines of*

[14] Le Bon, *The Psychology of Socialism* (no tr.) (London: Fisher Unwin, 1899), 328–9.
[15] Le Bon, *Les Lois psychologiques*, 165.
[16] Le Bon, *Psychology of Socialism*, 326.   [17] *Ibid.*, 342.

Sociology (1885),[18] Gumplowicz presented races as the units of evolution, which equated with species defined by durable hereditary characteristics (161, 177, 217). Motivated by economic self-interest, races were engaged in ceaseless competition for resources, which generated conflict and exploitation, the dynamics of evolution (205–6).[19] The state was a coercive institution for the protection of the interests of a dominant class. Hence even within a society, group conflict was endemic: though it could be temporarily confined to peaceful competition by the state, the adversarial nature of group interests was such that 'each group that is able, tends to become exclusive like a caste, to form a consanguineous circle. In short it becomes a race' (227). Racial war was, therefore, ubiquitous, and the potential possessed by any group to consolidate into a race ensured the continual formation of new races.

Gumplowicz concluded from this that moral progress was chimerical. From the earliest forms of social organisation, the horde, to the nation-states of the present, groups were motivated by 'blind natural law' rather than by ethical considerations. 'Lying and deceit, breach of confidence and betrayal is on every page of their history', exactly like the relations between primitive hordes.

Indeed, it is generally recognised that states oppose each other like savage hordes; that they follow the blind laws of nature; that no ethical law or moral obligation, only the fear of the stronger, holds them in check; and that neither right nor law, treaty nor league, can restrain the stronger from seeking its own interests when the opportunity is offered (229).

Ethics constituted no more than a camouflage for group interests, and right was defined to suit the strongest. In addition, since the individual reflected the morality of the horde or state to which he or she belonged, there could be no question of the progressive individuation regarded by earlier Social Darwinists as an essential facet of progress. For the more liberal among them, like Royer and Spencer, this involved the gradual emancipation of the individual from collective constraints and his or her self-realisation as an autonomous, rational being. No such evolution was envisaged by Gumplowicz. Although his sociology assigned a certain amount of importance to the development of structural complexity within social systems, from the horde to the nation-state, this did not entail a corresponding expansion of human freedom and autonomy.[20]

As with Le Bon, what we see in the sociology of Gumplowicz is not so much a theory of *evolution* as one of *social change*, and a severely

---

[18] L. Gumplowicz, *Outlines of Sociology*, tr. F. Moore (New York: Paine-Whitman, 1963).

[19] See also Gumplowicz, *Sociologie et politique* (no tr.) (Paris: Giard et Brière, 1898), 157.

[20] For further discussion of Gumplowicz's Social Darwinism, see my 'The Struggle for Existence', 55–8.

constrained theory of change at that. Once the primeval horde has been superseded, social and psychological transformations seem to be cyclic in form, consisting of political growth, fragmentation and decline. Gumplowicz warned his readers that a catastrophic annihilation was quite conceivable for modern European states for, though they were no longer menaced by barbarian tribes, the absence of any moral distinctions between primitive and modern mentality meant that the instincts of such tribes 'lie latent in the populace of European states' (304–5, 309). Thus Gumplowicz adhered to the Darwinist tenet that new species (i.e. races) could be formed and existing ones become extinct through conquest, inter-mixing and closure, but his theory amounted to a denial that, in *social* terms, changes were cumulative and directional and hence could lead to the creation of novel modes of social and political organisation.[21] This denial was made even more forcefully in my next example of racial Social Darwinism.

The calibration of racial worth

The distinctive features of the race theories of Le Bon and Gumplowicz – biological determinism, racial essentialism, group selection and the implicit representation of evolution as preservation rather than change – are even more pronounced in the writings of the Frenchman, Georges Vacher de Lapouge (1854–1936). Lapouge, a former public prosecutor turned librarian, has earned a reputation as an uncompromising theorist of race, even to the extent of anticipating Nazism.[22] The following exegesis seeks to identify the main contours of what he designated as the discipline of 'anthropo-sociology' and to relate it to the world view of Social Darwinism.

Lapouge was convinced that Darwinism would revolutionise political science. Rejecting the inheritance of acquired characters on the authority of Weismann's experiments, Lapouge announced heredity and selection to be the only forces at work in evolution, acting throughout nature with the same universality and irresistibility as gravity. These forces operated upon humans, who were part of nature. 'We must never forget that man is not a being apart, but simply a primate.' Humans could be classified

---

[21] It is perfectly possible for cyclic conceptions of change to coexist with linear conceptions within Darwinism; indeed Gould has argued (*An Urchin in the Storm*, 165) that both notions – time's arrow and time's cycle – are essential. But Gumplowicz seems to deny, or at least seriously underplay, the idea of time's arrow.

[22] According to Clark (*Social Darwinism in France*, 131), the Nazis reprinted Lapouge's *L'Aryen* in 1939. Lapouge, in an interview given in 1933, apparently accused the Nazis of distorting his theories, although J. Colombat (*La Fin du monde civilisé*, Paris: Vrin, 1946) refers to him as 'Hitler's French master' (9–10).

into races which were discrete biological units, species in the process of formation. 'What enables the recognition of race is the presence of physical, physiological and psychic characteristics which constitute the type.' Races were created and maintained through the actions of heredity and selection rather than culture and language, which made race a 'zoological' concept for Lapouge.[23]

Although Lapouge did not consider himself to have been influenced by de Gobineau, he dated the birth of anthropo-sociology from the publication of the latter's *Essay on the Inequality of the Human Races*.[24] Lapouge agreed with de Gobineau that: 'The psychology of race is the fundamental factor in historical evolution ...'[25] Once there had been pure races, but through inter-breeding these had been replaced by races of varying degrees of purity. Such crossings were the cause of decadence and decline. Lapouge invoked an anthropological analogue to Gresham's law in economics, according to which good coin was driven out of circulation by bad coin: when two races were mixed, the inferior would eventually predominate over the superior.[26] In regions where racial inter-breeding was long established, 'there is an infinity of individuals who no longer belong to any race by dint of belonging to several, and whose blood is contaminated in a definitive manner. In other words, to the notion of race it is necessary to oppose that of the individual outside of any race, the zoological pariah.'[27]

Racial differences were innate and ineradicable and therefore any notion of the unification and integration of races was a mere pipe-dream, contrary to the elementary laws of biology.[28] Throughout his work, Lapouge portrayed heredity as an inexorable determinant of both physique and character. The individual could not alter his physical appearance, and nor could he efface 'from his soul the tendencies which make him think and act as his ancestors thought and acted'. Education was powerless to alter a person's character because traits such as independence and initiative could not be taught but only acquired through inheritance. The individual was constrained by the iron laws of nature: 'The blood that he carries in his veins from birth he keeps all his life. The individual is crushed by his race, he is nothing. The race, the nation, are everything.'[29] The psychology of the race dominated that of the individual, and the idea of free will – of the individual as an autonomous agent – was illusory. It was impossible for individuals to

[23] Lapouge, *Sélections*, 1, 11, 5, 8.
[24] Lapouge, 'The Fundamental Laws of Anthropo-sociology', tr. C. Closson, *Journal of Political Economy*, 6(1898), 56.
[25] Lapouge, *L'Aryen*, 369.   [26] Lapouge, *Sélections*, 67.   [27] *Ibid.*, 7.
[28] Lapouge, *L'Aryen*, 369.   [29] *Ibid.*, 351, 511.

escape their racial heritage: the belief that inferior races were improvable through contacts with more advanced races was contrary to the lessons of science.[30]

According to Lapouge, useful variations of a physical or psychological nature allowed some individuals to survive and reproduce while others died out.[31] But because man was a social animal, the struggle for existence became modified into a conflict between different groups 'in which the individuals found themselves united against the common enemy'.[32] This transformation was of momentous consequence for the course of human evolution. 'The struggle of man against man through war has not ceased, but it has acquired a social character . . .'[33] As social solidarity grew, natural selection diminished in importance and was replaced by *social selection*, a form of struggle no less murderous than its natural counterpart but one producing very different results. In fact, social selection perverted evolution by eliminating the best individuals and allowing inferior specimens to survive and propagate their kind. This was how the great civilisations of antiquity had perished and a similar fate now threatened modern Europe.[34]

Lapouge argued that Europe was populated by three major racial groups. The first was *Homo Europaeus* – tall, pale-skinned, blue-eyed and long-skulled. Lapouge considered the 'cephalic index' afforded a good measure of racial type, and *Homo Europaeus* was dolichocephalous, with an index of 75 or less.[35] This race had become popularly referred to as 'Aryan', a term Lapouge found acceptable on condition that the anthropo-sociologist bore in mind its zoological rather than linguistic connotations. The second race was *Homo Alpinus*, smaller and darker complexioned than the Aryan, with black hair, brown eyes and brachycephalous heads (i.e. short skulls with an index of over 80). This race was a product of inter-breeding with several others. The third race was the Mediterranean type, long-headed but possessing the darker skin and shorter stature of *Alpinus*. Lapouge was primarily concerned with the first two races.

Psychological differences augmented the physical distinctions between the Aryan and *Alpinus*. The former was a natural leader and

---

[30] *Ibid.*, 352–3, 405.   [31] Lapouge, *Sélections*, 82.
[32] Lapouge, *L'Aryen*, 374.   [33] Lapouge, *Sélections*, 60.
[34] *Ibid.*, chap. 7 and 443–4; Lapouge, *L'Aryen*, 512, 406.
[35] The cephalic index is obtained by dividing the width of the skull by its length and multiplying the result by 100. However, anthropologists disagreed over the respective virtues of dolichocephaly and brachycephaly, and many, *contra* Lapouge, were of the opinion that brachycephaly was a sign of superiority. See Schneider, *Quality and Quantity*, 251; Haller, *Outcasts From Evolution*, 38. Havelock Ellis associated dolichocephaly with degeneration in his *Man and Woman*, eighth edn (London: Heinemann, 1934), 186.

innovator, excelling in intellectual work, whether in science, letters or the arts, as well as in the business world. This made the Aryan 'a great promoter of progress', a natural conqueror, robust, intelligent, possessed of boundless energy, though of a sad and cold disposition.[36] In all these respects, he contrasted sharply with the brachycephalous *Alpinus*; Lapouge even considered the greater tendency of Aryans to ride bicycles a mark of superiority.[37] He speculated that *Alpinus* had originally 'lived in forests and mountains in an almost simian state, and had been enticed out of their lairs only to serve as slaves to the dolichocephals'.[38] This had generated an innate desire for a master: 'The instinct of servitude is so anchored in the psychology of the brachycephal that immediately he is free, he is compelled to seek a master who will guarantee his security.' These psychological differences were reflected in a 'natural division of labour' in which the Aryans occupied the most important social positions while the brachycephals performed menial tasks and manual labour.[39]

In spite of their natural inferiority – indeed, *because* of it – the brachycephals were becoming the dominant race in Europe. *Homo Alpinus* was seemingly indestructible: 'He is inert, he is mediocre, but he multiplies.'[40] Since the Middle Ages the brachycephals had increased at the expense of the dolichocephals because the social milieu progressively favoured servility and mediocrity, subverting the natural division of labour throughout Europe. Social selection was destroying the most eugenic families and leaving in its wake a racial debris incapable of resisting the challenge of new conquerors.

Lapouge identified several forms of social selection. First, there was political selection, functioning through civil wars, exile and persecution. The French Revolution was an important instance of this, marking the violent transfer of power from one race – the Aryans – to another, *Alpinus*, who maintained this dominance through the device of democracy.[41] Lapouge regarded democracy as an unmitigated disaster in France, where it failed to express French racial realities in the way that a parliamentary system did in Britain and the USA (where the Aryans were still numerous). Though weak and vacillating due to the mutual paralysis of the executive and legislature, this regime continued to oppress individuals left unprotected after first the absolute monarchy and then the Revolution had destroyed the institutional life of France and created a 'human dust' of atomised individuals. Yet the brachyce-

---

[36] Lapouge, *L'Aryen*, 399, 151.   [37] Lapouge, 'The Fundamental Laws', 63.
[38] Lapouge, *L'Aryen*, 236.   [39] Lapouge, *Sélections*, 76; *L'Aryen*, 238.
[40] Lapouge, *L'Aryen*, 481; see also *Sélections*, 67.
[41] Lapouge, *Sélections*, 251; *L'Aryen*, 464.

phal thrived in this environment: 'He is the perfect slave, the ideal serf, the model subject, and in a republic like our own, the best-regarded citizen, as he tolerates every abuse.'[42]

Modern warfare also had a deleterious selective impact. Among primitives and barbarians, war was beneficial because it eliminated weak individuals. With the advent of civilisation it became a veritable scourge, ensuring that the bravest and strongest were exposed to death while the lunatics, criminals and misfits were protected. War had been virtually eliminated within societies, but at the international level it was as fierce and relentless as ever, making the proposal for a United States of Europe an empty utopia. 'War is the essential and necessary mode of international selection, and it appears to augment rather than diminish in intensity.' The decline of the militaristic Aryan spelled disaster for European nations in the forthcoming conflicts which, for Lapouge, were unavoidable. 'The struggle of large nations is a natural necessity.'[43]

Religion exerted another adverse selective influence, especially Catholicism, where celibacy among the priesthood reduced the ranks of the most ardent, and hence usually better, individuals. Worse still was the fact that Christianity encouraged moral conformity and intolerance, which worked against the independently minded Aryans.[44] Lapouge was convinced that society had need of a shared system of values which could act as a moral bond because selection had produced in man a biological need to believe in such values which made them as necessary as bread, but the religion he endorsed was Haeckel's monism rather than Christianity.[45]

Closely linked to religion was moral selection, in which prudish norms and prohibitions hindered reproductive activities and forced people to wear too much clothing, which restricted the ability of the skin to breathe and caused diseases like tuberculosis. Charitable endeavours were equally regressive, 'protecting from the effects of selection those elements which cannot and will not work, and multiplying them in an artificial manner'.[46] This allowed racial degeneration to become the norm in modern societies 'where the incompetent, far from being eliminated, can live at the expense of others and multiply the more so as they are psychically closer to animality'. Humanitarian concern for the criminal had also created a form of legal selection. Lapouge insisted that the criminal should not be allowed to reproduce because all of his

[42] Lapouge, L'Aryen, 233; also 376–8, 381.
[43] Lapouge, Sélections, 224; L'Aryen, 501.
[44] Lapouge, Sélections, 264–6, 281.
[45] Lapouge, 'Préface' to Haeckel, Le Monisme, 1, 8; L'Aryen, vi.
[46] Lapouge, Sélections, 312–17, 318.

progeny would carry the germ of criminality. Imprisonment he decried as both ineffectual and expensive: the most certain, selective and economical penal sanction was the death penalty.[47]

Finally, there existed a mode of economic selection which was helping to destroy the Aryan who, while eminently suited to entrepreneurial and even speculative activities, was disadvantaged by the untrammelled egoism of the modern world. This favoured an aristocracy whose wealth was based upon chance rather than upon merit, one which became softened and corrupted by success, lazy and decadent.

All these forces, along with the emigration of the best Aryan stock to the New World and the degenerative consequences of cross-breeding, combined to reduce the number of dolichocephals in Europe, particularly in France, Spain and Southern Germany. Hence Lapouge's writings were punctuated with jeremiads prophesying the imminent destruction of European civilisation. Europe was finished, and in the forthcoming global confrontation he foresaw the triumph of Russia and the implementation of a bureaucratic regime congenial to the brachycephals, although it was just conceivable that victory could go to the Aryan United States.[48] Sometimes Lapouge predicted the total eclipse of civilisation in a tone which came close to the subsequent Nazi rhetoric of apocalypse:

The final times will see men emancipated from all civilisation, returned to their elementary liberty, ensconced in caves, borrowing their coats from the denizens of the forest, begging their repast from wild boars and wolves. One will no longer see any inequality among men, except one, the inequality between he who is on the spit and he who turns it. *Dies irae!* ['Day of wrath!'][49]

Lapouge did offer some hope of salvation if nations could harness the immensely powerful forces of heredity to work in favour of their eugenic elements. 'Systematic selection appears to be the only means possible to escape from the coming mediocrity and the final fall.'[50] Public opinion must be educated about the effects of racial mixing and of the urgent need for eugenic policies. Polygamy, abortion and even incest he approved as eugenically sound practices, and Lapouge suggested that the provision of free alcohol to the worst social types might encourage them to kill themselves off in their inevitable excesses.[51] His ideal was a society in which the superior racial elements were in complete control

---

[47]   *Ibid.*, 119, 321–4.   [48]   Lapouge, *L'Aryen*, 492, 495, 502.

[49]   Lapouge, '*Dies irae*! La fin du monde civilisé', *Revue Europe* (1923), cited in Colombat, *La Fin du monde civilisé*, 219. Statements like this, common throughout Lapouge's publications, caused him to become associated with pessimistic and iconoclastic versions of Social Darwinism. See C. Fages, 'L'Evolution du darwinisme sociologique', *L'Humanité nouvelle*, 3(1899), 30, 32–4, 36–7.

[50]   Lapouge, *Sélections*, 489.   [51]   *Ibid.*, 486.

and remained strictly segregated from the remainder of the population. 'The system of closed, specialised castes, artificial sub-species, is the last word in evolution.'[52]

Though Lapouge was marginalised in his own country and played a limited role in the French eugenics movement, it would be too simple to explain this by reference to the sentiments outlined above.[53] First, Lapouge's ideas were not qualitatively different from those of his contemporaries, even if somewhat less tactfully presented. Second, Lapouge did enjoy a considerable reputation in the wider international eugenics movement, and even in France his status improved somewhat with the development of a more racially oriented eugenics during the 1930s and 1940s.[54] Third, Lapouge's ideas on race were also unremarkable by the standards of his time and were hence unlikely to have been responsible for his lack of popularity among his countrymen. Lapouge described the Jews as an ethnic group rather than a zoological race – one founded upon religion and with a psychic identity forged over centuries of selection. They were everywhere the same: intelligent, ruthless, gifted money-makers, arrogant in success and servile in defeat, and congenitally odious, as evinced by their history of persecution, which antedated the birth of Christ by several centuries. In the leadership vacuum created by the decline of the Aryans, the Jews would undoubtedly become prominent, perhaps even to the extent of taking over Europe, but they were unable to reproduce themselves sufficiently rapidly to become a master race, and were likely to remain a powerful but detested caste.[55]

Arguments of this nature would have been offensive to many French citizens in the highly charged atmosphere surrounding the Dreyfus case, but they were mild by comparison with the anti-Semitic rhetoric of the radical, nationalistic right.[56] Yet Lapouge does not appear to have found an audience among these groups. The reason surely lies in

---

[52] *Ibid.*, 484.
[53] For details of Lapouge's reception in France, see Clark, *Social Darwinism in France*, 143–54, 158; Clark, 'Le Darwinisme social en France', 197–8; W. Schneider, *Quality and Quantity*, 61.
[54] See Schneider, *Quality and Quantity*, 251. Schneider underlines the originality of Lapouge's ideas on eugenics at their time of publication, 61. Lapouge was cited in books on heredity, as well as by social theorists. See J. A. Thomson, *Heredity* (London: Murray, 1908), 562, 593; Sumner *Folkways*, 42; T. Veblen, in M. Lerner, ed., *The Portable Veblen* (New York: Viking Press, 1948), 215; C. Spiess, *Impérialismes* (Paris: Eugène Figuière, 1917); C. Closson, 'Social Selection', *Journal of Political Economy*, 4(1896), 449–66.
[55] Lapouge, *L'Aryen*, 465–8, 474.
[56] See, for example, *Campagne nationaliste, 1899–1901* (Paris: Imprimerie de la Cour d'Appel, 1902) by Jules Soury (a Social Darwinist), which contains numerous pejorative references to Jews, including fantasies about sticking them like pigs (91).

the overwhelming thrust of his publications, which was directed against not only the political institutions of the Third Republic – dislike of which he shared with the nationalist right – but against contemporary French culture in general. Like de Gobineau, who also had few French disciples, Lapouge located the cause of French decline and decadence in the racial composition of the nation. His anthroposociology was not focused upon the relationships between whites and non-whites, which was the case with much of the literature on race, but with relationships within the national community. His unflattering description of the brachycephals, especially his derogatory assessments of their character and capabilities, was aimed at the mass of the French population. Even to those who repudiated the values and institutions of republicanism, Lapouge must have appeared to have relegated the vast majority of the French nation to the status of permanent and irremediable worthlessness.

In effect, Lapouge went beyond a critique of the Third Republic to challenge the entire heritage of the Enlightenment and the Revolution. His assertion that the individual was 'crushed by his race' controverted the universalist claim of autonomous, enlightened reason to chart the course of human destiny. To the formula 'Liberty, Equality and Fraternity' Lapouge opposed the slogan 'Determinism, Inequality, Selection'.[57] He was unequivocal in his condemnation of democracy, progress and pacifism. Science demonstrated the accidental, contingent nature of life and was inimical to any ideal of progress.[58] The notion of individual rights was ludicrous, for there could be no question of rights against force; on the contrary, rights were created and maintained by force. Finally, Lapouge poured scorn on the goal of fraternity: 'Let there be fraternity, but woe to the vanquished! Life maintains itself only through death.'[59]

Lapouge's ambition was to achieve a 'scientific explanation of the historical development of civilisations by showing them to depend upon the processes of biological evolution'.[60] In this he had a great deal in common with Otto Ammon (1842–1915) in Germany. Both theorists sought to quantify physical racial differences and to correlate these with psychological traits, and both used their results to oppose those political and social tendencies in their countries of which they disapproved.[61] Darwinism held out the hope of a genuine science of society and politics,

---

[57] Lapouge, 'Préface' to Le Monisme, 2.   [58] Lapouge, Sélections, 451; L'Aryen, ix.
[59] Lapouge, L'Aryen, 512.   [60] Lapouge, 'The Fundamental Laws', 54.
[61] See Ammon's critique of socialism in his Der Darwinismus Gegen die Sozialdemokratie (Hamburg: Verlagstalt und Druckerei, 1891). For a discussion of Ammon, see Stark, 'Natural and Social Selection'; Bellomy, ' "Social Darwinism" Revisited', 109–13.

and the task of anthropo-sociology was to communicate the importance of race for an understanding of history and to measure and explain the course of racial degeneration in Europe.

However, Lapouge's methodology, which, like that of Lombroso, relied upon cranial measurements as indices of racial type, waned in popularity during the twentieth century. The dubiousness of the attempt to correlate intelligence and other mental attributes with the cephalic index was apparent from Lapouge's own data. He alleged that the dolichocephals made up the bulk of the intelligentsia and the high-status professions, but his statistics actually showed the intellectual classes to have a mean cephalic index that was *higher* than the average for the population as a whole. The implications of this were evaded by invoking the absence of large numbers of brachycephals in the populations concerned.[62]

Lapouge was also unable to maintain a consistent explanation of social and political phenomena by means of the biological reductionism he espoused. The point of his work was to show that modern nations were amalgams of different races, and the obvious inference to be drawn from this was that nation-states were artificial units within which racial conflicts were endemic. Many of Lapouge's strictures against the racial pollution caused by the brachycephals, including his interpretation of the French Revolution, drew precisely this inference. But he also argued on occasions that a nation was an immense family within a certain geographical area, linked to its dead by traditions which would in turn be bequeathed to its posterity. This implies a much more harmonious (and traditionalist) conception of nationality stressing the role of *cultural* bonds in cementing a people into a community.[63] Yet this perspective was contradicted by his critique of the idea of naturalisation, which he labelled biological nonsense; hoping to turn a foreigner into a national was akin to wanting to change a man into a woman. 'Nations are as real as races, they are biological entities', subject to a common selection which fused their various racial components.[64] But this thesis – that racial inter-breeding established the basis for national identity – contradicts the repeated attacks on racial crossings for causing the appearance of 'racial pariahs', people pulled in different directions by plural hereditary forces, biologically incoherent specimens doomed to extinction.[65]

---

[62] Lapouge, 'The Fundamental Laws', 90–1. Lapouge sometimes grouped mesocephals – people with a cranial index of 75–9 – with dolichocephals in order to obtain a sufficient contrast between the latter and brachycephals. See 'The Fundamental Laws', 82–3.
[63] Lapouge, *L'Aryen*, 367.   [64] Lapouge, *Sélections*, 225.   [65] *Ibid.*, 161, 184.

There is a paradox at the centre of Lapouge's theory of social selection, namely that biological forces, alleged to be inexorable causal processes at work in human history, were implicitly acknowledged to be powerless against countervailing social factors. Previous civilisations were supposed to have declined due to race-mixing; modern civilisation was, in addition, threatened by social dynamics which perverted the course of 'natural evolution'. There is a great deal of intellectual opportunism here. Phenomena were explained in either biological or cultural terms depending on how they were evaluated. The psychological attributes of the Aryans which fitted them for mastery and creativity, as well as the corresponding traits of the brachycephals which rendered them suitable for servility and drudgery, were ascribed to immutable biological laws. The factors responsible for the decline of the Aryans and the numerical ascendancy of *Alpinus*, however, derived from social processes which gave the latter an 'unfair' advantage, and should therefore be checked.

This inconsistency of argument derived in part from the way in which ideological considerations dominated the underlying world view, and partly from the enterprise of trying to construct an account of culture upon the presumed workings of nature. In the case of Lapouge, it is ironic that the outcome of his efforts was a view of evolution in which natural selection actually played very little part in bringing about *change*, and instead functioned to *preserve* the dominance of the blue-eyed, long-headed, bicycle-riding Aryan. In short, nature in his work provided less a model of how social change actually took place than a normative model of how society should be ordered. In this framework, the struggle for existence was as potent a force as ever, but its consequences had little to do with changing the physical and mental properties of races. Thus, contrary to a constant emphasis on the ubiquity of change, Lapouge adopted an essentialist position on race: for him, racial traits were, for all intents and purposes, fixed. Transformation was possible, but only as corruption and decadence.

The race problem in the South

In the USA Brace had yoked Darwinism to a theory proposing a common origin for all races and attacking the enslavement of negroes in the South. Later theorists experienced little difficulty in arguing the opposite, i.e. that races were distinct species of unequal capabilities, and that the stronger races eliminated the weaker in the struggle for survival. In the context of the USA, this reasoning was often applied to post-bellum black–white relations to argue that, severed from the protection afforded by slavery, negroes were doomed to extinction in the struggle for existence.[66]

The Race Problem in the South[67] by Joseph Le Conte (1823–1901) is representative of this style of argument. The author was a respected geologist and president of the American Association for the Advancement of Science when the book appeared in 1892. He began by stating that the evolutionary theories of Darwin, and their extension by Spencer, had revolutionised every department of thought, especially sociology. He went on: 'The law determining the effects of contact of species, races, varieties, etc. among animals may be summed up under the formula, "The struggle for life and the survival of the fittest". It is vain to deny that the same law is applicable to the races of man also' (359). Inherited from the animal kingdom, the right of the strongest at one time naturally entailed either slavery or extinction of the vanquished. The difference between humans and animals resided in the reason of the former, but the development of this varied according to the stage of evolution attained by each race. The inevitable result of the two races which differed widely in the 'grade of race evolution' coming into close proximity 'will be, must be, ought to be, that the higher race will assume control and determine the policy of the community' (359).

The character of the lower race determined the form of this subordination. If, like the negro, the race was at an early stage of evolution and hence plastic, docile and imitative, then slavery was appropriate: if, like the redskin, the race had become more specialised and so more rigid, then 'extermination is unavoidable' (360–1). Le Conte contended that slavery was initially optimal for the negro, but by the time of the Civil War he had evolved to a point where this institution was no longer appropriate and some degree of freedom was essential. The problem was that the negro's inferiority meant that his probable fate was the second 'natural' outcome of racial competition – extinction (362). If this conflicted with constitutional amendments, so much the worse for the latter, since they were in conflict with the laws of nature, which were the laws of God: 'There is a law of self-preservation for communities as well as for individuals, and this law takes precedence over all other laws. It is a higher law if you like' (364).

The differences between blacks and whites could not be eradicated through education because although Le Conte was not of the opinion that individual acquirements were totally refractory to inheritance, he was certain that only a very small proportion of such modifications could be passed on to future generations and thus took millennia to produce

---

[66] Haller, *Outcasts From Evolution*, especially chap. 2.
[67] Evolution Series no. 29: Man and the State (New York: Appleton and Co., 1892).

any important effects. True, the higher the race, the more scope there was for these effects, but Le Conte was adamant that heredity furnished the greater part of every person's 'intellectual and moral capital' (366). The negro was therefore constitutionally incapable of looking after himself: 'The Negro race is still in childhood; it has not yet learned to walk alone in the paths of civilisation.' This was why, in those parts of the South where blacks predominated and white influences were minimal, 'the Negroes are rapidly falling back into savagery' (367).

For Le Conte, races were distinctive species, and their sexual union produced infertile offspring, which was contrary to nature. This was why racial prejudice was not wholly pernicious: 'It is probably an instinct necessary to preserve the blood purity of the higher race' (365). Inter-mixture of varieties within the five or six 'primary races' was beneficial, but the crossing of these races themselves was deleterious, producing races (like mulattos) lacking the strength and endurance to compete with other races. So faced with the struggle for survival, inferior races had two options – extermination or mixture with other races. But since the latter bred an even weaker race then extermination was inevitable anyway as an outcome of 'the pitiless law of organic evolution' (373).

Le Conte softened this harsh verdict somewhat by insisting that lower races possessed valuable qualities that could be incorporated into a 'perfect humanity', and he envisaged a 'final civilisation' which seemingly reflected the diverse traits of this humanity (375). When he returned to the immediate problem of race relations in the South, however, this idealism vanished. He insisted that blacks were unworthy of the vote and should be disenfranchised through educational and property qualifica-tions, which had the useful side-effect of disqualifying undesirable whites as well (376–7). Racial differences reflected real differences in the evolutionary advance of two races and should be maintained unless race mixture could be shown to be both feasible and beneficial. Le Conte asserted that it was not possible to speak with confidence on this matter at the present time, belying the dogmatism of his own pronouncements throughout the book on the evils of race mixture.

Le Conte's views on race were quite unremarkable for the period. Sumner had argued that the South should be left to work out its racial problems free from outside interference. He also maintained that the experience of the South demonstrated that the negro was incapable of exercising the vote. He concluded: 'The negro is unquestionably entitled to good government, but giving him political rights has made it harder to give him good government.'[68] Similar views could be entertained even

---

[68] Sumner, *Collected Essays*, 130.

by persons who did not believe that races were equivalent to species. Thus the geologist Nathaniel Southgate Shaler (1841–1906) wrote that humans belonged to a single species and races were 'mere varieties of the same stock'.[69] These varieties were nonetheless exposed to the struggle for survival, and Shaler claimed that the frequency of Indian and French place names in the United States was 'a startling suggestiveness of the incapacity of certain peoples to hold their places in the struggle for existence'.[70] As for the situation of blacks, Shaler insisted that both sides in the Civil War had been motivated by honourable considerations, and that while slavery was an evil, blacks had flourished under its regimen and their masters had been humane.[71] Racial prejudice he attacked as unwarranted in educated people; but he asserted that it had once functioned to keep 'kinds' separate in order to avoid race mixing, which Shaler deemed to be a cause of degeneracy, despite his insistence that humans were one species.[72]

It must be stressed that one did not need to be a Social Darwinist in order to adhere to this position on race. As Haller has argued, different perceptions of the course of evolution had little impact on racist doctrines.[73] What Social Darwinism contributed to race theory was an apparently scientific rationale for racial hierarchy and a mechanism – the struggle for survival – for legitimating the predicted fate of blacks and the actual fate of native Americans.

Imperialism

During the late nineteenth and early twentieth centuries the imperialist policies pursued by the great powers were often perceived in terms of racial conflict. This provided a context in which Social Darwinism could be harnessed to the explanation and justification of imperialist policies, and historians have indeed argued that this ideological linkage was an intimate one.[74] In fact there is a dearth of detailed investigations of the role of Social Darwinism in imperialist thought and practice, a lacuna particularly marked with regard to the soldiers, entrepreneurs and administrators who were actively engaged in colonialism.

[69] N. S. Shaler, *The Citizen: A Study of the Individual and Government* (New York: Barnes, 1904), 13.
[70] *Ibid.*, 53.   [71] *Ibid.*, 60, 318.   [72] *Ibid.*, 234–5, 319–20.
[73] Haller, *Outcasts From Evolution*, 210.
[74] Williams, 'Social Darwinism,' 122; Young, 'Malthus and the Evolutionists', 137–8; Moore, 'Varieties of Social Darwinism', 36; Jones, *Social Darwinism*, 149–53; J. Joll, *Europe After 1870* (Harmondsworth: Penguin, 1983), 101–5; B. Semmel, *Imperialism and Social Reform* (London: Allen and Unwin, 1960); H. W. Koch, 'Social Darwinism as a Factor in the "New Imperialism"', in Koch, ed., *The Origins of the First World War*, second edn (London: Macmillan, 1984), 319–42.

Two additional points need underlining. First, it is evident from some of the figures already discussed that there was no single Social Darwinist perspective on imperialism: to Woltmann's and Royer's endorsement must be contrasted the hostility evinced by Sumner and Spencer. Second, one could be an enthusiastic imperialist without being a Social Darwinist. The German explorer and adventurer in East Africa, Carl Peters, was convinced of the civilising mission of the Anglo-Saxons. By opening up Africa, Europe would not only become enriched but would realise a great duty, 'namely, to elevate a race from a lower plane, and to draw it into the stream of the active development of mankind'.[75] On a less elevated level, he was equally set on the aggrandisement of the German Reich in the face of what he saw as the British ambition of world hegemony.[76] In neither cause did he resort to Social Darwinism; when he lapsed into a philosophical register it was to stress the importance of the will in overcoming obstacles and the need for stoical acceptance of the mysterious workings of Providence.[77]

As with its associations with *laissez-faire* and racial conflict, then, Social Darwinism's connections with imperialist ideology were complex, and neither entailed the other. This being so, there were nevertheless Social Darwinist rationalisations of imperialism. An excellent example is furnished by the publications of the adventurer, hunter and businessman, Frederick Courtney Selous (1852–1917). In 1889, Selous christened a mountain in South-East Africa Mount Darwin 'after that illustrious Englishman whose far-reaching theories ... have revolutionised modern thought, and destroyed for ever many old beliefs that had held men's minds in thrall for centuries'.[78] Selous was deeply involved in the annexation of what was to become Rhodesia, which entailed some bloody confrontations with the warlike Matabele. In his description and rationalisation of these conflicts, Selous drew heavily upon Social Darwinism.

Selous defied his readers to judge his actions in the Matabele Wars according to the dictates of conventional morality. He admitted to shooting at fleeing blacks 'with as little compunction as though they were a pack of wild dogs'.[79] But he maintained that human beings,

[75] Carl Peters, *The Future of Africa* (London: Waterlow, 1897), 15.

[76] See Peters, *England and the English* (London: Hurst and Blackett, 1904), chap. 10. Peters' efforts in East Africa were actually an embarrassment to the German government which was lukewarm about colonial expansion in this area.

[77] Peters, *New Light on Dark Africa*, tr. H. W. Dulken (London: Ward Locke, 1891), 91.

[78] F. C. Selous, *Travel and Adventure in South-East Africa* (London: Rowland, Ward, 1893), 286. For a discussion of Selous and his views on empire, see K. Tidrick, *Empire and the English Character* (London: Taurus, 1990), chap. 2.

[79] Selous, *Sunshine and Storm in Rhodesia* (London: Rowland, Ward, 1896), 64.

including the civilised inhabitants of Western Europe, were initially descended from wild beasts and then from the equally savage peoples of pre-historic times. Hence even with civilised persons it was not necessary to scratch very deep 'in order to discover the savage ancestors from whom they are descended'.[80] In the context of the Matabele Wars, the horrors of the natural environment, the fear of insurrection and the spectacle of massacred white women and children, were responsible for awakening the 'slumbering fiend' which lies latent within us all:

in the smooth and easy course of civilised existence it is possible for a man to live a long life without ever becoming aware that somewhere deep down below the polished surface of conventionality there exists in him an ineradicable leaven of innate ferocity, which, although it may never show itself except under the most exceptional circumstances, must and ever will be there – the cruel instinct which, given sufficient provocation, prompts the meekest nature to kill his enemy – the instinct which forms the connecting link between the nature of man and that of the beast.[81]

As far as the indigenous peoples of south-east Africa were concerned, Selous was convinced of their inferiority relative to the white colonisers. The latter despised the blacks and regarded them as occupying a lower scale of humanity. Empathy between the races was out of the question, and Selous proclaimed it to be 'impossible for a European to understand the workings of a native's mind'.[82] History showed that when a civilised race tried to govern a savage race, the latter rebelled. The conquest of the savage race was therefore a pre-requisite for the development of civilisation, even though this undoubtedly involved bloodshed and injustice against the primitive race.

Therefore Matabeleland is doomed by what seems a law of nature to be ruled by the white man, and the black man must go, or conform to the white man's laws, or die in resisting them. It seems a hard and cruel fate for the black man, but it is a destiny which the broadest philanthropy cannot avert, whilst the British colonist is but the irresponsible atom employed in carrying out a preordained law – the law which has ruled upon this planet ever since, in the far-off misty depths of time, organic life was first evolved upon the earth – the inexorable law which Darwin has aptly termed the 'Survival of the Fittest'.[83]

Here a Darwinist perspective on the animal origins of mankind and the role of struggle in evolution is appealed to as a vindication of white colonial policies in Africa. Selous made the love of hunting, adventure and colonisation criteria of national fitness. When youths no longer wished to leave the comfort of their homes to seek their fortunes in 'wild

[80] Ibid., 193–4.   [81] Ibid., 193.
[82] Ibid., 25. See also Selous, Travel and Adventure, 9–10, 135.
[83] Selous, Sunshine and Storm, 67.

and distant lands', 'then will the decadence of England have set in. As a nation we are probably already past our prime; but that we still possess a vast fund of vigour and energy there can be no doubt.'[84] Selous certainly practised what he preached: he was killed in action against German forces in Tanganyika in 1917.

The tribunal of the battlefield

The publications and the career of Selous offer graphic testimony to the reality of violent conflict in the modern world. The intensification of international disagreements during the opening years of the twentieth century increased the likelihood of such conflict, establishing a climate in which putative national interests could assume a high degree of ethical saliency.[85] Social Darwinism, with its stress on struggle, would seem to furnish a ready-made rationale for warfare and the aggressive assertion of national interests as expressions of a law of nature, and some historians have, indeed, assigned it a contributory role in the outbreak of World War I.[86]

In fact the situation was far more complex, as recent research has demonstrated.[87] As is apparent from the cases investigated in this book, many Social Darwinists adopted an evolutionary interpretation of war. Once an indispensable selective device, it was replaced by peaceful modes of competition as evolution advanced, and actually became an obstacle to additional progress. Other theorists approved of war between races at different stages of evolution, but not between 'advanced' races, where struggle assumed a non-violent form. Plainly, therefore, not all Social Darwinists endorsed warfare as a social analogue of natural selection.

Another complicating factor is the proliferation of alternative standpoints from which warfare could be legitimated. A case in point is the German historian and theorist of *Machtpolitik*, Heinrich von Treitschke

---

[84] Selous, *Travel and Adventure*, 383–4.
[85] D. Pick, *War Machine: The Rationalisation of Slaughter in the Modern Age* (London: Yale University Press, 1993). For analyses of the significance of war and related matters, such as conscription, in Britain and other European nations between 1900 and the outbreak of World War I, see J. Gooch, 'Attitudes to War in Late Victorian and Edwardian England', in B. Bond and J. Roy, eds., *War and Society* (London: Croom Helm, 1975), 88–102; V. G. Kiernan, 'Conscription and Society in Europe before the War of 1914–18', in M. R. D. Foot, ed., *War and Society* (London: Eleck, 1973), 141–58; Koch, 'Social Darwinism as a Factor in the "New Imperialism" '. For the role of Social Darwinism in Anglo-American relations during this period, see S. Anderson, *War and Rapprochement* (London: Associated University Press, 1981).
[86] For example, F. Gilbert, *The End of the European Era, 1890 to the Present*, third edn (London: Norton, 1984), 31–4.
[87] Most notably that of Crook in his *Darwinism, War and History*.

(1834–96). Although Treitschke's aggressive doctrine of power politics has been linked to Social Darwinism,[88] there is no connection between the two, even if some isolated passages in his *Politics*[89] can give the contrary impression. Thus Treitschke asserted: 'Brave peoples alone have an existence, an evolution or a future; the weak and cowardly perish, and perish justly. The grandeur of history lies in the perpetual conflict of nations, and it is simply foolish to desire the suppression of their rivalry. Mankind has ever found it to be so' (I, 21). When we inquire into the reason for this struggle, we find that it stems from the assertion of national interests in a world of competing states – 'War is nothing but foreign policy expressed in terms of force' (II, 404). The state exists as power precisely in order to assert itself against other independent sovereign entities. Treitschke did not explain this by reference to the need for resources or land. In fact, he eschewed any materialist rationale for war, insisting instead that: 'The rational task of a legally constituted people, conscious of a destiny, is to assert its rank in the world's hierarchy and in its measure to participate in the great civilising mission of mankind' (I, 22). This enabled Treitschke to extol the 'moral majesty' of warfare, during which men 'overcome the natural feelings of humanity' in order to slaughter their fellows and sacrifice their own lives 'for the sake of patriotism; here we have the sublimity of war' (II, 395–6).

These arguments demonstrate that nationalism and militarism could be elevated to the rank of moral imperatives without any help from Social Darwinism. Despite this, and notwithstanding the powerful deployment of Darwinism by pacifists, it is important not to lose sight of the fact that Social Darwinist rationalisations of warfare did exist and were highly influential. These accounts were typically structured around two themes: the centrality of struggle and group selection. This discursive tactic allowed for the assertion of the moral supremacy of group over individual welfare, a theme already firmly established in a certain genre of Social Darwinist literature. Consequently, Social Darwinist legitimations of warfare were invariably closely linked to nationalism, which made the integrity of the nation-state and its interests the supreme moral value to which all other interests and values were subordinate.[90]

One of the most notorious examples of a Social Darwinist defence of

---

[88] K. H. Metz, 'The Politics of Conflict: Heinrich von Treitschke and the Idea of *Realpolitik*', *History of Political Thought*, 3(1982), 276.

[89] Heinrich von Treitschke, *Politics*, 2 vols., tr. B. Dugdale and Torben de Bille (London: Constable, 1916).

[90] I. Berlin, *Against the Current* (Oxford University Press, 1981), 338.

international warfare was written by the German general, Friedrich von Bernhardi. His *Germany and the Next War* (1912)[91] sold well and was translated into several languages. In it Bernhardi deplored the opposition to warfare mounted by people who were devoted to personal comfort at the expense of national values and interests. Such sentiments were symptomatic of moral decay, of a turning against nature's laws and the 'biological necessity' of war:

The struggle for existence is, in the life of Nature, the basis of all healthy development. All existing things show themselves to be the result of contesting forces. So in the life of man the struggle is not merely the destructive, but the life-giving principle ... The law of the stronger holds good everywhere. Those forms survive which are able to procure themselves the most favourable conditions of life, and to assert themselves in the universal economy of Nature. The weaker succumb. This struggle is regulated and restrained by the unconscious sway of biological laws and by the interplay of opposite forces (10–11).

Bernhardi maintained that all the laws of nature reduced to one: the law of struggle. This had a dual aspect: *intra-social*, which occurred in everyday life within a society, in the realm of science, thoughts and wishes as well as that of actions; and *super-social*, consisting of violent clashes between nations. Struggle and war were not identical therefore, since the former could be peaceful, as in the case of intra-social conflict, where laws and the state established limits and controls. But no power existed capable of arbitrating the interactions among states, which inevitably resulted in warfare (11–13).

Bernhardi, in orthodox Darwinian fashion, inferred the inevitability of conflict from the pressure of population on resources. Healthy nations had a tendency to expand their populations. Since the globe was now almost entirely inhabited, this growth could be accommodated only through conquest, emigration and colonisation. If the last two options were foreclosed, as they were to Germany, then 'the instinct of self preservation leads inevitably to war, and the conquest of foreign soil' (15). To the pressures created by population growth as motives for war, Bernhardi added the need for foreign markets as an outlet for German goods, and the imperative of protecting the domestic market from foreign imports. His conclusion was: 'The knowledge, therefore, that war depends on biological laws leads to the conclusion that every attempt to exclude it from international relations must be demonstrably untenable. But it is not only a biological law, but a moral obligation, and, as such, an indispensable factor in civilisation' (17).

[91] Trans. A. H. Powles (London: Arnold, 1912). See Crook, *Darwinism, War and History*, 82–3.

The moral imperatives of the nation entailed the subordination of individual rights to national duties (17–18, 41, 59), and meant that the actions of the state could not be assessed in accordance with the standards of personal morality. Bernhardi proclaimed that in the arena of international relations: 'Might is at once the supreme right, and the dispute as to what is right is decided by the arbitrament of war. War gives a biologically just decision, since its decisions rest on the very nature of things' (57).

There are strong echoes of Treitschke's doctrine of *Machtpolitik* in these arguments, which has prompted some commentators to downplay the general's Social Darwinism, relegating it to a marginal role in the text, or seeing it as a mere gloss of 'disconnected catchwords'.[92] These judgements underestimate both the coherence and the rhetorical significance of Bernhardi's Darwinism. The world view was clearly formulated and invoked at those points in his arguments where Bernhardi went beyond Treitschke to argue that the interests of the nation-state had to be understood within the context of biological imperatives. The pressure of population on resources made struggle 'a universal law of nature', a law which grounded the interactions among states and which justified the subordination of the individual to the nation. This materialist rationale for power politics and reason of state would have been anathema to Treitschke.

There is another reason for taking Bernhardi's Social Darwinism seriously, namely that his thesis that nations struggled for space and resources resonated, and indeed may have been influenced by, the *Lebensraum* theory of the zoologist-turned-geographer, Friedrich Ratzel (1844–1904). Ratzel argued that all organisms were engaged in a *Kampf um Raum* – a struggle for space – in which the strongest sought to expel or eliminate the weakest. This struggle for *Lebensraum* (living space) was extended to humans, and Ratzel made it clear that nations were inevitably engaged in the struggle to expand their living space if they wished to avoid decline.[93] Thus Bernhardi's own use of Social Darwinism was hardly eccentric but echoed an established tradition among respectable academic thinkers in Germany.

Furthermore, very similar rationalisations of war were produced by thinkers outside of Germany. 'God's Test by War' was published in an

---

[92] For the first interpretation see Crook, *Darwinism, War and History*, 83, 117; for the second, see Zmarlik, 'Social Darwinism in Germany', 455–6.

[93] For analyses of Ratzel's theories and their relationship to Social Darwinism, see Smith, *Politics and the Sciences of Culture*, 142–7, 219–30; Weikart, 'The Origins of Social Darwinism in Germany', 485–6.

influential British journal in 1911 by Harold F. Wyatt.[94] It opened with the assertion that 'the biological law of competition still rules the destinies of nations as of individual men'. The author then enquired of England: 'Is the heart that once was hers still strong to dare and to resolve and to endure? How shall we know? By the test. What test? That which God has given for the trial of peoples – the test of war' (591–2).

According to Wyatt nations, which now constituted the main divisions of the human race, were analogous to individual organisms. Every healthy organism 'feels the same impulse to grow and to compete with its rivals for increased means of subsistence' (595). Since nations were part of nature, they too were subjected to the struggle for existence, with victory going to the strongest and most efficient organism. Without death the world would be rapidly overpopulated, and among humans war was the 'scythe' that brought death. But it was also the 'condition of human advance', something ignored by those who stigmatised warfare as a relic from mankind's barbarous past:

Defeat in war is the fruit of naval and military inefficiency, and that inefficiency is the inevitable sequel to moral decay. Victory in war is the method by which, in the economy of God's providence, the sound nation supersedes the unsound, because in our time such victory is the direct offspring of a higher efficiency, and the higher efficiency is the logical outcome of the higher morale (595).

Unless human nature was radically transformed, the absence of warfare would produce stagnation rather than progress 'because the terrific punishment which war provides for human degeneracy would be removed' (597). Wyatt was adamant that in war the morally righteous win, so that 'victory is the crown of moral quality', and 'the "survival of the fittest" means the survival of the ethically best'. War was the enemy of sloth, apathy and decadence, and the test of a nation's fitness and moral worth was decided before 'the Court of God, which is war' (599, 602). The author lambasted the Anglo-Saxons for the absence of the 'spirit of self-sacrifice' which he saw manifest in the refusal of their women to bear children and their menfolk to bear arms, in contrast to the Japanese and Germans (600).

Despite Wyatt's resort to religious metaphors and the language of sin and retribution, Social Darwinism provided the intellectual scaffolding for his argumentation. Societies were assimilated to the laws regulating biological organisms, and struggle derived from superfecundity and was made the motor of evolution and progress. This essay was not merely a reflection of jingoistic fervour, therefore, but resonated a number of

---

[94] H. F. Wyatt, 'God's Test by War', *The Nineteenth Century and After*, 69(1911), 591–606.

well-established themes in Social Darwinist discourse, both in Britain and elsewhere.

The notion that, in the polity of nature, warfare acted as the ultimate test of a nation's fitness was also articulated by the Frenchman, George Valois (1876–1945). Valois pursued a veritable ideological pilgrimage across the entire political spectrum, from anarchism through monarchism, to Fascism and finally socialism, a journey that finally ended in a Nazi concentration camp. Throughout these peregrinations, Valois sought the same goal: a united France, organised for the purpose of industrial efficiency, and bound together by a moral consensus. While he changed his mind about the optimal socio-political framework within which this goal could be achieved, the view of the world and human nature which underpinned it was first adumbrated in *L'Homme qui vient*, published just prior to his joining the extreme nationalist and pro-monarchist Action Française in 1906.[95]

Valois was influenced by a recent study by a French biologist, René Quinton, entitled *L'Eau de mer, milieu organique* (1904). Quinton proposed that the earth had been slowly cooling since its formation. This forced each organism to struggle to maintain the temperature of its 'internal milieu', i.e. the biochemical conditions of its physiological existence. A contemporary commentator summarised Quinton's research as a demonstration that life should not be seen as unstable and ruled by caprice and accident, because the external adaptations of an organism acted to preserve its internal milieu.[96] For Valois, Quinton's book facilitated a reworking of Darwinism in which progress and conservation could both be shown to be part of nature's law. Each organism struggled incessantly to augment its protection against a hostile environment. Among animals, this was achieved through organic modifications; in humans, by work and the organisation of work.

Unfortunately, humans were, by nature, disinclined to labour. Civilisation commenced when energetic individuals coerced their fellows into organised efforts, meaning that the need for leadership and authority was universal and perpetual: 'The domination of the man with the whip is eternal' (27). Even after centuries of civilisation, human nature had not changed: 'The beast of yore is still within us, ready at any moment to lead us back to the forest' (14). The coercive and

---

[95] G Valois, *L'Homme qui vient: philosophie de l'autorité*, second edn (Paris: Nouvelle Librairie Nationale, 1909). According to Y. Guchet, *Georges Valois* (Paris: Edition Albatros, 1975), 44–5, 205, this text was the best known and most philosophical of Valois' books, and he remained faithful to the world view sketched therein until at least 1930.

[96] J. Weber, 'Les Théories biologiques de M. René Quinton', *Revue de métaphysique et de morale*, 13(1905), 138.

organisational abilities of the man with the whip were constantly required to prevent human nature from reasserting its primeval slothfulness. What motivated *him* was the struggle for survival. The very success of the dominant individual was an incentive for others to take his place. Thus the master had to be constantly vigilant: 'There is the fear of the other aristocrat who had armed himself in order to take his slaves and the wealth he accumulates in his house; there is the fear of the slave who would like to take his place ...' (12–13). This worked to the benefit of the species, for the aristocrat could only maintain his position of dominance if he continued to perform the functions of discipline and organisation.

The need for authority was eternal, but the *forms* of constraint, domination and social coordination evolved over time. Valois believed that with the emergence of industrial civilisation, the intra-social form of the struggle for existence was transformed. In the modern world, the industrialist and businessman, motivated by the spirit of struggle and risk and subject to the selective pressures of economic competition, complemented the activities of the warrior, while among ordinary people poverty acted as a spur to effort and a punishment for degeneracy and idleness (86). But this did not imply that war became dysfunctional during the industrial era. On the contrary, it was still a 'law of the world' (132), but one that now applied to nations rather than to individuals. Industrial activities required domestic stability which was achieved within the framework of the nation-state. But each nation was in a state of nature *vis-à-vis* its neighbours, so that 'war between nations is a fortunate necessity for civilisation' (175). It was fortunate because armed conflict or its threat prevented laziness and decadence and forced each country to improve its industrial, and hence military, capacity, to the full. Selection, which had formerly operated upon individuals, now acted upon nations. Weak nations, like weak individuals, were inclined to whine about justice and self-determination, but rights could only be established by submission to the ultimate 'tribunal of the Field of Battle' (181). Valois admonished nations to halt their clamour for peace and to prepare for war if they wished to survive. Nature recognised only one form of justice, 'the decline, the death of every living being which abdicates, which renounces, effort' (188). He additionally proposed that a victorious nation ought to replace the work-force of a defeated nation with its own rather than attempt to incorporate the vanquished since this was more beneficial to the species. The victors, by extending their own brave and diligent race and eliminating weak, idle and lax races, contributed to the creation of an ever higher humanity (194–5).

This text is an eclectic one and a number of influences are discernible, especially Nietzsche, from whom Valois borrowed a number of expressions and ideas. But the Darwinian world view is no mere gloss, for it once again provided a set of background assumptions that were brought to the fore when Valois required a scientific counter to liberal and socialist celebrations of individual freedom, egalitarianism, emancipation from labour and peace. As with Bernhardi and Wyatt, group selection through warfare, presented as a biological law, established the rationale for the supremacy of the state and the nation over the individual.

My final case study was written during World War II by Sir Arthur Keith (1866–1955), a distinguished British anatomist and physical anthropologist. Interestingly, in his *Essays on Human Evolution*[97] Keith confessed that until the war of 1914–18 he had subscribed to the view that modern warfare was dysgenic, depriving a nation of its fittest members and thus rendering it less capable of conducting the struggle for existence. Thereafter he came to believe that war 'is part of the machinery which has determined, and is now determining, the fate of nations and of races' (129). In light of the use then being made of Social Darwinism by Nazi theoreticians it is interesting to examine Keith's arguments in some detail.

The foundation of Keith's theory was the premise that among social animals struggle took place between relatively isolated groups, whether of the same or dissimilar species. This required unity and cooperation within the group but resistance to any amalgamation with other groups. Thus intra-group solidarity was complemented by hostility and aggression towards other groups. Since man was a social animal, this held true of the most basic form of association, the 'tribe', which was a specific assortment of genetic material. In biological terms, a tribe was a success if it managed to maintain its genetic integrity over time; if it failed to do so by a slackening of parental and other social bonds, or lack of courage and skill in defence, or by inter-breeding with neighbouring tribes, it was an evolutionary failure (5).

In these conditions, tribesmen evolved a 'dual mentality' consisting of two codes of conduct, the 'ethical' and the 'cosmical'. The former was oriented to the group and stressed altruism, cooperation and solidarity, while the latter stressed antagonism and violence against other tribes and inevitably entailed warfare. The pacifists and the militarists were therefore both correct in their assessment of human nature, but they each concentrated on only one of its facets: the truth was that man was

---

[97] Sir A. Keith, *Essays on Human Evolution* (London: Scientific Book Club). These essays have no date of publication, but according to the author's testimony they were written between 1942 and 1944, and published towards the end of 1944. See vi–vii, 92.

instinctually fitted for both peace and war. 'Human nature was fashioned or evolved just to secure these two conditions – continuity through time and separation in space. Hence the duality of man's nature – the good, social, or virtuous traits serving intra-tribal economy; the evil, vicious, or anti-social qualities serving the inter-tribal economy and the policy of keeping its genes apart' (23).

The breaking up of tribal communities by the formation of city-states and then nations had been a vital step in the progress of civilisation, allowing the rule of law to replace that of custom, and nurturing individual liberty and independence. But there were limits to this process. First, the dual code was so deeply entrenched in human nature 'that it cannot be rooted out; by effort and education the individual may control the cosmical side of his nature, but he cannot annihilate it' (123). Second, 'nations are in the scheme of evolution, the lineal successors of tribes' (146). As a consequence, individuals simply transferred their allegiance from the tribe to the nation-state. 'Free peoples value their liberties above all else save one thing: that one exception is the integrity and independence of the tribe or nation of which they form part ...' (35). This explained the nature and the cause of war: 'any threat of injury to the life or integrity of a nation, any attack on its homeland or on its means of supply, calls forth the old defensive mechanism which Nature has implanted for the protection and perpetuation of her evolutionary units. War is indeed a factor, and a very powerful one, in the evolution of mankind' (133).

Keith derived several moral and political inferences from this theory. He apparently saw no possibility of social evolution beyond the modern nation-state, and regarded universal brotherhood as an impossibility because of the tribal foundations of human nature and the ineradicability of the cosmic code. Christianity was doomed to failure because it sought to apply the ethical code to the whole of humanity, hence 'its methods are discordant with human nature, and are therefore anti-evolutionary. Nationalism, on the other hand, is a growing force because it is in harmony with human nature, and is therefore pro-evolutionary' (68). People had to recognise the existence of the dual code within themselves. Those who sought to regulate their lives according to only one code – the ethical – would be prone to unhappiness, such as was the case with conscientious objectors (195). Moreover, Keith did not regard civilisation as a force capable of eliminating the cosmic ethos. On the contrary, some of the most civilised modern states were also the most ferocious, cruel and warlike, e.g. the Japanese, Western Europeans and North Americans (38–9).

Keith acknowledged the dysgenic impact of modern warfare on a nation's population but insisted that the effects of war had to be measured in national rather than in individual terms. 'War, particularly war as now waged, is the ultimate test, not only of armies, but also of nations. The whole national fabric is tested' (193). War was a powerful factor in national integration, producing a strengthening of the ethical code and the bonds of fellowship and altruism even if the cosmic code of hatred was also reinforced (106). But Keith's position was not without its difficulties. Nazi Germany he presented as a nation that had succumbed to tribalism, although he praised Hitler for understanding the laws of evolution and applying them to the German people (8–11). In fact Keith found it difficult to condemn Nazi Germany for its belligerence since he described nationalism as the successor of tribalism, and regarded nations as incipient species (140). He also celebrated the rejuvenating effects of war on a nation's sense of identity and solidarity and proposed that 'if mankind is to be vigorous in mind and progressive in its spirit, its division into nations and races must be maintained' (175). His paradoxical recipe for peace in Europe was 'each nation being prepared for war and ready to give its blood and its treasure to maintain peace' (206). Finally, although he praised the expansion of individual freedom in countries such as Britain, he considered these liberties dangerous in times of war when they should be abrogated in order to achieve unity of action. He even suggested that periodic outbreaks of war were required in order to prevent individualism from corroding group solidarity: 'When individual selfishness eats into this capital of altruism, then the pyramid of civilisation begins to crumble.' War, by comparison may 'damage a civilisation, but cannot destroy it' (84, 113).

Keith's ideas were remarkably close to Hitler's pronouncements on war and individualism (which are discussed in chapter 11), as well as exhibiting continuity with those of Wyatt, Bernhardi and, earlier, Lapouge and Gumplowicz. The linking of a hereditarian, group selectionist version of Social Darwinism to positions in which national interests assumed moral paramountcy, and ethnic characteristics were virtually timeless, had taken place well before the end of the nineteenth century and had been reinforced by the eugenics movements of the early twentieth. The use of Social Darwinism to construct a moral celebration of international and inter-racial war was not, therefore, a marginal or perverse ideological activity, but rather an important instance of how the world view could be adapted to the perceived moral and political imperatives of the moment.

9   The eugenic conscience

Introduction

The story of the various national eugenics and racial hygiene movements has been told many times, and it is not my intention to reproduce these histories here.[1] My interest is in the relationship between these movements and Social Darwinism. As I argued in the introduction, eugenics and Social Darwinism should not be conflated for it was possible to endorse one and not the other. Nevertheless, Darwin himself prefigured the concerns of the eugenics movements. In his *Descent* Darwin signalled his anxiety about the possibility of biological decline caused by social practices that cushioned the unfit from the impact of natural selection. Whereas among 'savages' mentally and physically defective individuals were quickly eliminated, in civilised societies such persons were sustained by various medical and charitable practices:

Thus the weak members of civilised society propagate their kind. No one who has attended to the breeding of domestic animals will doubt that this must be highly injurious to the race of man. It is surprising how soon a want of care, or care wrongly directed, leads to the degeneration of a domestic race; but excepting in the case of man himself, hardly any one is so ignorant as to allow his worst animals to breed (205–6).

[1]   The most recent studies are: for Britain, G. Jones, *Social Hygiene in Twentieth Century Britain* (London: Croom Helm, 1986); R. Soloway, *Demography and Degeneration* (London: University of North Carolina Press, 1989); P. M. H. Mazumdar, *Eugenics, Human Genetics and Human Failures* (London: Routledge, 1992); for Britain and the USA, D. Kevles, *In the Name of Eugenics* (Harmondsworth: Penguin, 1986); the USA, M. H. Haller, *Eugenics* (New Brunswick, NJ: Rutgers University Press, 1984); for France, Schneider, *Quality and Quantity*; for Germany, Weindling, *Health, Race and German Politics*. Material on France and Germany is also contained in M. Adams, ed., *The Wellborn Science* (New York: Oxford University Press, 1990), which also includes essays on Brazil and Russia. There is an excellent history of various attempts to measure intelligence in S. J. Gould, *The Mismeasure of Man* (Harmondsworth: Penguin, 1992). For investigations of other national eugenics movements, see M. Nash, 'Social Eugenics and Nationalist Race Hygiene in Early Twentieth Century Spain', *History of European Ideas*, 15(1992), 741–8; N. L. Stepan, 'Race, Gender and Nation in Argentina: The Influence of Italian Eugenics', *History of European Ideas*, 15(1992), 749–56.

In the closing pages of the book Darwin returned to this topic to suggest that 'all ought to refrain from marriage who cannot avoid abject poverty for their children', pointing out that 'if the prudent avoid marriage whilst the reckless marry, the inferior members tend to supplant the better members of society'. Darwin underlined the role played by natural selection in human evolution, and claimed that man must remain subject to a severe struggle for existence: 'Otherwise he would sink into indolence, and the more gifted men would not be more successful in the battle of life than the less gifted. Hence our natural rate of increase, though leading to many and obvious evils, must not be greatly diminished by any means' (945).

There were a number of assumptions in these arguments which reappeared in, and indeed structured, subsequent discourses on eugenics and racial hygiene. There was, first, the supposition that 'inferiority' and 'superiority' could be objectively ascertained. Second, there was the assumption that the factors responsible for this distinction were mainly due to heredity rather than to social conditions. Third, there was a presumption of the appropriateness of the analogy between stockbreeding and human reproduction – a presumption that was widespread throughout Europe at the time.[2] Finally, there was the proposition that the beneficial action of natural selection had been replaced by social mechanisms facilitating the propagation of inferior specimens. There was a potential dilemma within this proposition, however, because concern for the unfit derived from the strengthening of social sentiments which themselves were the products of natural selection. Natural forces were hence ambivalent in their social outcomes.

These themes were central to the work of Darwin's cousin Francis Galton (1822–1911). In 1883 Galton proposed the 'science' of eugenics in the belief that it was objectively possible to recognise the undesirable elements in a population and reduce their numbers through relevant social controls – negative eugenics – while at the same time encouraging the reproduction of the better elements – positive eugenics.[3] These suggestions were not initially influential, but by the early twentieth

[2] On the importance of animal breeding in furnishing models for the breeding, control and elimination of humans, see E. U. Da Cal, 'The Influence of Animal Breeding on Political Racism', *History of European Ideas*, 15(1992), 717–25.
[3] For a full elaboration of his ideas on the eve of the formation of eugenics movements across the world, see F. Galton, 'Eugenics: Its Definition, Scope and Aims', *American Journal of Sociology*, 10(1904), 1–25. For a discussion of Galton's work, see Kevles, *In the Name of Eugenics*, chap. 1; Soloway, *Demography and Degeneration*, chaps. 2–6. For Galton's influence on contemporary anthropology see D. Lorimer, 'Theoretical Racism in Late Victorian Anthropology', *Victorian Studies*, 31(1988), 430.

century they acquired considerable currency as the various eugenics movements urged government action to prevent national and racial decline. The German Race Hygiene Society was founded in 1905, followed by the Eugenics Education Society in England (1907), and the French Eugenics Society (1912). A similar body was established in the USA in 1910, and the First International Eugenics Congress was held in London in 1912. The reasons for this transition from the *laissez-faire* stance of Royer and Spencer to the demand for government action typical of the eugenics and racial hygiene movements are complex, but important to an understanding of the role of Social Darwinism in these movements.

Perhaps the most direct impact was the discovery that after a period of steady population increase the trend was reversed, with all European nations experiencing a sharp fall in birth-rates.[4] Moreover, this decline was not socially uniform but mainly confined to the middle and upper classes, thus fuelling anxieties about the future quality of the nation. Statistics also revealed increases in crime and prostitution, the incidence of diseases like tuberculosis, and the numbers of feebleminded persons. The worthless appeared to be thriving at the expense of the worthy.

There were other factors at work as well. Historians have shown how eugenics and social hygiene programmes in some countries served the interests of the practitioners in the various branches of medicine and related professions in their efforts to achieve professional status and public recognition.[5] Urbanisation and industrialisation created social conditions in which ill-health, poverty and crime could thrive, providing opportunities for experts of various descriptions to supply services to a state apparatus increasingly concerned with monitoring and controlling its subjects.[6] The tensions brought about through class and ethnic conflicts and the demands of organised labour and feminists helped establish a climate in which these social conditions could become the focus of political controversy. Reformers advocated programmes of environmental engineering aimed at removing what they saw as the social causes of crime, poverty and disease. But those who believed that

---

[4]   Soloway, *Demography and Degeneration*, xii.
[5]   Weindling, *Race, Health and German Politics*; Schneider, *Quality and Quantity*. Jones does not regard these motives to have been significant in the formation of the British social hygiene movement, though she believes they may have subsequently come to play this role; Jones, *Social Hygiene*, 52. Although physicians played an important role in British eugenics, the majority of the British medical profession appear to have been opposed to eugenics. See D. Porter, ' "Enemies of the Race": Biologism, Environmentalism and Public Health in Edwardian England', *Victorian Studies*, 34(1991), 160–78.
[6]   See J. Donzelot, *The Policing of Families* (London: Hutchinson, 1980).

the environment exerted a negligible impact on the formation of character and physique demanded policies which placed the emphasis on heredity. Not that the two political agendas were mutually exclusive; some reformers like Wallas were able to combine a commitment to social change with a belief in the importance of eugenics. But the increasingly hereditarian bias of eugenics and social medicine during the course of the twentieth century encouraged the promotion of action aimed at elevating the biological quality of the population rather than restructuring the social system in ways that would redistribute opportunities and rewards in favour of the disadvantaged.

Another factor was the concern of many intellectuals with something mentioned in the above citation from Darwin's *Descent* – degeneration. Fiction, medicine and social thought were replete with data, images and explanations concerning the degenerative consequences of modernity. Urbanisation and industrialisation produced a fascination with mental and physical disease, with suicide and crime, prostitution and sexual deviance. In some versions, degeneracy was vested with a wider significance as the manifestation of a deep-seated malaise, endemic to Western culture and morality.[7] This was the thesis of the physician and Jewish nationalist, Max Nordau (1849–1923), the pseudonym of Max Simon Südfeld. In his widely read *Degeneration* of 1892,[8] Nordau wrote of 'a severe mental epidemic; a sort of black death of degeneracy and hysteria . . .' (537). Degeneracy was a pathological condition, a deviation from normalcy that was hereditary and hence transmissible to descendants. It was manifested in a number of physical stigmata – squint eyes, imperfect ears, stunted growth – but above all in a series of mental morbidities, such as hysteria, exaggerated egoism, pessimism, apathy, impulsiveness, emotionalism, mysticism, and a complete absence of any sense of right and wrong (18–22).

Although Nordau's text was important for popularising the notion of degeneracy, it differed from later eugenics literature on two points. First, the main target of his attacks was not the 'lower classes' as was so often the case for eugenicists. For Nordau, the peasantry and the majority of the working class and bourgeoisie were untainted by degeneracy, which was confined the aristocracy and the urban intelligentsia – to the 'upper ten thousand' (2). Second, Nordau did not advocate political intervention as a remedy for degeneracy. The latter was a condition brought

---

[7] Pick, *Faces of Degeneration*; Chamberlin and Gilman, eds., *Degeneration*.
[8] Published in German as *Die Entartung*. The text I have used is the English translation of the second German edition (London: Heinemann, 1895). For a more detailed account of Nordau's views on degeneracy, see S. E. Aschheim, 'Max Nordau, Friedrich Nietzsche and *Degeneration*', *Journal of Contemporary History*, 28(1993), 643–57.

about by the failure of the human organism to adapt to the enormous changes in the conditions of life experienced during the past half century or so. During this period, lives had been dramatically altered by steam, electricity, the railways and newspapers. This new lifestyle incurred a tremendous increase in 'organic expenditure', leading to nervous exhaustion (39). It was, though, precisely through the agencies of adaptation and the struggle for existence that the problem of degeneracy would be eventually resolved, since degenerates were incapable of adaptation (540). Their elimination was hastened if they were surrounded by normal, healthy people, for in such a case the former 'have to fight in the struggle for existence, and there is no leisure for them to perish in a slow decay by their own incapacity for work' (540–1). Hence Nordau was fairly optimistic about the future of civilisation. Normal people would either adapt to the changing circumstances of civilisation or else, if this proved too difficult, abandon the innovations responsible for undue stress. As for the degenerates, their sterility and dysfunctionality doomed them to elimination: 'They can neither adapt themselves to the conditions of Nature and civilisation, nor maintain themselves in the struggle for existence against the healthy' (541).

Nordau's account of degeneracy, therefore, reproduced the optimism of the early pioneers of Social Darwinism insofar as he believed that the course of evolution was ultimately progressive.[9] By the end of the nineteenth century, however, Darwinian theory had itself been reinterpreted in ways that made degeneracy an evolutionary possibility. This was the overt thesis of the eminent British naturalist E. R. Lankester in his *Degeneration: A Chapter in Darwinism* (1880).[10] Warning his readers against a complacent faith in the benignity of future evolution, Lankester asserted that natural selection could have one of three possible outcomes for an organism: the maintenance of a balance between it and its milieu; organic development; or degeneration. The last of these outcomes he defined as a gradual change in structure by means of which an organism became adapted to a less varied and complex form of life (32). Its causes – and human relevance – were clarified thus:

Any new set of conditions occurring to an animal which renders its food and safety very easily attained, seem to lead as a rule to Degeneration; just as an active healthy man sometimes degenerates when he becomes suddenly possessed of a fortune; or as Rome degenerated when possessed of the riches of the ancient

---

[9] Nordau retained this optimism in his later publications. Despite the carnage of World War I, he maintained that war would eventually be eliminated through the taming of the 'wolfish instincts' within humans. See Nordau, *Morals and the Evolution of Man*, tr. M. A. Lewenz (London: Cassell, 1922), 183, 246.

[10] London: Macmillan.

world. The habit of parasitism clearly acts upon animal organisation in this way (33).

Indeed, the moral implications of this conception of degeneracy were never very far beneath the surface of Lankester's arguments. He reminded his readers that 'we are subject to the general laws of evolution, and are as likely to degenerate as to progress' (60). Such a fate had befallen civilisations in the past, and was possible once more due to the prevalence of 'a contented life of material enjoyment accompanied by ignorance and superstition' (61). He looked to science to enable people to avoid this fate: 'The full and earnest cultivation of Science – the Knowledge of Causes – is that to which we have to look for the protection of our race – even of this English branch of it – from relapse and degeneration' (62).

Lankester elevated degeneracy to the status of a natural process by demonstrating how it could occur in nature as a consequence of evolutionary dynamics. Two points are noteworthy about his presentation of this issue. The first has already been remarked upon: the moral judgements implicit in the criteria proposed for deciding when an organism was degenerating. The fact that degeneration could only be inferred from the existence of these alleged criteria gave the theorist a great deal of latitude for interpreting change and discriminating between elaboration, stasis or decay. The second point concerns the prescribed role of the scientist in detecting and remedying degeneracy. If the course of evolution was such that pathological outcomes were not only possible but probable, then the scientist, social scientist or physician, possessed expertise relevant to diagnosis and cure. The ground was prepared for intervention and redirection in social affairs on the basis of scientific expertise in order to ensure that the course of evolution remained wholesome. Lankester himself was to underline this point in subsequent publications in which he insisted that only scientific knowledge of heredity and breeding could avert the potentially disastrous consequences of overpopulation.[11] This was exactly the message of eugenics.

Eugenics was a convenient framework for thinking about these issues. It brought together a configuration of phenomena – crime, mental and physical illness, poverty, moral depravity, childcare, parenthood, the structure and functions of the family, abortion, birth control, and the respective powers and responsibilities of public and private agencies. It allowed these problems to be addressed either within a cosmopolitan perspective stressing concern for the future of the entire human species

[11] E. Ray Lankester, *The Kingdom of Man* (London: Watts and Co., 1911), 32, 35, 40–1, 53.

or, much more commonly, within a context of national or racial consciousness in which the survival of the community was deemed paramount. This chapter examines samples of this reasoning within four national contexts.

Eugenics in Britain

One of the earliest calls for eugenics policies in Britain was made by a professor of physiology, John Berry Haycraft (1857–1922) in his *Darwinism and Race Progress*.[12] Haycraft represented a shift towards the more exclusive hereditarianism heralded by Weismann's theories, rejecting any significant role for environmental factors in racial improvement in favour of selection acting through the death or non-reproduction of inferior specimens, falsely claiming that Darwin himself had gradually come to favour selection over the inheritance of acquired characters (28). He drew attention to differential fertility rates within advanced societies and raised the spectre of the 'swamping' of the capable by the incapable (150). But the main thrust of his work was to highlight the beneficial effects of fatal diseases such as smallpox, whooping cough, tuberculosis and leprosy, which were 'friends to humanity' because they carried off the weaker members of society. Modern medicine and social policies, however, were eradicating these diseases, allowing large numbers of the unfit to survive and reproduce (50–1). It being a law of nature that the world would be dominated by the producers of the largest number of progeny, Haycraft insisted: 'Let us be sure that in our own nation it shall not be the offspring of the deteriorated ...' (153). This entailed replacing 'the selection of the microbes by the selection of human forethought' (58).

Haycraft dissociated himself from any desire to deprive individuals of the benefits of modern medicine, but he argued that there were additional considerations to be borne in mind, including the ramifications of medical care for the health of the race. He took heart from what he perceived to be a diminution in the 'clamorous appeals for personal rights' in favour of a 'growing sense of obligation and a desire to further the interests of others' (156).

Haycraft's recommendations were for the prevention of marriage and reproduction among those with innate criminal tendencies, and among the 'undeserving poor' who were capable of work and should therefore be treated as criminals (98–102). Those suffering from hereditary defects should be segregated – though well treated – because such

[12] London: Swan Sonnenschein, 1895. A translation was published in Germany with a foreword by Weismann. See Weindling, *Health, Race and German Politics*, 97.

people 'are obviously unfit to perpetuate themselves, and in the best interests of the human species, they should be prevented from so doing' (109). He also opposed the prohibition, or restriction in the sale, of alcohol. Though there was no evidence that alcoholism was hereditary, it often accompanied a 'vicious temperament', which was. Excessive alcoholic consumption was, accordingly, an excellent selective device, one 'constantly thinning the ranks of those who are weak enough by nature to give way to it, and leaving unharmed those with healthy tastes and sound moral constitutions' (86).

Haycraft pointed out that in addition to the struggle for existence between nations, making the need for a healthy nation an urgent imperative, another struggle took place within societies for the possession of property and wealth, although this was based almost entirely on brain-power. Success in this conflict encouraged idleness and decadence, so Haycraft suggested that there was a need to equalise conditions in order to increase competition, leading to the formation of an aristocracy of talent recruited from all social classes (130). Although this suggestion was left undeveloped, it was evidently not prompted by any egalitarian sentiments, which Haycraft dismissed as 'ridiculous'. His goal was a new class system based upon 'real organic differences', although he warned his readers that this new elite, through its very success in the struggle, would be likely to be selfish and devoid of generosity (131–3). He side-stepped this issue by drawing attention to an expansion in altruism, although he gave no clue as to the origins of this trend. He concluded by insisting on the need to educate the masses into an awareness of mankind's relationship to animals and to the general laws of evolution, and on the need to prevent the marriage of the unfit: 'If the community undertakes its own selection we can dispense with the selective influence of the micro-organism of whooping-cough, scarlet fever, or tubercle' (170).

Haycraft's text reproduced the four assumptions underpinning eugenics identified in Darwin's *Descent*. In addition, it drew upon the premise of a struggle for existence between nations as justification for the elevation of the rights of the nation over those of the individual in the name of national survival. Another striking example of this type of argument is afforded by the British idealist philosopher, Francis Herbert Bradley (1846–1924). An admirer of Hegel, Bradley was opposed to materialist and empiricist metaphysics. For him, ultimate reality – the Absolute – was spiritual but, *contra* Hegel, could not be adequately comprehended in thought but through feeling.[13] This idealist perspec-

---

[13] See F. H. Bradley, *Appearance and Reality*, second edn (Oxford: Clarendon Press,

tive hardly seems compatible with Social Darwinism, and yet in a pungently argued essay on punishment, Bradley unflinchingly adopted a Social Darwinist position.[14]

Bradley declared that while Darwinism was unlikely to lead to any revolutionary conclusions as far as the ends of morality were concerned, it could force a radical reassessment of the means of achieving these ends, taking us beyond Christianity back to Hellenic principles (269–70). The Chief Good was 'the welfare of the community realised in its members'. Darwinism demonstrated that the survival and progress of the race in the past was due to the struggle for existence among its members and the natural selection of the fittest. Bradley insisted that it was impossible to reinstate this state of affairs because no community could tolerate an unchecked struggle in its midst. At the same time, in terms of the Chief Good, it was equally the case that the principle of natural selection could not be totally disregarded. 'We do not deny that progress has been made largely by natural selection, and we must admit that in this process the extinction of the worse varieties is essential. It is clear again that with this struggle and this extinction the community now interferes' (271). The unchecked competition of the past was replaced by a 'competition of fertilities' in which the 'higher types' were being outbred by the 'weaker and lower'.

In response to this development, Bradley argued that there was an urgent need to divorce punishment from considerations of guilt and justice. The latter was 'but a subordinate and inferior principle. It can hear no appeal from the tribunal of the common welfare' (276). He stipulated the right of a community to perform 'moral surgery' on its membership if this was required for the good of the whole. 'Once admit that life in this world is an end in itself, and the pure Christian doctrine is at once uprooted. For, measured by that end and standard, individuals have unequal worth, and the value of each individual is but relative, and in no case infinite' (277). It was meaningless to appeal to the rights of the individual, for 'over its members the right of the moral organism is absolute' (278).

Bradley's aim in adumbrating these arguments was to highlight the need for eugenics – one of the cardinal lessons of Darwinism. 'It teaches, in a word, the necessity of constant selection. It insists that the way to improve – the way even not to degenerate – is on the whole unchanging. That way consists in the destruction of worse categories, or

1897). For a brief but accessible introduction to Bradley's metaphysics, see J. Passmore, *A Hundred Years of Philosophy*, second edn. (Harmondsworth: Penguin, 1968), 60–71.

[14] F. H. Bradley, 'Some Remarks on Punishment', *International Journal of Ethics*, 4(1894), 269–84.

at least in the hindrance of such varieties from reproduction' (280). To do otherwise was to sustain the unfit at the expense of the fit. What was required was 'social amputation' because wholesale confinement, even mutilation, of the worse specimens was inadequate, burdening the community with the maintenance of 'useless lives' and condemning the members of this latter group to a cruel existence: capital punishment was far kinder. Bradley left his readers in no doubt as to his feelings on this matter:

I am oppressed by the ineffectual cruelty of our imprisonments. I am disgusted at the inviolable sanctity of the noxious lunatic. The right of the individual to spawn without restriction his diseased offspring on the community, the duty of the state to rear wholesale and without limit an unselected progeny – such duties and rights are to my mind a sheer outrage on Providence (283–4).

Bradley took care to pay homage to traditional values which, he avowed, were fully consistent with Darwinism, including mutual assistance, benevolence, charity and mercy. Indeed, these virtues were actually implied by Darwinism which taught that 'within the whole the principle of competition has become subordinate. It has ceased to be absolute, and is overruled less or more by the main principle of general advantage.' Nor did it license individual self-seeking or tribal and national selfishness. 'Regard for a whole beyond my social group', purred Bradley, 'for humanity, indeed for all sentient beings, is certainly not opposed to Darwinism.' What the latter doctrine demonstrated was that ethical surgery was a true form of benevolence if unflinchingly exercised for the common good, and not therefore vulnerable to the criticisms of humanitarian opponents, whom Bradley found hypocritical: 'There is no one … so remorseless as the humanitarian, no one more ruthless and more bloody than the sentimentalist, no one so pitiless as the rider on Christian principles. And it is not a rational world where the surgeon is charged with cruelty' (280).

These are chilling sentiments, emanating as they did from the pen of an Oxford don with a considerable academic reputation. Moreover, although the overt subject of Bradley's essay was the punishment of criminals, his target was obviously much more extensive. He included among the unfit who were to be denied the right to life lunatics, persons with hereditary diseases, and the children of these groups. His tactic was to take the national community as the unit of evolution and then to assume the moral priority of this community in the struggle for existence. I say 'assume' because Bradley offered no arguments to this effect, but simply took the precedence of the whole over its parts for granted. He then proposed that for the community to survive in the struggle for existence it must find a substitute for natural selection which could no longer be countenanced within its boundaries. The use of euphemisms like 'moral/ethical surgery' and 'social amputation' created the impression that the morally diseased could be scientifically identified. Their removal was intimated to be a clinical operation which, though conducted principally in the interests of society as a whole, would be a blessing to the individuals concerned. In this way, Bradley mounted a challenge to a whole congeries of Christian and liberal precepts relating to justice, individual liberties and moral agency.

These tasks assumed practical urgency during the Boer War in South Africa between 1899 and 1902. Recruitment to the British army during this conflict exposed the prevalence of low levels of health and education among the urban working classes, provoking a great deal of speculation about the causes of this situation, and its implications for 'national efficiency'. *National Life From the Standpoint of Science*[15] by Karl Pearson (1857–1936), a British pioneer in the application of statistical techniques to biological data, was an intervention in these debates – initially in the form of a wartime lecture – which was intended to invest them with some scientific content. It linked the perceived crisis in the vitality and health of the nation to a Social Darwinist vision of human evolution and a call for eugenic policies capable of reversing the trend in national deterioration while it was still possible to do so.

Humans, maintained Pearson, were the products of an evolutionary process generated by the struggle for existence in the form of warfare, as well as 'the more silent, but none the less intense' peaceful competition for markets, resources and commercial supremacy (13). The struggle took place between herds, tribes or nations rather than between individuals, and Pearson considered it imperative that people should be aware that the 'continual progress of mankind, is the scarcely recognised outcome of the bitter struggle of race with race, the result of man, like all other life, being subject to the stern laws of the survival of the fitter, to the victory of the physically and mentally better organised' (64).

Successful nations in this struggle were those effective in mobilising the abilities of their most talented members and these abilities were, in great part, hereditary. Education could modify an individual's behaviour, but such modifications could not be inherited by his or her descendants. 'You cannot change the leopard's spots', proclaimed Pearson, 'and you cannot change bad stock into good' (19), so that a nation had to ensure the continual reproduction and 'dominant fertility'

---

[15] Second edn (London: Adam and Charles Black, 1905). The lecture was originally delivered in Newcastle in 1900.

of its 'better elements' or else it would destroy itself 'far more effectively than its foes could ever hope to destroy it in the battlefield' (ix).

The data on army recruits demonstrated that Britain could no longer rely upon the blind workings of natural selection to guarantee the dominant fertility of its superior members. This was because a number of social forces were removing or weakening the checks which 'the unrestrained struggle for existence places on the fertility of the unfit', while simultaneously contributing to the diminishing fecundity of the fit. In the latter category, he hinted vaguely at 'love of ease, a mistaken sense of duty, insidious new social habits' (viii). In the former he targeted charitable endeavours and state welfare programmes which encouraged the multiplication of the 'feckless and improvident', in addition to criminals, lunatics and the chronically sick (29–30, 31). Elsewhere, Pearson criticised minimum wage legislation, proposals for an eight-hour working day, and the public provision of free medical advice for the same reasons.[16]

Having described the world as an arena of struggle Pearson then converted moral issues into questions of group survival. 'By moral conduct . . . we mean that which tends to the welfare and progress of the group of which we are members, and by immoral conduct the reverse' (96–7). In this light, parenthood acquired new significance as a matter of national importance, yet people persisted in falsely regarding it as a realm of individual preference and choice. 'From the point of view of the nation', insisted Pearson, 'we want to inculcate a feeling of shame in the parents of a weakling, whether it be mentally or physically unfit' (28). Equally at fault was the public's indulgent attitude to criminals. Crime and 'health, sanity, conscientiousness and ability are inherited characters', but this was ignored by people who wanted to suspend the principle of natural selection. 'A hundred years ago you hung a rogue if you caught him. Nowadays you provide him with soup-kitchens and night-shelters up and down the country, and leave him to propagate his kind at will' (101).

The result of the failure to perceive these issues within the context of national – as opposed to individual – welfare was a situation whereby the less worthy elements in society multiplied while the stocks from which the nation's leaders should be recruited, which Pearson estimated to be about one half of one per cent of the population, married late and had small families. Pearson drew a stark conclusion and, by implication,

---

[16] Kevles, *In the Name of Eugenics*, 34. At the same time, Pearson was supportive of many feminist goals, and did not subscribe to the view that women were innately inferior to men; see Kevles, *In the Name of Eugenics*, 34; Soloway, *Demography and Degeneration*, 111–21.

offered his audience an equally stark choice: 'The problem is simple in the extreme. We have two groups in the community – one parasitic on the other. The latter thinks of tomorrow and is childless, the former takes no thought and multiplies. It can only end as the case so often ends – the parasite will kill its host, and so end the tale for both alike' (106).

Pearson hastened to add that recognition of these facts did not require the hanging of rogues or the refusal of medical assistance to the physically and mentally sick, only the prevention of the unfit from reproducing themselves. His use of the expression 'parasite', however, suggests a contemptuous and punitive attitude that is reflected in his actual recommendations, which included sending criminals to a 'sub-tropical climate', and the institutionalisation and strict surveillance of paupers and the insane (105).

Pearson also attacked the dysgenic consequences of a social system which allowed aristocrats to be recruited into important posts on the basis of wealth rather than ability. Nevertheless, Pearson did not propose any radical restructuring of the class system because he thought that existing inequalities had a biological basis:

If we look upon society as an organic whole, we must assume that class distinctions are not entirely illusory; that certain families pursue definite occupations because they have a more or less specialised aptitude for them. In a rough sort of way we may safely assume that the industrial classes are not on the average as intelligent as the professional classes and that the distinction is not entirely one of education.[17]

Pearson's position was that inequalities of health and education should not be allowed to compromise the sense of national solidarity. Class conflict was disruptive and impaired national efficiency: 'The true statesman has to limit the internal struggle of the community in order to make it stronger for the external struggle' (54). This struggle, involving warfare and commercial competition with other nations and races, made it imperative that the nation should achieve a strong sense of unity and identity. Insisting that 'national spirit is not a thing to be ashamed of', Pearson admonished his countrymen for their lack of patriotism. A nation containing a large number of people imbued with fraternal regard for the entire human species and devoid of the patriotic spirit would experience serious difficulties in the struggle for survival (52–3).

Pearson's refusal to countenance a social explanation for the existence and alleged proliferation of the 'unfit' was bound up with his attitudes to class and racial inequalities, which he attributed to biological causes that were refractory to modification through ameliorative social action. Thus

[17]   Pearson, *The Groundwork of Eugenics* (1912), 33. Cited in Jones, *Social Darwinism*, 114.

for him the black races were inherently and therefore permanently inferior to whites, a situation which had been brought about by selective forces and was hence unalterable by education. Racial inter-mixing was deleterious for the 'good stock', and even the physical proximity of differently endowed races was demoralising. Pearson recognised that to many people this might appear a bleak representation of the human condition, but struggle was a law of evolution, and 'intense suffering' was the price of progress: 'This dependence of progress on the survival of the fitter race, terribly black as it may seem to some of you, gives the struggle for existence its redeeming features; it is the fiery crucible out of which comes the finer metal' (26).

Since national survival was at stake in the struggle for existence it was vital to reverse the counter-selective policies and actions that were swelling the numbers of the unfit. Urgent action was needed if the 'parasites' were not to overwhelm the host and destroy it. These included the indigent, criminals, the feebleminded and insane, vagrants, prostitutes and 'weaklings'. Their various conditions were caused by hereditary defects, and they had to be prevented from reproducing their kind, given the obvious dysgenic consequences this would entail.

It has been suggested that among British eugenicists, Pearson, with his strident nationalism and his endorsement of war, was something of a maverick.[18] Yet the reasoning, as well as the tone, of Pearson's text does not differ in essentials from those of Bradley or Haycraft. Furthermore, an examination of seemingly more moderate proposals reveals the same features: the subordination of the individual to the nation-state in the interests of national survival, and a call for the reduction of the unfit as a substitute for the seemingly defunct culling action of natural selection.

These features are fully apparent in the publications of Darwin's son, Major Leonard Darwin (1850–1943), who was president of the British Eugenics Education Society from 1911 to 1928. Towards the end of his period in office, Darwin produced a lengthy tome on eugenics, followed by a scaled-down version for more popular consumption.[19] In both he presented a Darwinian view of man as an animal that had evolved through natural selection and about whom much could be learned by observing the breeding practices of farmers. As with livestock, superior humans should be encouraged to reproduce as much as possible, the

---

[18] For comparisons between Pearson's ideas and those of other British eugenicists, see Searle, *Eugenics and Politics in Britain, 1900–1914* (Leyden: Noordhoff International Publishing, 1976), 36–9; Soloway, *Demography and Degeneration*, chap. 7. Pearson only approved of war between civilised and inferior races. Struggle between the former took the form of competition for markets, trade-routes and raw materials.

[19] L. Darwin, *The Need For Eugenic Reform* (London: Murray, 1926), and *What is Eugenics?* (London: Watts, 1928).

inferior encouraged to reproduce less. Eugenics demonstrated that good breeding practices were crucial to the future welfare of the country: 'Eugenics calls upon us to include all future generations amongst our neighbours ... for whom we ought to be prepared to sacrifice our own immediate interests.'[20]

Darwin surmised that it was folly to allow 'parents with bad natural qualities' to reproduce at a faster rate than the better endowed.[21] In the former category he included not only the mentally and physically handicapped, but a large 'inferior class' living on low wages, comprising 'the stupid, the careless, the inefficient, the intractable, the idle, the habitual drunkard, as well as those too feeble in body or in health to do a good day's work'.[22] Finally, for good measure he added manual labourers, for whom parenthood had been made less onerous than it should be by both public and private philanthropy.[23]

Similar anxieties are discernible in the eugenics writings of Julian Huxley (1887–1975), a distinguished biologist and a grandson of T. H. Huxley. In a series of essays entitled *What Dare I Think?*,[24] Huxley depicted heredity as a lottery, a throw of the genetic dice determining an individual's biological constitution and physical and mental capabilities (74). But he went on to draw attention to the doubling of the number of morons and defectives in Britain during the previous quarter of a century, which he attributed to improvements in public health, infant welfare and preventive medicine. Huxley then evoked Social Darwinism to highlight the counter-selective impact of these measures: 'By reducing the rigour of natural selection, we are allowing an undue proportion of unfit types to survive.' The only 'civilised' course of action was to prevent mental defectives from having children, though whether this was best achieved by prohibiting marriage, by segregation or by sterilisation, he described as not 'our present concern'. What Huxley sought was 'a general agreement that it is not in the interests of the present community, the race of the future, or the children who might be born to defectives, that defectives should beget offspring' (97, 98).

Huxley constructed a gloomy scenario. He was convinced that the genetic changes taking place in the population were for the worse, and believed alteration of the socio-economic system, though perhaps an ultimate goal, could only be achieved slowly, during which time degeneration would advance unchecked. These problems all stemmed from the fact that society had deflected the workings of natural selection and 'without attempting to put anything in its place, has allowed harmful mutations to accumulate instead of weeding them out or prevented

---

[20] L. Darwin, *What is Eugenics?*, 5–12, 24.   [21] *Ibid.*, 19.   [22] *Ibid.*, 57, 58.
[23] *Ibid.*, 63–4, 70–1.   [24] London: Chatto and Windus, 1932.

them from appearing, and in fine has neglected eugenic measures' (115–16).

Huxley propounded a form of 'scientific humanism' in which humanistic values and science could be harmonised. He did not want to see science enthroned as a dictator to which every human value had to be referred for approval. But he was equally opposed to the current tendency to push certain values – for example, those pertaining to the sanctity of life – to absolute limits. In such circumstances: 'The value of human life becomes so absolute that it is murder to put away a deformed monster at birth, and criminal to suggest euthanasia; and we push on with our reduction of infant mortality until we save an excess of cripples and defectives to breed from' (165). It was essential to realise that humanity was implicated in a 'gigantic evolutionary experiment'. Science could furnish 'impersonal guidance and efficient control' over the workings of this process, and this was the responsibility and the promise of eugenics. 'On its negative side it becomes racial preventive medicine: on its positive side, racial hope' (119).

Although there are considerable differences in tone in the proposals of Darwin and Huxley (who subsequently abandoned eugenics) on the one hand, and Haycraft, Bradley and Pearson on the other, there are also a number of striking continuities. In all of these thinkers there can be discerned an elitism which attributed social hierarchies to differences in biological worth; which subordinated the welfare of individuals to that of the race or nation; and which, in the name of evolutionary science, consigned large portions of their co-nationals to the realm of the biologically worthless. In all of these examples, the need to improve the race or nation – these concepts tended to be employed interchangeably – against the pernicious actions of counter-selective practices was propounded as an evolutionary imperative. This need was invested with added urgency by invoking the spectre of the struggle for existence in which only the fittest, healthiest and socially efficient nations/races would survive. Thus Huxley, during the 1920s, foresaw a time when eugenics would become 'practical politics' and raise the quality of the population 'by altering the proportion of good and bad stock, and if possible eliminating the lowest strata in a genetically mixed population'.[25] Genetics became an analytical tool for diagnosing the racial health of the population, and Social Darwinism furnished the rationale for eugenic intervention, while science legitimated the claim to expertise in these matters.

---

[25] Huxley, *Essays of a Biologist* (London: Chatto and Windus, 1928), 51.

Germany and the science of racial hygiene

In Germany, interest in questions of racial hygiene increased during the last decade of the nineteenth century, and soon became salient among biologists and anthropologists, as well as in the health professions. In these early years it was a heterogeneous movement containing many advocates of policies aimed at improving the quality of life for the masses. After World War I there occurred a change of emphasis, with hereditarian explanations of ill health, linked with a conception of race as a biological entity, achieving prominence. The consequence was the emergence of a phobia about racial decline and the need for appropriate remedial policies. According to Weindling, the political disruption and mass starvation and sickness which were rampant between 1919 and 1924 'broke down precepts of humanity and benevolence', and fears for national survival encouraged widespread discussion among doctors and lawyers about the role of euthanasia and other radical eugenic measures in preventing the collapse of the German *Volk*.[26]

An example of this reaction is a text on the 'destruction of worthless life' which appeared in 1920. The authors, Binding and Hoche, argued that in current circumstances it was impossible to devote a large measure of resources to 'living burdens', i.e. those who were 'mentally dead'. The criteria by which such persons could be recognised were extremely vague, leaving a great deal of discretion to the authorities. Binding and Hoche cited 'the alien character of the mentally dead within the context of human society, the lack of any productive achievements, a condition of complete helplessness with the necessity of being looked after by others . . .' Eliminating these people was neither a crime nor an immoral act, but one that would benefit the nation. The authors argued:

There was a time which we regard as barbaric, in which the elimination of those who were born or became unviable was regarded as natural. Then came the phase we are in now, in which finally the maintenance of any, even the most worthless, existence was considered to be the highest moral duty; a new period will come which, on the basis of a higher morality, will cease continually implementing the demands of an exaggerated concept of humanity and an exaggerated view of the value of human life at great cost.[27]

The arguments employed in this text were not qualitatively different from those expressed by Haycraft, Lapouge, Bradley, Pearson or even

---

[26] Weindling, *Race, Health and Politics*, 393–4.

[27] K. Binding and A. E. Hoche, *Die Freigabe der Vernichtung Lebensunwerten Lebens: Ihr Mass und Ihre Form* (Leipzig: 1920). Extract in J. Noakes and G. Pridham, eds., *Nazism, 1919–1945: A Documentary Reader*, 3 vols. (University of Exeter, 1983–8), III, 1000–1.

Huxley. What the shock of defeat in Germany did was produce circumstances in which these ideas could attain widespread currency, something which never happened in Britain or France.[28] The concept of racial hygiene enunciated by German theorists during the early years of the century could thus acquire added plausibility and their proposals could achieve the urgency of racial survival. An indication of what this would entail is contained in an internal Nazi Party memorandum circulated by a party official, Franz von Pfeiffer, in 1925. 'No pity is to be shown to those who occupy the lower categories of the inferior groups: cripples, epileptics, the blind, the insane, deaf and dumb, children born in sanatoria for alcoholics or in care, orphans (= children born out of wedlock), criminals, whores, the sexually disturbed, etc.' Such people constituted an immense waste of resources. Hence: 'This bottom category means destruction and death. Weighted and found wanting. Trees which do not bear fruit should be cut down and thrown into the fire.'[29] The Third Reich provided the opportunities for the realisation of these proposals.

Chapter 11 will examine Nazi eugenic ideology in some detail. Here I want to explore the academic rationalisation of eugenics which linked genetics, eugenics and race prior to the Third Reich. A good example of this is an influential textbook on heredity.[30] Written by established experts in their fields and often highly technical and mathematical, this text cited Ammon's work in its bibliography of 'important and comprehensive books'. Continuity with earlier race theories was signalled even more clearly by its approval of de Gobineau's *Essay*, of which the authors observed: 'Notwithstanding manifold errors, this is an inspired book whose fundamental ideas remain incontrovertible. It stands unrivalled as a pioneer book on the racial problem' (706).

In a section entitled 'Racial Differences in Mankind', Eugen Fischer (1874–1967) rejected the cranial index as a measure of race while remaining convinced of the reality of race (117). 'Technically speaking',

---

[28] Although both countries had supporters of radical eugenic measures. In Britain, Winston Churchill, when Home Secretary, tried in 1910 to convince the Prime Minister, Asquith, and the Cabinet, of the need for forcible sterilisation and incarceration of the feebleminded and insane. See C. Ponting, 'Churchill's Plan for Racial Purity', *The Guardian*, 20 June 1992. In France, the defeat of 1940 paved the way for a racially inspired eugenics under the Vichy regime. See Schneider, *Quality and Quantity*, chap. 10.

[29] Reading no. 62 in R. Griffin, ed., *Fascism* (Oxford University Press, 1995), 119.

[30] Bauer, Fischer and Lenz, *Human Heredity*. Weindling describes this book as 'authoritative in linking genetics and medicine with racial hygiene', which 'established the scientific status of the concept of a Nordic race'. First published in 1921, it went to a revised fifth edition in 1940. See Weindling, *Health, Race and German Politics*, 473, 306.

he wrote, 'there is no such generalised being as "man"; there are only men and women belonging to particular races or particular racial crossings.' This was because 'in human heredity the innumerable characters which differentiate individuals and groups (races) are tenaciously and inalterably transmitted from generation to generation ...' (209). This held true for psychology as for physiology: 'The various races of men differ from one another to an extraordinary degree in mental respects no less than in bodily' (181). Mental aptitudes were inheritable, established 'once and for all', which meant that races varied considerably in their capabilities (130, 181).

Fischer argued that humans were descended from an anthropoid ancestry and their evolution had been, and still was, governed by natural selection, although the rigour of this tended to diminish with the advance of civilisation. The extinction of races could not be accounted for by applying the metaphors of senescence: 'The races of man no more grow old and die than do the races of lower animals or of plants. They can only be eliminated by selection, thus dying an unnatural death' (183). Nor was racial inter-crossing necessarily the cause of a race's elimination. Such crossings could be deleterious, but they also gave rise to new varieties and were a source of regeneration and development (182). The answer he gave was one of a 'reverse selection' which altered the racial composition of a people and deprived it of effective leadership, thus making it a less functional biological unit. The author hinted darkly that the present fate of Germany had precisely such an 'anthropological cause' (183). 'We are coming to recognise more and more clearly', he wrote, 'that racial factors, and especially hereditary mental endowments ... are among the most influential in determining the course of a nation's history' (182).

These themes were extended in the contributions by Lenz, professor of racial hygiene at the University of Munich. Like many of his countrymen, Lenz was affected by an acute sense of crisis brought about by Germany's defeat in the Great War. Faced with the contingency and transience of human values and achievements he looked to race for permanence and certainty.[31]

Lenz contended that the distinction between health and sickness turned upon the adaptational capacity of an organism. However, he made it clear that the significance of this distinction lay in its bearing upon 'racial rather than individual survival' (216). 'Thus every adaptation upon which we make the concepts of health and disease turn, is in the last analysis directed towards the preservation not of the individual

---

[31] Weindling, *Health, Race and German Politics*, 302–3.

but of the race. Individual-survival is only a means to the end of race-survival' (216).

What did Lenz mean by race? In constructing a racial classification, he disclaimed any intention of ranking races in a hierarchy because this implied a standard of value other than race itself (696–7). But the entire thrust of his analysis of racial differences was aimed at precisely the creation of such a hierarchy, and then to draw out the implications of this for the future of Germany. The criteria he adopted for this task were psychological, on the grounds that the mental differences between races were even more pronounced than bodily differences and equally rooted in heredity to the extent that environmental influences, including education, 'can do no more than help or hinder the flowering of hereditary potentialities'. Lenz completely rejected the inheritance of acquired characters and insisted on the need to abandon Lamarckian prejudices in order to arrive at an accurate understanding of the genetic determinants of race (565, 604, 607). Notwithstanding the scholarly apparatus deployed by Lenz, his classification reproduced all the standard racial prejudices and stereotypes found in the writings of de Gobineau, Lapouge and Chamberlain.

At the bottom of his scale Lenz located 'primitive races', such as the Veddahs and Australian Blackfellows, whom he described as feeble-minded and 'closely akin to our simian forefathers' (628). The negro races he considered more advanced than primitives, but lacking in foresight and initiative, influenced by their senses, unintelligent and displaying many of the mental traits of children (628–34). In his description of the next level, Lenz succeeded in combining racial stereotypes with shibboleths on gender. Mongoloids were hard-working and frugal, but unimaginative. They related to Europeans in the same way as women to men, 'for Mongols are receptive rather than creative; and are at the same time frugal, contented, and patient' (634–9).

After describing a series of 'intermediary' races, Lenz reached the summit of the hierarchy, the Nordic race, which created the Aryan languages and civilisation (647–61). The Nordic possessed great intelligence and creativity, enormous energy and a vivid imagination, but was an individualist, devoid of a sense of community. 'The Nordic finds it difficult to put himself in another's place. His instincts are individualistic rather than social, his craving for independence makes him resist being enrolled in a community.' Above all, the Nordic was motivated by a will-to-power and proclivity for war, tempered by an aristocratic capacity for self-restraint (658–9).

The implication that individualism was a vice mirrored the claim that the individual was only a means to the end of racial survival. But from whence did the threats to this survival derive? Lenz was far from explicit on this point. One such threat obviously came from people afflicted with hereditary diseases. But the physical and mental descriptions of the Nordic race, and Lenz's concentration on the racial divisions within Europe, were redolent with other implications. Some of these appeared in his discussion of Jews. According to Lenz the Jews were not a unified race, but their solidarity and closedness made them something of a 'mental' race. They possessed a great talent for economic activities, and were capable of intellectual greatness, as shown by Einstein. Indeed, Lenz went so far as to argue: 'Next to the Teutonic, the Jewish spirit is the chief motive force of modern civilisation' (674). But these positive assessments were interspersed with familiar negative stereotypes. Thus Jews lived within other cultures, which they mimicked; they induced other races to accept Jewish leadership; they were averse to physical labour and inept at warfare. They were partially composed of the Near Eastern race, 'which has been selected to excel, not so much in the control and the exploitation of nature, as in the control and exploitation of man' (644). Lenz maintained that whereas the Jew could not exist without the Teuton, the latter would be perfectly capable of getting along without the Jew (677). While such comments were not so overtly disparaging as the more virulent anti-Semitic rhetoric of the period, they relied upon a similar set of contrasts with the psychic disposition of the Nordic race, against which they acted mainly as a negative counterpoint. Thus Lenz, who maintained that racial mixing could be advantageous, insisted that the reverse was true if the races were widely divergent and, in spite of his acknowledgements of Jewish achievements, condemned the crossing of Teutons and Jews (692–3).

For Lenz, the realities of racial and other hereditary differences rendered idealistic dreams of equality biologically untenable: 'The inequalities among human beings are mainly dependent upon the hereditary equipment, and this cannot be transformed in any simple way either by material or by spiritual influences. In the individual it cannot be changed at all, and in the race it can only be changed by selection' (698). This did not justify inaction on the part of a nation. To the contrary, membership of a superior race should not lull one into a false sense of security, because the 'biological heritage of the mind' is just as perishable as that of the body. 'If we continue to squander that biological heritage as we have been squandering it during the last few decades, it will not be many generations before we cease to be the superiors of the Mongols. Our ethnological studies must lead us, not to arrogance, but to action – to eugenics' (698).

Lenz was convinced that the reason for the collapse of classical civilisation was to be sought in the 'extermination of the creative racial elements' responsible for their achievements (696). His views contain the same mixture of elitism and biological reductionism that occur in the writings of the British eugenicists and Lapouge and, as we shall see, the American Stoddard. Moreover, selection and struggle were implied to be forces of preservation rather than change. A politics geared towards guarding the forces of nature against subversive social practices was offered as the only hope for the future. The consequences of this politics were to be fully realised under the Third Reich.

Richet and human selection

French scientists were, as already noted, relatively unreceptive to Darwinism. This was reflected in the eugenics and social hygiene movements in France, which tended to retain a marked environmentalist as opposed to hereditarian orientation. The thinker I am about to discuss was not typical of French eugenicists because he was convinced that heredity dominated all aspects of social life. But Charles Richet (1850–1935) was an influential figure. Professor of physiology at the University of Paris and winner of the Nobel Prize in physiology in 1913, Richet became a vice president of the French Eugenics Society after the Great War, and Schneider maintains that his status assisted the popularisation of his eugenic ideas among the French public.[32] The text in which these ideas were systematically presented was *Sélection humaine*, an influential book published in 1919 but written some time earlier in 1912.[33]

In *Sélection humaine* Richet asserted that man was no exception to nature's laws, one of which was the pursuit of happiness, a universal proclivity not confined to man and the cause of progress. But this pursuit was made difficult by another law, the struggle for existence: 'Life is a ceaseless struggle against the sundry hostile forces which besiege us from all sides and at every instant. These forces are colossal, innumerable, indefatigable, inexorable' (3–4). They derived from climatic conditions; organic needs which condemned us to labour; from our vices and from parasites which caused disease. The struggle against these enemies was led by science, which improved with the advancement of human intelligence. This made paramount the improvement of man – the science-creating tool – or rather, the improvement of his mind. However, here, according to Richet, we encountered widespread

---

[32] Schneider, *Quality and Quantity*, 110.
[33] C. Richet, *La Sélection humaine* (Paris: Alcan, 1919). See Schneider, *Quality and Quantity*, 109–10.

indifference: 'Nothing is more extraordinary that our lack of concern for human selection' (15). Man was prepared to improve everything – livestock, flowers and vegetables – except himself. Living matter was plastic, and through judicious and patient selection it was capable of taking on multiple forms, just like the clay in the hands of a potter (25). But humanity remained oblivious to the need for applying the selective practices of the stockbreeder and horticulturalist to itself.

What rendered this need imperative was the perversion of natural and sexual selection in civilised conditions. In savage societies the eternal combat against a pitiless nature ensured the survival of the strongest. But with civilisation came altruism, conscience and notions of rights, with the result that the sick and insane were nurtured and recidivist criminals tolerated (17). Marriage was no longer entered into with the future of the race in mind, but was governed by chance or cupidity. 'Thus civilisation, which has perverted natural selection, has perverted sexual selection even more' (19). Individually, people were able to improve their situation through increased standards of living and education, while collectively, progress was not simply at a standstill, for the race was menaced by decline. Selection was distorted by social institutions while civilisation threatened to bring about 'the degradation of the species' (22).

Richet was convinced that heredity was a dominant influence in human existence. Not only did it determine physical traits like hair colour, height, beauty, strength and health, but it also governed character and intelligence. The latter was particularly important, because intelligence distinguished man from the animals and facilitated continued evolutionary progress. But Richet, in keeping with the general tenor of French eugenics at the time, did not relegate environmental factors to a non-existent or even minor role (39). He obviously endorsed the inheritance of acquired characters, claiming improvements to the body and the mind through better conditions and education would be inherited by the next generation (178, 188), and arguing that women needed to be encouraged to develop their intellectual potential during adulthood by allowing them opportunities to work and think (40, 194). Nor did he believe that the current occupants of important social positions reflected a natural distribution of intelligence, since many of them owed their status to birth rather than ability. In fact, social inequality he castigated as one of the worst perversions of civilisation because it ensured the progeny of a millionaire would be victors in the struggle for life no matter how stupid, lazy and weak they were (21). Nonetheless, in his espousal of the policies necessary to restore selective processes to social life, Richet adopted a biologically reductionist stance.

This is evident in Richet's analysis of race. Initially he gave the impression that he was concerned with the happiness of the entire human species, claiming that selection was capable of securing a more noble and brilliant future for the whole of humanity (ii–iii), in which he included not just the existing generations but their future descendants (2–3). These universalist sentiments are misleading though, for Richet effectively confined the notion of humanity to the white races only, stating baldly: 'I do not at all believe in the equality of the human races' (58). Using skin colour as the criterion of racial difference, he proposed a hierarchy of races based upon intelligence as the most distinctively human attribute. He then produced an extremely disparaging assessment of blacks whom he presented as close to monkeys in terms of their skull and brain measurements, possessing an infantile intelligence, and having contributed absolutely nothing to the sciences, the arts, or to social and political institutions (67–72). His conclusion was stark: 'The black race is an inferior race' (70). As for the 'yellow' races, they were capable of advanced civilisation, but were imitative rather than creative, and their thought showed no evidence of progress (73–7).

The essential principle Richet derived from his classification of races was the absolute necessity of preventing any mixing of the superior white races with the black or brown races (58). The deleterious consequences of miscegenation for the superior race was an incontestable biological fact; while the occasional sexual liaison between whites and inferior races was admissible, marriage was not (91). Hence 'the first principle of human selection is strictly to forbid the union of whites with the women of another race, yellow or black' (84). The inhabitants of the great cities in Europe were a pretty unedifying spectacle, but they had potential for improvement, a potential that would be irremediably lost if they became a population of mulattos (85–6).

The next selectionist principle was aimed at individuals within the nations of the white races. Richet thought Europeans consisted of a number of white races (including Semites), and nations were communities in which these different races were fused together by such factors as history, language, religion and tradition (80). Once these communities were safeguarded against pollution by inter-mixing with non-whites, the next task was to purge them of inferior specimens. Here physical and mental normality were the yardsticks, and all those who were abnormal must be 'pitilessly rejected' (161). This criterion was both 'simple and precise' and encompassed the defective, the deformed, criminals, maniacs and imbeciles (161–2). Richet conceded that his proposals would be branded by some as monstrous, but he was adamant that: 'Our task must be to fortify Nature's disdain for the weak ...'

(165). He advocated the killing of newly born infants with hereditary defects. In this stage they were incapable of thought and hence could not suffer, and if they could think, they would be grateful for being spared a lifetime of suffering (168). As for those who exhibited these defects after birth, Richet believed castration to be the rational solution, though in the current state of public opinion the next best policy was prohibition of marriage. In this category Richet included people suffering from tuberculosis, rickets, syphilis and epilepsy; individuals who were too short or too weak; criminals; and people unable to read, write or count (176).

Richet dismissed philanthropic or humanitarian counter-arguments as simply irrelevant to the future welfare of the race: 'What do criminals, deaf-mutes, hydrocephalics, rachitics and epileptics matter to us? Shall we allow our human race to be perverted by these tainted seeds? I too am philanthropic, but my philanthropy leads me to hope for a human race that is noble and strong. What do the lazy, the ignorant, the stupid and the puny matter to me?' (207).

These arguments reveal the close kinship between Richet's selectionism and the eugenics of Pearson, Lapouge and the German advocates of racial hygiene, a kinship that extended to the world view within which these proposals were embedded. Richet depicted a cosmos governed by the laws of adaptation, heredity and natural selection, though these laws had been obstructed or distorted by social institutions and practices. Elevating the good of the 'race' above any considerations of individual rights or welfare, he justified the rigid separation of races and radical programmes of negative eugenics in order to ensure continued evolution. The most important difference between Richet and the other Social Darwinist supporters of eugenics was to be found in his concept of struggle. He did not list population pressures as one of its causes, and neither did he regard war as one of its forms, at least among civilised nations. He was a vociferous critic of militarism, wanting the resources hitherto devoted to warfare to be used for the promotion of science, the goal of which was to replace international conflict with union (5), while perceiving peaceful competition within societies to be essential to progress. Paradoxically, given his description of inequality as a perversion of natural selection, he argued that liberty and equality were incompatible values. We must, he insisted, reject socialism and egalitarianism because any form of collectivism suppressed individual effort. Liberty was therefore essential, and Richet proposed anarchism as the ideal system – a stateless federation of families and communes (94–9). 'For the grandeur of future humanity', he wrote, 'individualist societies are necessary which, by means of an inexorable struggle for life, reward effort and vigorously punish laziness' (105). The object of these societies was not the creation of some aristocratic elite but the improvement of the race as a whole to establish a 'universal aristocracy' (112). These sentiments seem to distance Richet from the authoritarianism of Pearson, Lapouge and the German racial hygienists. This is misleading, for Richet recognised that this ideal had to be compromised for the sake of racial improvement. In fact, the state would prohibit inter-racial marriage, forbid the marriage of other categories of person, supervise the elimination of unfit new-born infants, and castrate and sterilise adult degenerates. To the objection that these policies were tyrannical, Richet replied that all policies aimed at social preservation were inevitably tyrannical, including sending children to school and paying taxes (90). In any case, Richet was convinced that eugenics accorded with nature's rules, restoring the selectionism that had been blunted by civilisation.

Before leaving France it is interesting to note the similarity between the ideas of Richet and those of another Nobel Prize winner, Alexis Carrel (1873–1944). Carrel lived and worked for many years in the USA, researching cell tissue cultivation at the Rockefeller Institute for Medical Research. In 1941, in Vichy France, Carrel established the Fondation pour l'Etude des Problèmes Humaines, the goal of which was to study measures for the improvement of the French population.[34] In 1935 he made his views on eugenics public in *Man the Unknown*,[35] a book which sold well in the USA and France.

Carrel was a thorough-going Social Darwinist who deplored the fact that natural selection no longer played its former role of conserving and improving the race (20). He rejected the inheritance of acquired characters, but pointed out that the germ-plasm was not immune to environmental influences in the form of disease, alimentary factors and other items, which meant that it was often difficult to ascertain the respective roles of environment and heredity in producing defects in a population (263, 268). Eugenics, accordingly, though essential, had its limits: 'It has no magic power, and is not capable, when unaided, of greatly improving the individual' (254). Nonetheless, eugenics was 'indispensable for the perpetuation of the strong. A great race must propagate its best elements' (299). This entailed, among other things, euthanasia by gassing of dangerous criminals and the criminally insane; whipping and temporary hospitalisation for petty criminals (318–9); the refraining from marriage by people suffering from hereditary defects

[34] For details of Carrel's career and work at the Fondation, see Schneider, *Quality and Quantity*, 272–80.
[35] London: Harper, 1935.

(300); and the suppression of 'all forms of the proletariat' (302), with factory work performed by conscription and people living in small communities so as to avoid the debilitating influences of city life (315).

Carrel was fully aware that these proposals ran counter to the moral prescriptions of human rights, democracy and humanitarianism, all of which he condemned as disastrous because illusory. 'The feebleminded and the man of genius should not be equal before the law' (271). Democracy had promoted the interests of the weak at the expense of the strong (272). This situation must be reversed, and modern society should 'organise itself with reference to the normal individual. Philosophical systems and sentimental prejudices must give way before such a necessity. The development of human personality is the ultimate purpose of civilisation' (319). In the light of these sentiments it is small wonder that Carrel found the authoritarian and racist atmosphere of the Vichy regime congenial.

The USA

Eugenics took hold in the USA more so than in any European nation excepting Nazi Germany, which expressed great interest in American policies and practices.[36] The state of Indiana enacted the first sterilisation law in 1907; by 1933 twenty-nine other states had followed suit, although three states had by then repealed their acts.[37] At this time, officially over 16,000 people had been sterilised, many involuntarily. Furthermore, recent research has shown that these practices did not disappear with the discrediting of eugenics after revelations of Nazi excesses, but continued until well after the conclusion of World War II into the 1970s.[38] On this evidence some scholars have surmised that the real magnitude of enforced sterilisation in the USA between 1907 and 1974 involved hundreds of thousands of victims.[39] Despite the considerable amount of research devoted to American eugenics, the success of

[36] The connections between Nazi and US eugenics are documented in S. Kühl, *The Nazi Connection* (New York/Oxford: Oxford University Press, 1994).

[37] Kevles, *In the Name of Eugenics*, 100; *Report of the Departmental Committee on Sterilisation*, Cmd. 4485 (London: HMSO, 1933), 35, 109–12.

[38] According to the Channel Four TV documentary of 17 February 1994, 'The Lynchburg Story', involuntary sterilisations of inmates of an institution in Lynchburg, Virginia, continued until 1972. In all, some 8,300 people were sterilised, primarily young, white vagrants, paupers, petty criminals and the 'feebleminded'. The rationale for this policy was the prevention of racial deterioration and the promotion of national success in the struggle for existence.

[39] For an analysis of eugenics in the USA which estimates sterilisations in hundreds of thousands, see A. Chase, *The Legacy of Malthus* (New York: Knopf, 1980). For an overview of the evidence see A. Cockburn, 'Social Cleansing', *New Statesman and Society*, 5 August 1994, 16–18.

these policies in a nation which prides itself on its tradition of individualism and personal freedom still requires an adequate explanation. As with other eugenics movements discussed in this chapter, my concern is not with American eugenics *per se* but with the interaction between eugenic ideas and Social Darwinism. The treatment is selective but aims to convey the flavour of this interaction.

One of the earliest supporters of eugenics has already been encountered in an earlier chapter, the feminist and radical Victoria Woodhull. By the time she published her eugenicist views Woodhull was residing in England and had tempered much of her earlier radicalism. But her writings of the early 1890s anticipated most of the themes propounded by later eugenicists. Woodhull demanded that artificial laws should be predicated upon the laws of nature, and called for a new religion based upon scientific truths.[40] Insisting that criminality, feeblemindedness and pauperism were hereditary and incurable, she argued that the current growth of these phenomena was contrary to the survival of the fittest.[41] It was imperative, therefore, that nations refrain from breeding from the unfit and instead encourage the breeding of the fit, which she heralded as the 'first principle of the breeder's art'. There was no reason why societies could not be organised so as to assign prominence to this principle. This entailed a new creed that would 'make a religion of the procreative principle'.[42] But it also required governmental policies aimed at preventing the birth of unfit people. 'A humanitarian government', opined Woodhull, 'would stigmatise the marriages of the unfit as crimes; it would legislate to prevent the birth of the criminal rather than legislate to punish him after he is born.'[43] False ideas of liberty which permitted the procreation of the unfit imposed a heavy burden on the provident who had to support them. 'And it is these false ideas of liberty which makes the struggle for existence so terrible.'[44] Moreover, Woodhull did not confine the label of unfit to the urban underclass, but gave it an additional racial signification. Thus, in contrast to her youthful support for the enfranchisement of blacks, she asked rhetorically: 'Eventually, if America is owned and governed by negroes, would it be the survival of the fittest?'[45]

---

[40] Victoria C. Woodhull, *Humanitarian Government* (London: no pub., 1890), 25, 29.
[41] *Ibid.*, 30; Woodhull, *The Rapid Multiplication of the Unfit* (London/New York: no pub., 1891), 18.
[42] Woodhull, *Rapid Multiplication*, 38, 39.
[43] Woodhull, *Humanitarian Government*, 49.   [44] *Ibid.*, 55.
[45] Woodhull, *Rapid Multiplication*, 18–19. For Woodhull's earlier support of black (and female) suffrage, see her *Origin, Tendencies and Principles of Government*, 38–40c. In 1872 Woodhull had nominated herself the presidential candidate of her Equal Rights Party and asked the black leader Frederick Douglas to stand as her running mate. Douglas ignored the request – wisely as it happened, since Woodhull spent the election

Woodhull did not develop her eugenic proposals in any detail and her writings did not sustain a consistently hereditarian position since she sometimes attributed indigence, alcoholism, crime and illness to environmental conditions. But her eugenic publications were a remarkable anticipation, both in substance and tone, of later eugenicists such as D. Colin Wells (1858–1911). In a provocative conference paper entitled 'Social Darwinism',[46] Wells advocated the application of Darwinian evolutionary theory 'to the investigation of the manner in which social institutions and doctrines influence the competition, elimination, survival of individuals and groups of individuals' (697). He postulated that natural selection had been superseded by social selection, and that 'society is the sieve by which human beings are sifted ...' (698). This prompted the question of what kind of persons were favoured by the selective actions of modern industrial societies. Wells' response was gloomy but predictable, namely that modern conditions reversed the action of natural selection and favoured the multiplication of the unfit. He then linked this claim to an attack on contemporary political and social developments. Trade unionism, socialism, heavy taxation, urbanisation and higher education for women were all implicated in facilitating the postponement of marriage and small families among the worthier sections of society coupled with the survival and procreation of the 'incapable and weak' (702). Thus while Wells possessed a more sophisticated knowledge of Darwinian theory that Woodhull, and was conversant with current (particularly European) theoretical developments, his paper displayed essentially the same concerns: the substitution of social for natural selection and a concomitant multiplication of the unfit.

The continuity of these themes in eugenic discourses is illustrated by *The Revolt Against Civilisation* by Lothrop Stoddard (b. 1883), a text which was popular in Britain and the USA and which appeared in German translation.[47] Stoddard's theme was the racial impoverishment that he deemed to be endemic to modern civilisation. Civilisation was the consequence of 'the creative urge of superior germ-plasm. Civilisation is thus fundamentally conditioned by race' (2). The progress from animality through savagery and barbarism to civilisation was an uneven one, with many races confined to the earlier phases of evolution. Only superior races reached civilisation, and within them it was the actions of

in jail on an adultery charge. See G. Blodgett, 'Victoria Woodhull', *Notable American Women 1607–1950: A Biographical Dictionary* (Cambridge, MA: Belknap Press, 1971), III, 654.

[46] Published in *The American Journal of Sociology*, 12(1907), 695–708.

[47] London: Chapman and Hall, 1922. The German edition was published in 1925. See Weindling, *Health, Race and German Politics*, 311.

an elite which caused advancement. Elite qualities were hereditary – Stoddard completely rejected the inheritance of acquired characters – and were developed through natural selection. Unfortunately, with civilisation natural selection was substituted by social selection allowing the weak and degenerate to thrive and reproduce. Hence 'instead of dying at the base and growing at the top, civilised society was dying at the top and spreading out below' (18).

Stoddard enumerated several types of inferior person. There were savages and barbarians, people who were arrested at early evolutionary phases and therefore congenitally incapable of achieving civilisation. Then there were true 'degenerates' – the insane and neurotic – and finally the 'border-liners', consisting of those with 'neither the wit nor the moral fibre to meet the sterner demands of high, complex civilisations'. Collectively, these inferior specimens constituted the 'Under-Men', 'the vast army of the unadaptable and incapable' (21). They represented a reservoir of potential discontent; inimical to the demands of civilised existence, they were a threat to social order and had to be controlled (23). Failure to do so would result in revolution.

Invoking an 'iron law of inequality', Stoddard insisted that the IQ tests performed by the US Army on 1.7 million servicemen during World War I demonstrated conclusively that intelligence was hereditary (52). The declining birth-rates in the upper echelons of American society, accompanied by the high rate of reproduction among the lower, meant that 'intelligence is today being steadily *bred out* of the American population' (64, original emphasis). The Under-Man was on the increase while the racially valuable elements responsible for civilisation were declining. Since the Under-Man was unconvertible to the demands of civilisation Stoddard concluded – in terms reminiscent of those used by Lombroso – that 'we have among us a rebel army – the vast host of the unadaptable, the incapable, the envious, the discontented, filled with instinctive hatred of civilisation and progress, and ready on the instant to rise in revolt' (80–1). The world was in fact a vast battleground – the war against chaos (202–3).

Faced with this problem, Stoddard ruled out any possibility of returning to natural selection. The solution was to be found in eugenics, which was 'an *improved* social selection based upon natural law . . .' (86, original emphasis). Social rebels – by which he apparently meant Bolsheviks – should be 'hunted down and extirpated' (215). As for degenerates, Stoddard was a firm advocate of negative eugenics on the grounds that: 'Race cleansing is the obvious starting-point for race betterment' (226). He proposed that habitual paupers should be prevented from having children, while the insane and feebleminded should be institutionalised or sterilised and birth control encouraged among other inferior groups. This entailed the emergence of new social ideals through the development of the 'eugenic conscience', which would also 'impel the well-endowed to raise larger families, prefer children to luxuries' and think more of duties than of rights (236).

Stoddard was unquestionably a hardliner on eugenic issues. He met German eugenicists such as Lenz and Fischer as well as Nazi politicians like Himmler, and continued to enthuse over Nazi eugenic and racial measures into the 1940s.[48] It would be wrong, however, to dismiss him as a marginal figure in American eugenics. The racist and elitist perspectives which grounded Stoddart's eugenic proposals were common to all the American and European examples considered in this chapter. Equally common was the Social Darwinism which was employed to explain the proliferation of the unfit through the suspension or obstruction of natural selection. The continuity of these themes in the overwhelming majority of eugenicist arguments is attested by the appearance, in 1949, of a biology textbook by Garrett Hardin (b. 1915).[49] In the final chapter of this text, Hardin reported data which purported to show that the birth-rate was negatively correlated with educational attainment. Since higher education signified high IQ, and the latter was partly due to heredity, then Hardin concluded that under present social arrangements *'there will be a slow but continuous downward trend in the average intelligence'* (612, original emphasis).[50]

Hardin's response to this trend was more nuanced than that of Stoddard. Nevertheless, he argued: 'It is difficult, on rational grounds, to object to the sterilisation of the feebleminded' (613). Similarly, he proposed that only full knowledge of their public responsibilities – the 'eugenic conscience'? – would encourage high IQ individuals to have more children (615). People needed to be aware of the selective consequences of their actions: 'When one saves a starving man, one may thereby help him to breed more children' (619). Hardin's conclusion was that 'the logic of our situation is clear. Either there must be a relatively painless weeding out before birth or a more painful and wasteful elimination of individuals after birth' (618). The language may have been more sophisticated than Stoddard's, but the concerns of both he and Hardin were similar, as were their diagnoses and recommenda-

---

[48]   Kühl, *The Nazi Connection*, 53, 59–63.

[49]   *Biology: Its Human Implications* (San Francisco: Freeman and Co., 1949).

[50]   There is a clear continuity in American concern with what is currently referred to as the 'dumbing down' of the population, exhibited in the writings of Wells, Stoddard and Hardin and its most recent advocates, Murray and Hernnstein. See C. Murray and R. J. Hernnstein, *The Bell Curve: Intelligence and Class Structure in American Life* (New York: Free Press, 1994).

tions. In this they were part of an international tradition of eugenicist thinking which typically drew upon Darwinian premisses for its support.[51]

Conclusion

Soloway's verdict on British eugenics as a biological way of thinking about socio-economic, political and cultural change, has a wider relevance.[52] The biology in question was invariably Darwinian, with its stress on inheritance, selection and survival of the fittest. In eugenics discourses the unit of concern became the race, a term which could still be used in a number of senses, even by the same theorist, but which increasingly tended to be conceived as a biological entity whose defining traits were resistant to cultural forces. The fusion of eugenics, racial theories and Social Darwinism, therefore, produced a graphic picture in which racial survival in a world of incessant conflict was predicated upon the maintenance of a healthy population purged of those elements which threatened its integrity. Given the increasing tendency of Social Darwinists to present collectivities rather than individuals as the agents of adaptation and survival and thus to assign moral priority to the group, these developments provided a powerful rationale for policies aimed at the elimination of racially undesirable elements.

The fit between eugenics and Social Darwinism was a coherent one because most proponents divorced natural selection from cultural processes. Darwin, it will be recalled, derived altruism – and hence charitable institutions and policies – from social and moral sentiments that developed through natural selection, resulting in ambivalence towards the maintenance of the unfit. Subsequent eugenicists invariably depicted a rupture between nature and culture: natural selection had been replaced by selective forces which were social in *origin* and which usually acted contrary to the former. Eugenic policies were, in contrast, social practices modelled upon the workings of nature.

Yet the effect of this device was, as we saw with Lapouge, to break the continuity between nature and culture which was central to Social

---

[51] The vitality of eugenics is evidenced by its continuing relevance in the modern era. China embarked upon a eugenics programme in 1995 as part of its policy of birth control. See Linda Jakobson, 'China Brings in Tough Law to Stamp Out Birth Defects', *Guardian*, 6 June 1995. In the West, welfare cutbacks in Britain and the USA, coupled with advances in genetic engineering, have aroused interest in the 'new eugenics'. See Cockburn, 'Social Cleansing', and D. King, 'The State of Eugenics', *New Statesman and Society*, 25 August 1995. Though the context of these policies differs from pre-World War II, it would be interesting to examine their relationship to Social Darwinism.

[52] Soloway, *Demography and Degeneration*, xviii.

Darwinist thought. Cultural practices arose which were not only inexplicable on Darwinist principles but which overrode the supposedly ineluctable laws of nature. Thus eugenics was harmonised with Social Darwinism by depicting nature as a model rather than a threat, with social practices and values portrayed as the source of pathology. But the virulence of the latter was such that nature itself seemed threatened unless bolstered by social intervention.

10   Social Darwinism, nature and sexual difference

Introduction

Sexual – like racial – characteristics have visible manifestations capable of being ordered and classified, read as symbols for other differences, and assigned values. Concern with such characteristics, both physical and mental, and with their meaning, have a long pedigree in Western thought. What invested this concern with particular urgency from the mid-nineteenth century on was the interface of two processes: political agitation for female emancipation and a reinterpretation of nature.

The growth of movements throughout Europe and the USA dedicated to the extension of civil and political rights to women created an intense interest in what became known, both to sympathisers and opponents, as the 'Woman Question'.[1] These movements challenged prevailing notions of the appropriate division of labour between the sexes and in so doing raised issues about the respective 'nature' of men and women and the extent to which these natures were biologically or culturally determined. Feminism, therefore, posed a comprehensive and disturbing challenge in ways not matched by class or even racial issues. As Cynthia Eagle Russett has argued, it not only encompassed education, occupation and legal issues, but intruded into such intimate areas as personal and matrimonial relationships.[2]

The debate was complicated by the fact that while nature often acted as a court of appeal for the protagonists, the understanding of nature was itself undergoing a transformation. There was a long-standing tendency – general if not universal – to personify nature as a female, as at once both a physical and spiritual presence, nurturing, caring and erotic. But this imagery, as much a conception of femininity as of nature, had been undergoing revision even prior to the publication of the *Origin*. The palaeontological record had disclosed the impermanence of species,

---

[1] For the development of women's emancipation movements, see R. J. Evans, *The Feminists* (London: Croom Helm, 1977).
[2] C. E. Russett, *Sexual Science* (Cambridge, MA: Harvard University Press, 1989), 10.

revealing a fossilised chronicle of elimination and extinction.[3] This was accompanied by a shift in the image of woman/nature, evident in Tennyson's 'In Memoriam' (1850). Here nature was still represented as a female, but one 'red in tooth and claw', not a nurse but a monstrous and impersonal agent of death which even destroyed her own dependants. Hence this reassessment of nature was mediated through a revaluation of femininity in which woman was conceived as a much more threatening and subversive figure.[4]

Yet this symbolisation of nature was nuanced, with the angel of death imagery sometimes juxtaposed with a more nurturing and optimistic representation, as is evident in Tennyson's great poem, where the red in tooth and claw portrait of nature in stanzas LIV–LVI contrasts with the more optimistic imagery of stanza CXVIII.[5] This dualism and the tension it reflects were reproduced within Darwinism itself, as I have frequently argued. It also resonated an additional set of images surrounding the notion of womanhood and the revisions to this notion occasioned by women's fight for emancipation. It is for this reason, perhaps, that the ambivalent status of nature as both model and threat is particularly pronounced in Social Darwinist discourses on women.

Modern feminist historiography has tended to depict Social Darwinism (and nineteenth-century science in general) as broadly supportive of patriarchal values and as reinforcing traditional gender stereotypes.[6] Even feminist appropriations of Social Darwinism are perceived as succumbing to these stereotypes in that their promotion of women's causes was premised on notions of distinctive but complementary sexual difference.[7] These interpretations are surely correct; evolutionary science was enlisted in the cause of patriarchy. But this is not the whole story and I shall argue that Social Darwinism could be, and was, turned against patriarchy and conventional Victorian views on gender. Moreover, some of the most innovative and influential efforts in this direction were made by women themselves. In arguing thus I am developing a point made some years ago by Rosaleen Love, namely that women

---

[3] Bowler, *The Invention of Progress*, 167–8.
[4] J. E. Adams, 'Woman Red in Tooth and Claw: Nature and the Feminine in Tennyson and Darwin', *Victorian Studies*, 33(1989), 7–27.
[5] I am grateful to Gail Cunningham for drawing my attention to this contrast.
[6] Russett, *Sexual Science*; J. Conway, 'Stereotypes of Femininity in a Theory of Sexual Evolution', *Victorian Studies*, 14(1970–1), 47–62; F. Alaya, 'Victorian Science and the "Genius" of Woman', *Journal of the History of Ideas*, 38(1977), 261–80; R. Jann, 'Darwin and the Anthropologists: Sexual Selection and Its Discontents', *Victorian Studies*, 37(1994), 287–306.
[7] See Alaya's discussion of Olive Schreiner and Charlotte Perkins Gilman, 'Victorian Science', 277–8.

exhibited great ingenuity in manipulating 'scientific' theories of gender for their own purposes.[8]

The evolution of sexual characteristics

In the *Descent*, Darwin argued that as a consequence of natural and sexual selection the sexes had evolved distinctive but complementary mental and physical traits. Man was not only physically larger than woman, but also 'more courageous, pugnacious and energetic', and psychologically more competitive, ambitious and selfish. 'Woman seems to differ from man in mental disposition, chiefly in her greater tenderness and less selfishness', and had retained the faculties of 'lower races' for intuition, rapid perception and imitation (847, 857). As to intellectual differences, Darwin asserted that the 'chief distinction in the intellectual powers of the two sexes is shewn by man's attaining to a higher eminence, in whatever he takes up, than can woman – whether requiring deep thought, reason, or imagination, or merely the use of the senses and hands' (858).

However, although women were innately inferior to men in matters of physical strength and intellectual prowess they possessed a number of psychological proclivities which endowed them with moral ascendancy, complementing, completing and refining the aggressive and egoistic traits of men. Darwin, like Huxley, was in favour of the extension and improvement of the education of females, but both men were convinced that because of their biologically determined disadvantages women could not compete with men on equal terms in the same spheres.[9] The true domain of woman, the one for which she had been shaped by nature, was the domestic one, as wife and mother, nurturer and carer. Nature had, therefore, in the evolution of women, produced beings capable of offsetting, to an extent at least, the ravages of the struggle for existence, of counteracting the seemingly harsh regimen to which all life was subjected.

This representation of sexual difference in which males were aggressive, egoistic and rational and females, though physically and intellectually inferior, possessed a moral supremacy on account of their altruism and maternal functions, was widely accepted long before Darwinism. For Darwin these differences were natural because they had evolved

---

[8] R. Love, 'Darwinism and Feminism: The "Woman Question" in the Life and Work of Olive Schreiner and Charlotte Perkins Gilman', in Oldroyd and Langham, *Wider Domain*, 127.

[9] For a detailed analysis of Darwin's and Huxley's views on women, see Richards, 'Darwin and the Descent of Woman'; Russett, *Sexual Science*, chap. 3.

from pre-human organisms through the forces of natural and sexual selection. Spencer proposed a somewhat different rationale derived from the principle of the conservation of force, namely that women used up so much energy in the performance of their procreative and childraising functions that little remained for mental development. This was why women remained at a less advanced evolutionary stage than men, an argument also adopted by Ferri.[10] Indeed, the recapitulation thesis was widely used to rationalise female inferiority.[11] But these arguments did not entail a uniform political position. Thus Spencer employed the 'evidence' for male superiority to argue against female suffrage, while both Ferri and Lombroso – the latter being one of the most assiduous documenters of women's inferiority – supported the extension of political rights to women.[12]

An influential variation on this theme was presented in the widely read *The Evolution of Sex*, published in 1889 by two Scottish biologists, Patrick Geddes (who had studied under Huxley) and J. Arthur Thomson.[13] The authors argued that maleness involved the dissipation of energy, femaleness the conservation of energy. Thus male cells were the source of variation in evolutionary dynamics, while female cells maintained continuity and stability. Cell metabolism, therefore, provided the foundation for the energetic male and the altruistic, passive female. For Geddes and Thomson a more cooperative society could be envisioned in the future if female altruism was given expression, but this necessitated retention of the sex differences produced through evolution, which would be threatened if women assumed masculine roles.

The rediscovery of Mendel's laws and advances in the study of genetics did nothing to dispel these stereotypes. In the 1920s the German racial hygienist Lenz proclaimed the existence of 'essential differences' between the sexes which were the outcome of evolutionary specialisation and hence 'natural and normal'. 'Men', wrote Lenz, 'are specially selected for the control of nature, for success in war and the chase and in the winning of women, whereas women are specially selected as breeders and rearers of children and as persons who are successful in attracting the male ...' As a result of these selective forces men were more egoistic and materialistic than women, who were altruistic and capable of empathy with others. Lenz also had no doubt about the respective abilities of the sexes: '"Great women" endowed

[10] Ferri, *Socialism and Positive Science*, 9–11.
[11] For numerous examples, see Russett, *Sexual Science*, chap. 2.
[12] See M. Gibson, 'On the Insensitivity of Women: Science and the Woman Question in Liberal Italy', *Journal of Women's History*, 2(1990), 11–41.
[13] There is a detailed account of the contents of this text in Conway, 'Stereotypes of Femininity', 49–57.

with "greatness" in the sense of outstanding creative faculty are practically unknown.'[14]

The 'fact' that the division of functions between the sexes had arisen through evolution rather than through human agency could be directed against advocates of sexual equality and greater female participation in civic and economic affairs. In Britain, Darwin's son Leonard attacked the efforts by women to secure employment in 'male' occupations on the grounds that such objectives had 'blinded the eyes of some of them to the fact that women's special duties stand out as amongst the noblest and most important of all human duties'. The duties in question were, of course, those of the bearing and socialising of children.[15] Similar views were held by the French scientist, Alexis Carrel, who castigated feminists for their ignorance of the differences between the two sexes in proposing that they should receive the same education and assume the same social responsibilities. Women differed from men in their cellular construction, a fact which must be accepted as biologically ineluctable. Carrel concluded that it was absurd to educate boys and girls along similar lines and turn women against maternity, since: 'Between the two sexes there are irrevocable differences. And it is imperative to take them into account in constructing the civilised world.'[16]

Such claims savour of male prejudice and a vested interest in the maintenance of patriarchal relations, but these models of sexual difference were deeply ingrained in Western thought and were capable of structuring the thought of women as well as men, and of theories of female equality as well as inequality. Two examples are illustrative of this claim. The first consists of Cesare Lombroso's daughter Gina who, after a distinguished career in criminal anthropology and medicine, wrote *The Soul of Woman*[17] in defence of what she regarded as the true mission of women. Having supported the movement for female emancipation for many years, Gina Lombroso claimed that she had come to realise that this movement confused women by dividing them between the pursuit of worldly success and the cravings of their innermost natures. 'Woman', she proclaimed, 'sways like a pendulum between her interests, as reflected today in the woman's rights movement, and her passions, represented by her altruistic, alterocentrist and maternal instinct, love' (18).

The natures of the sexes had been welded by evolution and heredity. Whereas men were egocentric, motivated by power and success, women were alterocentric, instinctively orientated to the welfare of others. Gina

[14] Lenz, 'The Inheritance of Intellectual Gifts', 597–8, 599.
[15] L. Darwin, *What is Eugenics?*, 77.   [16] Carrel, *Man the Unknown*, 92.
[17] No tr. (London: Jonathan Cape, 1924).

Lombroso inferred from this that women's nature provided them with an inherent sense of justice and furnished a model for social relationships in general:

Woman does not need laws, nor even education or religion, to respect the lives and property of others, or to have pity on the fallen, the weak and the sick, to feel gratitude, love and respect for her father and mother; nor does she need laws to remain chaste and pure. Her passions coincide with the object of all law and order, that is, with general well-being. Woman alone can dare erect her passion into a standard, to consider her heart a legal code (22).

Attempts to give women the same education as men were unnatural. 'Woman is born to be a mother. Logic, abstract ideas, deductive arguments would not help her to bring up her children' (150). Whereas the pursuit of philosophy and the social and natural sciences helped to clarify a man's mind, they served only 'to dull the minds of woman' (155). Thus, concluded Lombroso: 'It is hindering things and confusing the whole issue to say that we are the equals of man.' Women suffered because men were ignorant of the ways in which the sexes differed (97).

The fact that Gina Lombroso, who had achieved success in a male-dominated world, could reassert the altruistic/egoistic dualism as exemplifying sexual difference surely attests to the powerful hold exercised by this dualism. This claim is reinforced by my second example, the English philosopher, J. S. Mill. In his *The Subjection of Women* (1869) Mill rejected the thesis that nature predetermined the position of a particular group of people in a social hierarchy, asking 'was there ever any domination which did not appear natural to those who possessed it?' (229). Females had been socially conditioned to display certain characteristics and adopt certain roles. There was no convincing evidence of any innate intellectual inferiority of women, and when given the relevant opportunities they revealed themselves to be just as capable as men in all spheres of mental and occupational activity. Femininity was culturally, not biologically determined, so much so that it was impossible to know what the actual 'nature' of woman was – 'what is now called the nature of women is an eminently artificial thing – the result of forced repression in some directions, unnatural stimulation in others' (238).[18]

Mill was uncompromising in his condemnation of the family as the site of male domination and a school for inculcating the continued subjection of women. Moral progress could take place only when this

---

[18] Darwin was critical of Mill's insistence that moral feelings were acquired rather than innate, and had responded to the *Subjection of Women* by avowing that Mill 'could learn some things' from biology. Darwin, *Descent*, 149–50; Desmond and Moore, *Darwin*, 572.

'most fundamental of the social relations' was transformed into one of equality between husband and wife (311). But Mill still regarded marriage and the family as vital institutions and this partly because he saw them as frameworks within which distinctively female qualities could be exercised, despite his denial of such qualities. Thus he was dismissive of the stereotypes which portrayed men as selfish and women as altruistic, intellectually inferior to men, but morally superior and hence naturally suited to the roles of wife and mother. He described this as a 'silly depreciation of the intellectual, and silly panegyric on the moral, nature of women' (293). Yet only a few pages after this statement he wrote approvingly of the genuine moral influence of women in 'softening' the aggressive temperament of males and maintained that in matters of sentiment, spirit and generosity, women's standard is higher than that of men, 'in the quality of justice, somewhat lower' (302). Nature was smuggled into Mill's analysis to reproduce the very stereotypes his arguments sought to refute.

If this model of sex differences could emerge in the discourse of an opponent of sexual stereotyping like Mill, or be explicitly endorsed by a woman of the calibre of Gina Lombroso, then it must have been deeply rooted in the culture of the period. Small wonder, then, that it was also manifest in the writings of Social Darwinists who supported feminism. In Britain, for example, Ritchie rejected the proposition that sexual equality violated any evolutionary law of increasing specialisation and was highly sceptical of the claim that women possessed smaller brains than men. He reasoned that if men on the average displayed more ability than women, then 'this must be due to the way in which the two sexes are respectively treated'.[19] He attacked the 'patriarchal family' as a source of female subordination and proposed the extension of political and civil liberties to women. He launched a blistering critique of Comte's idealisation of the feminine psyche – symbolised by Comte's notion of the 'Divine Woman' – which he described as 'one of the worst enemies that women have to contend with in their struggle towards recognition as complete and responsible persons'.[20] Yet in responding to Spencer's allegation that allowing women to vote was tantamount to introducing family ethics into affairs of state, Ritchie approvingly agreed that this 'would mean the moralisation of politics'.[21] Despite his critique of the model of femininity as altruistic and moral, then, Ritchie apparently subscribed to a version of this model himself.

This paradox is equally apparent in the work of the British sexologist and physician, Havelock Ellis, who was both a supporter of women's

---

[19] Ritchie, *Darwinism and Politics*, first edn, 83.   [20] *Ibid.*, 87.   [21] *Ibid.*, 89.

rights and a convinced Darwinist. Ellis undertook a detailed examination of the scientific evidence on sexual difference in his *Man and Woman*, first published in 1894 and going to eight editions by 1934.[22] Ellis opposed the prevalent belief in masculine superiority but at the same time took issue with the feminist credo of sexual equality. His conviction was: 'The more comprehensive our investigation the more certainly we find that we cannot speak of inferiority or superiority, but that the sexes are perfectly poised in complete equivalence' (v). Ellis carefully reviewed the data on sexual differences in cranial capacity, brain size and intellectual ability, and concluded that these gave no grounds for belief in female inferiority (203, 221, 405). What the available anthropological, physiological and psychological evidence indicated was that men were 'more variable' than women. He remarked, apropos this evidence: 'The progressive and divergent energies of men call out and satisfy the twin instincts of women to accept and follow a leader, and to expend tenderness on a reckless and erring child, instincts often intermingled in delicious confusion' (440). Ellis argued that men and women had evolved separate but complementary spheres of activity. For the former this sphere consisted of the cultivation of the arts, industry and exploration; for women, it was the bearing and raising of children and domestic activities. From innumerable civilisations, races and historical epochs, the data confirmed the universality of these separate domains: 'Woman breeds and tends; man provides; it remains so even when the spheres tend to overlap' (448). This prompted Ellis to caution his readers about the dangers attendant upon the efforts of women to cross the 'natural' boundaries, arguing that: 'When women enter the same fields as men, on the same level and to the same degree, their organic constitution usually unfits them to achieve the same success, or they only achieve it at a greater cost' (447). Despite his denial of any grounds for believing in the innate inequality of the sexes, then, Ellis still reproduced the popular conception of womanhood in terms of its maternal and domestic functions accompanied by the model of the male as adventurer and breadwinner.

In fairness to Ellis, he was fully cognisant of the ways in which alleged sexual differences had been used to legitimate the subjugation of women and how the existing sexual division of labour had been excessively restrictive for both sexes (450, 457). He accepted, notwithstanding his own reservations, that modern social conditions rendered it inevitable that women should enter into competition with men for the same roles and occupations, and he admitted that where this had occurred, women

---

[22]   I have used the eighth revised edition (London: Heinemann, 1934).

had acquitted themselves well, sometimes with distinction (448). He additionally made it quite clear that the natural spheres of men and women furnished no justification for social conservatism or the introduction of artificial barriers to sexual equality. Ultimately, the respective fitness of men and women for various social tasks could only be decided by experiments, and even here, the changing contexts of such experiments entailed that nothing in this area could ever be definitively resolved. As in all things, nature was the final tribunal for deciding the legitimacy of social innovations: 'When such experiment is successful, so much the better for the race; when it is unsuccessful, the minority who have broken natural law alone suffer. An exaggerated anxiety lest natural law be overthrown is misplaced' (459). Here nature was invested with the status of arbitrating among social practices and innovations, success being equated with conformity to nature's ways.[23]

This strategy had been adopted earlier in Bebel's *Woman in the Past, Present and Future*. According to Bebel: 'Woman was the first human being that tasted bondage. Woman was a slave before the slave existed' (7). In the earliest stage of human evolution – the primitive horde – the sexes were equal, both physically and mentally, as was still apparent from the situation found in some contemporary 'savage races'. But because women were liable to pregnancy and childbirth they were periodically dependent on males for support and protection and it was this dependency which became transformed into permanent subordination. The current mental and physical inferiority of women, therefore, was the product of social causes – exploitation and oppression – and would be remedied by a socialist socio-political system. Where women had obtained the requisite opportunities, their achievements ranked with those of men. Restricted occupational roles and an education that trivialised the mind were responsible for the seemingly low number of female achievers. Economic, political and educational equality would, within a generation, eradicate these differences between the sexes (120–9).

These were powerful arguments, and the portrait of an original sexual equality becoming subverted by social processes would assume paradigmatic status in socialist and feminist circles. But Bebel at times fell back upon a more biologically reductive model of sexual difference. For example, he described motherhood as 'natural' and a service to the community, despite having earlier attacked the view that the family and home were the natural milieux for women (112, 145). On several occasions he posited the existence of innate dispositions in both sexes

[23] Ellis adopted a similar position on modern war, which he saw as contrary to nature. Nature was a 'Great Mother' that acted 'as the exalting and civilising element in the world's life': Ellis, *Morals, Manners and Men* (London: Watts, 1939), 124.

and of desires that were 'deeply implanted in human nature' (150, 190, 223). We have already encountered, in chapter 7, Bebel's thesis that bourgeois society induced people to go against their true natures and overstep natural sexual boundaries (122). Social conditions were responsible for a contradiction between people as 'natural' and sexual beings on the one hand and their membership of society on the other, thereby creating social and psychological pathologies. Socialism represented a return to nature, a release of natural proclivities from the bondage to which they had been enthralled by a perverse social order. Thus while Bebel's text did not reproduce the altruistic/egoistic model as such, it nevertheless implied the existence of original natures in both men and women and that each sex had 'a proper purpose'. Biological determinism was reinscribed into Bebel's otherwise cultural explanation of the emergence of sexual difference.

Bebel's theory posited an original primitive equality between the sexes: in the USA, the sociologist Lester Frank Ward produced an equally paradigmatic version in which females were initially *superior* to males. In his *Pure Sociology* he maintained that 'while female superiority is a perfectly natural condition, male development requires explanation' (323). His reasoning was that in nature, sexual selection ensured the maintenance of quality in a species. Males were driven to fecundate indiscriminately, but unlimited variations were potentially dangerous. They were held in check by female choice of mates: female discrimination preserved hereditary qualities (325). This was why females were the dominant sex in the animal kingdom, and were still so in primitive hordes. The transition from *gynaecocracy* to *androcracy* occurred when men discovered their roles in procreation and then used their superior strength to control the economic functions of women. According to Ward: 'The man saw that he was the master creature, that woman was smaller, weaker, less shrewd and cunning than he, and at the same time could be made to contribute to his pleasure and his wants, and he proceeded to appropriate her accordingly' (345).

A similar thesis of an originary female superiority was advanced by another eminent American sociologist, William Isaac Thomas (1863–1947). Thomas declared that in primitive communities women were the core of society, running the household and both economically creative and independent. The transition to male dominance occurred with the rise of settled agriculture, when men deployed their capacity for organised action to the purpose of usurping the economic functions of women. The result was the distortion of female nature.[24] Like racial

---

[24] W. I Thomas, 'The Adventitious Character of Woman', *American Journal of Sociology*, 12(1906–7), 32–44.

differences, therefore, sexual differences owed more to culture than to nature. This was particularly the case in the realm of science and intellectual activity in general. 'The world of modern intellectual life is in reality a white man's world. Few women and perhaps no blacks have ever entered this world in the fullest sense . . . ' Thomas urged greater equality of opportunity in order to realise the unexplored talents of women and blacks, concluding: 'Certain it is that no civilisation can remain the highest if another civilisation adds to the intelligence of its men the intelligence of its women.'[25]

In these types of argument Social Darwinism provided an emancipatory framework within which the position of women could be diagnosed. Far from legitimating male domination, Social Darwinism in these theories allowed for either the evolution of distinct but complementary sexual characteristics or for social explanations of patriarchy as a perversion of an originary sexual equality or even female superiority. This is not to deny the continuation of sexual stereotypes in these theories or to ignore the contradictions which could occur in explanations that shifted between the social and the biological. What is significant is that Social Darwinism was highly serviceable in the cause of women's liberation.

But what of women themselves? So far in this chapter the voices urging a change in the position of females have been male. Yet women also adapted Darwinism to their cause in ways which were often radical and innovative. Some, it is true, were dismissive of Darwinism, such as the English feminist and follower of Mill, Frances Power Cobbe.[26] Others undoubtedly saw in Darwinism a liberating potential. The remainder of this chapter will focus on some notable, albeit largely neglected, examples.

Sexual selection and sexual equality

A major contribution to the feminist appropriation of Social Darwinism occurs in the pioneering efforts of Clémence Royer who, even prior to her translation of Darwin, had argued for female equality in her *Introduction à la philosophie des femmes*, published in 1859.[27] Later, in a contribution to a debate on the reasons for the declining French birth-rate, she

---

[25] Thomas, 'The Mind of Woman and the Lower Races', *American Journal of Sociology*, 12(1906–7), 469.

[26] Frances Power Cobbe, *Darwinism in Morals and Other Essays* (London: Williams and Norgate, 1872). Darwin responded tartly to Cobbe's criticisms in the second edition of the *Descent*, 152. For an analysis of Cobbe's feminism, see B. Caine, *Victorian Feminists* (Oxford University Press, 1992), chap. 4.

[27] See Harvey, 'Strangers to Each Other', 322, note 5.

argued that women's upbringings kept them ignorant of the realities of pregnancy and maternity and their resulting fears and disappointments led them to avoid both. She also accused the Catholic Church of exacerbating this situation with its prudish attitudes towards sex.[28] As for male dominance, we have already encountered Royer's thesis that this was contrary to the natural course of evolution. Social conditions prevented women from realising their true potential by confining them to a limited set of roles and artificially encouraging certain traits. But Royer also believed that the sexual and maternal drives were natural components of woman's nature and that it was the weakening of these drives which was responsible for the decline in France's birth-rate. In fact, her analysis of the condition of women was couched in terms of natural proclivities that were thwarted by the conventions of patriarchalism; removal of the latter would facilitate the efflorescence of female genius, of which Royer apparently regarded herself as an exemplar.[29] As I argued in chapter 6, Royer was inconsistent in the explanatory roles she assigned to biology and society in her treatment of social divisions; but she deserves recognition for her attempt to provide an evolutionary account of male domination and for highlighting the blighting consequences of patriarchy for the lives of women.

This merging of theoretical interests, political goals and subjective experience was crucial to the work of the three theorists considered below.[30] It is apparent in Eliza Burt Gamble's preface to *The Evolution of Woman* (1894).[31] Here Gamble recorded her personal conviction that females were not inferior to males, a conviction confirmed by her subsequent reading of Darwin's *Descent*, despite the latter's misinterpretation of his data (v–viii). After accurately describing the roles of natural and sexual selection in evolution, Gamble emphasised a crucial feature of sexual selection, namely female choice of mating partner, something which Darwin ignored when considering human evolution.

Sexual selection, we are told, resembles artificial selection, save that the female takes the place of the human breeder. In other words, she represents the intelligent factor or cause in the operations involved. If this be true, if it is through her will, or through some agency or tendency latent in her constitution

[28] Royer, 'La Natalité', suppressed paper to the Société d'Anthropologie de Paris, July 1874. For details of this paper, and an analysis of its contents, see Harvey, 'Strangers to Each Other', 160–1, 322, note 2.

[29] Harvey, 'Strangers to Each Other', 160, 165.

[30] This merging has already been signalled by Rosaleen Love in her study of Gilman and Schreiner, 'Darwinism and Feminism', 120.

[31] E. B. Gamble, *The Evolution of Woman: An Enquiry into the Dogma of Her Inferiority to Man* (New York/London: Putnam's Sons, 1894). I have been unable to ascertain any details of Gamble's career and background.

that Sexual Selection comes into play, then she is the primary cause of the very characters through which man's superiority over woman has been gained. As a stream may not rise higher than its source, or as the creature may not surpass its creator in excellence, it is difficult to understand the process by which man, through Sexual Selection, has become superior to woman (29).

Gamble's alternative account of sexual difference maintained that natural selection evolved the maternal instinct in females which then, through sexual selection, became the foundation of parental bonding and all the social sentiments among humans (62). This was brought about through female choice of mates which not only selected for these qualities, but which also produced the distinctively male attributes of energy, perseverance and courage – to which Gamble contrasted the feminine traits of perception, intuition and endurance (65). This choice was still exercised in primitive tribes where the independence of women had often been misconstrued as evidence of promiscuity by ethnographers (91–8).

Gamble insisted that primitive tribal structures were democratic and solidaristic, with land held in common and descent reckoned through women, who enjoyed high status and autonomy (109–21). Male domination occurred with the emergence of wife-capture and the development of private property in land (140). Marriage then became based upon 'the power of a man over a woman and her offspring' (166), and women were reduced to the status of a possession. Since then, women had been subjected to the vilest slavery in which they had been systematically denied opportunities to develop their talents and were exposed to an 'excessive and useless maternity' (52), a position from which they were beginning to emerge although there was still a great deal to be done (347–8).

Gamble's treatise made novel use of sexual selection for the purpose of underlining the injustice of female subordination. For her, nature provided a model for the organisation of social relations and sexual selection based upon female mate selection should be once again allowed full expression. Gamble contended that the 'unnatural' condition of women illustrated how the survival of the fittest did not necessarily produce success for the best endowed (73). Indeed, she suggested that the restoration of sexual selection could even produce the elimination of the struggle for existence. She contemplated a future social condition in which 'man will no longer struggle with man for place or power, and that the bounties of the earth will no longer be hoarded by the few, while the many are suffering for the necessities of life; for are we not all members of one family, and dependent for all that we have on the same beneficent parent – Nature?' (78). In this imagery, nature is benevolent and women its true representatives and guardians. Yet the above passage also suggests a tension already encountered in other theorists, for natural selection is also one of nature's laws, and Gamble's comments indicate an ambivalence towards the struggle for existence and its social consequences. The dark side of nature is still present in Gamble's reinterpretation of sexual selection, just as it was for Darwin.

This dark side was also evident in the work of Charlotte Perkins Gilman (1860–1935), the American novelist, poet and social theorist. Gilman was a feminist and a socialist, an avid reader of popular science, and influenced by the sociology of Ward. The interests converged in her *Women and Economics* (1898), a biting attack on the subordinate status of contemporary women which achieved a very wide readership, having been reprinted seven times by the early 1920s and translated into seven languages.[32] In this text Gilman argued that in primitive times both women and men were agile, independent and strong, qualities evolved through natural selection. The male was larger and more ferocious because he fought with other males for the right to mate; females selected the victors. At a certain point in time, the male realised that it was easier to fight a small female than a large male, and so enslaved the female, depriving her of her independence. From then on women, confined to narrow domestic functions, were excluded from the direct action of natural selection. Instead, they developed only the faculties of sexual attraction required to secure a mate and ensure being fed. Fortunately, this situation was not irremediable due to the action of heredity. 'Heredity has no Sallic Law' (58). Each girl inherited some of her father's abilities: hence 'the daughter of the soldier and the sailor, of the artist, the inventor, the great merchant, has inherited in body and brain her share of his development in each generation, and so stayed somewhat human for all her femininity' (59).

When Gilman wrote: 'There are other purposes before us besides mere maintenance and reproduction' (55), she did so in painful personal awareness of the psychic costs to women caused by their imprisonment in these roles, an awareness used to harrowing effect in her fiction.[33] The argument about the relationship between natural and sexual selection, however, was developed in her *The Man-Made World*, published in 1911.[34] Here Gilman proposed that there were sexual traits

---

[32] Love, 'Darwinism and Feminism', note 4, 128. The text used here is the extract in Hollinger and Capper, *American Intellectual Tradition*, II, 55–60.
[33] C. P. Gilman, *The Yellow Wallpaper* [1892] (London: Virago, 1983).
[34] C. P. Gilman, *The Man-Made World Or Our Androcentric Culture* (London: Fisher Unwin, 1911).

specific to males and females, but there were also common traits deriving from a shared humanity: 'Woman's natural work as a female is that of the mother; man's natural work as a male is that of the father. Every handicraft, every profession, every science, every art, all government, education, religion, the whole living world of human achievement – all this is human' (27).

Gilman's thesis was that the original relations between the sexes were matriarchal, due to the principle of female mate selection. This was subverted by the enslavement of women and their conversion into possessions, with the concomitant usurpation of their economic activities and the conversion of the family into a patriarchal institution (36–40). As a result, in a history both made and recorded by men, specifically male attributes had become identified with human nature *per se* (20, 24).

The human species thus represented an aberration in the natural order for, according to Gilman, it was the only one where the male selected females and where the female was dependent for her livelihood on the male (64–5). The outcome was a situation in which females were excluded from the action of natural selection, while males escaped the effects of sexual selection. 'Nothing was required of woman by natural selection save such capacity as should please her master; nothing was required of the man by sexual selection save power to take by force, or buy, a woman' (56). The impact on the race could not fail to be deleterious. 'Nature did not intend him [the male] to select; he is not good at it. Neither was the female intended to compete – she is not good at it' (34–5). By 'compete' Gilman was not referring to the struggle for existence within a certain milieu but to the exercise of what she saw as peculiarly male impulses to fight and destroy (117). Whereas women originally organised for gathering and maternal activities, men organised for hunting and, later, for warfare (186). Hence warfare was not a human but a male process for eliminating the unfit, whereas by contrast: 'The female process is to select the fit; her elimination is negative and painless.' Gilman continued: 'Greater than either is the human process, *to develop fitness*' (190, original emphasis).

This equation of warfare with masculinity points to a contradiction in Gilman's analysis. She argued that a number of contemporary evils were the product of the exclusive action of male traits. Thus punishment was androcentric, based on the principle of if hit, hit back harder; for Gilman, apart from the odd pervert, criminals were made rather than born, hence punishment was archaic (205, 210–12). Similarly, *laissez-faire* and economic competition reflected the spirit of the predatory male. Thus economic development was hindered 'by this artificially maintained "struggle for existence", this constant endeavour to eliminate what, from a masculine standard, is "unfit" ' (251). Gilman insisted that life consisted of growth and combat belonged to lower levels of existence (228). But this raised the issue of how, if at all, natural selection operated in ideal modern social circumstances. In *Woman and Economics* Gilman extolled the action of natural selection when it acted upon both sexes 'with inexorable and beneficial effect' to develop the species (56). In the later text, she tended to equate the forces of natural selection with maleness, which then obstructed the development of the 'human instinct of mutual service' (246). Industry, on the other hand, portrayed as a human sphere in the clarification of male, female and human nature cited earlier, became attributed to women, later to be perverted by the male spirit of competitiveness (242).

These oscillations suggest that Gilman, like many radicals and reformers, was unhappy with the idea of natural selection continuing to hold sway in culturally advanced societies based upon equality and mutual cooperation. Nonetheless, her ideal did not require a complete abandoning of evolutionary laws because she believed that sexual equality would augment the action of sexual selection in species development. Equality would restore the primacy of female choice and men who were not selected for fatherhood would not be eliminated but would still be able to pursue full human lives (256).

Gamble and Gilman were creative in their adaptation of sexual selection for the feminist cause, and pioneering to the extent that only fairly recently has sexual selection been assigned prominence in Social Darwinism. Their strategy consisted in constructing biologically evolved sexual natures which were then stultified or perverted by social processes. In both instances, though, the remedies sought were social and political, and the normative standards, while still set by nature, reflected a nature seemingly shorn of the pernicious effects of natural selection. Thus Gilman became an opponent of eugenics – the attempt to pattern social upon natural selection – which she castigated as a 'primal process of promoting evolution through the paternity of the conquering male ...' (250).[35] Her hostility to eugenics may have been well founded, for it has been suggested that the adoption of eugenics by the women's movements in Germany gradually led to a weakening (though not a total renunciation) of their radical emancipatory programmes.[36] Yet my last example, though Swedish rather than German, shows that some women found it possible to unite Social Darwinism and eugenics with feminism, socialism and pacifism.

[35] See also Gilman's 'Response to Wells' "Social Darwinism" ', *The American Journal of Sociology*, 12(1906–7), 713–14.
[36] See R. J. Evans, *Rethinking German History* (London: HarperCollins, 1987), 226–9.

Key and the evolution of love

The Swedish educationalist Ellen Karolina Sofia Key (1849–1926), who achieved extensive acclaim for her *The Century of the Child* (1909), also published widely on the Woman Question. In her view, life entailed movement, which in turn implied diversity and transmutation, although this latter process could be either progressive or regressive. Among humans, sexual reproduction was the means through which hereditary traits were transmitted, which made sex of the utmost importance to human evolution.[37]

Sexual love was not unique to humans and could be found among animals. Like all instincts and behaviour patterns it had evolved over time and, in keeping with the general trends of evolution, had shown increasing individuation from its primitive manifestations.[38] Unfortunately, social and legal conventions had not kept pace with the development of love, and the stifling institution of monogamous marriage actually interfered with the individuating dynamics of sexual evolution. Key proclaimed that both the choice of sexual partners and the rearing of children should be based upon a union motivated by mutual love, and the propriety of the partnership should be judged by the capacity of the couple to assume parental responsibility rather than by outmoded ideas about the legality of the relationship. By the same token, divorce should be the prerogative of either one of the partners, which involved an equality of rights between the two sexes.[39] In this way, children would be born into and from relationships inspired by love which, other things being equal, 'produces the best children'. These offspring would themselves inherit 'a greater power to love' because of this affective milieu. Such an arrangement was infinitely more responsible than the present system, which encouraged the raising of children in loveless unions and even sanctioned childless marriages. For Key, love must become once again what it formerly was 'when nations looked upon life with reverence: Religion'.[40]

Key justified these calls for changes in legal and moral conventions by an appeal to their eugenic consequences. 'All other problems must be regarded from this one point of view: the elevation of the species', and we 'must strive for the elevation of the human race'.[41] Since the goal was species perfection, sexual practices had to be evaluated in relation to

[37] Ellen Key, *Love and Ethics* (no tr.) (London: Putnam's, 1912), 27–8.
[38] Key, *Love and Marriage*, tr. A. Chater (London: Putnam's, 1911), 62, 157, 158.
[39] Key, *Love and Ethics*, 22–3.
[40] Key, *Love and Marriage*, 157; Key, *Love and Ethics*, 28, 27, 23.
[41] Key, *Love and Ethics*, 13, 18.

this. For Key: 'The development of the race gains when the lives less worthy to survive are not reproduced in offspring ...' Immature and degenerate couples must be discouraged from procreating, which entailed both partners in a prospective union submitting to a medical examination in order to ascertain 'whether they are capable of fulfilling their duty to the race'.[42]

Key denied that this duty to the race entailed the sacrifice of the happiness of individuals on the altar of race ennoblement. On the contrary, the sensible selection of sexual partners was consistent with the individuating processes of evolution as well as with the dictates of racial hygiene.[43] Evolution was a matter of chance and change in which the future was indeterminate. This necessitated recognition of the incalculability of future outcomes and a realisation 'that life is not a hard and fast fact, but a growth with undivined possibilities, that it leads us and all other creatures along mysterious paths ...' Consequent on the development of individuality there arose a corresponding need for *freedom* in order to facilitate experiments, variations and changes, rather than blind obedience to authority, which would smother innovation and adaptation. 'The important thing, therefore, is to harmonise our concepts of right with nature, after we have learned to know nature by thorough investigation.'[44]

These arguments reveal Key to have made use of certain components of Social Darwinism – universal laws, evolution and heredity. This leaves the struggle for existence as the selective mechanism, and though this notion can be found in her writings on love and marriage, it was certainly not a salient feature of their argumentation. It is to her wartime defence of pacifism that we must turn to find a clarification of her position on struggle. Here she opposed war precisely because in its modern guise it failed to result in the survival of the fittest, and she chided those who wrongly equated modern warfare with the Darwinian struggle for existence.[45] Techniques of indiscriminate mass slaughter left women with the choice of either forgoing motherhood altogether or else mating with inadequate men who had been rejected for military service. 'War causes a contra-selection, that is, it furthers the survival of the defective.' Wars would only make sense as selective devices for raising national standards if they 'were fought by the degenerates of the nations'.[46]

The dysgenic consequences of modern warfare in no sense implied

---

[42] Key, *Love and Marriage*, 43–4, 141.   [43] *Ibid.*, 143; Key, *Love and Ethics*, 9, 18.
[44] Key, *Love and Ethics*, 14, 56.
[45] Key, *War, Peace and the Future*, tr. H. Norberg (London: Putnam's, 1916), 44, 87.
[46] *Ibid.*, 88–9, 85.

the elimination of the struggle for existence in human relations. For Key, this struggle had to take a form consonant with the levels of evolution attained by civilised nations, which meant that conflicts must be restricted to those permitted within the framework of the law. She mentioned public debate and argument and electoral contests as modes of selection which were appropriate to advanced societies. 'Strife and competition will not, therefore, be done away with.'[47] She gave no reason for this belief though, and it is hard to avoid the impression that Key had difficulty in reconciling her pacifism with the notion of natural selection. Indeed, the term played a relatively small role in her discourse relative to the other elements of the Darwinist world view. She was also unable to make use of a tactic available to liberals like Spencer, i.e. substituting industrial competition for warfare as civilisation progressed, because she was a socialist as well as a pacifist and therefore found industrial competition uncongenial as a selective device.

What Key certainly upheld was the need to harness the social counterparts of natural selection to the interests of the race through eugenic measures. The medical examination of prospective marriage partners was not the only way in which she envisaged racial improvement taking place. Key had great faith in the power of education to moderate the action of inherited traits, a faith that set her apart from current trends in neo-Darwinism. She believed education was especially necessary to eliminate atavistic instincts and passions which threatened to impede progress. For Key there was no fixed human essence or nature: the characteristics exhibited by humans were primarily governed by their level of physiological and mental development. The modern age was not compelled to accept passively the legacy of former evolutionary stages. On the contrary, the species must be prepared to 'reject what hinders and select what assists its struggle for the strengthening of its position as humanity and its elevation to superhumanity'.[48]

Education's potential for altering hereditary dispositions made all brutal and exploitative practices unacceptable to Key. Whether these involved warfare, or the domination of women by men or of one class by another, they could no longer be justified by appeals to inexpungable features of human nature. 'What are culture and civilisation if not the taming of the blind forces within us as well as in nature?'[49] Women could play a major role in this educative process, and Key articulated a conception of a gender-based division of labour which, on her own admission, earned her the label of 'reactionary' from many contemporary feminists. She perceived 'motherhood' to be the true vocation of

[47] Ibid., 130.   [48] Key, Love and Marriage, 53.
[49] Key, War, Peace and the Future, 4.

women, not through the mass production of children, but as a full-time educational activity devoted to the improvement of the quality of childhood and, ultimately therefore, of humanity as a whole.[50] Key was scornful of the 'amaternals', those 'fanatics' in the women's movement who believed that equality of rights entailed the performance of identical functions, or that equality between the sexes necessitated the sameness of the sexes.[51] She accused advocates of the 'third sex' of ignoring an important dimension of the women's struggle, namely its focus upon 'erotic, religious and social emancipation'.[52] Key did not underestimate the importance of the fight for equal political and legal status with men or deny the need to remove obstacles to women's employment in the many professions and careers still closed to them. She insisted that women 'must have free choice of work' as a right and also for the sake of improved social efficiency, and opposed restriction on female employment because 'the right to limit the choice of work the law does not possess; nature assumes that right herself . . .'[53] But for Key the worth of a married woman could not be measured simply by her ability to earn a living. Raising children was a full-time occupation and women could not be expected to perform this task and at the same time compete with men in holding down a full-time job. Furthermore, the evolution of increasing specialisation had produced females who, for millennia, had specialised in the production and rearing of children. To remain in harmony with the direction of evolution, this role should be enhanced in order that 'woman *in an ever more perfect manner shall fulfil what has hitherto been her most exalted task*: the bearing and rearing of the new generation'.[54]

Key was convinced that women had a natural propensity for educational roles due to their innate capacity for sympathy, which developed out of the reciprocity inherent in the bond between mother and child. This relationship constituted a primal form of the 'law of mutual help' and was, accordingly, 'the root of altruism'. There was, therefore, a happy congruence between a woman's biological evolution and her social position: 'The very fact that woman's *primitive instinct* coincided with her *greatest* cultural *office* has been an essential factor in the harmony of her being.'[55] But the importance of this cultural office had yet to be fully appreciated; society must recognise motherhood as a fundamental state service, rewarded by some form of state payment.[56]

[50] *Ibid.*, 161, 182–4.
[51] Key, *The Woman Movement*, tr. M. B. Borthwick (London: Putnam's, 1912), 181.
[52] Key, *Love and Marriage*, 70.   [53] Key, *Woman Movement*, 182.
[54] Key, *Woman Movement*, 187, original emphasis.
[55] Key, *Woman Movement*, 186, 197, original emphases.
[56] Key, *War, Peace and the Future*, 182–3.

Key's eugenic proposals at times had an ominous ring, although in fairness her notion of race, though vague, was invariably applied to humanity as a whole rather than to a particular ethnic group. It is possible to interpret her thesis as legitimating stereotypes of male and female sexuality to justify confining women to procreative and maternal functions. On the other hand, the radicalism of her critique of marriage and her ideas on love should not be overlooked and was certainly not lost on her contemporaries.[57] Similarly, her proposals for state-funded maternity benefits were prophetic. However, what is particularly striking about Key's ideas in the context of this study is the methodological inconsistency they exhibit over the role of education. She proposed an evolutionary basis to motherhood, with its roots in instinctual feelings and primal bonds, insisting that to ignore these latter sentiments was to go against the specialised functions for which women had been equipped by nature. Yet in different contexts she celebrated the transformative power of education with respect to deep-seated instincts – for instance, those giving rise to war and exploitation. A tension is apparent in Key's writings between her desire to enlist the hereditarian and selective features of Darwinism in the twin causes of social explanation and social reform, and the need to interpret certain facets of human behaviour as 'unnatural' and capable of modification by cultural processes. Nature vacillates between something to be emulated and something to be conquered in Key's discourse, just as in so much Social Darwinist thinking.

Conclusion

The literature scrutinised in this chapter shows that Social Darwinism was certainly enlisted in the defence of patriarchy, but that this was not its exclusive function. The world view was also used in the service of feminism and some of its most notable adaptations were by women writers. Their theories were not devoid of tensions and aporia, but I have argued that these were similar to those encountered in much Social Darwinist thought, particularly if of a radical orientation. The evidence suggests that at least some women experienced Darwinism as an enlightening and emancipatory intellectual current containing the potential for alternative – i.e. gynaecocentric – evolutionary histories.

The radicalism displayed in the attacks by Gamble, Gilman and Key on monogamy and marriage, and in their gynaecocentrism, is apparent

---

[57] See, for example, E. Faguet, *Le Feminisme* (Paris: Société Française d'Imprimerie et de Librairie, 1910). The chapter entitled 'L'Anarchie morale' contains an attack on Key's views on these topics.

even within the framework of Darwinism. This can be illustrated by comparing their work with that of the Finnish sociologist, Edward Alexander Westermarck (1862–1939). In 1891 Westermarck published *The History of Human Marriage*,[58] a highly influential Darwinian account of the evolution of marriage and incest prohibitions. His thesis was that marriage – 'a more or less durable connection between male and female' (19) – had its origins in the animal kingdom, was particularly strong in primate species and, contrary to the stereotype of primitive promiscuity, much in evidence among savages. This bonding was instinctual and had been spread by natural selection. In contrast to Gilman and Gamble, Westermarck emphasised the importance of *paternal* care as a primal factor in consolidating marriage ties:

when the father helps to protect the offspring, the species is better able to subsist in the struggle for existence than it would be if this obligation entirely devolved on the mother. Paternal affection and the instinct which causes male and female to form somewhat durable alliances, are thus useful mental dispositions which, in all probability, have been acquired through 'the survival of the fittest' (20–1).

Westermarck also equivocated over the relationship between natural and sexual selection, acknowledging the possibility of conflict between them, but in the end entirely subordinating the latter to the former (252). He did not, therefore, accord female choice the powerful selective effects ascribed to it by Gilman. Westermarck concluded his treatise with these words: 'The history of human marriage is the history of a relation in which women have been gradually triumphing over the passions, the prejudices, and the selfish interests of men' (550). But he had earlier suggested that the cause of this process was to be found in the development of altruism among *men* (361), and he saw monogamy as the culmination of evolution rather than, as for Gilman and Key, an obstacle to further evolutionary advances.

This chapter commenced with the observations that nature had often been personified as female and that the mid-nineteenth century witnessed a transformation in the images of both the natural and the feminine. It is interesting to note that Gilman, Gamble and Key did not overtly personify nature as female. This could well reflect one of the consequences of Darwinian biology (and natural science in general), i.e. the depersonalisation of nature as its laws became known and popularised. At the same time, all three writers hinted at a transcendence of the more brutal features of natural law through the agency of natural proclivities and sentiments that were deemed to be specifically female.

---

[58] London/New York: Macmillan. This book went to five editions by 1921, and expanded to three volumes.

Positing an evolutionary foundation for sexual difference these theorists then looked to one of the sexes as the seedbed of future change – change which was sometimes presented as a development, perhaps even transformation, of the laws governing evolution itself.

This strategy is clearly exemplified in another female writer, the poet Mathilde Blind (1841–96). Blind's family were Germans exiled to England after the abortive insurrection of 1848, and her poetry often reflects a radical political persuasion. She was also influenced by Darwinism, which is clearly in evidence in her *The Ascent of Man* (1889).[59] Here she graphically described the struggle for existence as a relentless slaughter – 'A dreadful war, where might is right, / Where still the strongest slay and win, / Where weakness is the only sin' (12–13). Humanity was forged through this process, and the struggle for life was continued by man against man. However, Blind found the manner in which this struggle was culturally represented (to the benefit of the rich and powerful) hypocritical. 'Better far for the plain, carnivorous fashion/ Which is practiced in the lion's den' (104). At times, a powerful feeling of meaninglessness and despair pervaded the poem, for example, 'Life is but a momentary blunder / In the cycle of the Universe' (105). Yet Blind finished on an optimistic note, proclaiming the triumph of God and Love from man's martyrdom. The explanation for this transcendence of blind struggle and carnage was vague, but hinted that it would appear through the agency of women:

> O redeem me from my tiger rages,
> Reptile greed, and foul hyaena lust;
> With the hero's deeds, the thoughts of sages,
> Sow and fructify the passive dust;
> Drop in dew and healing love of woman
> On the bloodstained hands of hungry strife,
> Till there break from passion of the Human
> Morning – glory of transformed life (109).

Blind's poem reproduces two themes highlighted in the analysis of female Social Darwinists. First there is the ambivalence over nature – the model/threat dualism which is so prevalent in Social Darwinist discourses. Second, though nature as a whole is not accorded a female persona, those features of nature through which salvation is possible are invested with features designated as feminine. The nurturing/caring model of womanhood is still retained as natural, even if no longer typical of nature in its entirety.

---

[59] M. Blind, *The Ascent of Man* (London: Chatto and Windus, 1889). The 1899 reissue of this poem had a foreword by A. R. Wallace. (I am grateful to Christine Pullen for drawing my attention to this poem.)

11   Nazism, Fascism and Social Darwinism

Introduction

There is an enormous scholarly literature on Nazism and Fascism, one that is marked by controversy over how the two movements are to be defined, over their origins, sources of support, ideologies and significance. The genocidal policies of the Nazi regime in Germany from 1933 to 1945, culminating in the Holocaust against the Jews, raise additional issues concerning the causes of such actions and the roots of anti-Semitic and racial thinking and policies in German, and more generally, European, culture and history. It has also inclined some commentators to question the extent to which Fascism and Nazism can be considered as members of the same ideological and political family, and to suggest that the latter may be a distinctive and unique phenomenon.[1]

One point on which scholars do seem to have reached a consensus relates to the role of Social Darwinism in both Nazi and Fascist ideology. Social Darwinist ideas are cited as underpinning Nazi policies on war, eugenics and race,[2] and providing a rationale for the emphasis on struggle and conflict found in Italian and French Fascism.[3] Yet there is to date no detailed analysis of the nature and function of Social Darwinism within Nazism and Fascism, or of whether the two ideologies

---

[1] For an overview of the pros and cons of this latter debate, see I. Kershaw, *The Nazi Dictatorship*, second edn (London: Edward Arnold, 1989), chap. 2.

[2] For examples, see Kershaw, *The Nazi Dictatorship*, 74, 129, 146; J. Noakes and G. Pridham, eds., *Nazism 1919–1945*, III, 610–11, 617–8; H. Krausnick and M. Broszat, *Anatomy of the SS State*, tr. D. Long and M. Jackson (London: Granada, 1970), 27–35; Burleigh and Wipperman, *The Racial State*, 28–33; H. Dicks, *Licensed Mass Murder* (London: Heinemann, 1972), 112, 267.

[3] See A. Lyttleton, *Italian Fascisms From Pareto to Gentile* (London: Jonathan Cape, 1973), 32; Z. Sternhell, 'Fascist Ideology', in W. Laqueur, ed., *Fascism: A Reader's Guide* (Harmondsworth: Penguin, 1976), 334–5; Sternhell, *Ni droite ni gauche* (Paris: Editions du Seuil, 1983), 47, 141; P. Milza, *Les Fascismes* (Paris: Imprimerie Nationale, 1985), 51–2; R. Eatwell, *Fascism: A History* (London: Chatto and Windus, 1995), 26, 166.

exhibited any significant differences in these respects. The purpose of this chapter is to make a start at filling this lacuna by conducting such an investigation. For the sake of convenience I will deal with German Nazism and Italian Fascism separately, and then conclude by making some general comparative observations. Given the sheer volume and complexity of the material under consideration, I must emphasise the provisional nature of this enterprise and the tentativeness of the conclusions, although the latter do indicate some fruitful lines of further inquiry. I will also be confining the analysis to the period up to 1945, since an investigation of the development of these ideologies after World War II is beyond the scope of this study.

The foundations of the Nazi world view

In analysing Nazi ideology I shall initially concentrate on the writings and speeches of Adolf Hitler (1889–1945). The danger of so doing is that Nazi ideology can become exclusively identified with one man to the neglect of the other contributors to Nazi discourse, creating the impression that National Socialism was a monolithic and unified doctrine. On the contrary, Nazism was the work of many contributors and like any other creed exhibited variations in the emphasis given to its various components, as well as contradictory positions on some issues.[4] My reason for focusing upon Hitler is largely one of convenience, i.e. the need to limit the field of inquiry in order to conduct a detailed analysis of the structure and content of a number of texts. Moreover, there can be little doubt about the importance of Hitler's ideas for an understanding of Nazism in the light of the centrality of the dictator within the movement, particularly after the seizure of power in 1933. The Nazi regime itself became suffused with Hitler's rhetoric on matters of both domestic and foreign policy soon after this point, as will become evident in the following section, so Hitler's ideas are an excellent guide to the ideology and practice of Nazism in general.

One of the most significant texts for an understanding of Hitler's world view is a book written in 1928 but only published after the war as *Hitler's Secret Book*. Here Hitler announced: 'History itself is the presentation of the course of a people's struggle for existence. I deliberately use the phrase "struggle for existence" here because in truth that struggle for daily bread, equally in peace and war, is an eternal

---

[4] Material from Nazi ideologues other than Hitler has been published in B. Lane and L. Rupp, eds., *Nazi Ideology Before 1933: A Documentation* (Manchester University Press, 1978); Griffin, ed., *Fascism*, Readings 60–89.

battle against thousands upon thousands of resistances just as life itself is an eternal struggle against death.'[5]

According to Hitler, the twin dynamics of life were hunger and love, the first of which promoted self-preservation, the second the preservation of the species. However, the space in which these instinctive drives had to be satisfied was limited – here Hitler was undoubtedly endorsing a version of the earlier *Lebensraum* theories – with the result that organisms were compelled to struggle for space and resources. It is out of this struggle that evolution occurred through the survival of the fittest. 'From the invisible confusion of the organisms there finally emerged formations, clans, tribes, peoples, states. The description of their origins and their passing away is but the representation of an eternal struggle for existence.'[6]

Among the lowest organic beings, self-preservation was confined to survival of the individual. With increasing development the focus was transferred to spouse and offspring, and among the highest creatures, to the 'entire species'. Men, therefore, acted in accordance with the instinct of self-preservation when they sacrificed themselves for their people.[7] By 'people' and 'species', Hitler meant 'race'. In *Mein Kampf* he wrote: 'The racial question gives the key not only to world history, but to all human culture.'[8] Race was not a matter of language or historical continuity, but of blood. Since nature did not reserve the use of the soil to particular nations and races, the acquisition of space and resources could only be decided by conflict. Nature established no political boundaries, but rather conferred 'the master's right on her favourite child, the strongest in courage and industry'.[9] This was an unalterable law: 'Providence has endowed living creatures with a limitless fecundity; but she has not put in their reach, without the need for effort on their part, all the food they need. All that is very right and proper, for it is the struggle for existence that produces the selection of the fittest.'[10] It was through the survival of the fittest that nature contrived the elimination of the weak and the improvement of the race:

Those whom she permits to survive the inclemency of existence are a thousand-fold tested, hardened, and well adapted to procreate in turn, in order that the process of thorough-going selection may begin again from the beginning. By thus brutally proceeding against the individual and immediately calling him back to

[5] A. Hitler, *Hitler's Secret Book*, tr. S. Attanasio (New York: Grove Press, 1961), 5.
[6] *Ibid.*, 7.   [7] *Ibid.*, 5.
[8] Hitler, *Mein Kampf*, tr. R. Manheim (London: Hutchinson, 1974), 308.
[9] *Ibid.*, 123.
[10] Hitler, *Hitler's Table Talk 1941–1944*, tr. N. Cameron and R. Stevens (Oxford University Press, 1988), 134.

herself as soon as he shows himself unequal to the storm of life, she keeps the race and species strong, in fact, raises them to the highest accomplishments.[11]

To abolish this struggle would deprive men of 'the highest driving power for their development'.[12] Struggle determined the worth of both individuals and races by establishing a hierarchy according to their capabilities for preservation and development, and for Hitler the task of National Socialism was to ensure that society mirrored this principle of nature:

the folkish philosophy finds the importance of mankind in its basic racial elements. In the state it sees on principle only a means to an end and construes its end as the preservation of the racial existence of man. Thus, it by no means believes in the equality of the races, but along with their differences it recognises their higher or lesser value and feels itself obligated, through this knowledge, to promote the victory of the better and stronger, and demand the subordination of the inferior and weaker in accordance with the eternal will that dominates this universe. Thus, in principle, it preserves the basic aristocratic idea of Nature and believes in the validity of this law down to the last individual. It sees not only the different value of the races, but also the different value of individuals.[13]

One of nature's rules which Hitler thought it vital to observe was the deleterious effects of race mixing. Nature, he proclaimed, 'has little love for bastards', as evinced by the punishment in the form of decadence and defeat inflicted on races which violated this rule. 'Eternal Nature inexorably avenges the infringement of her commands.'[14] The mixing of the blood of higher with lower races must therefore be resisted at all costs, for: 'The stronger must dominate and not blend with the weaker ...'[15] Anything which represented a racial danger must be resisted, 'for in a bastardised and niggerised world all the concepts of the humanly beautiful and sublime, as well as all ideas of an idealised future of our humanity, would be lost forever'.[16]

Needless to say, it was the Aryan, Nordic or Germanic race – Hitler employed these terms interchangeably – which represented the height of human development, whereas the Jew was a parasite, a bacillus, a 'world plague' threatening to poison and destroy the Aryan unless counteracted with appropriate measures. With these images of the Jew as an alien 'otherness', whose materialism and lack of 'rootedness' in his own native soil contrasted with the idealistic and racially superior Aryan, Hitler was drawing upon a long tradition of anti-Semitic and Volkish racial stereotyping in Germany.[17] He argued that the Jewish race possessed a

---

[11] Hitler, *Mein Kampf*, 121.   [12] Hitler, *Secret Book*, 16; also Hitler, *Mein Kampf*, 259.
[13] Hitler, *Mein Kampf*, 348.   [14] Ibid., 363, 60.
[15] *Ibid.*, 259; Hitler, *Secret Book*, 28.   [16] Hitler, *Mein Kampf*, 348.
[17] For an analysis of the interplay between Volkish and anti-Semitic currents in German

great instinct for survival but this only acted at the level of the self-preservation of the individual; hence Jews lacked sufficient idealism to form their own state. Instead they sought to corrupt and then subjugate the states which harboured them.[18] But the Jews were not the only 'racial danger' which the 'culture-creating' Aryan needed to guard against, and one of the crucial functions of the state was to maintain and improve the racial health of its people. In keeping with a long-standing feature of a certain genre of Social Darwinist thought, Hitler was of the opinion that modern civilisation tended to substitute social for natural selection, with highly damaging consequences for racial hygiene. Modern warfare, for example, tended to eliminate the healthiest specimens in the population while sparing the weaklings, and modern judicial and penal practices likewise preserved the lives of criminals. Birth control had created a situation in which people sought to limit the size of their families while paying little attention to the racial value of the children they did beget. It was racial suicide to countenance the continued propagation of defective and incurably sick infants. Hitler lauded the eugenic practices of ancient Sparta on the grounds that the destruction of weak, sickly and deformed children 'was more decent and a thousand times more humane than the wretched insanity of our day'.[19] In a speech to the Nuremberg Party Rally on 5 August 1929, Hitler denounced 'sentimental humanitarianism' and the 'sense of charity' which he considered responsible for 'maintaining the weak at the expense of the healthy'. He complained 'that even cretins are able to procreate while more healthy people refrain from doing so ... Criminals have the opportunity of procreating, degenerates are raised artificially and with difficulty. And in this way we are gradually breeding the weak and killing off the strong.'[20]

Hitler's writings and speeches portrayed nature in rigidly deterministic terms. Expressions such as 'eternal', 'inexorable' and 'iron' were used to refer to nature and its laws. Sometimes 'God' or 'Providence' were substituted for nature, but it is evident that Hitler was not appealing to any Christian deity, for he defined God as 'the dominion of natural laws throughout the whole universe', and referred to Providence as 'the unknown, or Nature, or whatever name one chooses'.[21] These natural laws were inescapable realities which could not be ignored without courting disaster: 'Nothing that is made of flesh and blood can escape

culture and their relationship to National Socialism, see G. Mosse, *The Crisis of German Ideology* (New York: Schocken, 1981).

[18] Hitler, *Mein Kampf*, 273, 299. Cf. Hitler, *Table Talk*, 117.
[19] Hitler, *Secret Book*, 8–9, 17–18.
[20] Noakes and Pridham, eds., *Nazism*, III, 1002.   [21] Hitler, *Table Talk*, 6, 44.

the laws which determined its coming into being.' Man must continue to be subjected to 'Nature's stern and rigid laws' because he 'has never yet conquered Nature in anything'.[22] The task of the politician was to recognise this and seek to harmonise policies with nature's rules so as to ensure the 'preservation and the continuance of the life of a people ...' This became the yardstick against which the success or failure of actions and policies must be judged: 'All human thought and invention, in their ultimate effects, primarily serve man's struggle for existence on this planet ...' And Hitler harboured no doubts about the efficacy of National Socialism in this respect, since 'the folkish philosophy of life corresponds to the innermost will of Nature ...'[23]

In conformity with this deterministic conception of nature, Hitler adopted a hereditarian stance with regard to the social and political problems of the day. Character for him was largely a matter of nature rather than upbringing. True, some traits vital to racial survival, such as loyalty, self-sacrifice and discretion, could be instilled through the right education. But ability was inborn, a gift of nature, not something that could be inculcated through instruction. 'Assuredly', wrote Hitler, 'the most essential features of character are fundamentally preformed in the individual: the man of egotistic nature is and remains so for ever ... The born criminal is and remains a criminal ...'[24]

The limits of education became particularly apparent with regard to racial differences. Hitler was adamant that racial traits were refractory to any modification. It was impossible to make Germans out of Poles, which rendered assimilationist programmes ludicrous in his eyes. As for the efforts to educate negroes to become lawyers, teachers and pastors, this was an offence against nature and reason, for 'it is a criminal lunacy to keep on drilling a born half-ape until people think they have made a lawyer out of him ... For this is training exactly like that of a poodle ...'[25]

This exegesis of Hitler's ideas reveals him to have endorsed the elements comprising Social Darwinism: laws common to humans and nature in general, a struggle for existence deriving from pressure on space and other resources which operated both at the level of individuals and social aggregates, of which races were the most important, and heredity constituting the mechanism whereby adaptive traits were transmitted to successive generations. This Social Darwinist world view was not only central to Hitler's ideology, but underpinned the most

[22] Hitler, *Secret Book*, 5; Hitler, *Mein Kampf*, 262, 261.
[23] Hitler, *Secret Book*, 7; Hitler, *Mein Kampf*, 405, 348.
[24] Hitler, *Mein Kampf*, 378, 377.
[25] Hitler, *Secret Book*, 47; Hitler, *Mein Kampf*, 391.

distinctive and essential features of Nazi theory and practice. This will be illustrated by a brief examination of some areas of Nazi thought and policy during their period in power.

Social Darwinism in Nazi thought and practice

The National Socialist vision of the world as an arena of competing states among which the only principle in operation was that of 'might is right' had fairly obvious repercussions for the field of foreign policy. The Nazi ideologue, Alfred Rosenberg (1893–1946), spelled this out as early as 1924 when he asserted that 'the world-political task of National Socialism consists of knocking one state after the other out of the world-political power system of today and, in the end, leaving no peoples under international management, but only a series of organic, folkish state systems on a racial basis'.[26] When the Nazis came to power this brutal message, if not always apparent to foreign statesmen of the period, was made clear to the German people. For example, the official guidelines for the teaching of history in secondary schools issued in 1938 by the German Central Institute of Education stated:

The German nation in its essence and greatness, in its fateful struggle for internal and external identity is the subject of the teaching of history. It is based on the natural bond of the child with his nation and, by interpreting history as the fateful struggle for existence between the nations, has the particular task of educating young people to respect the great German past and to have faith in the mission and future of their own nation and to respect the right of existence of other nations.

Apparently, the authors of these guidelines perceived no inconsistency between teaching history as a struggle for national survival and inculcating respect for the existence of other nations. They continued with an injunction to emphasise the enduring racial forces of the German nation, and added: 'Insight into the permanence of the hereditary characteristics and the merely contingent significance of environment facilitates a new and deep understanding of historical personalities and contexts ...'[27] In like vein, the notes for speeches by a Nazi party official to civil servants and other party officials in 1939 contained the following statement: 'The struggle for existence and the racial self-assertion of a nation is a process which eternally repeats itself. There is no end to it, for there are always new tasks since each new

[26]   A. Rosenberg, *Der Völkishe Staastgedanke* (Munich: Eher, 1925). There is an excerpt from this entitled 'The Folkish Idea of State', in Lane and Rupp, eds., *Nazi Ideology Before 1933*, 71.
[27]   Noakes and Pridham, eds., *Nazism*, II, 438.

generation must once again be turned into a body capable of resistance through education, work, and the supervision of its morale.'[28] Paul Josef Goebbels (1897–1945) conveyed the essence of this message in an entry in his diary in 1940: 'All means are justified. Our end is clear: a new world empire of Germans.'[29]

Closely connected to the foreign policy goals of National Socialism was war and the need for the total mobilisation of the population and national resources in order to achieve success. Despite his awareness of the dysgenic consequences of modern warfare, Hitler subscribed to the view that wars were good for a nation, encouraging its inhabitants to have more children. Hence: 'For the good of the German people, we must wish for a war every fifteen or twenty years.' War, in fact, was 'life's most potent and most characteristic expression', the ultimate test of a nation's capabilities and moral fibre.[30] This meant involving the entire nation in the war effort 'as if they were passionate participants in a sports contest'.[31]

The need for effectiveness in the struggle with other states, coupled with the biological determinism typical of Nazi versions of Social Darwinism, provided the rationale for a comprehensive eugenics programme aimed at purifying the population of its criminals and mental and physical defectives. The Nazi sterilisation law of 1933 made sterilisation compulsory for certain categories of people deemed to be suffering from hereditary illnesses (including alcoholism). However, additional criteria (e.g. 'anti-social behaviour', which included homosexuality, and 'moral weakness', which encompassed unmarried mothers) were often employed by medical officials. By 1945, 360,000 men and women had been sterilised under this programme, to which must be added an unknown number of foreign workers and members of ethnic minorities.[32]

Even more brutal was the euthanasia programme applied to mentally handicapped persons from 1939 to 1945. As previously noted, there had been serious discussion of the costs of maintaining 'idiots' during the

---

[28] *Ibid.*, 242.
[29] P. J. Goebbels, *The Goebbels Diaries, 1939–1941*, ed. and tr. F. Taylor (London: Sphere, 1983), 160.
[30] Hitler, *Table Talk*, 28, 397.
[31] Notes taken from a speech by Hitler to a conference of Gauleiters, 2 February 1934, in Noakes and Pridham, eds., *Naxism*, II, 235–6.
[32] See Noakes and Pridham, eds., *Nazism*, II, 458; Weindling, *Health, Race and German Politics*, 533. On the persecution of homosexuals in the Third Reich, which included castration and imprisonment, see Burleigh and Wipperman, *The Racial State*, 182–97; G. J. Giles, '"The Most Unkindest Cut of All"': Castration, Homosexuality and Nazi Justice', *Journal of Contemporary History*, 27(1992), 41–61; R. Plant, *The Pink Triangle: The Nazi War Against Homosexuals* (Edinburgh: Mainstream, 1987).

Weimar Republic, including proposals for the elimination of the 'mentally dead'.[33] Opportunity to implement such policies was provided by the Nazis, who embarked upon a programme of 'mercy-killing' of handicapped children in 1939, a process often involving the gradual starvation of the victims.[34] This was accompanied by the gassing of mentally handicapped adults from 1939, although Hitler officially put a stop to this in August 1941 as a result of opposition to the programme. By then, over 70,000 people had been 'disinfected', a figure that was to be greatly augmented by unofficial euthanasia practices conducted in the concentration camps after 1941, often including people who were not sick but considered undesirable on racial grounds.[35] In this manner, Hitler's vision of a state which employed the ancient Spartan practice of eliminating the weak, the unfit and the socially unacceptable members of the community was realised in a most brutal fashion. These policies received their legitimation from the Social Darwinist world view which saw in such categories of people a threat to the survival capabilities of the nation in the struggle for existence due to their possession of traits deemed to be genetically determined. This also applied to criminals and political subversives. As Goebbels put it: 'The asocial elements must not be preserved for a later revolution. They will always be a threat to the state, particularly in the large cities. Therefore: liquidate them and create a healthy social life for the *Volk*. Authority is, of course, nothing but a fiction. If the asocial elements succeed in devaluating it – or even denting it – then the door is open to anarchy.'[36]

The most horrific manifestation of this perspective took place in the domain of Nazi racial policies, primarily, though not exclusively, directed against the Jews. So thorough-going was the Nazi persecution of Jews, gypsies and Slavs – people considered to be so racially inferior as to be virtually sub-human – that some commentators have interpreted these actions as expressing the essence of the Nazi revolution. This was a revolution directed, not against the prevailing social and economic system, but at the realisation of a racial utopia.[37] Hitler had proclaimed: 'All who are not of good race in this world are chaff',[38] and the policies of the National Socialists, from their assumption of power in 1933, were dedicated to separating the chaff from the wheat. This culminated in the

---

[33] See Noakes and Pridham, eds., *Nazism*, III, 997–1002.
[34] *Ibid.*, 1008.   [35] *Ibid.*, 1041, 1043–8.
[36] Goebbels, *Diaries*, 124–5.
[37] See, for example, H. Arendt, *The Origins of Totalitarianism* (London: André Deutsch, 1986), part III; Mosse, *Crisis*, chaps. 16–18; Burleigh and Wipperman, *The Racial State*; M. Hauner, 'A German Racial Revolution?', *Journal of Contemporary History*, 19(1984), 669–87.
[38] Hitler, *Mein Kampf*, 269.

mass murder of millions of Jews, but also at least half a million Sinti and Roma ('gypsies'), and millions of Russians and Poles. To the Nazis these were *untermenschen* – sub-people who at best were fit only to serve their Aryan masters in the most menial capacities. Thus Hitler counselled no remorse over the fate of the subject populations in the conquered Eastern Territories: 'There's only one duty: to Germanise this country by the immigration of Germans, and to look upon the natives as Redskins.' Improvements in health, education and social conditions were definitely not on Hitler's agenda, and he recommended that subject races 'know just enough to understand our highway signs, so that they won't get themselves run over by our vehicles!'[39] The extraordinary ferocity of the war on the Eastern Front has been partially attributed to National Socialist propaganda which stressed the racial character of the struggle against the USSR.[40]

Another consequence of the biologically grounded racism of the Nazis was the continual underestimation by their leaders of the military capabilities of the Russians. Goebbels, for example, repeatedly wrote in his diaries that the Bolsheviks would collapse like a 'house of cards', that their army was 'scarcely battleworthy', probably because 'the low intelligence level of the average Russian makes the use of modern weapons impossible'.[41] These judgements were not confined to the enemies of Nazism. After denigrating the ability of the Italian army, he observed, by way of explanation: 'The Italians are, after all, a Romance race.'[42] Military prowess, like other traits, was unevenly distributed among the different races, and a notable speciality of the Aryan.

When faced with impending defeat, the leaders of National Socialism tended to give even greater prominence to the racial core of Nazi ideology. In their exhortations to the German people they stressed that the conflict was a struggle for survival between different races on which would depend the future of the Nordic race and the civilisation it had created. Thus in a military directive dated 25 November 1944, Hitler maintained: 'The war will decide whether the German people shall continue to exist or perish. It demands selfless exertion from every individual.'[43] A few weeks before his suicide, Hitler gave orders for his retreating armies to adopt a 'scorched earth' policy within the Reich itself in order to prevent resources from falling into the hands of the enemy. The order was prefaced by the statement: 'The struggle for the

---

[39] Hitler, *Table Talk*, 69.
[40] See O. Bartov, *The Eastern Front, 1941–45* (London: Macmillan, 1985), chap. 3.
[41] Goebbels, *Diaries*, 343; also 48, 59, 87, 411, 414.
[42] *Ibid.*, 214.
[43] *Hitler's War Directives 1939–1945*, ed. H. R. Trevor-Roper (London: Pan, 1966), 288.

existence of our people compels us, even within the territory of the Reich, to exploit every means of weakening the fighting strength of our enemy, and impeding his further advance.'[44] The Führer's rationalisation of this policy to his subordinates showed a consistent adherence to the premisses of Social Darwinism to the very end, for he asserted that Germany had shown itself to be weaker than its eastern opponents and did not therefore deserve to survive.[45]

Nazism and Social Darwinism

Hitler and other ideologues of National Socialism clearly endorsed the main tenets of Social Darwinism. Heredity, struggle and selection were integral to their conception of both the natural and the social realms, and the task of Nazism was to create a community in harmony with the eternal laws of nature.

The primary unit upon which the forces of natural selection acted was that of the race, although there was also a role for the struggle for survival within the *Volksgemeinschaft* as well. The economy, for example, was regarded as an arena of competition in which only the most efficient and competent firms would succeed. Hitler observed, in a speech made on 20 May 1937: 'Business is quite brutal. You know, one notices a businessman who has made it, but one doesn't notice the tens of thousands of others who have gone bust. But it is in the nation's best interests for its economy to be run only by able people and not by civil servants.' And he concluded with a judgement that those businessmen who failed were 'merely good-for-nothings, incompetents – they can go bust'.[46] But the main thrust of Nazi rhetoric was to present the *Volk* as the major protagonist in the battle for life to which the welfare of the individual must be subordinated at all times. Hence marriage, for example, was perceived not an end in itself but rather a means to attaining a higher goal, namely 'the increase and preservation of the species and the race. This alone is its meaning and its task.'[47] The 'natural' role of women was confined to the task of producing and nurturing the next generation.

The Nazi veneration of motherhood reflected their general attitude to nature as a virtually sacred domain so that a genuinely authentic existence consisted of living in harmony with natural laws. Hitler insisted

[44] Order dated 19 March 1945, *Hitler's War Directives*, 293.
[45] See R. Pois, *National Socialism and the Religion of Nature* (London: Croom Helm, 1986), 109.
[46] Noakes and Pridham, eds., *Nazism*, II, 264.
[47] Hitler, *Mein Kampf*, 229. See also Noakes and Pridham, eds., *Nazism*, II, 454; Reading 71 in Griffin, ed., *Fascism*.

that there was no gap between organic and inorganic nature, and regarded the destruction of the belief in the separation of these two domains by the 'battering-ram of science' as vital to the task of discrediting Christianity.[48] This type of attitude, however, did not preclude a mystical conception of nature as a life-force to which those who were in possession of its secrets were attuned.[49] The celebration of spiritual values and concern with an 'inner revolution' of the soul was held to be the objective of National Socialism, involving the creation of a New Man, of which the SS warriors were the prototype. This stress seems antithetical to the biological reductionism of other aspects of Nazi thought, and particularly with the deterministic features of the racial struggle for survival.

There is certainly one point on which the Nazi version of Social Darwinism differed from those articulated by early pioneers such as Darwin and Haeckel, namely the common ancestry of apes and humans. Some Nazi texts unequivocally repudiated an ape-like ancestry.[50] Such also seems to be the message contained in the following statement by Hitler in a private conversation in 1942:

Where do we acquire the right to believe that man has not always been what he is now? The study of nature teaches us that, in the animal kingdom just as much as in the vegetable kingdom, variations have occurred. They've occurred within the species, but none of these variations has an importance comparable with that which separates man from the monkey – assuming that this transformation really took place.[51]

At the very least, this implies scepticism about the alleged ape-like origins of mankind and possibly even about the idea of species transmutation. As an inveterate racist Hitler would of course have been opposed to any idea of a common ancestor for all the human races. The evidence, however, is equivocal. Only a few days prior to this observation the dictator, in one of his diatribes on the virtues of vegetarianism, insisted: 'The monkeys, our ancestors of prehistoric times, are strictly vegetarian.'[52] In October 1941, Hitler apparently claimed that 'there have been human beings, in the baboon category, for at least three hundred thousand years. There is less distance between the man-ape and the ordinary modern man than there is between the ordinary modern man and a man like Schopenhauer.' Goebbels reported a conversation with Hitler at the end of December 1939 as follows: 'He [Hitler] has little regard for *homo sapiens*. Man should not feel so superior to the animals. He has little reason to. Man believes that he

[48] Hitler, *Table Talk*, 59, 84–5.
[49] For a detailed analysis of this dimension of Nazi ideology, see Pois, *National Socialism*.
[50] Pois, *National Socialism*, 43.   [51] Hitler, *Table Talk*, 248.   [52] *Ibid.*, 231.

alone has intelligence, a soul, and the power of speech. Has not the animal these things?'[53] It is, moreover, worth noting that around this time a number of respected European and American palaeo-anthropologists were seeking to eliminate the apes from human ancestry.[54]

Even if Hitler and other Nazi ideologues had displayed complete consistency in their denial of the ape-like lineage of humanity, there can be no doubt that as far as *Social* Darwinism is concerned both their theory and praxis were predicated upon the world view to a remarkable degree. What Nazi ideology exemplifies is a development already noted in the history of Social Darwinism, in which the struggle for existence becomes transmuted. It becomes a dynamic not so much responsible for evolution – although this term was employed in Nazi texts, equivocation about the origins of mankind, and celebration over the seemingly 'eternal' achievements of the Aryan renders its meaning problematic – as with the *preservation* of an existing, and seemingly timeless, racial ideal. Social and political forms may change, as may economic and military technologies, but human nature remains essentially fixed. The struggle for survival takes the form of an age-long conflict between the embodiment of different forms, and levels, of this nature. In this respect, National Socialism replicates a development noted in the work of earlier theorists like Vacher de Lapouge in which the play of natural laws and forces serves to maintain certain essences rather than acting as agents of perpetual transformation.

What of the model/threat dualism in Nazi representations of nature? By endorsing the struggle for existence and virtually eradicating individual welfare as an ethical goal, Nazism avoided this dichotomy. Nature and its laws represented an ideal, the main threats to which emanated from social institutions and value systems. The aim of Nazism was to remove these threats by harmonising nature and society, which entailed reorganising the latter so as to render its processes and outcomes concordant with the putative workings of nature's laws.

The world view of Italian Fascism

Italian Fascism exhibits considerable ideological diversity, and this is notably apparent with regard to Social Darwinism. An example where this world view provided a scaffolding for Fascist ideas is furnished by

---

[53] *Ibid.*, 86; Goebbels, *Diaries*, 77.
[54] See P. Bowler, *Theories of Human Evolution: A Century of Debate, 1844–1944* (Oxford: Blackwell, 1989), chap. 5. A notable example was the American, Henry Fairfield Osborn, who in the aftermath of the Scopes 'monkey trial' in Tennessee, 1925, sought to liberate mankind from what he referred to as 'the bar sinister of ape descent'. Cited by Bowler, *Theories*, 128.

some of the speeches and publications of Alfredo Rocco (1875–1935), who was Mussolini's Minister of Justice from 1925 to 1932. In a text written just after the Great War, Rocco depicted the world as a plurality of distinctive states, each one representing an organism with autonomous needs and goals, as evinced by history and 'by the biological and moral laws governing social life'. The form of these laws is conveyed in the following citation:

Conflict is in fact the basic law of life of all social organisms, as it is of all biological ones; societies are formed, gain strength, and move forwards through conflict; the healthiest and most vital of them assert themselves against the weakest and less well adapted through conflict; the natural evolution of nations and races takes place through conflict.[55]

Rocco emphasised that within social organisms there must be unity, based upon discipline, hierarchy and organisation. All competition was directed outwards, at other nations, whether in the form of economic competition or armed conflict. This took place 'in order that, as a result of their inequality, those nations should assert themselves who are best prepared for and best adapted to the function that devolves on every powerful and capable nation in the evolution of civilisation'.[56] The rise of the state was explicable by, and subject to, this 'ineluctable law of the struggle for existence'. At various stages of history, certain state forms predominate among the most advanced nations: for example, the city-state among the ancient Greeks, and the nation-state in modern times. More recently, this latter form was being replaced by empires – the outcome of a century of evolution.[57]

These arguments quite plainly smack of Social Darwinism. On other occasions, however, the relationship between conflict and socio-political evolution in Rocco's outlook was less obvious. In a speech delivered two years later, Rocco denied the existence of a unilinear pattern to historical change. Developing a point made in the earlier text, in which he had repudiated the notion of an evolutionary sequence from smaller to larger social aggregates,[58] Rocco described history as a series of distinct but recurring cycles, in which political communities expanded and then disintegrated into smaller units.[59] He still interpreted this process as reflecting a biological law, but one rather different from the adaptational dynamic he had invoked previously. The model stressed in this speech was that of the life-cycle. In history 'we see the birth of the state, we see

[55] A. Rocco, 'Politica Manifesto', 15 December 1918, in Lyttleton, Italian Fascisms, 258–9.
[56] Ibid., 259.   [57] Ibid., 259, 263–4.   [58] Ibid., 262.
[59] Rocco, 'The Syndicates and the Crisis Within the State', Speech to the University of Padua, 15 November 1920 in Lyttleton, Italian Fascisms, 271.

it become organized, gain strength and prosperity and then become disorganized, decline and perish, just as any biological organism is born, develops, grows old and dies'.[60]

This life-cycle model of history is an ancient one and does not need the motor of conflict to explain adaptations and transformations. The status of Social Darwinism in Rocco's thought is, therefore, problematic, and one can hardly assign it an important functional role, despite its intimation in some of his discourses. In other expressions of Fascism, Social Darwinism was completely absent. In *The Origins and Doctrine of Fascism* (1934) of Giovanni Gentile (1875–1944), the underlying structure was Hegelian, as exemplified in such statements as: 'The nation is never complete and neither is the state ... The state is always becoming.'[61] Gentile conferred great importance on conflict, announcing that 'mankind progresses only through division, and progress is achieved through the clash and victory of one side over another ...'[62] But there was no suggestion that division and conflict were the manifestations of biological laws. Indeed, such a conception would contradict his view that human beings were motivated primarily by spiritual considerations. This position was set forth by Benito Mussolini (1883–1945) in collaboration with Gentile in *The Doctrine of Fascism* (1932). Once again, the existence of, and necessity for, conflict, was presented as axiomatic.

> Above all, Fascism ... believes neither in the possibility nor in the utility of perpetual peace. It thus repudiates the doctrine of Pacifism – born of the renunciation of the struggle as an act of cowardice in the face of sacrifice. War alone brings up to their highest tension all human energies, and puts the stamp of nobility upon the peoples who have the courage to meet it.[63]

The struggle referred to, though, was not derived from any premises about a natural law of struggle for existence. In fact, the accent was on the transcendence of the animal features of human nature – consisting primarily of concern with personal welfare – through heroic self-abnegation and sacrifice. The Fascist strives to achieve 'a life in which the individual, through the denial of himself, through the sacrifice of his own private interests, through death itself, realises that completely spiritual existence in which his value as a man resides'.[64] Hence the imperialist ambitions signalled in this text were not derived from any inexorable struggle for survival, but presented as the sign of vitality and

[60] *Ibid.*, 271.
[61] G. Gentile, *The Origins and Doctrine of Fascism* in Lyttleton, *Italian Fascisms*, 310.
[62] *Ibid.*, 304.
[63] B. Mussolini, *The Doctrine of Fascism* (1932), in Lyttleton, *Italian Fascisms*, 47.
[64] *Ibid.*, 40.

strength as opposed to the decadence and weakness that typified the renunciation of expansionist goals.[65]

Not only would reducing humanity to the effects of biological laws constitute a denial of the expressly human features of mankind, it would also be guilty of the sins of fatalism and determinism. In a speech made just prior to the march on Rome, Mussolini asserted that: 'We don't believe that history repeats itself; we don't believe that history follows a hard and fast itinerary . . .'[66] History was made by people in the attempt to impress their values on the world through the expression of will. This Nietzschean perspective was inconsistent with determinism of any kind, and Mussolini rejected Marxian economic determinism and class struggle, and liberal doctrines of progress, as examples of attempts to impose a pattern on historical change. Life 'is a continual change and coming to be', and Fascism insists that man 'with his free will can and must create his own world', must 'conquer for himself that life truly worthy of him . . .'[67]

A similar critique of historical determinism in any form can be found in the attempt by an Englishman, Barnes, to distil the universal content of Fascist ideology in a text prefaced by Mussolini himself.[68] Barnes criticised the view of history as 'an unfolding, inevitable pageant, containing no might have beens . . .'[69] He believed in the existence of two sorts of laws – the moral law which derived from God, and natural laws which were uniformities established through scientific induction. Natural laws were transcended by moral laws, but not in a manner which involved any contradiction between them. The struggle for existence was an example of a law of nature, and its relationship to moral imperatives he described as follows:

The natural tendency of all organisms is to fight for their continued existence; and Sociology demonstrates that States exhibit this tendency as powerfully and instinctively as any other living organisms. This is a natural law which the Moral Law transcends, but does not lay aside. The Moral Law can never be in essential conflict with Natural Law. So here we have a law of life; and the manner in which the Moral Law transcends it is by sanctioning the sacrifice of individual

---

[65] *Ibid.*, 56.
[66] Mussolini, speech at San Carlo Opera House, 24 October 1922, in C. Delzell, ed. and tr., *Mediterranean Fascism, 1919–1945: Selected Documents* (London: Macmillan, 1970), 42.
[67] Mussolini, *Doctrine of Fascism*, 41, 40.
[68] Barnes, who was raised in Italy, was a personal friend of Mussolini and a member of the Italian Fascist Party. See G. Webber, *The Ideology of the British Right 1918–1939* (London: Croom Helm, 1986), 143–4.
[69] J. S. Barnes, *The Universal Aspects of Fascism* (London: Williams and Norgate, 1928), 94. Barnes was antagonistic to the Hegelian conception of history favoured by theorists like Gentile.

life whenever thereby a richer, more vigorous life and a generally higher (more moral) life is rightly judged to be the consequence.[70]

Barnes was here walking a very thin line between determinism and the power of humans to change the course of history. He often assimilated the state to other living organisms, 'subject to growth and decay', evolving through adaptation to changed circumstances and possessing 'a natural instinctive force' directed at its own survival. The struggle for existence was 'a law of life, from which none of us can withdraw'.[71] This is close to the Nazi rhetoric of iron laws of nature. Yet Barnes also suggested that a law of nature could be acknowledged as much by resisting as by submitting to it. He insisted that the means to adaptation were not scientifically determined but had to be realised through rationally directed political action, while denying that warfare was a natural human condition.[72] Such arguments are more typical of the stress on *élan*, dynamism and heroic effort found in the Mussolini/Gentile texts. Thus while Barnes undoubtedly construed the struggle for existence as a law of life that encompassed human societies as well as biological organisms, it cannot be said that this notion belonged to an expressly Social Darwinist outlook, or formed a central component of his ideology as was the case for Hitler and Nazism in general.

In keeping with their denial of history as a process reducible to the play of one particular set of factors, both Mussolini and Barnes were critical of racial interpretations of the nation and its historical role. Mussolini defined the nation in non-racial terms and was hostile towards Nazi race theory.[73] Barnes likewise refused to identify nation and race, and described racism as a 'materialist illusion, contrary to natural law and destructive of civilisation'.[74] Racism, i.e. a systematically formulated theory of racial difference and superiority/inferiority, did not play a significant role in these discourses. The term race was often employed, usually as a synonym for nation or people, but did not form a part of a wider system of significations denoting a hierarchy of peoples based upon biological differences. This is not to argue that Italian Fascism lacked a racist faction,[75] or that racialist assumptions played no

---

[70] *Ibid.*, 70–1.   [71] *Ibid.*, 69, 105, 156.   [72] *Ibid.*, 6n, 105, 92–3.

[73] Mussolini, *Doctrine of Fascism*, 43. Note also Mussolini's critique of racism in his 1935 essay 'The Irrefutable Fact', Reading 35 in Griffin, ed., *Fascism*. For Mussolini's criticisms of Nazi race theory, see R. Thurlow, 'Nazism and Fascism: No Siamese Twins', *Patterns of Prejudice*, 14(1980), 12–13.

[74] Barnes, *Universal Aspects*, 43, 60.

[75] But even the racialist faction of Italian Fascism was usually wary of biological conceptions of race. On this, see R. Sodi, 'The Italian Roots of Racialism', *UCLA Historical Journal*, 8(1987), 40–70. According to Sodi (54), Italian racialist authors used the words *sangue*, *stirpe*, *nazione* and *popolo* (blood, race, nation and people) interchangeably to connote a cultural, rather than a biological, identity.

role in Mussolini's foreign policy, particularly in Africa, where Fascist foreign policy was conducted with great brutality.[76] But the majority of Europeans were convinced of their superiority *vis-à-vis* the indigenous populations in Africa, Asia and the New World, and such an attitude would hardly serve to distinguish Fascism as an ideological entity in its own right. In the writings of Ammon or Vacher de Lapouge, or the ideologues of Nazism, on the other hand, race constituted precisely the key to history which Fascism denounced.

As far as Social Darwinism is concerned, the texts examined above reveal elements of this world view, especially in the early writings of Rocco, but it would be misleading to argue that Social Darwinism acted as a foundation for the theoreticians of Italian Fascism in the way that it did for German National Socialists.

Conclusion

If the position adopted in this study is accepted – i.e. that Social Darwinism comprises the philosophical infrastructure of a social theory or ideology – then, on the basis of the material reviewed in this chapter, it is reasonable to conclude that German Nazism and Italian Fascism, during the period studied here, reposed upon different intellectual foundations. In the former case, these foundations were Social Darwinist, in the latter not. The world view underpinning Fascism was one which regarded historical time as a dimension devoid of any pattern, and though it accepted the existence of laws of nature, it denied the ability of these to set limits to human endeavour or to dictate the course and content of public policies. In this, Fascism can be seen to be partially inspired by the philosophies deriving from Hegelian doctrines of conflict and synthesis, Sorelian celebrations of myth and violence, the Nietzschean advocacy of self-transcendence and Bergson's notion of evolution as a process of self-creation.

This is not the place to examine the precise ways in which these various components of Fascism were articulated and elaborated, but it does seem clear that in this formulation there would be little scope for biological determinism or, indeed, for any kind of determinism. Fascism would therefore be inimical to one of the core assumptions of Social Darwinism, namely, that human beings are, both morally and culturally,

---

[76] See E. Robertson, 'Race as a Factor in Mussolini's Policy in Africa and Europe', *Journal of Contemporary History*, 23(1988), 37–58. The release of material from United Nations archives in early 1988 exposed the viciousness and brutality of the Italian occupation of Abyssinia and Europe. See William Scobie, 'Revealed: Italy's Savage War Crimes', *Observer*, 24 January 1988.

governed by natural laws. Thus while they placed a high value on struggle and conflict, Fascists did so for reasons other than those invoked by Social Darwinists, seeing in adversarial conditions the opportunities for men (or, rather, some men – those of the elite) to display the heroic qualities that differentiated the spiritual from the material realms.

This stress on heroism and spirituality can also be found in Nazism. But in this instance, heroism consists in expressing values that are consistent with the dictates of nature, in accordance with the natural order. To fight against the determinism of the latter is to court disaster. In this way, the different metaphysical foundations of Nazism and Fascism have important ideological consequences, not least of which is the salience of race in the former creed. For Nazism, race was genetically based and hence hereditary, its features produced by selection and adaptation and threatened by miscegenation. The exigencies of the struggle for survival justified the most radical measures in eugenics and racial hygiene. There is, consequently, a relentless continuity between the Nazi conception of human nature and history on the one hand, and the racial and eugenic practices of the Third Reich on the other.

There are a number of caveats which need to be made at this juncture. First, I have no desire to argue that Nazi praxis was an inevitable consequence of its ideological premises. Though ideologies make up an important aspect of reality, they are not the whole of that reality and do not possess the power of independent causation. The history of the Third Reich does not flow inexorably from the pages of *Mein Kampf*, and Nazi ideology is only one factor in the conditions in which policies of war, racial purification and genocide occurred. My points are simply that: (a) there is a great deal of consistency between the Nazis' ideology and the policies that they implemented; (b) this ideology is one in which race occupies a central role; (c) race is, in turn, predicated upon a Social Darwinist world view in which the struggle for survival is a prescient fact of life.

My second caveat relates to the role of race in Fascist thought. Racism was, as we have seen, rampant throughout the West during this period, and few Europeans or white colonialists harboured any doubts over their superiority *vis-à-vis* the indigenous populations of Asia, Africa and the New World. Italian Fascism contained racist factions, and the initial success of Nazism would have encouraged imitation of their ideas. Such could well be the reason for the anti-Semitic legislation of 1938, which was criticised by some Italian Fascists precisely for this reason.[77] This

---

[77] For condemnations of this legislation for imitating Nazism, see Carlo Costamagna (1881–1965), reproduced in J.-P. Faye, *Langages Totalitaires* (Paris: Hermann, 1973), [84–90]; Gioacchino Volpe (1876–1971) in Griffin, ed., *Fascism*, Reading 39.

being said, the texts analysed here show race not to have been an integral feature of Fascist theorising. Some commentators have responded to this difference by referring to Nazism as 'Fascism + racism'.[78] But Nazism cannot be adequately conceived in these terms: racism was not a simple accretion to the world view of Fascism but, on the contrary, reflected a different, even incompatible, view of nature, time and humanity. If all references to race were removed the essential structure of Fascist ideology would remain intact, whereas a similar excision for Nazism would remove its central core. This has implications for Fascist practice, for the experience of Fascism in Italy for Jews, brutal and distressing as it undoubtedly was, did not approach the genocidal horror of the Third Reich.[79]

I have argued that whereas Nazi racism was legitimated by a Social Darwinism of a particularly deterministic ilk, Fascism was anti-deterministic, and its concept of national community therefore was less exclusive than one based upon race. Or rather, the exclusionary criteria employed by Fascists in their conception of national identity were less rigid than those adopted by Nazis. Once again, I am not arguing that ideas are the sole (or even major) determinants of social processes, only pointing to a certain degree of congruence between world view, ideology and praxis.

These conclusions are tentative. The analysis has been confined to two countries, and I have only examined a small sample of individual texts rather than surveying the entire corpus of Fascist literature. Furthermore, there is *some* evidence of the language of Social Darwinism, notably in some of the writings and speeches of Rocco. What are needed are detailed comparative investigations of the ideology of the various Fascist movements and ideologues of the period. Though much progress has been made in recent years in the understanding of Fascist ideology it is still a neglected area of study. Hopefully the analyses conducted in this chapter have suggested some interesting lines of inquiry.

[78] Ball and Dagger, *Political Ideologies and the Democratic Ideal*, 192.
[79] Mussolini's position on the Jews tended to fluctuate, but seems to have been governed by pragmatic rather than by ideological considerations. See M. Michaelis, *Mussolini and the Jews* (Oxford: Clarendon Press, 1978).

Postscript: Social Darwinism old and new: the case of sociobiology

Introduction

There is a widely held view among historians and social scientists that Social Darwinism declined in popularity after World War II due to its association with racism and Nazism. The belief is that in the post-war democratic consensus that emerged in the Western states there was little tolerance for theories which apparently gave a biological justification for racism, war or exploitation. The American historian Degler considers these circumstances were not just uncongenial for Social Darwinism but actually fatal to it. 'Social Darwinism', he writes, 'was definitely killed, not merely scotched ...'[1]

The thesis that Social Darwinism is dead is false, as will be shown below. The weaker claim that it declined in importance during the immediate post-war period is plausible although the detailed studies required to substantiate it have yet to be made. In any case, by the mid-1960s Social Darwinism had re-emerged and was reaching wide audiences in Britain and the USA. It took the form of popular writings about the evolutionary heritage of humans that were the forerunners of sociobiology which itself, I shall argue, is a particularly powerful example of Social Darwinism. It is possible that Social Darwinism was manifested in other currents of thought in the post-war era, and that accounts of its decline have been exaggerated, but an investigation of this possibility is outside the scope of this study.[2] In confining this chapter to sociobiology the intention is not to engage in a critical appreciation of this discipline but to examine its relationship to Social Darwinism. The aims are to test the robustness of the model of the

---

[1] Degler, *In Search of Human Nature*, ix.

[2] Social Darwinism has certainly been appropriated by neo-Fascist and extreme right-wing groups in Europe. Examples for Britain are cited later in this chapter and there is evidence to suggest that the Front National in France has also adopted Social Darwinist rhetoric. See P. A. Taguieff, 'La Métaphysique de Jean-Marie Le Pen', in N. Mayer and P. Perrineau, eds., *Le Front National à découvert* (Paris: Presses de la Fondation Nationale des Sciences Politiques, 1989), 173–94.

world view constructed in chapter 1 for a different historical epoch and to explore the continuing relevance of Social Darwinism to Western culture.

Before embarking on this exercise it is useful to take cognisance of developments in biology since the Modern Synthesis. The discovery of the structure of DNA in 1953 paved the way for advances in molecular biology which have greatly enhanced knowledge about the processes of genetic mutation and transmission. Developments in population genetics and evidence from ecology and detailed ethological studies have deepened our understanding of selection and evolution. 'Fitness' is defined as the differential success of organisms in survival and the leaving of offspring. Since the 1960s a consensus has emerged over the unit of selection, with group selection rejected by the majority of biologists in favour of individual selection, although some persist in retaining a notion of species selection.[3] Others maintain that since it is genes which are actually replicated, selected and transmitted then the gene is the appropriate level of analysis. Gene and individual-level models are broadly compatible and are both opposed to group selection.

The trend towards individual or gene-based models of evolution has developed out of attempts to solve the hoary problem of altruism. Actions apparently favouring the group at the expense of the individuals performing them, as in the case of the warning cries emitted by certain species of birds in the presence of predators, are explained as examples of 'kin selection'. Altruistic actions can increase the likelihood of an organism preserving copies of its own genes in its relatives. On average an organism's offspring or siblings will possess half of its own genes; hence even a self-sacrificing action which leaves two or more siblings alive promotes 'inclusive fitness'. The inclusive fitness of a gene is therefore defined as 'the reproductive rate of its bearer plus that of the copies of the gene carried by relatives to whom the bearer may extend help'.[4]

Another important concept is that of 'reciprocal altruism'. Animals that extend help to other (unrelated) animals in their group improve the chances of receiving aid themselves in times of need. In these cases (as was suggested by Darwin), seemingly altruistic actions in fact derive from individual self-interest. Here, then, as with inclusive fitness, behaviour which potentially benefits the group at the expense of the

---

[3]   For discussions of these different positions, see Smith, *Did Darwin Get it Right?*, chap. 16; Wilson, *Diversity of Life*, 81–5.
[4]   D. J. Futuyma, *Evolutionary Biology* (Sunderland, MA: Sinauer Associates, 1979), 305. For a brief overview of the development of the notion of inclusive fitness, see Smith, *Did Darwin Get it Right?*, chap. 13; Gould, *Ever Since Darwin*, chap. 33.

individual is explained by reference to the selective advantages accruing to the individual.

Modern evolutionary theory is therefore Darwinian in its explanatory structure. It combines genetics, ecology, ethology and mathematics in its models of evolutionary dynamics. Palaeontology continues to be closely relevant to Darwinian theory, particularly the spectacular discoveries of early hominid fossils in Africa. The outcome is a theory of evolution which is more powerful but more abstruse than the original version. Whereas Darwin's technical writings could be readily assimilated by non-specialist audiences, modern Darwinism is much less accessible. Despite this, Darwinism continues to excite public controversy and debate and scientists have been remarkably successful in producing popular accounts of the latest developments in evolutionary theory. This is the intellectual context in which sociobiology made its appearance.

Sociobiology

Sociobiology as a discipline is usually traced to the publication, in 1975, of the bestselling *Sociobiology: The New Synthesis* by the Harvard biologist, Edward Osborne Wilson. Wilson defined sociobiology as 'the systematic study of the biological basis of all social behaviour'. According to his own testimony he had concluded his *Insect Societies* (1971) with the hypothesis that the principles of population biology and comparative zoology that had worked so well for the analysis of the social insects could be extended to the study of vertebrate animals. This goal was realised in *Sociobiology*, the final chapter of which contains Wilson's controversial assertion that these principles could be applied to the study of human social behaviour, thereby closing the gap between the natural and the social sciences. His *On Human Nature* (1978) was a first step in the achievement of this synthesis.[5] Since then there has been a veritable efflorescence of literature devoted to this project. This has in turn inspired an enormous level of criticism and a great deal of debate – much of it acrimonious – over the methods, conclusions and alleged political implications of sociobiology. The existence of this body of criticism coincident with the continued thriving of sociobiology – especially in the USA – provides an important lesson for an understanding of the history of Social Darwinism: hostility towards a body of ideas in certain social circles provides no warrant for assuming its overall unpopularity.

[5]   This account of Wilson's ideas is taken from his *On Human Nature*, ix–x.

A recurrent theme in this criticism has been the accusation that sociobiology is a renascent Social Darwinism. The claim was made at the birth of the discipline and has remained a basis of condemnation ever since.[6] Sociobiologists are accused of espousing a rigid biological determinism in their efforts to explain phenomena such as incest prohibitions, rape, adultery, warfare, homicide and homosexuality – among many others – as the consequences of a genetic heritage shaped by natural selection. Such efforts are deemed by some critics to provide a justification, at least implicitly, for capitalism, class inequalities, racism, patriarchy and armed conflict. For them, there is nothing novel about the proposed 'New Synthesis', which reprises the basic themes of the Social Darwinism of the 1870s.[7]

Sociobiologists and their supporters have been vociferous in their rejection of these allegations. While without exception they claim to be Darwinists, the majority seem to agree with the political scientist Lopreato that the link between Darwinism and Social Darwinism was 'theoretically disastrous' as the latter was bad science and bad Darwinism. This was because Social Darwinism 'was to a large extent an ideology and an apologia for the worst form of capitalism, ethnocentrism, and racism'.[8] Degler likewise insists on the ideological discontinuity between the politically liberal sociobiologists and conservative defence of the capitalist status quo which he sees as typical of Social Darwinism.[9] The psychologist Crawford bemoans the 'heavy burden' placed on evolutionary theory by Social Darwinist defences of predatory business practices, racism, inequality and imperialism, while the philosopher Ruse, in denying the connection, stresses the scientific authenticity of sociobiology.[10]

Both accusers and accused share one point in common: they agree in

---

[6] P. Samuelson, 'Sociobiology, a New Social Darwinism', *Newsweek*, 7 July 1975; Sahlins, *The Use and Abuse of Biology*, 72; J. Thompson, 'The New Social Darwinism: The Politics of Sociobiology', *Politics*, 17(1982), 121–8.

[7] Rose, Lewontin and Kamin, *Not in Our Genes*, 243.

[8] J. Lopreato, *Human Nature and Bio-Cultural Evolution* (Boston: Allen and Unwin, 1984), 8. Wilson distances himself from the 'absolute Social Darwinist', Sumner, in *Human Nature*, 208.

[9] Degler, *In Search of Human Nature*, 13, 42, 112.

[10] C. Crawford, 'Sociobiology: Of What Value to Psychology?' in C. Crawford, M. Smith and D. Krebs, eds., *Sociobiology and Psychology* (London/New Jersey: Lawrence Erlbaum Associates, 1987), 4–5; M. Ruse, 'Sociobiology and Knowledge', in Crawford *et al.*, *Sociobiology and Psychology*, 63–5. Sarah Hrdy admits that sociobiology is 'social Darwinism' because it applies Darwinism to human society, but denies it is 'Social Darwinism' because it does not attempt to justify social inequalities. S. B. Hrdy, *The Woman That Never Evolved* (1981), cited in Bellomy, ' "Social Darwinism" Revisited', 16.

equating Social Darwinism with certain ideological positions such as racism, imperialism, patriarchy and, especially, pro-capitalism. Socio-biologists then refute the charge of Social Darwinism by denying any connection with such positions, by pointing to their own liberal political persuasions, or by separating Darwinism from the ideological perversions to which it has been subjected.

From the perspective of this study both the allegations and their denials are irrelevant. Social Darwinism cannot be defined by its ideological functions or equated with a particular political position. Whether or not sociobiology is Social Darwinist depends on whether or not its practitioners adhere to the five components of the world view identified earlier. In the remainder of this chapter I argue that socio-biologists *do* adhere to the components of this world view and are quite unambiguously Social Darwinists. This is followed by an assessment of the salient characteristics of this Social Darwinism and its relationship to earlier manifestations. I make no pretence to have covered the socio-biological literature comprehensively but I believe that the selections used convey an accurate portrait of the assumptions underpinning the discipline.

My focus, for reasons of convenience, is on the literature published from 1975, but it is worth underlining a connection – one which others have already highlighted – between modern sociobiology and what has been termed the 'pop ethology' of the previous decade.[11] The works in question include Robert Ardrey's *African Genesis* (1961) and *The Territorial Imperative* (1967); *The Naked Ape* (1967) by Desmond Morris; *On Aggression* (1966) by Konrad Lorenz; and *The Imperial Animal* (1970) by Lionel Tiger and Robin Fox. These books were, albeit in rather different ways, concerned with human nature and looked to ethology and evolutionary biology for enlightenment. They linked humans to other animal species through the shared possession of innate capacities for aggression, territoriality and predation which had evolved in our hominid predecessors through natural selection. These predispositions remained a powerful legacy in modern times and underpinned such phenomena as war, patriotism, private property and sexual difference.

The free (and in some instances, dubious) speculations of pop ethology earned the hostility of some professional biologists, and modern sociobiologists like Wilson and Dawkins have dissociated themselves from this literature.[12] Its relevance to this study resides in its

[11] The expression 'pop ethology' is taken from Gould, *Ever Since Darwin*, 240. The connections with sociobiology are noted in Rose *et al.*, *Not in Our Genes*, 239–40.
[12] For a critique of this material see Gould, *Ever Since Darwin*, chap. 30. Dawkins

explicit utilisation of Darwinism as a means to an understanding of human nature and certain social institutions and practices. Having established (at least to their satisfaction) the existence of behavioural uniformities among humans and other social animals the authors then ascribed these uniformities to natural selection. Evolved over millennia these patterns derived from innate features of human nature and were discernible in such cross-cultural practices as incest taboos, territoriality and war. Because these phenomena were deeply rooted in the human evolutionary heritage they were usually held to be immune to radical alteration.

These claims will be illustrated by a single example, Robert Ardrey's *The Territorial Imperative.*[13] Ardrey, a former American playwright, had a personal mission to counteract, through the popularisation of recent discoveries and developments in population genetics, ethology and palaeontology, what he saw as widespread misunderstandings about human nature and society. The particular theme of this publication was the universal human need – shared with some other social animals – for territory. 'The territorial nature of man', asserted Ardrey, 'is genetic and ineradicable' (116). It had evolved through natural selection in our pre-human ancestors on the African savannah and, in conjunction with other psychological and behavioural attributes evolved in like manner, was responsible for a good deal of social action. 'We act as we do for reasons of our evolutionary past, not our cultural present ...' (5). The 'biological nation' was an example of this kind of programming. It was defined as a social group with at least two mature males, in exclusive possession of a piece of territory, isolated 'from others of its kind through outward antagonism', and within which there was social cooperation (191). According to Ardrey, this form of social organisation had been in existence in the animal kingdom for fifty million years (192). Patriotism, therefore was a 'predictable force' elicited by the appropriate circumstances just as in any 'territorial species' (232).

Ardrey was adamant that 'the basic evolutionary unit is not the individual but the population of which he is a part' (138). He went even further than this, insisting that 'through natural selection evolution is capable of fostering inborn traits ... restraining the individual to the ultimate benefit of his species. I see no reason to regard this as other

describes this literature as 'totally and utterly wrong', primarily for its insistence on group as opposed to individual selection. Dawkins, *Selfish Gene*, 2. For Wilson's reaction, see Rose *et al.*, *Not in Our Genes*, 240. J. Diamond is dismissive of Ardrey in his *The Rise and Fall of the Third Chimpanzee* (London: Vintage, 1992), 33.

[13] London: Collins, 1967.

than a biological morality' (79). Hence there was 'no qualitative break between the moral nature of the animal and the moral nature of man' (78). This morality, however, was confined to the ingroup. Resurrecting the arguments of Arthur Keith on the 'dual code', Ardrey insisted that aggression and warfare – the 'code of enmity' – were equally deeply ingrained in human nature as the result of selective forces (286–8).

Ardrey's books were bestsellers and so these ideas reached a large public. Of significance to this study are a number of features which these writings shared with the other pop ethologists. First, there was a clear endorsement of Darwinian evolutionary theory, with particular emphasis on the importance of natural selection and competition. Second, there was an unhesitating application of this theory to human psychology and culture in order to grasp the fundamental attributes of human nature. Thus the pop ethologists reproduced both the discursive substance and the ambitions of earlier Social Darwinists.

There was one point, though, on which these modern Social Darwinists differed from their earliest counterparts like Bagehot, Spencer, Royer and Haeckel. The latter had posited a socio-psychological development from primitive to modern – usually from military to industrial types of social organisation and mentality. True, all believed in the possibility of arrested development and atavism at both the individual and the social levels: the primitive legacy could still assert its presence in modern civilisation. But as I have sought to show, the primary function of the primitive in these theories was to define the starting point of evolution by marking the threshold of animality/ humanity. In pop ethology this threshold was erased and evolutionary time no longer acted to distance the modern from the primitive but served to underscore the continuity of the primitive *in* the modern. The Social Darwinism of Ardrey *et al.* collapsed the distance not only between the primitive and the modern but between the animal and the human. In this, they continued a form of Social Darwinism already developed by, for example, Lapouge, in which human nature appears as an unchanging essence. As we shall see, this tendency is maintained in sociobiology.

The world view of sociobiology

As stated above, sociobiologists are unequivocally Darwinian in outlook. Wilson has summarised what this means in the context of human evolution. Genes predisposing their carriers to adopt traits that enhanced their adaptiveness would be spread through the population by natural selection.

Adaptiveness means simply that if an individual displayed the traits he stood a better chance of having his genes represented in the next generation than if he did not display the traits. The differential advantage among individuals in this strictest sense is called genetic fitness. There are three basic components of genetic fitness: increased personal survival, increased personal reproduction, and the enhanced survival and reproduction of close relatives who share the same genes by common descent. An improvement in any one of the factors or in any combination of them results in greater genetic fitness.[14]

The driving force of evolution is selection deriving from competition for resources. Dawkins depicts the most intense manifestation of this competition occurring among conspecifics, but the relationship between predator and prey can also be seen in these terms since the evolutionary goals of the antelope and the lion hunting it are 'mutually incompatible'.[15] However, what distinguishes sociobiology and gives it analytical (and polemical) bite is its assertion that evolutionary theory facilitates a scientific understanding of many aspects of human psychology and culture. Parallels – sometimes close ones – are posited between certain human social practices like murder, pair-bonding, warfare and rape, and behaviour patterns in other social animals. Matt Ridley, in his book on sex and human evolution, argues that if we were chimpanzees we would still exhibit many of our characteristics, i.e. 'we would be family based, urban, class-conscious, nationalist and belligerent, which we are'. Where humans differ profoundly from chimpanzees is in the realm of sexual behaviour. Here the appropriate comparison is with birds. Ridley asserts that 'man is just like an ibis or a swallow or a sparrow. He lives in large colonies. Males compete with each other for places in a pecking order. Most males are monogamous.'[16] Jared Diamond has likewise proposed animal precursors for two seemingly uniquely human capacities, language and art.[17]

The assumption is that if evolutionary theory can explain the emergence of pair-bonding, adultery, aggression and incest avoidance in animal societies, it can do so for humans. Culture is not denied all relevance: on the contrary, most sociobiologists acknowledge an interactive relationship between genes and culture which they refer to as co-evolution.[18] Yet ultimately most see genetic evolution as the determinant of cultural possibilities. In the words of Wilson: 'The genes hold culture on a leash. The leash is very long, but inevitably values will

---

[14] Wilson, *On Human Nature*, 32–3.   [15] Dawkins, *Selfish Gene*, 67, 83.
[16] M. Ridley, *The Red Queen* (Harmondsworth: Penguin, 1994), 208, 226.
[17] Diamond, *Rise and Fall*, chaps. 8 and 9.
[18] Lopreato, *Human Nature*, chap. 3; C. J. Lumsden and E. O. Wilson, *Genes, Mind and Culture: The Coevolutionary Process* (Harvard University Press, 1981).

be constrained in accordance with their effects on the human gene pool.'[19]

One of the most provocative examples of sociobiology challenging conventional approaches to a topic is the theory of rape advanced by the Thornhills. After studying 'rape' – i.e. forced copulation of a female by a male – among scorpion flies, the authors turn their attention to human rape. Rejecting alternative explanations, the Thornhills argue that, as with scorpion flies, human rape is 'an evolved mating tactic'. It occurs when low-status males are denied mating opportunities, allowing these males some opportunity to spread their genes and increase their inclusive fitness. Although the reproductive benefits of rape are very low, in evolutionary terms they could prove to be important. According to the Thornhills: 'A small difference in fitness between men who raped when other avenues of reproduction were closed compared to men who did not rape in this context during evolutionary history would be expected to lead to major evolutionary change.'[20]

Another controversial focus has been on sexual differences. Wilson claims that men and women have evolved different physical and mental traits through evolutionary history. Among our early forebears, men hunted and competed with other males for women, hence men, as with males in most species, tend to be aggressive, women much less so.[21] Males can in principle impregnate many females, while females have to invest much time and effort in childbearing. These different reproductive strategies have produced different traits in males and females, with the latter, according to Ridley, favouring monogamous relationships and the former more promiscuous, prone to opportunistic mating 'and to use wealth, power and violence as means to sexual ends in the competition with other men . . .'[22] Ridley goes on to argue that while, in contrast to chimpanzees and gorillas, humans tend to form monogamous pairs in which the males invest time and effort in childcare, adultery nevertheless can be advantageous to both sexes, which is why it is a 'chronic problem throughout human society . . .'[23] Ridley believes that these evolved sex differences explain much social behaviour. Thus for men he maintains that 'deep in the mind of modern man is a simple male hunter–gatherer rule: strive to acquire power and use it to lure women who will bear heirs; strive to acquire wealth and use it to buy affairs with other men's wives who will bear bastards.'[24]

[19] Wilson, *On Human Nature*, 167.
[20] R. Thornhill and N. W. Thornhill, 'Human Rape: The Strengths of the Evolutionary Perspective', in Crawford *et al.*, *Sociobiology and Psychology*, 283.
[21] Wilson, *On Human Nature*, 125–8.   [22] Ridley, *Red Queen*, 198.
[23] *Ibid.*, 220.   [24] *Ibid.*, 236.

Ridley insists that: 'Men and women have different minds. The differences are the direct result of evolution.'[25] Equally adamant that difference does not entail inequality he nonetheless insists that the differences are real and cannot be attributed to social conventions.[26] A similar position is upheld by Wilson, who proposes that: 'Even with identical education for men and women and equal access to all professions, men are likely to maintain disproportionate representation in political life, business and science. Many would fail to participate fully in the equally important, formative aspects of child rearing.'[27]

These examples suffice to demonstrate the Social Darwinist credentials of sociobiology, the entire rationale for which is predicated on the fifth assumption of the world view, namely that Darwinian theory can explain important aspects of human society, culture and psychology. Moreover, despite their protestations to the contrary, sociobiologists are in this respect closely allied to the pop ethologists of the 1960s. Whatever the sophistication of the former, in both instances the project of synthesising evolutionary theory with ethology and ecology and applying this synthesis to problems erstwhile deemed to be the province of psychology, anthropology and sociology is clearly articulated. In this, the pop ethologists may actually have facilitated the wide acceptance of sociobiology by introducing some of its central ideas to the general public.

There are two other areas in which sociobiology evinces close links with pop ethology, and before that with early Social Darwinist texts. First, sociobiologists concede nothing to previous generations of Social Darwinists when it comes to speculative audacity. Wilson has proposed genetic explanations for crime, murder, ethnocentrism and aggression and homosexuality and speculated as to how these traits might improve genetic fitness.[28] Others have advanced evolutionary explanations for suicide, fasting, drug taking, and why modern (as opposed to pre-modern) men prefer slim women.[29] Sociobiology excels in the construction of evolutionary narratives that relate current institutions, fashions and social practices to the selection of genes in the evolutionary past.

Second, like their predecessors, sociobiologists have been conspicuous

---

[25] *Ibid.*, 240.   [26] *Ibid.*, 253.   [27] Wilson, *On Human Nature*, 133.
[28] *Ibid.*, 44, 83–100, 143–7.
[29] On suicide see D. de Catanzaro, 'Evolutionary Pressures and Limitations to Self-Preservation', in Crawford *et al.*, *Sociobiology and Psychology*, 311–33; for dieting, Lopreato, *Human Nature*, 214; for drug addiction, Diamond, *Rise and Fall*, chap. 11; for slim women, Ridley, *Red Queen*, 279–84. There is a resounding critique of these attempts to explain current social practices through the selection of genes for which no evidence actually exists in R. C. Lewontin, *The Doctrine of DNA* (Harmondsworth: Penguin, 1993), 100–4.

for both proclaiming the ethical neutrality of the science of sociobiology *and* advertising its relevance to moral debates. Thus Lopreato writes: '*Free* competition – that is at once the game and the fundamental principle of the ethics implicit in biocultural science.'[30] Wilson adopts a similar position, believing that human biology 'will fashion a biology of ethics, which will make possible the selection of a more deeply understood and enduring code of moral values'.[31] In fact Wilson betrays his affinities with older (and allegedly discredited) modes of discourse in a disturbing passage where he contends that in the light of our current knowledge 'we are justified in considering the preservation of the entire gene pool as a *contingent* primary value until such time as an almost unimaginably greater knowledge of human heredity provides us *with the option of a democratically contrived eugenics*'.[32] Even Dawkins, who is sensitive to the charge of biological reductionism, draws ethical conclusions from his thesis of the selfish gene. Organisms, he argues, are vehicles made by genes in order that the latter can replicate themselves. Nevertheless, human mental capacities mean that we 'have the power to defy the selfish genes of our birth ...'[33] But Dawkins, in language close to that of Wilson and other sociobiologists, makes plain the fact that this power renders humans unique in nature:

Be warned that if you wish, as I do, to build a society in which individuals cooperate generously and unselfishly towards a common good, you can expect little help from biological nature. Let us try to *teach* generosity and altruism, because we are born selfish. Let us understand what our own selfish genes are up to, because we may then at least have the chance to upset their designs, something that no other species has ever aspired to.[34]

In the light of this discursive continuity I am sympathetic to Crook's verdict that sociobiologists are inflicted with 'collective amnesia about their forebears'. Reading them induces a feeling of *déjà vu*, because: 'The same old issues keep cropping up, although the language is now more sophisticated ...'[35] The remainder of this chapter examines in more detail the relationship between the Social Darwinism of the sociobiologists and that espoused by their intellectual ancestors.

---

[30] Lopreato, *Human Nature*, 340, original emphasis.
[31] Wilson, *On Human Nature*, 198.   [32] *Ibid.*, my emphasis.
[33] Dawkins, *Selfish Gene*, 200.
[34] *Ibid.*, 3, original emphasis. A similar conclusion occurs in M. Konner, 'Human Nature and Culture: Biology and the Residue of Uniqueness', in J. J. Sheehan and M. Sosna, eds., *The Boundaries of Humanity: Humans, Animals, Machines* (Oxford: University of California Press, 1991), 120.
[35] Crook, *Darwinism, War and History*, 196, 198. Greta Jones also arrived at this conclusion in 1980; *Social Darwinism*, 187.

Continuities and contrasts

Since 1859 Darwinian theory has been revised and enriched by advances in genetics and other pertinent sciences. What are the consequences of these developments for the application of Darwinism to social and psychological phenomena, i.e. are there any substantial differences between early and contemporary versions of Social Darwinism? Answering this question is difficult due to the range of Social Darwinist applications subsumed under the rubric of 'early', i.e. covering the period 1859–1945. Bearing in mind the potential this creates for overgeneralisation and oversimplification, it is possible to arrive at some preliminary conclusions by focusing upon a number of themes in Darwinism, particularly upon those which constituted the indeterminacies of the earlier versions.

The struggle for existence

Natural selection through the struggle for existence was the mechanism adopted by Darwin to explain evolution. We have seen how the application of this mechanism to human affairs generated a variety of interpretations, ranging from the presentation of human conflict in its several manifestations as the analogue of natural selection to the thesis of an evolution of struggle itself from violent to peaceful modes as civilisation advanced. The interpretation of the social equivalents of natural selection was, accordingly, a key issue for Social Darwinists and one that provided a rich rhetorical resource.

It is interesting to note that after the Modern Synthesis Darwinian biology tended to downplay the notion of a struggle for existence. Biologists continued to acknowledge a role for direct conflict in natural selection but denied that this was inevitably the case since selection 'may simply be a matter of differential birth-rates'. If two strains of bacteria are placed in identical conditions and one has a higher rate of division, it will eventually replace the other completely without any violent struggle occurring.[36] Sociobiologists, in contrast, tend to stress competition and conflict as integral to selective dynamics. Some, certainly, have objected to the equation of natural selection with a nature 'red in tooth and claw'.[37] These dissenters are in the minority.

[36] Futuyma, *Evolutionary Biology*, 291–2. Smith, in his popular *Theory of Evolution* (first edition 1958, third edition 1975), refers to the struggle for existence only twice (32, 42).

[37] Crawford, 'Sociobiology', 7. Wilson also denies natural selection is necessarily lethal, *Diversity of Life*, 74. However, in his analysis of human behaviour he has stressed the ubiquity of murder and aggression. See Wilson, *On Human Nature*, 83, 99.

Dawkins explicitly endorses this equation, stating 'I think "nature red in tooth and claw" sums up our modern understanding of natural selection admirably.'[38] This perception of nature is unflinchingly applied to human societies. The anthropologist Konner maintains that all forms of conflict, up to and including homicide, can be found in every type of human society as well as in 'virtually all animal species for which there is sufficient evidence'.[39] He castigates social scientists for falsely assuming that society is an organism in which conflict is aberrant. On the contrary, conflict is endemic in all social relations and 'among *unrelated* individuals can be expected at times to be extreme'.[40] Even within families there is conflict because members have different evolutionary goals which will periodically lead to competition: between husband and wife, parents and progeny, siblings. 'Such conflict is not inadvertent friction in a system that should, by design, function smoothly but is an inherent and inevitable expression of the purposes of social life itself.'[41]

By making conflict arising from the attempts by individuals to improve inclusive fitness a central feature of social reality, socio-biologists have reinstated the view of some earlier thinkers. Darwin and his supporters were engaged in the attempt to redefine nature and stress the importance of struggle, death and extinction. At the social level, many Social Darwinists supported the notion of violent inter-social conflict coupled with peaceful intra-social competition, a tradition that has been reasserted by sociobiology. Wilson, for example, explains warfare as a consequence of ethnocentrism, which is 'the emotionally exaggerated allegiance of individuals to their kin and fellow tribesmen'.[42] Human brains are programmed to divide people into friends and aliens just as some birds are predisposed to learn certain songs. Hence: 'We tend to fear deeply the actions of strangers and to solve conflict by aggression.'[43] But the sociobiologists seem to go much further than even the most conflict-oriented of the earlier theorists, who while perhaps regarding warfare between rival states and races as inevitable would have shrunk from the implications that murder, rape, adultery and child abuse were universal – and perhaps ineradicable – features of social systems because they were encoded in human genes. In this respect, sociobiology adopts an even more uncompromising perspective on the struggle for existence than did early Social Darwinism.

---

[38] Dawkins, *Selfish Gene*, 2.   [39] Konner, 'Human Nature and Culture', 109, 111.
[40] *Ibid.*, 111, original emphasis.   [41] *Ibid.*, 119.
[42] Wilson, *On Human Nature*, 111.   [43] *Ibid.*, 119.

Sexual selection

Few of Darwin's followers assigned much significance to sexual selection as an evolutionary mechanism, although there were exceptions, and I have underlined the efforts of feminists like Gamble and Gilman to enlist sexual selection in the cause of female equality. Modern biologists recognise the role of sexual selection in evolution. Although it is ultimately subsumed under natural selection, sexual selection is assigned importance because traits which foster reproductive success could conflict with survival, as in the case of the peacock's tail.

Sociobiologists have made sexual selection an important part of their explanation of sexual dimorphism and have not shrunk from extending the analysis to human sexual differences. The differences they accentuate are almost identical to those emphasised by earlier Social Darwinists although, unlike some of the latter, sociobiologists are quick to repudiate any implication of female inferiority. As with the earlier period, such theorising is not exclusively male: several prominent sociobiologists are female and some feminists have insisted on the need to recognise the importance of sex differences.[44] Other feminists, while recognising the relevance of biology to the formation of sexual identities, reject sociobiological accounts of these identities as excessively reductionist.[45]

Sociobiologists dismiss these accusations while at the same time insisting on the reality of differences established through evolution and the constraints these differences place upon socio-political action. In Wilson's words: 'The consequences of genetic history cannot be chosen by legislatures.'[46] As with early forms of Social Darwinism, then, sociobiologists tend to use sexual and natural selection to represent certain aspects of the sexual division of labour as reposing upon 'natural' distinctions, although in ways which would have been most uncongenial to Gamble and Gilman.

The unit of selection

From the outset, Darwinism contained an indeterminacy over the unit of selection, i.e. whether it was the individual or the group. This permitted different social applications in which struggle occurred

[44] Examples are cited in Ridley, *Red Queen*, 255; Degler, *In Search of Human Nature*, chap. 12.

[45] L. Birke, *Women, Feminism and Biology* (Brighton: Harvester, 1986), 11–43; E. F. Keller, 'Language and Ideology in Evolutionary Theory: Reading Cultural Norms into Natural Law', in Sheehan and Sosna, eds., *Boundaries of Humanity*, 86–7, 99.

[46] Wilson, *On Human Nature*, 7.

primarily between individuals or groups (clans, classes, nation-states, races or empires) according to the ideological predilection of the theorist. These debates continue, although the present consensus is that selection acts upon individual organisms or their genes. Modern biology and sociobiology seem to have narrowed, if not closed off, one of the original indeterminacies in the Darwinian world view.

One consequence has been a marked emphasis on self-interested behaviour, whether at the level of individuals or genes. Altruism is reduced to the unconscious effort to maximise inclusive fitness or else to the expectation of reciprocal aid in the future, which is a form of self-interest. Thus Wilson contends that: 'Our societies are based on the mammalian plan: the individual strives for personal reproduc tive success foremost and that of his immediate kin secondarily; further grudging cooperation represents a compromise struck in order to enjoy the benefits of group membership.'[47] Dawkins insists that: 'Much as we might wish to believe otherwise, universal love and the welfare of the species as a whole are concepts that simply do not make evolutionary sense.'[48] Daly and Wilson are sceptical about the existence of supposedly social as opposed to individual interests. They argue that evolutionary theory 'suggests that the individual is a more basic mode of unitary self-interest than is the larger society, and hence that appeals to society's interests may often be self-serving smoke screens'.[49] Indeed, they erect self-interest into a normative standard by arguing that insanity occurs when individuals no longer recognise or wish to pursue their self-interest. Since in evolutionary terms self-interest equates with inclusive fitness, 'sanity is characterised by the intelligible pursuit of nepotistic self-interest' while insanity consists in 'the forswearing of that pursuit'.[50]

In sociobiology groups still compete with one another but, as we have seen, this stems from genetically rooted ethnocentricity – a blind allegiance to one's tribe which probably originated in kin-selection. Most sociobiologists, however, avoid discussion of one of the most salient forms of group conflict in early Social Darwinism – race. Wilson correctly observes that scientists agree that it is impossible, on biological grounds, to identify discrete races, and insists that 'almost all' differences between societies are cultural rather than hereditary.[51] Others

---

[47] Ibid., 199.   [48] Dawkins, Selfish Gene, 2.

[49] M. Daly and M. Wilson, 'Evolutionary Psychology and Family Violence', in Crawford et al., Sociobiology and Psychology, 294. See also Dawkins, Selfish Gene, 255: 'The group is too wishy-washy an entity. A herd of deer, a pride of lions or a pack of wolves has a certain rudimentary coherence and unity of purpose. But this is paltry in comparison to the coherence and unity of purpose of the body of an individual lion, wolf or deer.'

[50] Daly and Wilson, 'Evolutionary Psychology and Family Violence', 303.

[51] Wilson, On Human Nature, 48–9. See also Diamond, Rise and Fall, 199–200, 213–14.

have denied racism any foundations in evolutionary theory, while acknowledging that racist ideology may have been adaptive in consolidating ingroup solidarity.[52] Needless to say, this has not prevented the appropriation of sociobiology by racist individuals and movements, as ever seeking a scientific legitimation for their beliefs. One example must suffice. In Britain during the 1970s the racist National Front Party was quick to seize upon sociobiology in order to validate its doctrines of European racial supremacy and its opposition to liberalism and Marxism.[53] Despite the atomistic methodological bias of sociobiology, then, and the liberal persuasion of many of its Anglo-American practitioners, it can and has been deployed to explain both group and individual antagonisms.

Heredity

Modern Darwinism is unremittingly hereditarian and the action of the environment through the inheritance of acquired characters is rejected by sociobiologists. Here one of the original indeterminacies is definitely closed off in that a Social Darwinist would find it very difficult nowadays to endorse Lamarckism. The debate about nurture versus nature is as fierce as ever, although it now takes place between Social Darwinists and their opponents rather than, additionally, within Social Darwinism itself as was once the case.

Most sociobiologists acknowledge the importance of culture as a determinant of human behaviour and even concede a dialectical interplay between genes and culture, with the latter having a selective impact on the former. In practice, as I have already indicated, when it comes to accounting for certain key institutions and practices, sociobiologists assign causal primacy to inherited biological traits. Thus Lopreato, in challenging Weber's thesis on the importance of Calvinist ideas of predestination in the development of early capitalism, comments: 'ideas may indeed have been powerful forces in the maturation of modern capitalism, but only because they were "public images" of a biological substratum. Without the latter, they would have fallen on deaf ears.'[54]

An important arena for the contest between sociobiological and

---

[52] I. Silverman, 'Race, Race Differences and Race Relations: Perspectives from Psychology and Sociobiology', in Crawford *et al.*, *Sociobiology and Psychology*, 217–18.
[53] See R. Verral, 'Sociobiology: The Instinct in Our Genes', *Spearhead*, 127(March, 1979), 10–11. The same journal later carried an article on Darwin in its 'Great British Racists' series. See *Spearhead*, 130(August 1979), 11. I am grateful to Steve Woodbridge for these references.
[54] Lopreato, *Human Nature*, 92.

cultural explanations has been the topic of incest prohibitions. Since these can be found in animal societies as well, they are deemed to have an instinctual basis. In humans, individuals who had a genetic aversion to mating with close kin would have left more descendants than those without this trait, and hence incest aversion would have been implanted through natural selection.

This kind of explanation is not new and a version of it was advanced over a century ago by Westermarck – as sociobiologists acknowledge.[55] Westermarck surmised that if selection favoured those who avoided injurious sexual unions, then an instinct for incest avoidance would develop. 'Of course', he continued, 'it would display itself simply as an aversion on the part of individuals to union with others with whom they lived; but these, as a matter of fact, would be blood-relations, so that the result would be survival of the fittest.'[56] Sociobiologists claim that Westermarck's conjectures have been confirmed by modern ethnology: unrelated children that are brought up together are unlikely to marry and when they do they tend to produce fewer offspring than couples who were brought up separately.[57] Some sociobiologists have inferred from this that incest rarely occurs and so-called incest taboos actually prohibit adultery and inbreeding (i.e. cross-cousin unions) 'and are made to enhance the fitness of powerful men, the rule-makers'.[58] An anthropologist has gone so far as to proclaim that 'purely cultural explanations' of incest avoidance are simply untenable.[59]

These views are contentious and tend to receive a hostile reception from cultural anthropologists.[60] I lack the time and competence to engage in these debates, but fortunately there is no need. All that requires emphasis is the 'hard' hereditarianism of modern sociobiology linking it with pop ethology and, before that, with the Weismann-inspired versions of Social Darwinism which emerged towards the end of the nineteenth century. The effect is that *within* Social Darwinism an indeterminacy has been closed off.

---

[55] For example, Ridley, *Red Queen*, 274–7.
[56] Westermarck, *The History of Human Marriage*, 352.   [57] Ridley, *Red Queen*, 275.
[58] N. Thornhill and R. Thornhill, 'Evolutionary Theory and Rules of Mating on Marriage Pertaining to Relatives', in Crawford *et al.*, *Sociobiology and Psychology*, 397.
[59] P. L. van den Berghe, 'Incest Taboos and Avoidance: Some African Applications', in Crawford *et al.*, *Sociobiology and Psychology*, 353.
[60] For a balanced assessment of cultural and instinctive explanations of incest taboos, see A. Kuper, *The Chosen Primate* (London/ Cambridge, MA: Harvard University Press, 1994), 156–66. This study is an excellent critical review of sociobiological accounts of aggression, pair-bonding, kinship and gender differences in the light of the ethnographic record.

Human nature

Darwinism represented a challenge to the idea of species essentialism which in turn undermined the notion of a fixed human essence. Very quickly, however, evolutionary theory itself was used to underwrite the view that human nature changed so slowly that within the compass of the historical record and the foreseeable future it could be taken as fixed. Versions of Social Darwinism appeared and gained wide credence in which human institutions and behavioural attributes – particularly those associated with race – were presented as virtually timeless.[61] This assumption was also an important component of pop ethology, as we saw above.

It is also a premiss of sociobiology whose practitioners, almost without exception, maintain that the nature of modern humans was, in essentials, established thousands of years ago. Modern people possess the emotional and behavioural repertoire of the hunter–gatherers who were their remote ancestors, much of which is in turn shared with primates and even other animals. In the words of Wilson: 'Human nature is ... a hodgepodge of special genetic adaptations to an environment largely vanished, the world of the ice-age hunter–gatherer. Modern life, as rich and rapidly changing as it appears to those caught in it, is nevertheless only a mosaic of cultural hypertrophies of the archaic behavioural adaptations.'[62] We have already encountered a similar explanation by Ridley, namely the 'hunter–gatherer rule' to acquire wealth and power for the purpose of acquiring women. In a recent publication Wilson bases his hope for conservationist policies aimed at protecting biological and ecological diversity partly on the existence of innate features of human nature. These he refers to as *biophilia*: 'the connections that human beings subconsciously seek with the rest of life'. The human heritage, he argues, is at least two million years old, stretching back to the appearance of the genus *homo*. In intimate contact with nature, our ancestors struggled to understand it. 'The imprint of that effort cannot have been erased in a few generations of urban existence.'[63]

The effect of arguments such as these is to reinstate human nature as the foundation of ethical and social thought and practice, as noted above; a human nature which, to all intents and purposes, we can take as fixed. Its main parameters were determined perhaps two million years ago and despite the vast cultural changes that have occurred since then, these parameters still provide the key to an understanding of much

[61] See my 'The Struggle for Existence in Nineteenth Century Social Thought'.
[62] Wilson, *On Human Nature*, 196.   [63] Wilson, *Diversity of Life*, 334, 332–3.

social action and many institutions. I am not concerned here with the veracity of these arguments, for it seems perfectly consistent with Darwinism to maintain that some species undergo little change over long periods. My point is that evolutionary theory – a theory of change – has been used to reinsert what is in practice a human essence into the fundamental premises of socio-political thought. In this, sociobiologists are continuing a long-standing tendency in Social Darwinism.

Sociobiologists are not therefore interested in social change.[64] Unlike the early Social Darwinists, they do not seek to construct stages of social and/or mental evolution. Like the pop ethologists, they do not ask how modern people were differentiated from primitives and primates: on the contrary, they seek to demonstrate that modern traits and institutions can be found in primitives and primates because they have been selected for by evolution. The chronological distance between modern humans, primitives, hominids and apes is condensed. Time's arrow becomes Zeno's arrow.[65] Whereas this distances socio-biologists sharply from someone like Spencer, it does show continuity with certain developments in early Social Darwinism, for example the theories of Gumplowicz and Lapouge, and the writings of Graham Wallas.

It is their insistence on the presence of timeless and universal features of human nature deriving from a genetic basis selected by evolution which has earned sociobiologists their reputation as conservatives. However much sociobiologists insist on their ethical neutrality or liberal credentials, their critics charge them with furnishing justifications for the status quo. Thus the American geneticist Lewontin sees sociobiology as 'the latest and most mystified attempt to convince people that human life is pretty much what it has to be and perhaps even ought to be'.[66] There is substance to these charges, as the examples cited here testify. But this political orientation should not be confused with the Social Darwinism of sociobiology and nor should it preclude the possibility that there exist modern examples of Social Darwinism employed in the service of more radical programmes, just as in the past (compare Lapouge and Wallas).

---

[64] It is instructive to recall Greta Jones's verdict on Wilson: 'Wilson is searching less for a scientific theory of human social evolution than for an ontology of human nature in which there is a strong biological component': Social Darwinism, 192.

[65] Zeno was a fifth-century BC Eleatic philosopher who endeavoured to prove that an object in motion was apparently at rest.

[66] Lewontin, Doctrine of DNA, 89. Lewontin continues: 'After all, if 3 billion years of evolution have made us what we are, do we really think that a hundred days of revolution will change us?' (90).

Nature as model and threat

Throughout this study I have drawn attention to the dual resonance of nature within Social Darwinism as both a model for and a threat to social existence. This duality varied in both the extent of its presence and in its discursive consequences. In some versions of Social Darwinism, such as Nazism, it was muted: nature was a model for social practices. What tended to fluctuate in Nazism was the status of nature, which alternated between an inexorable force against which culture was impotent and a rather fragile balance that required socio-political intervention for its preservation. This conception of nature was, as we have seen, prefigured in Lapouge and other late nineteenth-century thinkers.

In sociobiology the model/threat duality inclines to the muted variant. I have sought to show how sociobiologists tend to reify nature as a powerful causal force and as a normative guideline for cultural practices. In the words of Ridley: 'Nurture always reinforces nature; it rarely fights it.'[67] In some cases, nature is depicted as inimical to certain values. Thus Dawkins cautions those who wish to live in a world of peace and cooperation not to look to nature for practical guidance: disinterested altruistic behaviour must be taught. But even he perceives the possibility of a moral myth in the proclivity of vampire bats to assist non-related fellow cave inhabitants in times of need. 'They could herald the benignant idea that, even with selfish genes at the helm, nice guys can finish first.'[68]

The valuation of nature takes on a new twist in sociobiological writings that decry the environmental hazards created by humans. In these texts, nature is itself under threat. No longer is nature something which potentially threatens humans, but also something which is itself menaced by human agency. Green issues are very much a late twentieth-century concern and their salience inevitably feeds into a revaluation of nature and the place of humanity within it. In sociobiology this may account for the perception of nature as much more a model than a threat, with the latter emanating from culture rather than from within nature.

I would not, however, wish to push this point too far. The history of Social Darwinism shows that the notion of a struggle for existence was not an easy one for social theorists to handle. It is also problematic for sociobiologists. No matter how much they extol competition and emphasise the evolutionary legacy of human nature, they invariably fall

[67] Ridley, *Red Queen*, 244.   [68] Dawkins, *Selfish Gene*, 233.

back on human reason as a resource which enables humanity to recognise this legacy and perhaps even to achieve cooperation and international solidarity. Though rarely articulated there is an implicit recognition that murder, rape, nepotism, adultery, aggression and xenophobia, however 'natural', are morally unacceptable. Yet if these actions have a genetic basis established thousands of years ago through natural selection then the only way in which they can be eradicated or suppressed is through culture. One can expect, therefore, that our current Social Darwinists will continue to exhibit the dilemmatic features of their predecessors. Competition, aggression and the battle of the sexes will continue to appear in their writings as natural expressions of human evolutionary history. But unless the theorists in question are prepared wholeheartedly to endorse these actions or – which is most unlikely – to refrain altogether from any ethical judgement, then they will persist in representing nature as janiform – as model and threat.

Conclusion

The Social Darwinist world view described in chapter 1 is clearly recognisable in the writings of modern sociobiologists. All of the original five elements have been retained; what has altered are some of the indeterminacies within the world view due to developments in biology and related sciences. Not only the original world view but many of the substantive theoretical concerns and tactics of early Social Darwinism – even many of the same ideas – are reproduced in sociobiology. Social Darwinism, consequently, is thriving nearly a century and a half after the appearance of the *Origin*. Through the publicity accorded their ideas, the sales of their books, and the dissemination of their theories via academia, the sociobiologists have reached a very wide audience. Hence Social Darwinism has likewise been widely popularised and one could expect it to be manifest in many other areas, though this point cannot be pursued here.[69]

It is pointless and misleading to present this popularisation as a vulgarisation of Darwinism. The application of Darwinian theory to human society and psychology was an explicit goal of Darwin and the early Darwinians. There is, therefore, no such thing as 'vulgar' or 'crude' Social Darwinism. What varies between theories is the under-

---

[69] Casual evidence for the penetration of popular culture by Social Darwinism is readily available. For example, a recent editorial in a utilities magazine on competition within the industry following privatisation was headed 'Natural Selection'. It began: 'Competition is a basic instinct. The survival of the fittest determines which species survive and which ones don't': *Utilities Week*, 13 October 1995.

standing of Darwinism and the rigour with which it is applied to social phenomena. Many sociobiologists are rigorous in both respects but then so were Spencer, Haeckel and Royer given the state of knowledge of their time, as were Lapouge, Wallas and Lenz later. Sociobiologists are, then, quite wrong to insist on their differentiation from Social Darwinism, an insistence which is based upon an ignorance both of the nature and the history of Social Darwinism.

In the light of this history it is also apparent that sociobiologists are naive to disclaim any responsibility for the socio-political implications of their theories, especially as their own writings are usually redolent with such implications. It is certainly true that Darwinism does not under-write any specific ideological position or political programme, but as a contemporary cultural anthropologist, Kuper, has observed, 'it is well to bear in mind that any persuasive theory about human nature is bound to become the basis for policies – about child-rearing, social mobility, educational selection, immigration, even war and peace ...'[70] Social Darwinism can underpin more than one theory of human nature, but this study has demonstrated that such theories *are* persuasive and have precisely the consequences enumerated by Kuper. Since the explicit goal of sociobiology has been the construction of a scientifically based theory of human nature, and since sociobiologists themselves have been prominent in the popularisation of this theory, they should not be surprised at the consequences. Theirs is a long-standing ambition, and although conversance with its history can hardly be expected to daunt it, such awareness would at least make innocence as to its implications impossible.

[70] Kuper, *Chosen Primate*, 17.

Bibliography

This bibliography includes all items referred to in the chapters except for newspaper and magazine articles, full references to which are given in the footnotes.

SOURCES WRITTEN/PUBLISHED BEFORE 1945

(The date of first publication appears in square brackets where appropriate.)

Ambon, Gabriel. 'Darwinisme social', *Journal des économistes*, fifth series, 39(1899), 343–52

Ammon, Otto. *Der Darwinismus Gegen die Sozialdemokratie: Anthropoligische Plauderein* (Hamburg: Verlagstalt und Druckerei, 1891)

Bagehot, Walter. *Physics and Politics, or Thoughts on the Application of the Principles of 'Natural Selection' and 'Inheritance' to Political Society* (London: Kegan Paul, Trench, Trübner, 1903) [1867–8; book form, 1872]

    The English Constitution (Glasgow: Fontana/Collins, 1963) [1865; book form, 1867]

Bailey, L. H. 'Neo-Lamarckism and Neo-Darwinism', *The American Naturalist*, 28(1894), 661–78

Barnes, John Strachey. *The Universal Aspects of Fascism* (London: Williams and Norgate, 1928)

Bauer, Erwin, Eugen Fischer and Fritz Lenz. *Human Heredity*, tr. from third edn [1927] Eden and Cedar Paul (London: Allen and Unwin, 1931)

Bebel, August. *Woman in the Past, Present and Future*, tr. H. B. Adams Walther; reprinted with an introduction by Moira Donald (London: Zwan, 1988) [1879]

Bernhardi, Freidrich von. *Germany and the Next War*, tr. A. H. Powles (London: Arnold, 1912)

Bernstein, Eduard. *Evolutionary Socialism* (New York: Shocken, 1961) [1898]

Blind, Mathilde. *The Ascent of Man* (London: Chatto and Windus, 1889)

Boelsche, Wilhelm. *The Descent of Man* (no tr.) (London: Simpkin, Marshall, 1926) [1923]

Bourgeois, Léon. *Solidarité* (Paris: Colin, 1897)

Brace, Charles Loring. *The Races of the Old World: A Manual of Ethnology* (London: John Murray, 1863)

The Dangerous Classes of New York and Twenty Years of Work Among Them (New York: Wynkoop and Hallenback, 1872)

Brace, Emma, ed. *The Life of Charles Loring Brace Chiefly Told in His Own Letters* (London: Sampson, Low, Marston and Co., 1894)

Bradley, F. H. *Appearance and Reality*, second edn (Oxford: Clarendon Press, 1897) [1893]

    'Some Remarks on Punishment', *International Journal of Ethics*, 4(1894), 269–84

Brinton, Crane. *English Political Thought in the Nineteenth Century* (London: Benn, 1933)

Büchner, Ludwig. *Man in the Past, Present and Future: A Popular Account of Recent Scientific Research as Regards the Origins, Position and Prospects of the Human Race*, tr. W. S. Dallas (London: Asher and Co., 1872)

Carrel, Alexis. *Man the Unknown* (New York/London: Harper, 1935)

Closson, Carlos. 'Social Selection', *Journal of Political Economy*, 4(1896), 449–66

Cobbe, Frances Power. *Darwinism in Morals and Other Essays* (London: Williams and Norgate, 1872)

Comte, Auguste. *Plan des travaux scientifiques nécessaires pour réorganiser la société* (Paris: Aubier-Montaigne, 1970) [1822]

    Cours de philosophie positive, 6 vols. (Paris: Bachelier, 1830–42)

    Système de politique positive, 4 vols. (Paris: Mathias, Carilian-Goury et Delmont, 1851–4)

Condorcet, Marquis de. *Esquisse d'un tableau historique des progrès de l'esprit humaine* (Paris: Editions Sociales, 1966) [1795]

Cope, Edward Drinker. *On the Hypothesis of Evolution: Physical and Metaphysical* (New Haven, CT: Chatfield and Co., 1870)

    The Origin of the Fittest: Essays on Evolution (London/New York: Macmillan, 1887)

    'The Energy of Evolution', *The American Naturalist*, 18(1894), 205–19

Darwin, Charles. *Journal of Researches into the Natural History and Geology of the Countries Visited During the Voyage Round the World of HMS 'Beagle' Under Command of Captain Fitz Roy, RN* (London: Murray, 1909) [1839]

    On the Origin of Species by Means of Natural Selection, or the Preservation of Favoured Races in the Struggle for Life, ed. J. W. Burrow (Harmondsworth: Penguin, 1968) [1859]

    The Descent of Man and Selection in Relation to Sex, second revised and augmented edn (London: Murray, 1896) [1871]

Darwin, Charles and T. H. Huxley. *Autobiographies*, ed. Gavin de Beer (Oxford University Press, 1983)

Darwin, Francis, ed. *Charles Darwin: His Life Told in an Autobiographical Chapter, and in a Selected Series of His Published Letters*, rev. edn (London: Murray, 1902)

Darwin, Leonard. *The Need for Eugenic Reform* (London: Murray, 1926)

    What is Eugenics? (London: Watts, 1928)

Dewey, John. *Human Nature and Conduct: An Introduction to Social Psychology* (London: Allen and Unwin, 1922)

Experience and Nature (La Salle, IL: Open Court, 1971) [1925]

John Dewey: The Essential Writings, ed. David Sidorsky (New York: Harper Torchbooks, 1977)

Durkheim, Emile. *The Division of Labour in Society*, tr. W. D. Halls (London: Macmillan, 1984) [1893]

Edmonds, Thomas Rowe. *Practical, Moral and Political Economy, or the Government, Religion and Institutions Most Conducive to Individual Happiness and to National Power* (London: Effingham Wilson, 1828)

Ellis, Havelock. *Man and Woman: A Study of Secondary and Tertiary Sexual Characters*, eighth revised edn (London: Heinemann, 1934)

Morals, Manners and Men (London: Watts, 1939)

Evrie, John H. van. *White Supremacy and Negro Subordination; or Negroes a Subordinate Race and (So-Called) Slavery its Normal Condition*, second edn (New York: van Evrie, Horton and Co., 1868)

Fages, C. 'L'Evolution du darwinisme sociologique', *L'Humanité nouvelle*, 3(1899), 28–42

Faguet, Emile. *Le Feminisme* (Paris: Société Française d'Imprimerie et de Librairie, 1910)

Ferguson, Adam. *An Essay on the History of Civil Society*, ed. D. Forbes (Edinburgh University Press), 1966 [1767]

Ferri, Enrico. *Socialism and Positive Science. (Darwin – Spencer – Marx)*, tr. from the French edn E. C. Harvey (London: Independent Labour Party, 1905) [1894]

Fischer, Eugen. 'Racial Differences in Mankind', in Bauer, Fischer and Lenz, *Human Heredity*

Fiske, John. *Outlines of Cosmic Philosophy Based on the Doctrine of Evolution with Criticisms of the Positive Philosophy*, 2 vols. (London: Macmillan, 1874)

Darwinism and Other Essays (London/New York: Macmillan, 1879)

The Life and Letters of Edward Livingstone Youmans (London: Chapman and Hall, 1894)

The Meaning of Infancy (Boston: Houghton Mifflin, 1909)

Galton, Francis. 'Hereditary Talent and Character', *Macmillan's Magazine*, 12(1865), 157–66, 318–27

Hereditary Genius (London: Macmillan, 1869)

'Eugenics: Its Definition, Scope and Aims', *American Journal of Sociology*, 10(1904), 1–25

Gamble, Eliza Burt. *The Evolution of Woman: An Inquiry into the Dogma of her Inferiority to Man* (New York/London: Putnam's Sons, 1894)

Gilman, Charlotte Perkins. *The Yellow Wallpaper* (London: Virago, 1983) [1892]

Women and Economics, extracts in Hollinger and Capper, eds., *The American Intellectual Tradition*, II, 55–60 [1898]

'Response to Wells' "Social Darwinism"', *The American Journal of Sociology* 12(1906–7), 713–14

The Man-Made World or Our Androcentric Culture (London: T. Fisher Unwin, 1911)

Goebbels, Paul Josef. *The Goebbels Diaries, 1939–1941*, ed. and tr. F. Taylor (London: Sphere, 1983)

Gumplowicz, Ludwig. *Outlines of Sociology*, tr. F. W. Moore [1899] (New York: Paine-Whitman, 1963) [1885]

Sociologie et politique (no tr.) (Paris: Giard et Brière, 1898) [1892]

Haeckel, Ernst. *The History of Creation, or the Development of the Earth and its Inhabitants by the Action of Natural Causes*, revised tr. E. R. Lankester, 2 vols. (London: King, 1876) [1868]

The Evolution of Man, 2 vols., tr. J. McCabe (London: Watts, 1910) [1874]

Freedom in Science and Teaching (no tr.) (London: Kegan Paul, 1879)

Le Monisme: lien entre la religion et la science, tr. G. Vacher de Lapouge (Paris: Schleicher, 1902) [1892]

The Riddle of the Universe, tr. J. McCabe (London: Watts, 1900) [1899]

Last Words on Evolution: A Popular Retrospect and Summary, tr. J. McCabe (London: Owen, 1906)

Haycraft, John Berry. *Darwinism and Race Progress* (London: Swan Sonnenschein, 1895)

Hegel, Georg Wilhelm Friedrich. *Elements of the Philosophy of Right*, ed. Allen W. Wood, tr. H. B. Nisbet (Cambridge University Press, 1991) [1821]

Helvétius, Claude Arien. *De l'homme: de ses facultés intellectuelles et de son éducation*, 2 vols. (London: Société Typographique, 1773)

Hitler, Adolf. *Mein Kampf*, tr. R. Manheim (London: Hutchinson, 1974) [1925–6]

Hitler's Secret Book, tr. S. Attanasio (New York: Grove Press, 1961) [1928]

Hitler's War Directives, 1939–1945, ed. H. R. Trevor-Roper (London: Pan, 1966)

Hitler's Table Talk, 1941–1944, tr. N. Cameron and R. H. Stevens (Oxford University Press, 1988)

Hobbes, Thomas. *Leviathan*, ed. C. B. Macpherson (Harmondsworth: Penguin, 1968) [1651]

Huxley, Julian. *Essays of a Biologist* (London: Chatto and Windus, 1928) [1923]

What Dare I Think? (London: Chatto and Windus, 1932)

Evolution: The Modern Synthesis, third edn (London: Allen and Unwin, 1974) [1942]

Huxley, Thomas Henry. *Man's Place in Nature and Other Essays* (London: Dent, 1906) [1863]

Critiques and Addresses (London: Macmillan, 1873)

'The Struggle for Existence: A Programme', *The Nineteenth Century*, 23(1888), 161–80

Evolution and Ethics (London: Macmillan, 1893)

James, William. *The Principles of Psychology*, 2 vols. (London: Constable and Co., 1950) [1890]

The Will to Believe and Other Essays in Popular Philosophy (New York: Dover Publications, 1956) [1897]

Keith, Arthur. *Essays on Human History* (London: Scientific Book Club, n. d.) [1942–4]

Key, Ellen. *Love and Marriage*, tr. A. Chater (London: Putnam's, 1911)

Love and Ethics (no tr.) (London: Putnam's, 1912)

The Woman Movement, tr. M. B. Borthwick (London: Putnam's, 1912)

War, Peace and the Future: A Consideration of Nationalism and Internationalism, *and of the Relation of Women to War*, tr. H. Norberg (London: Putnam's, 1916)

Kidd, Benjamin. *Social Evolution* (London: Macmillan, 1894)

Kropotkin, Peter. *Mutual Aid: A Factor of Evolution*, ed. Paul Avrich (London: Allen Lane, the Penguin Press, 1972) [1902]

Lamarck, Jean Baptiste. *Zoological Philosophy: An Exposition With Regard to the Natural History of Animals*, tr. Hugh Elliot (London: Macmillan, 1914) [1809]

Lanessan, J.-L. de. *Etude sur la doctrine du Darwin: lutte pour l'existence et l'association pour la lutte* (Paris: Octave Doin, 1881)

La Lutte pour l'existence et l'évolution des sociétés (Paris: Alcan, 1903)

La Concurrence sociale et les devoirs sociaux (Paris: Alcan, 1904)

Lankester, Edwin Ray. *Degeneration: A Chapter in Darwinism* (London: Macmillan, 1880)

The Kingdom of Man (London: Watts and Co., 1911)

Lapouge, Georges Vacher de. 'Préface' to Haeckel, *Le Monisme*

Les Sélections sociales (Paris: Fontemoing, 1896)

'The Fundamental Laws of Anthropo-Sociology', tr. C. Closson, *Journal of Political Economy*, 6(1898), 54–92

L'Aryen: son role social (Paris: Fontemoing, 1899)

Laveleye, Emile de. 'L'Etat et l'individu, ou darwinisme social et le christianisme', in Laveleye, *Le Socialisme contemporaine*, fourth edn (Paris: Alcan, 1888)

Le Bon, Gustave. *L'Homme et les sociétés; leurs origines et leur histoire*, 2 vols. (Paris: Rothschild, 1881)

Les Lois psychologiques de l'évolution des peuples (Paris: Alcan, 1894)

Psychologie des foules (Paris: Alcan, 1895)

The Crowd: A Study of the Popular Mind (no tr.) (London: T. Fisher Unwin, 1896)

The Psychology of Socialism (no. tr.) (London: T. Fisher Unwin, 1899)

Le Conte, Joseph. *The Race Problem in the South*, Evolution Series no. 29: Man and the State (New York: Appleton and Co., 1892)

Lenz, Fritz. 'Morbific Hereditary Factors' and 'The Inheritance of Intellectual Gifts', in Bauer, Fischer and Lenz, *Human Heredity*

Lombroso, Cesare. *Crime: Its Causes and Remedies*, tr. from the French by H. P. Horton (Boston: Little, Brown, 1911) [1899]

Lombroso, Cesare and William Ferrero, *The Female Offender* (no tr.) (London: Owen, 1959) [1893]

Lombroso, Gina. *The Soul of Woman: Reflections on Life* (no tr.) (London: Jonathan Cape, 1924) [1923]

Lonsdale, Henry. *A Sketch of the Life and Writings of Robert Knox the Anatomist* (London: Macmillan, 1870)

Loria, Achille. 'Darwinisme social', *Revue internationale de sociologie*, 4(1896), 440–51

Malthus, T. R. *An Essay on the Principle of Population*, ed. Donald Winch (Cambridge University Press, 1992) [1798]

Marx, Karl. *The German Ideology*, Part I (London: Lawrence and Wishart, 1970)

Marx, Karl and Friedrich Engels. *Selected Works* (London: Lawrence and Wishart, 1968)

Meldola, Raphael. *Evolution: Darwinian and Spencerian* (Oxford: Clarendon Press, 1910)

Mill, John Stuart. *The Subjection of Women* (London: Dent, 1985) [1869]

Autobiography (New York: Columbia University Press, 1966) [1873]

Molinari, Gustave de. *L'Evolution économique du dix-neuvième siècle: théorie du progrès* (Paris: Reinwald, 1880)

Mosca, Gaetano. *The Ruling Class*, tr. Hannah D. Kahn, ed. A Livingston (New York: McGraw-Hill, 1939) [1896]

Nordau, Max. *Degeneration* (no tr.) tr. from second German edn (London: Heinemann, 1895)

Morals and the Evolution of Man, tr. M. A. Lewenz (London: Cassell, 1922) [1916]

Novicow, Jacques. *Les Luttes entre les sociétés humaines et leurs phases successives* (Paris: Alcan, 1893)

La Critique du darwinisme social (Paris: Alcan, 1910)

'The Mechanism and Limits of Human Association: The Foundations of a Sociology of Peace', tr. S. H. Otis, *American Journal of Sociology*, 23(1917), 289–349

Olivier, Sydney. 'Moral', in Shaw, ed., *Fabian Essays in Socialism*, 96–120

Pannokoek, Anton. *Marxism and Darwinism*, tr. Nathan Weiser (Chicago: Kerr, 1912) [1909]

Pareto, Vilfredo. *Sociological Writings*, tr. Derick Mirfin, ed. S. E. Finer (Oxford: Blackwell, 1966)

Parsons, Talcott. *The Structure of Social Action*, 2 vols. (London: Collier-Macmillan, 1968) [1937]

Pearson, Karl. *National Life from the Standpoint of Science*, second edn (London: Adam and Charles Black, 1905) [1900]

Peirce, Charles Sanders. 'The Fixation of Belief', in Hollinger and Capper, eds., *The American Intellectual Tradition*, II, 14–24 [1877]

Peters, Carl. *New Light on Dark Africa*, tr. H. W. Dulken (London: Ward, Locke, 1891)

The Future of Africa (London: Waterlow, 1897)

England and The English (London: Hurst and Blackett, 1904)

Reade, Winwood. *The Martyrdom of Man* (London: Watts, 1945) [1872]

Report of the Departmental Committee on Sterilisation Cmd 4485 (London: HMSO, 1934)

Richet, Charles. *La Sélection humaine* (Paris: Alcan, 1919)

Ritchie, David G. *Darwinism and Politics* (London: Swan Sonnenschein, 1889); second edn containing two additional essays (London: Swan Sonnenschein, 1891)

The Principles of State Interference: Four Essays on the Political Philosophy of Mr. Herbert Spencer, J. S. Mill, and T. H. Green (London: Swan Sonnenschein, 1891)

Rolle, Friedrich. *Der Mensch, Seine Abstammung und Gesittung im Lichte der Darwin'schen Lehre* (Frankfurt am Main: Germann'sche Verlagsbuchhandlung, 1866)

Romanes, George G. *Animal Intelligence*, sixth edn (London: Kegan Paul, Trench, Trübner, 1895)

Royer, Clémence-Auguste. *Théorie de l'impôt, ou la dîme sociale* 2 vols. (Paris: Guillaumin, 1862)
'Préface' to C. Darwin, *De L'origine des espèces, ou des lois du progrès chez les êtres organisés*, tr. Royer (Paris: Guillaumin, 1862)
'Avant Propos', *De L'origine des espèces par sélection naturelle, ou des lois de transformation des êtres organisés*, second edn (Paris: Guillaumin, 1866)
Origine de l'homme et des sociétés (Paris: Guillaumin, 1870)
Saleeby, C. W. *Evolution, the Master Key: A Discussion of the Principles of Evolution as Illustrated in Atoms, Stars, Organic Species, Mind, Society and Morals* (London: Harper, 1906)
Schmidt, Oscar. *The Doctrine of Descent and Darwinism* (no tr.) (London: King and Co., 1875)
Selous, Frederick Courtney. *Travel and Adventure in South-East Africa* (London: Rowland, Ward, 1893)
Sunshine and Storm in Rhodesia (London: Rowland, Ward, 1896)
Shaler, Nathaniel Southgate. *The Citizen: A Study of the Individual and Government* (New York: Barnes, 1904)
Shaw, George Bernard. *Back to Methuselah: A Metabiological Pentateuch* (London: Constable, 1931) [1921]
'Sixty years of Fabianism', in Shaw, ed., *Fabian Essays*, 207–31
Shaw, George Bernard, ed. *Fabian Essays in Socialism* (London: Allen and Unwin, 1948) [1889]
Fabianism and the Empire: A Manifesto by the Fabian Society (London: Grant Richards, 1900)
Small, Laurence. *Darwinism and Socialism* (London: Independent Labour Party, 1907/8)
Smiles, Samuel. *Self-Help; With Illustrations of Conduct and Perseverance*, revised edn (London: Murray, 1897)
Soury, Jules. *Campagne nationaliste 1899–1901* (Paris: Imprimerie de la Cour d'Appel, 1902)
Spencer, Herbert. 'A Theory of Population Deduced from the General Law of Animal Fertility', *Westminster Review*, new series, 1(1852), 468–501
The Principles of Psychology, third edn (London: Williams and Norgate, 1890) [1855]
First Principles, sixth edn (London: Williams and Norgate, 1922) [1862]
The Principles of Biology, 2 vols., enlarged and revised edn (New York: Appleton and Co., 1898) [1864–7]
The Study of Sociology, seventh edn (London: Kegan Paul, 1878) [1873]
The Data of Ethics (London: Williams and Norgate, 1879)
The Principles of Sociology, abridged, ed. S. Andreski (London: Macmillan, 1969) [1876–96]
The Man Versus the State, with Four Essays on Politics and Society, ed. D. Macrae (Harmondsworth: Penguin, 1969) [1884]
'Réponse à M. Laveleye', in Laveleye, *Le Socialisme contemporaine*
The Inadequacy of Natural Selection (London: Williams and Norgate, 1893)
Facts and Comments (London: Williams and Norgate, 1902)
An Autobiography, 2 vols. (London: Williams and Norgate, 1904)

Education: Intellectual, Moral and Physical (London: Williams and Norgate, 1906)

Herbert Spencer: Political Writings, ed. J. Offer (Cambridge University Press, 1994)

Spiess, Camille. *Impérialismes: la conception gobinienne de la race. Sa valeur au point du vue bio-psychologique* (Paris: Eugène Figuière, 1917)

Stephen, Leslie. *The Science of Ethics* (London: Murray, 1907) [1882]

'Ethics and the Struggle for Existence', *Contemporary Review*, 64(1893), 157–70

Stoddard, Lothrop. *The Revolt Against Civilisation: The Menace of the Underman* (London: Chapman and Hall, 1922)

Sumner, William Graham. *What Social Classes Owe to Each Other* (New York: Harper, 1883)

Collected Essays in Political and Social Science (New York: Henry Holt, 1885)

Folkways: A Study of the Sociological Importance of Usages, Manners, Customs, Mores and Morals (Boston: Ginn, 1906)

Social Darwinism: Selected Essays of William Graham Sumner, ed. Stow Persons (Englewood Cliffs, NJ: Prentice-Hall, 1963)

Thomas, W. I. 'The Adventitious Character of Woman', *American Journal of Sociology*, 12(1906–7), 32–44

'The Mind of Woman and the Lower Races', *American Journal of Sociology*, 12(1906–7), 435–69

Thomson, J. Arthur. *Heredity* (London: Murray, 1908)

Treitschke, Heinrich von. *Politics*, 2 vols., tr. B. Dugdale and T. de Bille (London: Constable, 1916) [1896]

Trotter, W. *Instincts of the Herd in Peace and War* (London: T. Fisher Unwin, 1916)

Tylor, Edward B. *Anthropology: An Introduction to the Study of Man and Civilization* (London: Macmillan, 1892)

Valois, Georges. *L'Homme qui vient: philosophie de l'autorité*, second edn (Paris: Nouvelle Librairie Nationale, 1909) [1906]

Veblen, Thorstein. *The Portable Veblen*, ed. Max Lerner (New York: Viking, 1948)

Wallace, Alfred Russel. 'The Origin of Human Races and the Antiquity of Man Deduced from the Theory of "Natural Selection"', in Biddiss, ed., *Images of Race* [1864]

Wallas, Graham. 'Property Under Socialism', in Shaw, ed., *Fabian Essays*, 123–39

Human Nature in Politics, third edn (London: Constable, 1927) [1908]

The Great Society (New York: Macmillan, 1920) [1914]

Men and Ideas (London: Allen and Unwin, 1940)

Ward, Lester Frank. 'Mind as a Social Factor', in Hollinger and Capper, eds., *The American Intellectual Tradition*, II, 40–7 [1884]

Pure Sociology: A Treatise on the Origin and Spontaneous Development of Society (New York: Macmillan, 1903)

Webb, Sydney. 'Historic', in Shaw, ed., *Fabian Essays*, 28–57

Weber, Jean. 'Les Théories biologiques de. M. René Quinton', *Revue de métaphysique et de morale*, 13(1905), 114–41

Weber, Max. *From Max Weber: Essays in Sociology*, tr. H. Gerth and C. Wright Mills (London: Routledge and Kegan Paul, 1948)
   The Methodology of the Social Sciences, tr. E. A. Shils and H. A. Finch (New York: The Free Press, 1949)
   The Agrarian Sociology of Ancient Civilizations, tr. R. I. Frank (London: NLB, 1976)
   'The Nation State and Economic Policy', in P. Lassman and R. Spiers, eds., *Weber: Political Writings* (Cambridge University Press, 1994)
Wells, D. Colin. 'Social Darwinism', *The American Journal of Sociology*, 12(1907), 695–708
Westermarck, Edward. *The History of Human Marriage* (London/New York: Macmillan, 1891)
Woltmann, Ludwig. *Die Darwinische Theorie und der Sozialismus: Ein Beitrag zur Naturgesichte der Menschlichen Gesellschaft* (Düsseldorf: Michels, 1899)
Woodhull, Victoria C. *The Origin, Tendencies and Principles of Government or a Review of the Rise and Fall of Nations* (New York: Woodhull, Claflin, 1871)
   Humanitarian Government (London: no publisher, 1890)
   The Rapid Multiplication of the Unfit (London/New York: no publisher, 1891)
Wyatt, H. F. 'God's Test By War', *The Nineteenth Century and After*, 69(1911), 591–606

SOURCES PUBLISHED AFTER 1945

Adams, James Eli. 'Woman Red in Tooth and Claw: Nature and the Feminine in Tennyson and Darwin', *Victorian Studies*, 33(1989), 7–27
Adams, Mark, ed. *The Wellborn Science: Eugenics in Germany, France, Brazil and Russia* (New York: Oxford University Press, 1990)
Alaya, F. J. 'Victorian Science and the "Genius" of Woman, *Journal of the History of Ideas*, 38(1977), 261–80
Alaya, F. J. and T. Dobzhansky, eds. *Studies in the Philosophy of Biology* (London: Macmillan, 1974)
Anderson, Stuart. *Race and Rapprochement: Anglo-Saxonism and Anglo-American Relations, 1895–1904* (London: Associated University Press, 1981)
Annan, Noel. *Leslie Stephen: The Godless Victorian*, revised edn (London: Weidenfeld and Nicolson, 1984)
Ardrey, Robert. *The Territorial Imperative* (London: Collins, 1967)
Arendt, Hannah. *On Revolution* (Harmondsworth: Penguin, 1973)
   The Origins of Totalitarianism (London: André Deutsch, 1986)
Aschheim, Steven E. 'Max Nordau, Friedrich Nietzsche and *Degeneration*', *Journal of Contemporary History*, 28(1993), 643–57
Badcock, Christopher. *Psycho-Darwinism* (London: HarperCollins, 1994)
Ball, Terence and Richard Dagger. *Political Ideologies and the Democratic Ideal* (New York: HarperCollins, 1991)
Bannister, Richard C. 'The Survival of the Fittest is our Doctrine: History or Histrionics?', *Journal of the History of Ideas*, 31(1970), 377–98
   'William Graham Sumner's Social Darwinism: A Reconsideration', *History of Political Economy*, 4(1973), 89–109

Social Darwinism: Science and Myth in Anglo-American Social Thought (Philadelphia: Temple University Press, 1979)

Banton, Michael, ed. *Darwinism and the Study of Society: A Centenary Symposium* (London: Tavistock, 1961)

Barnes, Harry Elmer. 'William Graham Sumner: Spencerianism in American Dress', in Barnes, ed., *An Introduction to the History of Sociology* (London: University of Chicago Press, 1966), 391–408

Barnett, S. A., ed. *A Century of Darwin* (London: Mercury, 1962)

Bartov, Omer. *The Eastern Front, 1941–45: German Troops and the Barbarisation of Warfare* (London: Macmillan, 1985)

Bellamy, Richard. *Liberalism and Modern Society* (Cambridge: Polity Press, 1992)

Bellomy, Donald C. ' "Social Darwinism" Revisited', *Perspectives in American History*, new series, 1(1984), 1–129

Benn, Sir Ernest. *The State the Enemy* (London: Benn, 1953)

Benton, Ted. 'Social Darwinism and Socialist Darwinism in Germany: 1860–1900', *Rivista di filosofia*, 73(1982), 79–121

Berghe, Pierre L. van den. 'Incest Taboos and Avoidance: Some African Applications', in Crawford *et al.*, eds., *Sociobiology and Psychology*, 353–71

Berlin, I. *Against the Current: Essays in the History of Ideas* (Oxford University Press, 1981)

Biddiss, Michael, ed. *Gobineau: Selected Political Writings* (London: Jonathan Cape, 1970)

Images of Race (Leicester University Press, 1979)

Billig, Michael. *Arguing and Thinking: A Rhetorical Approach to Social Psychology* (Cambridge University Press, 1987)

Billig, Michael, Susan Condon, Derek Edwards, Mike Gane, David Middleton and Alan Radley. *Ideological Dilemmas: A Social Psychology of Everyday Thinking* (London: Sage, 1988)

Birke, Lynda. *Women, Feminism and Biology: The Feminist Challenge* (Brighton: Harvester, 1986)

Blodgett, G. 'Victoria Woodhull', *Notable American Women 1607–1950: A Biographical Dictionary,* vol. III (Cambridge, MA: Belknap Press, 1971)

Bock, Kenneth E. 'Darwin and Social Theory', *Philosophy of Science*, 22(1955), 123–34

'Theories of Progress, Development, Evolution', in Bottomore and Nisbet, eds., *A History of Sociological Analysis*, 39–79

Boesiger, Ernest. 'Evolutionary Theories After Lamarck and Darwin', in Alaya and Dobzhansky, eds., *Studies in the Philosophy of Biology*, 21–44

'Evolutionary Biology in France at the Time of the Evolutionary Synthesis', in Mayr and Provine, eds., *The Evolutionary Synthesis*

Bond, Brian and Ian Roy, eds. *War and Society* (London: Croom Helm, 1975)

Boring, Edwin G. *A History of Experimental Psychology*, second edn (New York: Appleton-Century-Crofts, 1950)

Bottomore, Tom and Robert A. Nisbet. 'Structuralism', in Bottomore and Nisbet, eds., *A History of Sociological Analysis*, 557–98

Bottomore, Tom and Robert A. Nisbet, eds. *A History of Sociological Analysis* (London: Heinemann, 1979)

Boucher, David. 'Evolution and Politics: The Naturalistic, Ethical and Spiritual Bases of Evolutionary Arguments', *Australian Journal of Political Science*, 27(1992), 87–103

Bowler, Peter J. 'The Changing Meaning of Evolution', *Journal of the History of Ideas*, 36(1975), 95–114

'Malthus, Darwin, and the Concept of Struggle', *Journal of the History of Ideas*, 37(1976), 631–50

The Eclipse of Darwin: Anti-Darwinian Evolution Theories in the Decades Around 1900 (Baltimore: Johns Hopkins University Press, 1983)

Evolution: The History of an Idea (Berkeley: University of California Press, 1984)

Theories of Human Evolution: A Century of Debate, 1844–1944 (Oxford: Blackwell, 1986)

The Invention of Progress: The Victorians and the Past (Oxford: Blackwell, 1989)

Bristow, Edward. 'The Liberty and Property Defence League and Individualism', *The Historical Journal*, 18(1975), 761–89

Bronowski, J. 'Introduction', in Banton, ed., *Darwinism and the Study of Society*

Burkhardt, Richard W. Jr. 'Lamarckism in Britain and the United States', in Mayr and Provine, eds., *The Evolutionary Synthesis*

'Darwin on Animal Behaviour and Evolution', in Kohn, ed., *The Darwinian Heritage*, 327–65

Burleigh, Michael and Wolfgang Wippermann. *The Racial State: Germany 1933–1945* (Cambridge University Press, 1991)

Burrow, J. W. *Evolution and Society: A Study in Victorian Social Theory* (Cambridge University Press, 1966)

'Introduction' in Darwin, *On the Origin of Species*

'Social Darwinism', in D. Miller *et al.*, eds., *The Blackwell Encyclopaedia of Political Thought* (Oxford: Blackwell, 1987)

Caine, B. *Victorian Feminists* (Oxford University Press, 1992)

Canguilhem, Georges. *Etudes d'histoire et philosophie des sciences*, second edn (Paris: Vrin, 1970)

Carey, John. *The Intellectuals and the Masses: Pride and Prejudice Among the Literary Intelligentsia, 1880–1939* (London: Faber and Faber, 1992)

Catanzaro, Denys de. 'Evolutionary Pressures and Limitations to Self-Preservation', in Crawford *et al.*, eds., *Sociobiology and Psychology*, 311–33

Chamberlin, J. Edward and Sander L. Gilman, eds. *Degeneration: The Dark Side of Progress* (New York: Columbia University Press, 1985)

Chase, Allan. *The Legacy of Malthus* (New York: Knopf, 1980)

Chickering, Roger. *We Men Who Feel Most German: A Cultural Study of the Pan-German League, 1886–1914* (London: Allen and Unwin, 1984)

Clark, Linda. *Social Darwinism in France* (University of Alabama Press, 1984)

'Le Darwinisme social en France', *La Recherche*, 19(1988), 192–200

Clements, Harry. *Alfred Russel Wallace: Biologist and Social Reformer* (London: Hutchinson, 1983)

Collinson, Susan. 'Robert Knox Anatomy of Race', *History Today*, 40(1990), 44–9

Colombat, Jean. *La Fin du monde civilisé: les prophéties de Vacher de Lapouge* (Paris: Vrin, 1946)

Conry, Yvette. *L'Introduction du darwinisme en France au dix-neuvième siècle* (Paris: Vrin, 1974)

Conway, J. 'Stereotypes of Femininity in a Theory of Sexual Evolution', *Victorian Studies*, 14(1970–1), 47–62

Coren, Michael. *The Invisible Man: The Life and Liberties of H. G. Wells* (London: Bloomsbury, 1993)

Corsi, Pietro and Paul J. Weindling, 'Darwinism in Germany, France and Italy', in Kohn, ed., *The Darwinian Heritage*, 683–729

Coser, Lewis. 'American Trends' in Bottomore and Nisbet, eds., *A History of Sociological Analysis*, 287–320

Crawford, Charles. 'Sociobiology: Of What Value to Psychology?', in Crawford *et al.*, eds., *Sociobiology and Psychology*, 3–30

Crawford, Charles, Martin Smith and Dennis Krebs, eds. *Sociobiology and Psychology: Ideas, Issues and Applications* (London/New Jersey: Lawrence Erlbaum Associates, 1987)

Croce, P. J. 'William James' Scientific Education', *History of the Human Sciences*, 8(1995), 9–27

Crook, D. P. 'Darwinism: The Political Implications', *History of European Ideas*, 2(1981), 19–34
  Benjamin Kidd: Portrait of a Social Darwinist (Cambridge University Press, 1984)
  Darwinism, War and History (Cambridge University Press, 1994)

Da Cal, E. U. 'The Influence of Animal Breeding on Political Racism', *History of European Ideas*, 15(1992), 717–25

Daly, Martin and Margo Wilson. 'Evolutionary Psychology and Family Violence', in Crawford *et al.*, eds., *Sociobiology and Psychology*, 293–309

Dawkins, Richard. *The Selfish Gene*, second edn (Oxford University Press, 1989)

Degler, Carl. *In Search of Human Nature* (Oxford University Press, 1991)

Delzell, Charles F., ed. *Mediterranean Fascism, 1919–1945: Selected Documents* (London: Macmillan, 1970)

Dempster, W. J. *Patrick Matthew and Natural Selection* (Edinburgh: Paul Harris, 1983)

Desmond, Adrian. *The Politics of Evolution: Morphology, Medicine and Reform in Radical London* (London: University of Chicago Press, 1989)
  Huxley: The Devil's Disciple (London: Michael Joseph, 1994)

Desmond, Adrian and James Moore. *Darwin* (London: Faber and Faber, 1991)

Diamond, Jared. *The Rise and Fall of the Third Chimpanzee: How Our Animal Heritage Affects the Way We Live* (London: Vintage, 1992)

Dicks, Henry V. *Licensed Mass Murder: A Socio-Psychological Study of Some SS Killers* (London: Heinemann, 1972)

Di Gregorio, Mario A. *T. H. Huxley's Place in Natural Science* (New Haven/London: Yale University Press, 1984)

Dobzhansky, T. 'Species After Darwin', in Barnett, ed., *A Century of Darwin*, 19–55

Donzelot, J. *The Policing of Families* (London: Hutchinson, 1980)

Eatwell, Roger. *Fascism: A History* (London: Chatto and Windus, 1995)

Eley, Geoff. *Reshaping the German Right: Radical Nationalism and Political Change After Bismarck* (London: Yale University Press, 1980)

Evans, Richard J. *The Feminists: Women's Emancipation Movements in Europe, America and Australasia, 1840–1920* (London: Croom Helm, 1977)
    Rethinking German History: Nineteenth Century Germany and the Origins of the Third Reich (London: HarperCollins, 1987)
Faye, J.-P. *Langages totalitaires* (Paris: Hermann, 1973)
Feldman, J. 'Population and Ideology', *History of Political Thought*, 5(1984), 361–75
Field, Geoffrey G. *Evangelist of Race: The Germanic Vision of Houston Stewart Chamberlain* (New York: Columbia University Press, 1981)
Fishman, William J. *East End Jewish Radicalism, 1875–1914* (London: Duckworth, 1995)
Flew, Anthony. *Darwinian Evolution* (London: Paladin, 1984)
Florence, M. S., C. Marshall and C. K. Ogden. *Militarism Versus Feminism*, ed. M. Kemester and J. Vellacott (London: Virago, 1987)
Foot, M. R. D., ed. *War and Society: Historical Essays in Honour and Memory of J. R. Western, 1928–71* (London: Eleck, 1973)
Foucault, Michel. *Discipline and Punish: The Birth of the Prison*, tr. A. Sheridan (Harmondsworth: Penguin, 1977)
Fraser, D. *The Evolution of the British Welfare State* (London: Macmillan, 1973)
Freeman, Derek. 'The Evolutionary Theories of Charles Darwin and Herbert Spencer', *Current Anthropology*, 15(1974), 211–37
Futuyma, Douglas J. *Evolutionary Biology* (Sunderland, MA: Sinauer Associates, 1979)
Gale, Barry G. 'Darwin and the Concept of a Struggle for Existence: A Study in the Extrascientific Origins of Scientific Ideas', *Isis*, 63(1972), 321–44
Gasman, Daniel. *The Scientific Origins of National Socialism: Social Darwinism in Ernst Haeckel and the German Monist League* (London: Macdonald, 1970)
Ghiselin, Michael. *The Triumph of the Darwinian Method*, second edn (London: University of Chicago Press, 1984)
Gibson, Mary. 'On the Insensitivity of Women: Science and the Woman Question in Liberal Italy, 1890–1910', *Journal of Women's History*, 2(1990), 11–41
Gilbert, Felix. *The End of the European Era, 1890 to the Present*, third edn (London: Norton, 1984)
Giles, Geoffrey J. ' "The Unkindest Cut of All": Castration, Homosexuality and Nazi Justice', *Journal of Contemporary History*, 27(1992), 41–61
Glick, Thomas F., ed. *The Comparative Reception of Darwinism*, second edn (University of Chicago Press, 1988)
Gooch, John. 'Attitudes to War in Late Victorian and Edwardian England', in Bond and Roy, eds., *War and Society*, 88–102
Gould, Stephen Jay. *Ever Since Darwin: Reflections on Natural History* (Harmondsworth: Penguin, 1980)
    The Mismeasure of Man (Harmondsworth: Penguin, 1992) [1981]
    An Urchin in the Storm (Harmondsworth: Penguin, 1990)
Gray, T. S. 'Herbert Spencer: Individualist or Organicist?', *Political Studies*, 33(1985), 236–53
Greene, John C. *Darwin and the Modern World View* (Baton Rouge, LA: Mentor, 1963)

Science, Ideology and World View: Essays in the History of Evolutionary Ideas (Berkeley, CA: University of California Press, 1981)

Griffin, Roger, ed. *Fascism* (Oxford University Press, 1995)

Gruber, H. E. *Darwin on Man* (New York: Dutton, 1974)

Guchet, Yves. *Georges Valois: L'Action Française, le Faisceau, la République syndicale* (Paris: Edition Albatros, 1975)

Haller, John S. Jr. *Outcasts From Evolution: Scientific Attitudes of Racial Inferiority, 1859–1900* (New York: McGraw-Hill, 1971)

Haller, Mark H. *Eugenics: Hereditarian Attitudes in American Thought* (New Brunswick, NJ: Rutgers University Press, 1984)

Halliday, R. J. 'Social Darwinism: A Definition', *Victorian Studies*, 14(1971), 389–405

Hardin, Garrett. *Biology: Its Human Implications* (San Francisco: W. H. Freeman, 1949)

Harvey, Joy. ' "Doubly Revolutionary": Clémence Royer Before the Société d'Anthropologie de Paris', *Proceedings of the Sixteenth International Congress For the History of Science*, Symposium B (1981), 250–7

'Evolutionism Transformed: Positivists and Materialists in the *Société d'Anthropologie de Paris* from Second Empire to Third Republic', in Oldroyd and Langham, eds., *The Wider Domain of Evolutionary Thought*, 289–310

' "Strangers to Each Other": Male and Female Relationships in the Life and Work of Clémence Royer', in Pnina G. Abir-Am and Dorinda Outra, eds., *Uneasy Careers and Intimate Lives* (New Brunswick, NJ: Rutgers University Press, 1987), 147–71

Hauner, Milan L. 'A German Racial Revolution?', *Journal of Contemporary History*, 19(1984), 669–87

Hawkins, M. J. 'A Re-examination of Durkheim's Theory of Human Nature', *Sociological Review*, 25(1977), 229–52

'Comte, Durkheim, and the Sociology of Primitive Religion', *Sociological Review*, 27(1979), 429–46

'Comte's Theory of Mental Development', *Revue européenne des sciences sociales*, 22(1984), 71–90

'Reason and Sense Perception in Comte's Theory of Mind', *History of European Ideas*, 5(1984), 149–63

'The Struggle for Existence in Nineteenth Century Social Theory: Three Case Studies', *History of the Human Sciences*, 8(1995), 47–67

'Durkheim, the Division of Labour, and Social Darwinism', *History of European Ideas*, 22(1996), 19–31

Hayward, J. E. S. 'Solidarity: The Social History of an Idea in Nineteenth Century France', *International Review of Social History*, 4(1959), 261–84

'The Official Social Philosophy of the French Third Republic: Léon Bourgeois and Solidarism', *International Review of Social History*, 6(1961), 19–48

Helfand, Michael S. 'T. H. Huxley's "Evolution and Ethics": The Politics of Evolution and the Evolution of Politics', *Victorian Studies*, 20 (1977), 159–77

Herbert, Sandra. 'Darwin, Malthus and Selection', *Journal of the History of Biology*, 4(1971), 209–17

Himmelfarb, Gertrude. *Darwin and the Darwinian Revolution* (New York: Norton, 1962)

The Idea of Poverty: England in the Early Industrial Age (London: Faber and Faber, 1984)

Hirst, Paul Q. *Social Evolution and Sociological Categories* (London: Allen and Unwin, 1976)

Hofstadter, Richard. *Social Darwinism in American Thought 1860–1915*, revised edn (Boston: Beacon Press, 1955) [1944]

Hollinger, D. and C. Capper, eds. *The American Intellectual Tradition*, vol. II: *1865 to the Present*, second edn (New York: Oxford University Press, 1993)

Hughes, H. Stuart. *Consciousness and Society: The Reorientation of European Social Thought, 1890–1930* (St Albans: Paladin, 1974)

Hull, David. *Darwin and His Critics: The Reception of Darwin's Theory of Evolution in the Scientific Community* (Cambridge, MA: Harvard University Press, 1973)

'Darwinism as a Historical Entity: A Historiographic Proposal', in Kohn, ed., *The Darwinian Heritage*, 773–812

Jacob, François. *The Logic of Living Systems: A History of Heredity*, tr. B. E. Spillman (London: Allen Lane, 1974)

Jann, R. 'Darwin and the Anthropologists: Sexual Selection and Its Discontents', *Victorian Studies*, 37(1994), 287–306

Joll, James. *Europe After 1870* (Harmondsworth: Penguin, 1983)

Jones, Greta. 'The Social History of Darwin's *The Descent of Man*', *Economy and Society*, 7(1978), 1–23

Social Darwinism and English Thought: The Interaction Between Biological and Social Theory (Brighton: Harvester Press, 1980)

Social Hygiene in Twentieth Century Britain (London: Croom Helm, 1986)

Jordanova, L. J. *Lamarck* (Oxford University Press, 1984)

Keller, Evelyn Fox. 'Language and Ideology in Evolutionary Theory: Reading Cultural Norms into Natural Law', in James J. Sheehan and Martin Sosna, eds., *The Boundaries of Humanity: Humans, Animals, Machines* (Oxford: University of California Press, 1991), 85–102

Kelly, Alfred. *The Descent of Darwin: The Popularization of Darwin in Germany, 1860–1914* (Chapel Hill: University of North Carolina Press, 1981)

Kershaw, Ian. *The Nazi Dictatorship: Problems and Perspectives of Interpretation*, second edn (London: Edward Arnold, 1989)

Kevles, Daniel J. *In the Name of Eugenics: Genetics and the Uses of Human Heredity* (Harmondsworth: Penguin, 1986)

Kiernan, V. G. 'Conscription and Society in Europe before the War of 1914–18', in Foot, ed., *War and Society*, 141–58

Koch, H. W. 'Social Darwinism as a Factor in the "New Imperialism"' in Koch, ed., *The Origins of the First World War*, second edn (London: Macmillan, 1984), 319–42

Kohn, David, ed. *The Darwinian Heritage* (Princeton University Press, 1985)

Konner, Melvin. 'Human Nature and Culture: Biology and the Residue of Uniqueness', in Sheehan and Sosna, eds., *The Boundaries of Humanity*, 103–24

Korey, Kenneth, ed. *The Essential Darwin* (Boston: Little, Brown, 1984)

Krausnick, Helmut and Martin Broszat. *Anatomy of the SS State*, tr. D. Long and M. Jackson (London: Granada, 1970)

Kremer-Marietti, Angèle. *Le Projet anthropologique d'Auguste Comte* (Paris: Société d'Edition d'Enseignement Supérieur, 1980)

Kühl, Stefan. *The Nazi Connection: Eugenics, American Racism and National Socialism* (New York/Oxford: Oxford University Press, 1994)

Kuper, Adam. *The Chosen Primate: Human Nature and Cultural Diversity* (London/Cambridge, MA: Harvard University Press, 1994)

Kushner, Howard L. 'Suicide, Gender, and the Fear of Modernity in Nineteenth-Century Medical and Social Thought', *Journal of Social History*, 26(1993), 461–90

Lane, Barbara Miller and Linda Rupp, eds. *Nazi Ideology Before 1933: A Documentation* (Manchester University Press, 1978)

Laqueur, Walter, ed. *Fascism: A Reader's Guide* (Harmondsworth: Penguin, 1976)

Leeds, Anthony. 'Darwinian and "Darwinian" Evolutionism in the Study of Society and Culture', in Glick, ed., *The Comparative Reception of Darwinism*, 437–77

Lerner, Richard. *Final Solutions: Biology, Prejudice, and Genocide* (Pennsylvania State University Press, 1992)

Lewontin, R. C. *The Doctrine of DNA: Biology as Ideology* (Harmondsworth: Penguin, 1993)

Limoges, Camille. 'A Second Glance at Evolutionary Biology in France', in Mayr and Provine, eds., *The Evolutionary Synthesis*

Lopreato, Joseph. *Human Nature and Bio-Cultural Evolution* (Boston: Allen and Unwin, 1984)

Lorimer, Douglas A. *Colour, Class and the Victorians: English Attitudes to the Negro in the Mid-Nineteenth Century* (Leicester University Press, 1978)

 'Theoretical Racism in Late-Victorian Anthropology, 1879–1914', *Victorian Studies*, 31(1988), 405–30

Love, Rosaleen. 'Darwinism and Feminism: The "Woman Question" in the Life and Work of Olive Schreiner and Charlotte Perkins Gilman', in Oldroyd and Langham, eds., *The Wider Domain of Evolutionary Thought*, 113–31

Lumsden, C. J. and E. O. Wilson, *Genes, Mind and Culture: The Coevolutionary Process* (Cambridge, MA: Harvard University Press, 1981)

Lyttleton, Adrian, ed. *Italian Fascisms From Pareto to Gentile*, tr. D. Parmée (London: Jonathan Cape, 1973)

MacIntyre, Alasdair. *A Short History of Ethics: A History of Moral Philosophy from the Homeric Age to the Twentieth Century* (London: Routledge, 1967)

McClelland, J. S., ed. *The French Right from de Maistre to Maurras* (London: Jonathan Cape, 1979)

Mayr, Ernst. 'Prologue: Some Thoughts on the Evolutionary Synthesis', in Mayr and Provine, eds., *The Evolutionary Synthesis*

 'Darwin's Five Theories of Evolution', in Kohn, ed., *The Darwinian Heritage*, 755–72

 One Long Argument: Charles Darwin and the Genesis of Modern Evolutionary Thought (Harmondsworth: Penguin, 1992)

Mayr, Ernst and W. B. Provine, eds. *The Evolutionary Synthesis: Perspectives on the Unification of Biology* (Cambridge, MA: Harvard University Press, 1980)

Mazumdar, Pauline M. H. *Eugenics, Human Genetics and Human Failures: The Eugenics Society, its Sources and its Critics in Britain* (London: Routledge, 1992)

Meek, Ronald L. *Social Science and the Ignoble Savage* (Cambridge University Press, 1976)

Metz, K. H. 'The Politics of Conflict: Heinrich von Treitschke and the Idea of *Realpolitik*', *History of Political Thought*, 3(1982), 269–84

Michaelis, Meir. *Mussolini and the Jews* (Oxford: Clarendon Press, 1978)

Miller, William L. 'Herbert Spencer's Theory of Welfare and Public Policy', *History of Political Economy*, 4(1972), 207–31

Milza, Pierre. *Les Fascismes* (Paris: Imprimerie Nationale, 1985)

Montgomery, William H. 'Germany', in Glick, ed., *The Comparative Reception of Darwinism*, 81–106

Moore, James R. 'Varieties of Social Darwinism', Open University Course A309, *Conflict and Stability in the Development of Modern Europe c.1789–1970*, Block II (Milton Keynes: Open University Press, 1980)

Moore, James R., ed. *History, Humanity and Evolution: Essays for John C. Greene* (Cambridge University Press, 1990)

Mosse, George L. *The Crisis of German Ideology: Intellectual Origins of the Third Reich* (New York: Shocken, 1981)

Murray, Charles and Richard J. Hernnstein. *The Bell Curve: Intelligence and Class Structure in American Life* (New York: Free Press, 1994)

Myers, Greg. 'Nineteenth Century Popularizations of Thermodynamics and the Rhetoric of Social Prophesy', *Victorian Studies*, 29(1985), 35–66

Nash, Mary. 'Social Eugenics and Nationalist Race Hygiene in Early Twentieth Century Spain', *History of European Ideas* 15(1992), 741–8

Nisbet, Robert A. *Social Change and History: Aspects of the Western Theory of Development* (Oxford University Press, 1969)

Noakes, J. and G. Pridham, eds. *Nazism 1919–1945: A Documentary Reader*, 3 vols. (University of Exeter, 1983–8)

Nye, Robert A. 'Sociology and Degeneration: The Irony of Progress', in Chamberlin and Gilman, eds., *Degeneration*, 49–71

Oldroyd, D. R. *Darwinian Impacts: An Introduction to the Darwinian Revolution*, second edn (Milton Keynes: Open University Press, 1983)

Oldroyd, D. R. and I. Langham, eds. *The Wider Domain of Evolutionary Thought* (Boston, MA: Reidel, 1983)

Ospovat, Dov. 'God and Natural Selection: The Darwinian Idea of Design', *Journal of the History of Biology*, 13(1980), 169–94
  The Development of Darwin's Theory: Natural History, Natural Theology and Natural Selection, 1838–1859 (Cambridge University Press, 1981)

Passmore, John. *A Hundred Years of Philosophy*, second edn (Harmondsworth: Penguin, 1968)

Paul, Ellen Frankel. 'Herbert Spencer: The Historicist as Failed Prophet', *Journal of the History of Ideas*, 44(1983), 619–38
  'Liberalism, Unintended Orders, and Evolutionism', *Political Studies*, 36(1988), 251–72
  'Herbert Spencer – Second Thoughts: A Reply to Michael Taylor', *Political Studies*, 37(1989), 445–8

Peel, J. D. Y. *Herbert Spencer: The Evolution of a Sociologist* (London: Heinemann, 1971)

Pfeifer, Edward J. 'The United States', in Glick, ed., *The Comparative Reception of Darwinism*, 168–206

Pick, Daniel. *Faces of Degeneration: A European Disorder, c.1848–c.1918* (Cambridge University Press, 1989)

  War Machine: The Rationalisation of Slaughter in the Modern Age (London: Yale University Press, 1993)

Plant, R. *The Pink Triangle: The Nazi War Against Homosexuals* (Edinburgh: Mainstream, 1987)

Pocock, J. G. A. *Politics, Language and Time* (London: Methuen, 1972)

  The Machiavellian Moment: Florentine Political Thought and the Atlantic Political Tradition (Princeton University Press, 1975)

Popper, Karl. 'Darwinism as a Metaphysical Research Programme', in P. A. Schlipp, ed., *The Philosophy of Karl Popper* (La Salle, IL: Open Court, 1974)

Pois, Robert A. *National Socialism and the Religion of Nature* (London: Croom Helm, 1986)

Porter, Dorothy. ' "Enemies of the Race": Biologism, Environmentalism and Public Health in Edwardian England', *Victorian Studies*, 34(1991), 160–78

Qualter, Terence H. *Graham Wallas and the Great Society* (London: Macmillan, 1980)

Raphael, D. Daiches. 'Darwinism and Ethics', in Barnett, ed., *A Century of Darwin*, 334–59

Richards, Evelleen. 'Darwin and the Descent of Woman', in Oldroyd and Langham, eds., *The Wider Domain of Evolutionary Thought*, 57–111

Ridley, Matt. *The Red Queen: Sex and the Evolution of Human Nature* (Harmondsworth: Penguin, 1994)

Robertson, E. M. 'Race as a Factor in Mussolini's Policy in Africa and Europe', *Journal of Contemporary History*, 23(1988), 37–58

Rogers, James Allen. 'Darwinism and Social Darwinism', *Journal of the History of Ideas*, 33(1972), 265–80

Rorty, Richard. *Contingency, Irony and Solidarity* (Cambridge University Press, 1989)

Rose, Nikolas. *The Psychological Complex: Psychology, Politics and Society in England, 1869–1939* (London: Routledge and Kegan Paul, 1985)

Rose, Steven, R. C. Lewontin and L. J. Kamin. *Not in our Genes: Biology, Ideology and Nature* (Harmondsworth: Penguin 1990)

Runkle, Gerald. 'Marxism and Charles Darwin', *Journal of Politics*, 23(1961), 108–26

Ruse, Michael. *Darwinism Defended: A Guide to the Evolution Controversies* (Reading, MA: Addison-Wesley, 1982)

  'Sociobiology and Knowledge', in Crawford *et al.*, eds., *Sociobiology and Psychology*, 61–79

  The Darwinian Paradigm: Essays on its History, Philosophy and Religious Implications (London: Routledge, 1989)

Russett, Cynthia Eagle. *Sexual Science: The Victorian Construction of Womanhood* (Cambridge, MA: Harvard University Press, 1989)

Sahlins, Marshall. *The Use and Abuse of Biology: An Anthropological Critique of Sociobiology* (London: Tavistock, 1976)

Schneider, William H. *Quality and Quantity: The Quest For Biological Regeneration in Twentieth Century France* (Cambridge University Press, 1990)

Schweber, Sylvan S. 'The Origin of the *Origin* Revisited', *Journal of the History of Biology*, 10(1977), 219–316

'Darwin and the Political Economists: Divergence of Character', *Journal of the History of Biology*, 13(1980), 195–289

Scott, John A. *Republican Ideas and the Liberal Tradition in France 1870–1914* (New York: Octagon Books, 1966) [1951]

Searle, G. R. *Eugenics and Politics in Britain, 1900–1914* (Leyden: Noordhoff International Publishing, 1976)

'Eugenics and Class', in Webster, ed., *Biology, Medicine and Society*, 217–42

Semmel, B. *Imperialism and Social Reform: English Social-Imperial Thought, 1895–1914* (London: Allen and Unwin, 1960)

Shaw, C. 'Eliminating the Yahoo: Eugenics, Social Darwinism and Five Fabians', *History of Political Thought*, 8(1987), 521–44

Silverman, Irwin. 'Race, Race Differences and Race Relations: Perspectives from Psychology and Sociobiology', in Crawford *et al.*, eds., *Sociobiology and Psychology*, 205–21

Simon, W. M. 'Herbert Spencer and the "Social Organism"', *Journal of the History of Ideas*, 21(1960), 294–9

Smith, Anthony D. *The Concept of Social Change* (London: Routledge and Kegan Paul, 1973)

Smith, C. U. M. 'Evolution and the Problem of Mind: Part I. Herbert Spencer', *Journal of the History of Biology*, 15(1982), 55–88

Smith, John Maynard. 'Sexual Selection', in Barnett, ed., *A Century of Darwin*, 231–44

The Theory of Evolution, third edn (Harmondsworth: Penguin, 1975)

Did Darwin Get it Right? Essays on Games, Sex and Evolution (Harmondsworth: Penguin, 1993)

Smith, Woodruff D. *Politics and the Science of Culture in Germany, 1840–1920* (Oxford University Press, 1991)

Sober, Elliott. *The Nature of Selection: Evolutionary Theory in Philosophical Focus* (Cambridge, MA: MIT Press, 1985)

Sodi, Risa. 'The Italian Roots of Racialism', *UCLA Historical Journal*, 8(1987), 40–70

Soloway, Richard A. *Demography and Degeneration: Eugenics and the Declining Birthrate in Twentieth Century Britain* (London: University of North Carolina Press, 1989)

Stackelberg, Roderick. *Idealism Debased: From Völkish Ideology to National Socialism* (Ohio: Kent University Press, 1981)

Stark, W. 'Natural and Social Selection', in Banton, ed., *Darwinism and the Study of Society*, 49–61

Stebbins, Robert E. 'France', in Glick, ed., *The Comparative Reception of Darwinism*, 117–67

Stein, G. J. 'Biological Science and the Roots of Nazism', *American Scientist*, 76(1988), 50–8

Stepan, Nancy Leys. 'Race, Gender and Nation in Argentina: The Influence of Italian Eugenics', *History of European Ideas*, 15(1992), 749–56

Sternhell, Zeev. *Maurice Barrès et le nationalisme français* (Brussels: Editions Complexe, 1985) [1972]

'Fascist Ideology', in Laqueur, ed., *Fascism*

La Droite révolutionnaire 1885–1914. Les Origines françaises du fascisme (Paris: Editions du Seuil, 1978)

Ni droite ni gauche: l'idéologie fasciste en France (Paris: Editions du Seuil, 1983)

Sternhell, Zeev, Mario Sznajder and Maria Asheri. *Naissance de l'idéologie fasciste* (Paris: Fayard, 1989)

Strawbridge, Sheelagh. 'Darwin and Victorian Social Values', in Eric M. Sigsworth, ed. *In Search of Victorian Social Values* (Manchester University Press, 1988), 102–15

Sulloway, Frank J. *Freud, Biologist of the Mind: Beyond the Psychoanalytic Legend* (London: Fontana, 1980)

Taguieff, Pierre André. 'La Métaphysique de Jean-Marie Le Pen', in N. Mayer and P. Perrineau, eds., *Le Front National à decouvert* (Paris: Presses de la Fondation Nationale des Sciences Politiques, 1989), 173–94

Taylor, Michael. 'The Errors of an Evolutionist: A Reply to Ellen Frankel Paul', *Political Studies*, 37(1989), 436–42

Taylor, M. W. *Men Versus the State: Herbert Spencer and Late Victorian Individualism* (Oxford: Clarendon Press, 1992)

Thompson, Janna L. 'The New Social Darwinism: The Politics of Sociobiology', *Politics*, 17(1982), 121–8

Thornhill, Nancy Wilmsen and Randy Thornhill. 'Evolutionary Theory and Rules of Mating on Marriage Pertaining to Relatives', in Crawford *et al.*, eds., *Sociobiology and Psychology*, 373–97

Thornhill, Randy and Nancy Wilmsen Thornhill. 'Human Rape: The Strengths of the Evolutionary Perspective', in Crawford *et al.*, eds., *Sociobiology and Psychology*, 269–91

Thurlow, Richard C. 'Fascism and Nazism: No Siamese Twins', *Patterns of Prejudice*, 14(1980), 5–15, 15–24

Tidrick, Kathryn. *Empire and the English Character* (London: Taurus, 1990)

Turner, Jonathan H. *Herbert Spencer: A Renewed Appreciation* (London/Beverly Hills, CA: Sage, 1985)

Vincent, A. 'Classical Liberalism and its Crisis of Identity', *History of Political Thought*, 11(1990), 143–61

Vorzimmer, Peter. 'Darwin, Malthus and the Theory of Natural Selection', *Journal of the History of Ideas*, 30(1969), 527–42

Walt, S. 'Hegel on War: Another Look', *History of Political Thought*, 10(1989), 113–24

Watts, Cedric. *A Preface to Conrad* (London: Longman, 1982)

Webber, G. C. *The Ideology of the British Right 1918–1939* (London: Croom Helm, 1986)

Webster, Charles, ed. *Biology, Medicine and Society, 1840–1940* (Cambridge University Press, 1981)

Weikart, Richard. 'The Origins of Social Darwinism in Germany, 1859–1895', *Journal of the History of Ideas*, 54(1993), 469–88

Weindling, Paul J. 'Theories of the Cell State in Imperial Germany', in Webster, ed., *Biology, Medicine and Society*, 99–155

   Health, Race and German Politics Between National Unification and Nazism, 1870–1945 (Cambridge University Press, 1989)

   Darwinism and Social Darwinism in Imperial Germany: The Contribution of the Cell Biologist Oscar Hertwig (1849–1922) (Stuttgart: Gustav Fischer, 1991)

Weinstein, D. 'Equal Freedom, Rights and Utility in Herbert Spencer's Moral Philosophy', *History of Political Thought*, 11(1990), 119–42

Wells, David. 'Resurrecting the Dismal Parson: Malthus, Ecology and Political Thought', *Political Studies*, 30(1982), 1–15

Wells, Kentwood D. 'The Historical Context of Natural Selection: The Case of Patrick Matthew', *Journal of the History of Biology*, 6(1973), 225–58

Wheare, K. C. *Walter Bagehot: Lecture on a Master Mind* (London: Oxford University Press, 1974)

Whelan, F. G. 'Population and Ideology in the Enlightenment', *History of Political Thought*, 12(1991), 35–72

Wiener, Martin J. *Between Two Worlds: The Political Thought of Graham Wallas* (Oxford: Clarendon Press, 1971)

Wiener, P. *Evolution and the Founders of Pragmatism* (Cambridge, MA: Harvard University Press, 1949)

Willey, Basil. *The Eighteenth Century Background* (London: Chatto and Windus, 1965) [1940]

Williams, Raymond. 'Social Darwinism', in J. Benthall, ed., *The Limits of Human Nature* (London: Allen Lane, 1973), 114–30

Wilson, Edward O. *On Human Nature* (Cambridge, MA: Harvard University Press, 1978)

   The Diversity of Life (Harmondsworth: Penguin, 1994)

Wiltshire, D. *The Social and Political Thought of Herbert Spencer* (Oxford University Press, 1978)

Wokler, Robert. 'From *l'homme physique* to *l'homme moral* and Back: Towards a History of Enlightenment Anthropology', *History of the Human Sciences*, 6(1993), 121–38

Woodroffe, Martin. 'Racial Theories of History and Politics: the Example of Houston Stewart Chamberlain', in Paul Kennedy and Anthony Nicholls, eds., *Nationalist and Racialist Movements in Britain and Germany Before 1914* (London: Macmillan, 1981), 143–53

Young, R. M. 'Malthus and the Evolutionists: The Common Context of Biological and Social Theory', *Past and Present*, 43(1969), 109–41

   'Darwinism is Social', in Kohn, ed., *The Darwinian Heritage*, 609–38

   Darwin's Metaphor: Nature's Place in Victorian Culture (Cambridge University Press, 1985)

   'Herbert Spencer and Inevitable Progress', *History Today*, 37(1987), 18–22

Zmarlik, Hans-Günther. 'Social Darwinism in Germany Seen as a Historical Problem', in Hajo Holborn, ed., *Republic to Reich: The Making of the Nazi Revolution*, tr. R. Manheim (New York: Pantheon, 1972), 435–74

Index